The Good Research

The Good Research Guide

For small-scale social research projects

Fifth edition

Martyn Denscombe

Mc Graw Hill Education Open University Press

Open University Press
McGraw-Hill Education
McGraw-Hill House
Shoppenhangers Road
Maidenhead
Berkshire
England
SL6 2QL

email: enquiries@openup.co.uk
world wide web: www.openup.co.uk

and Two Penn Plaza, New York, NY 10121-2289, USA

First published 1998
Second edition published 2003
Third edition published 2007
Fourth edition published 2010
First published in this fifth edition 2014

A catalogue record of this book is available from the British Library

ISBN-13: 978-0-335-26470-4
ISBN-10: 0-335-26470-0
eISBN: 978-0-335-26471-1

Library of Congress Cataloging-in-Publication Data
CIP data applied for

Typeset by Aptara, Inc.

Fictitious names of companies, products, people, characters and/or data that may be
used herein (in case studies or in examples) are not intended to represent any real individual, company, product or event.

Printed by Bell and Bain Ltd, Glasgow

MIX
Paper from
responsible sources
FSC® C007785

Summary of contents

Contents

List of tables and figures

Acknowledgements

There are those close to home who contribute to the completion of a book by putting the author in a position to start, sustain and finish the book. For this reason, and many others, I would like to dedicate this book to my family.

Thanks especially to Viv – this book is for you.

Martyn Denscombe
Leicester

Introduction

A book for 'project researchers'

Social research is no longer restricted to a small elite of professionals and full-time researchers. It has become the concern of a far greater number of people who are faced with the prospect of undertaking small-scale research projects as part of an academic course or as part of their professional development. Such people:

- do not have large sums of money available to fund the research;
- need to complete the research within a relatively short time-span (perhaps within 6 months or less);
- must be responsible for doing the work themselves, rather than being able to use others to help with data collection and analysis.

The aim of this book is to present these 'project researchers' with practical guidance and a vision of the key issues involved in social research. It attempts to provide them with vital information that is easily accessible and which gets to the heart of the matter quickly and concisely. In doing this, the book is based on three premises:

1 Most of what needs to be known and done in relation to the production of competent social research can be stated in *straightforward language*.
2 The foundations of good social research depend on paying attention to *certain elementary factors*. If such factors are ignored or overlooked, the research will be open to criticism and serious questions may be raised about the quality of the findings.
3 Project researchers can safeguard against making elementary errors in the design and execution of their research by using *checklists* to assure themselves that they have attended to the 'minimum' requirements and have not overlooked crucial factors associated with the production of good research.

The book is pragmatic in its approach to social research. It does not present particular types of social research as being inherently better or worse than others but, instead, encourages project researchers to choose strategies and methods that are likely to work best in the context of the topic they are trying to investigate and the circumstances in which the research is being conducted.

The decisions and choices that project researchers make occur against a backdrop of two 'paradigms' of social research – two 'schools of thought'. The two paradigms for social research are commonly known as the *positivist* paradigm and the *interpretivist* paradigm. The *positivist paradigm* applies the natural science model of research to investigations of the social world. Social reality is treated in a similar way to physical reality as something that exists independently 'out there' with properties that can be studied scientifically. This allows the researcher to adopt an objective, detached approach to the study of social phenomena. The focus is generally on facts and figures relating to the causes and consequences of phenomena in the social world, and the approach tends to be associated with the use of quantitative data and statistics. The *interpretivist paradigm*, by contrast, challenges the idea that social researchers can view things from an objective position. It sees social reality as something that is subjectively constructed by people's thoughts and actions. This means that social researchers can never hope to be totally objective. They must always be 'insiders' – part and parcel of the social reality they are studying. A consequence is that, from this perspective, the role of social research must be to *interpret* social phenomena, recognizing that researchers' thinking will be shaped to some extent or other by their own experiences and identities as members of the social world within which their work takes place. The aim of research is to develop insights into people's beliefs and their lived experiences, and the approach tends to be associated with the use of qualitative data (text and images).

Each paradigm operates on a different set of beliefs about the nature of social reality and the ways that it ought to be investigated. Each offers a model of best practice when it comes to conducting research. And traditionally each has been regarded as holding a position that is incompatible with the other's position. The paradigms have been presented as competing alternatives, putting social researchers in the position of having to choose to conduct their research within one paradigm or the other.

However, the idea of a two-paradigm schism in social research is something that is hard to justify in practice and it vastly over-simplifies matters. It is a legacy of the past – and yet it continues to pervade the world of social research. It persists, though, not so much as a literal depiction of what goes on in social research so much as in the way that approaches to social research can be described and spoken about. It works as a short-hand term to capture broad notions about different styles of research and their underlying assumptions.

It is not the purpose of this book, however, to explore the underlying philosophy of social research – this is introduced in the companion book *Ground Rules for Social Research* (Denscombe 2010, also published by Open University Press). The focus here is on practice. And, in this respect, *The Good Research Guide* draws on the fact that social researchers can, and do, combine features of positivist and interpretivist paradigms within individual projects, crossing boundaries between the traditional paradigms. Chapter 10 on mixed methods develops this point. So, while it is wise for project researchers to understand where their choices fit in relation to these traditional paradigms a basic tenet of this book is that these paradigms need not ring-fence the choices that project researchers make when deciding 'what works best'.

Part **1**

Strategies for social research

There is no single pathway to good research: there are always options and alternatives. At any stage of any enquiry researchers need to take decisions, make judgements and use discretion in order to successfully complete a project. One of the biggest decisions to be made concerns the choice of research *strategy*, and the first section of this book outlines a variety of strategies that can be used. These are not the full range of possibilities that exist because this would be beyond the scope of this book and would include strategies more appropriate for large-scale, long-term and very costly investigations. The focus, instead, is on the range of strategies that are well suited to the needs of project researchers engaged with small-scale, low-budget research being conducted over relatively short periods of time.

What are research strategies?

A strategy is a plan of action designed to achieve a specific goal. In the context of social research this entails a broad approach that has:

- a distinct research logic and rationale that shapes
- a plan of action (research design) to address
- a clearly identified research problem (a specific goal that can be achieved).

A research strategy is different from a research *method*. Research methods are the tools for data collection – things like questionnaires, interviews, observation and documents (which are outlined in Part 2 of this book). Methods are the equivalent of a microscope when used by a scientist, a thermometer when used by a medic, or a telescope when used by an astronomer. They do a job. They are types of equipment that allow relevant data to be collected.

Which strategy to choose?

Is it suitable?

In themselves, research strategies are neither 'good' nor 'bad', nor are they 'right' or 'wrong'. It is only in relation to how they are used that they take on the mantle

Table P1.1 Research strategies and research purpose; some links

Strategy	Purpose of research
Surveys and sampling	• measure some aspect of a social phenomenon or trend • gather facts in order to test a theory
Case studies	• understand the complex relationship between factors as they operate within a particular social setting
Experiments	• identify the cause of something • observe the influence of specific factors
Ethnography	• describe cultural practices and traditions • interpret social interaction within a culture
Phenomenology	• describe the essence of specific types of personal experience • understand things through the eyes of someone else
Grounded theory	• clarify concepts or produce new theories • explore a new topic and provide new insights
Action research	• solve a practical problem • produce guidelines for best practice
Systematic reviews	• get an objective overview of evidence on a specific topic • evaluate the effectiveness of projects or interventions
Mixed methods	• evaluate a new policy and gauge its impact • compare alternative perspectives on a phenomenon • combine aspects of the other strategies

of being good or bad, right or wrong. They can only be judged in relation to the purpose for which they are used and, reflecting this point, it is better to think of strategies in terms of how *useful* they are and how *appropriate* they are. Thought of in this pragmatic way the justification for the choice of any specific strategy must depend on having a clear vision of the particular *purpose* for which it is being used. Unless we know what the research is trying to achieve, it is impossible to judge whether it is likely to be useful or appropriate. Table P1.1 indicates how the research strategies outlined in Part 1 can be valuable for different kinds of research purpose, and this should provide some initial guidance on the question of whether a particular strategy is suitable for the kind of research that is envisaged.

 Key point: The choice of strategy is a matter of 'horses for courses'
The researcher should choose a strategy that is likely to be successful in achieving the aims of the research, and be able to justify the choice of this strategy clearly and explicitly.

Is it feasible?

The choice of strategy needs to take into account certain practical aspects of conducting research. It is vital, for instance, that the researcher can get access to the kinds of people, contexts, events and documents that will be crucial for the success of the research. This might be a matter of getting the necessary authorization to contact people, enter locations or view documents. It might be a matter of getting agreement from people or organizations to collaborate with the research. Or, it might be a matter of having the resources for specialist equipment or travel to fieldwork locations. Whatever form it takes, the point is that *access to data sources* is crucial for the choice of research strategy.

Another practical consideration is the need to meet deadlines and to complete research within specified *time constraints*. Project researchers generally face deadlines for the completion of the research and it would be wrong to choose a strategy which could not possibly allow such deadlines to be met. Some strategies are relatively predictable in terms of their time-span and lend themselves to fairly tight time-planning (e.g. surveys, case studies, experiments). Others are less predictable (e.g. grounded theory) or tend to take a relatively long time (e.g. ethnography). This must be taken into account in terms of the feasibility of using specific strategies.

When choosing the strategy, researchers should also bear in mind the audience for the research and the particular *research community* within which the researcher is working. Different subject areas and disciplines tend to have different perspectives on research and, in practice, this means that they generally have a preference for certain styles of research rather than others. Project researchers need to be aware of this. In particular, those who need to conduct a small-scale piece of research as part of an academic qualification might be advised to make their choice of strategy mindful of the traditions of their own specific discipline and the predispositions of the people who are going to evaluate their research – their tutors and examiners.

Is it ethical?

Research ethics are an over-riding concern when it comes to the choice of strategy. It is hard to overstate the importance of research ethics in the context of contemporary social research and, for this reason, practical guidance on research ethics is provided in Chapter 17. These guidelines are based on some core principles of research ethics, the first of which is that no-one should suffer harm as a result of participation in the research. The notion of 'harm' in this context is wide-ranging and it calls on the researcher to anticipate possible ways in which participants *might* suffer as a consequence of their involvement with the research. A strategy that carries too many potential ethical risks is a strategy to be avoided, and so there needs to be some form of risk assessment right at the beginning of the research when choosing which strategy to use.

Checklist for the choice of research strategy

When choosing a research strategy you should feel confident about answering 'yes' to the following questions: ☑

Factors to be considered

| **Suitability**
Will it produce appropriate kinds of data? | • Has the purpose of the research been clearly identified? ☐
• Is there a clear link between the purpose of the research and the chosen strategy? ☐
• Will the strategy produce findings that can answer the research question(s)? ☐ |

| **Feasibility**
Can it be done? | • Is there sufficient time for the design of the research, collection of data and analysis of results? ☐
• Are sufficient resources available to cover the costs of the research (e.g. travel, printing)? ☐
• Is it possible and practical to gain access to necessary data (people, events, documents)? ☐
• Will the chosen strategy be favoured by the key evaluators of the research? ☐ |

| **Ethics**
Will it allow me to be ethical in my dealings with participants? | • Can I avoid any harm to participants resulting from their involvement in the research? ☐
• Can I get informed consent from potential participants? ☐
• Will the strategy permit me to work within an appropriate code of research ethics? ☐
• Can I guarantee the confidentiality of the information given to me during the research? ☐ |

---

1   Surveys

- What is a survey? • Types of survey • Which type of survey to choose?
- Postal surveys • Face-to-face surveys • Group-administered surveys
- Telephone surveys • Internet surveys • Web-based questionnaire
surveys • Social network sites • Facebook surveys • The research
population • Response rates • How to achieve good response rates
- Non-response bias • Advantages of surveys • Disadvantages of
surveys • Further reading • Checklist for the use of surveys

Surveys can take a number of forms. In social research the most common of
these are the kind that attempt to ask people questions. Using the phone, the
Internet, the postal service or face-to-face contact, their aim is to make contact
with suitable respondents in order to obtain information from those people. Questionnaires and interviews are the data collection methods that are normally used.

Surveys can also involve the observation of behaviour and they can involve
the analysis of documents as well. These type of survey, however, are less commonly used in small-scale social research and, for this reason, the focus of this
chapter will be on those types of survey that *ask people questions*.

What is a survey?

When something is surveyed, it is 'viewed comprehensively and in detail'. This
is clear in the case of geographical surveys, engineering surveys and ordnance
surveys which map out the landscape or the built environment of roads and
buildings. The principles, though, have been used to good effect on mapping
out the social world as well and, indeed, surveys have emerged in recent times
as one of the most popular approaches to social research. *Social* surveys tend
to share with their physical counterparts certain key characteristics. These are:

- *Empirical research.* Because 'to survey' carries with it the meaning 'to look',
  survey work inevitably brings with it the idea of empirical research. It involves
  the idea of purposefully seeking the necessary information from relevant people and relevant sites.

- *At a specific point in time.* Surveys are generally used to provide a snapshot of how things are rather than tracing events over a period of time. In most cases this is useful for 'bringing things up to date' and providing information about the current state of affairs. Although it is possible to use surveys as the basis for tracking changes over a period of time, this is relatively uncommon in the realms of small-scale research projects.
- *Wide and inclusive coverage.* In order to view things comprehensively surveys can try to get a panoramic view of the situation and strive for wide and inclusive coverage of the people or things being investigated. This kind of survey tends to cast the net wide to include the whole range of relevant people (or things) and, for this reason, they tend to be relatively large in terms of the number of participants involved. Such surveys are commonly associated with quantitative data and statistical analysis relating to trends, proportions and the prevalence of particular traits within the people or things being studied.
- *Detailed scrutiny.* Another aspect to the notion of a survey involves the idea of looking at things 'in detail'. This emphasizes a need for a 'close inspection' of the people or things of interest. Just as a house survey will focus its efforts on inspecting the structure of a specific building, social surveys can also examine things in depth and be small-scale rather than large-scale. This kind of survey tends to be based on a relatively small number of participants and be linked with qualitative data, exploratory research and the discovery of ideas about the people or things being investigated.

These characteristics of the survey approach include no mention of specific research methods. This is because *surveys are a research strategy* and, as such, they can be used with a variety of data collection methods – including questionnaires, interviews, documents and observation.

 Key point

Surveys are used for research into things like:
- consumer preferences and customer satisfaction;
- voting behaviour (opinion polls);
- health-related behaviour, diet, smoking and alcohol consumption;
- evaluation of innovations, programmes and educational courses;
- TV viewing and audience ratings.

Types of survey

Surveys differ in terms of the *technology* they use to communicate with respondents: postal services, telephone networks, the Internet, and face-to-face contact, each providing an alternative means for contacting people and obtaining data from them (see Table 1.1).

Table 1.1 Main types of survey and associated methods

Technology for distribution		Method of data collection
Postal	Mail	Questionnaire
Face to face	Individual	Interview
	Group	Questionnaire
Telephone	Landline	Interview
	Mobile	Questionnaire
Internet	Email	Interview
	Web-based	Questionnaire
Social networking sites	Facebook	Questionnaire
	Twitter	Questionnaire

Which type of survey to choose?

When deciding which type of survey to use, researchers need to appreciate that each of the different types of survey brings with it certain possibilities and certain limitations. The choice should be based on what works best in relation to the particular research project, bearing in mind:

- the *objectives* of the research, and whether this is to get data from a representative cross-section of people or whether it is to focus on particular kinds of people who are likely to have a special knowledge about the topic of the research;
- the *resources* available to fund the survey, and the constraints this puts on decisions about the size of the research population, the size of any sample that might be used (see Chapter 2 Sampling), the number of weeks or months required to complete the survey, and the facilities (equipment, software) that can be used;
- the *geographical area* to be covered by the survey, and whether participants are dispersed across widely scattered locations;
- the *methods* of data collection to be used in the survey, and whether there is a preference for questionnaires or interviews;
- the *speed* of responses, and any urgency that surrounds the collection of responses from participants;
- the *response rate*, and the amount of pressure there is to minimize the time and effort it takes to respond to the survey – the 'response burden' – so that busy people are not deterred from participating;
- the *contact* with potential participants, and the extent to which it is necessary to have a ready-made list or directory that researchers can use to select potential participants for inclusion in the survey;
- the need for *face-to-face contact*, and the extent to which the research will benefit from the 'personal touch'. Direct contact can be important for engaging with participants, establishing rapport and gaining trust. It also helps the researcher to informally assess the validity of the responses being given and

it allows the researcher to provide instant clarification on points if the participant is unsure;

- the need for *indirect contact*, and the way that remote and impersonal contact (e.g. using Internet surveys, postal surveys, self-completion questionnaires) can encourage people's willingness to answer openly and honestly when questions touch on things where there are particular social sensitivities (e.g. racism, sexism, homophobia, politics, religion);

- the *abilities/disabilities* of the respondents, and their capacity to complete the survey. If the type of survey includes forms some people cannot fill in, screens that some people cannot read, voices that some cannot hear, then obviously the survey will suffer. And this is not just a practical matter of increasing response rates. There is a larger ethical issue here concerned with *social inclusion* and the need to ensure that certain groups are not disadvantaged through exclusion from participation in the survey;

- the *validity* of the answers, and the need to avoid the '*social desirability*' factor where the respondent might be more inclined to provide answers which he/she feels are the expected ones, the correct ones or ones which put him/ her in a better light.

 Key point

'The major development of the twenty-first century, so far, is recognition that the use of all survey modes continues, and none seem likely to disappear. Each has strengths and weaknesses, allowing it to do things other modes cannot do' (Dillman et al. 2009: 495).

Postal surveys

Distributing a survey through the post used to be the most efficient and effective way of conducting a large-scale survey covering a wide geographical area. The postal network provided the researcher with the means for sending out self-completion questionnaires to a particular research population who could be identified through their names or addresses. Participants could then return the completed questionnaire, encouraged possibly by receiving a stamped envelope with the researcher's address on it. The process was fairly simple, straightforward and relatively cheap. And it remains a viable and often-used mode of distributing surveys today.

However, three things need to be borne in mind when considering the use of a postal survey. First, there is the cost. The printing, packing and postage costs can quickly mount up, particularly with larger surveys. Providing stamped addressed envelopes for the return of questionnaires, for instance, can double the postage costs. Project researchers with limited resources need to think carefully about the costs involved. Second, there is the time delay. Planning and preparation take time, as they do with all research, but there are specific delays that stem from the turn-round time involved with posting and returning questionnaires as part of a postal survey. In practice, the data collection is likely to take a number of weeks to complete even after the questionnaires have been posted out. Third, there is the response rate. The proportion of people who respond to postal surveys, as is often the case with surveys, tends to be quite low.

Face-to-face surveys

Face-to-face surveys involve direct contact between the researcher and individual respondents, and typically make use of questionnaires or interviews as the data collection method. The most easily recognized version of this kind of survey sees the researcher approaching people 'in the street' to ask if they will participate in the research. The sight of the market researcher with her clipboard and smile is familiar in town centres and shopping malls. Alternatively, the contact can be made by calling at people's homes. Sometimes this will be 'on spec' to see if the householder is willing and able to spare the time to help with the research. On other occasions, contact will be arranged in advance by letter or phone.

Either way, the face-to-face survey is a more expensive way of collecting data than the use of the post, Internet or telephone. Researcher time and travel costs are considerable. Weighed against this there is the prospect of probing beneath the surface to get a bit more depth to the information that is obtained. Plus, this kind of survey with its face-to-face contact offers some immediate means of validating the data. The researcher can sense if she is being given false information in the face-to-face context in a way that is not possible with questionnaires and less feasible with telephone surveys. And, with this kind of survey response rates pose less of a problem. Partly this is because the face-to-face contact allows the researcher to use her interpersonal skills and powers of persuasion to encourage the potential respondent to take part in the survey. Partly it is because with face-to-face surveys the researcher can continue making contacts until she has accumulated the total number of responses that are required.

> **Link up with**
> Quota sampling, p. 40.

Group-administered surveys

Like individual face-to-face surveys, group-administered surveys are conducted in person. They rely on the researcher travelling to a specific site to distribute and collect the research instrument – normally a questionnaire. But, unlike face-to-face surveys the data are collected from groups rather than individuals. Normally, these groups already exist. Rather than get a group of people together specifically for the purpose, it is easier from the researcher's point of view to use naturally occurring groups. For example, a survey of young people could involve the distribution of questionnaires in schools to whole classes – possibly 30 or more people at a time. The same approach could be taken with work-groups, community meetings or any occasions where there will be a (naturally occurring) collection of people who are suitable for the purposes of the research.

This approach does not really lend itself to use with thousands of people at a time. For practical purposes the group-administered survey tends to work best with fairly small numbers. In this context it is relatively easy to organize and can often draw on the researcher's personal knowledge about the context of the research. In terms of turn-round time this form of survey has advantages because the questionnaires are generally distributed, completed and returned in one process. And the personal, face-to-face contact means that response rates tend to be considerably higher than with postal, Internet or phone surveys. However, group-administered surveys are quite labour-intensive and, depending on the locations for research, can incur significant travel costs.

Link up with
Cluster sampling,
p. 37.

Telephone surveys

Telephone surveys tend to be used mainly in conjunction with one-to-one interviews and they have become a well-established alternative to postal or face-to-face surveys. One reason for this is that the evidence would suggest people are as honest and open on the phone as they are when answering postal questionnaires or being interviewed face to face (Dillman et al. 2009). Another reason is that conducting surveys via the telephone can have particular benefits in terms of time and costs. Researchers do not have to travel to all parts of the country to conduct the interviews – they only have to pick up a phone – and there are no significant delays with the return of data using a telephone survey because the responses are instantaneous. Local and national calls on landlines are not generally expensive, nor do calls to mobile phones need to incur significant costs. And the use of Skype or similar software provides the survey researcher with a means for making international calls via the Internet virtually free of cost. Skype also enables the interviewer to have visual face-to-face contact on screen with the interviewee if the contact is made online between computers.

Telephone surveys, like postal surveys, can target particular geographical areas. Researchers can select the area they wish to survey and identify the relevant dialling code for that area. They can then contact phone numbers at random within that area using *random-digit dialling*, where the final digits of the phone numbers are produced by computer technology which automatically generates numbers at random. Mobile phone numbers, however, are not allocated by geographical location (in the UK), which means that researchers cannot use prior knowledge about the geographical location of any mobile phone user as the basis for including them in a survey. As people come to use 'cell phones' instead of – not just in addition to – conventional land-line phones, this will pose something of a challenge for telephone surveys in terms of reaching a representative sample of the population.

Mobile phones, none the less, have introduced a new dimension to telephone surveys: they have enabled surveys to be conducted using SMS text questions and answers. In effect, they allow researchers to conduct questionnaire surveys (as distinct from the interview surveys associated with land-line phones). Such surveys need to keep things simple and short, and they are well suited to occasions when information is needed instantly by way of feedback from a situation. This could be an audience response to a performance, customer evaluation of a product or service, or some snap opinion poll on a matter 'of the moment'. Participants send their responses to a designated SMS text address – usually a short sequence of numbers.

Smartphones massively extend the range of possibilities for phone surveys. Surveys designed for smartphones (and tablet computers such as iPads) can include images and multimedia features that can make responding to a survey more interesting and more fun. Such surveys can also retrieve details about the location of respondents using GPS (Global Positioning Satellite).

Internet surveys

There are three main ways in which surveys can be conducted using the Internet. The first of these involves direct contact through *emails*. Potential respondents can be contacted by email and, if they agree to cooperate with the research, they can be sent a set of questions. If the questions are all sent within one message then it constitutes an email questionnaire. If an initial question sets in train a dialogue between the researcher and the respondent contained in a series of messages then it becomes an email interview. There is not too much to go wrong using this approach. It is a simple, cheap and fast way to collect data. But while email communication remains a viable means for doing an online interview, email questionnaires have been largely superseded by web-based surveys. As Sue and Ritter (2012: xvi) point out, 'The advent of free and easy-to-use survey software has rendered email questionnaires an unappealing choice for most purposes.' *Web-based questionnaire surveys* are 'hosted' on a 'server' linked to the Internet and respondents visit the host web-site to complete the questionnaire. They represent, in this respect, a second way of using the Internet to distribute a survey. A third possibility is to tap into online groups and social networks that already exist on the Internet, making use of instant messaging or forums that exist on the Internet such as chat rooms or discussion groups.

Internet surveys, in whatever form, are enticing for project researchers because:

- *They save time*: There are no delays involved in delivering questions or receiving answers.
- *They save money*: Online surveys eliminate the costs of printing, packaging and posting associated with postal surveys. Yes, there are still some costs associated with distributing questionnaires online (see below) but these will be relatively small.
- *They speed up data processing*: There is less burden in terms of data entry. Data can be downloaded directly without the need to transcribe text data or the manual entry of quantitative data into data files.
- *They allow wide geographical coverage*: Surveys are not restricted to particular localities. Online surveys can be national or international in scope with no additional burden in terms of the time or money needed to reach distant participants.
- *They provide an environmentally friendly approach to conducting research*: Online surveys reduce the need for paper and eliminate the need to travel. In these respects they save trees and avoid pollution.

Recent evidence, furthermore, would suggest that the quality of data obtained through Internet survey research is not significantly different from that obtained using more traditional methods. As the Internet is now part of everyday life for most people in developed societies there is little evidence that respondents provide significantly different kinds of answer or supply different amounts of information as a consequence of the online data collection method (Denscombe 2006, 2008, 2009; Sue and Ritter 2012; Tourangeau et al. 2013).

Web-based questionnaire surveys

The most widely used form of Internet survey is the web-based questionnaire survey. Its popularity stems from the availability of computer programs specifically designed for creating and distributing online questionnaires, and the fact that social researchers can gain access to this for little or no cost through online survey companies or computing facilities within their own organization.

Web-based questionnaire surveys involve three distinct processes: (1) design of the questionnaire; (2) distribution of the questionnaire; and (3) retrieval of the data.

Design

The first stage entails compiling the questions. The attraction of web-based questionnaires is that they can include a number of useful features that cannot be incorporated into paper questionnaires:

Link up with
Web-based
questionnaires,
p. 178.

things such as drop-down menus and the forced completion of questions. They can also include images and background designs that make them visually attractive, and online survey companies usually provide templates and examples that help with the design of a good questionnaire.

Delivery

Once the questionnaire has been designed then the next stage is to start the survey by distributing the questionnaire. A number of options are normally available (Table 1.2). With small-scale research, operating on a very limited budget, the most commonly chosen option is to deliver the questionnaire to participants who have been chosen specifically in relation to the research project. These participants are contacted via email, SMS text or social network site with an invitation to visit the website where the questionnaire is found. Other more expensive options include attracting people to the survey through publicity and advertising – for example, paying for 'pop-ups' on a website or a link via a social networking site. It is also possible to use a 'survey panel' – a list of people who volunteer to take part in such surveys and have been recruited on the basis of previous responses. Survey companies offer to provide access to suitable panels, for which they charge a fee.

> **Good practice**
>
> Web surveys work best when ...
>
> - Either: A list of email addresses is available for the research population because this allows the researcher to target relevant people (and allows more systematic sampling techniques).
> - Or: Self-selection to the survey is useful because it gives access to people specifically relevant for the topic of the research.

When the web survey is based on inviting specific people to participate, it is important to keep things simple and straightforward. To help with this the survey software provides a *unique web address* (URL) for each questionnaire that is made available on the host site. This is the web address that anyone answering the questionnaire will visit. When inviting people to participate in the survey it is good practice to put this web address in the message in the form of a hyperlink. All the person needs to do is click on the link to be taken directly to the questionnaire. Alternatively, it is possible to get a link to the survey via a QR code. Anyone with a smart phone or tablet (and with a suitable QR code app) will be able to access the survey by using their smart phone or tablet to read the 'Quick Response' barcode.

As a way of restricting access to the survey it is advisable to put *password restrictions* in place. Again, online survey companies normally include this facility. Using passwords makes the data more secure in the sense that it ensures the only people answering the questionnaire are those to whom the password has been revealed. From the researcher's point of view this can act as a safety device that eliminates the prospect of people outside the research population tapping into the survey and 'contaminating' the findings.

Table 1.2 Delivery options for web-based questionnaire surveys

Password protect	Only people who have been given the password can access the questionnaire
Prevent multiple responses	Prevents the accidental duplication of responses from one person or the malicious 'ballot-box stuffing' from anyone determined to fix the results of the survey
Hyperlink	Unique web address for the web location of the questionnaire
Link to social media	Put links to the questionnaire in Facebook pages, etc.
Email	Send the questionnaire to people on an email list

Retrieving the data

The answers from each questionnaire are automatically transferred into a data file and the *combined data* from all the completed questionnaires can be viewed online. Sometimes the results can be viewed in the form of graphs, which is useful. It is also possible to look at the results for *each individual questionnaire*. As well as listing the answers to each question, it is possible to see additional

Table 1.3   Retrieval options for web-based questionnaires

Data display	View individual respondent's details See summary of survey findings Produce graphs from data in PowerPoint
Data download	Download the data and save at a location that can be accessed later Export the graphics into a MS Word file and into a PowerPoint file
Respondent tracking	Survey tracking: views, started, completed, deleted survey counts Email tracking: tracking of respondent web or email addresses

information about each questionnaire – things like how long it took to complete and exactly when it was submitted.

Findings from the survey can be exported – and this is really useful. The benefits of being able to download the data directly into an Excel spreadsheet or statistics package are significant. It means that rather than the data being located on the remote server the researcher can 'take possession' of it, have it on his/her own computer, to process and analyse as desired (Table 1.3). However, this facility tends to come 'at a price', often requiring the researcher to upgrade from a free package to a subscription package.

Good practice

For a useful website for online web survey design and research findings connected with online surveys, visit http://www.websm.org.

Choosing an online survey company to host your questionnaire

The decision about which online survey company to use is obviously an important one that can affect the success of the web survey. The good news on this is that for many small-scale researchers the decision should be very straightforward. A number of large organizations have their own software for conducting online surveys or have a licence to use the survey facilities offered by companies who specialize in providing online survey services. Universities might have site licences that allow students to use the necessary software, and health service organizations, local authorities, government agencies, charities and large commercial businesses might already have the kind of survey software that their employees can use for research purposes. In the first instance, therefore, it is important to check whether you are eligible to use an existing online survey facility by virtue of belonging to a particular organization. If this is the case then it makes sense to use what is already available. The chances are that there will be no charges for using the survey software, and there is likely to be technical help on hand if it is needed.

If, however, you do not have this pathway for setting up a web-based questionnaire then it is still possible to conduct an online survey using the professional software with little cost involved. It might even be possible to collect the data for free. This is because there are a number of online survey companies who cater for the needs of small-scale researchers by offering low-budget packages.

Entry-level packages (with restricted functionality) are generally offered for free. These are 'taster' packages that allow you to explore the software and get the feel for what is on offer. It is feasible, on occasion, to rely entirely on these for small-scale projects. In practice, though, with the kind of surveys associated for instance with master's degrees and PhDs, it is likely that you will feel the need to upgrade to the next tariff. However, by shopping around it should still be possible to get the necessary online survey service for around £15–£25 per month (US$23–40). For a survey where data collection lasts for three months, then, the total cost could be estimated as £45–£75. Table 1.4 indicates a number of important factors that should be borne in mind when deciding which online survey company to use and which tariff to select.

Table 1.4 Key things to consider when choosing your online survey company

Contract	• How much does it *cost per month*? • Is there a *minimum sign-up period*? • Can you *stop payments* instantly when you want?
Data security	• How *'trustworthy'* is the organization? Will it survive? • What measures are taken to protect the *security and privacy* of data held on the server? • Is data or *personal information* shared with any third party?
Size of the survey	• Is there a cap on *number of respondents*? (e.g. 50, 100, 1,000) • Is there a limit to the *number of questions* allowed for each questionnaire?
Access to data	• Can data be *downloaded*? (free package or upgrade?) • In what *formats* can the data be downloaded? • Is the survey restricted to a specific period of *time*? (e.g. 1 week) • Are there *limitations* on the number of times data can be accessed or downloaded?
Data controls	• Can the software stop respondents submitting *multiple responses* by accident or on purpose? • Can access to the survey be restricted by using a *password*? • Are there blocks against computer-generated *mass submissions*? (e.g. where to gain access to the survey each respondent needs to 'decipher' a number displayed in a format which cannot be machine-read)
Design features	• Are *templates* and specimen questions provided? • Will the software allow you to add a *logo* and customize the appearance of the survey? • Is it possible to insert a *progress bar* to show respondent how far they are through the questionnaire? • Will the online survey company insist on inserting *advertisements* in the survey?
Survey tracking	• Is a *log of respondent activity* provided? (views, starts, completions, drop-outs?) • What kind of *respondent tracking* is offered? (e.g. respondent email addresses, web addresses)

Social network sites

Social network sites (SNS) offer an interesting and rapidly developing avenue for survey research. Specifically they provide new ways of making contact with potential participants and a new channel for distributing surveys (Wilson et al. 2012). Facebook is the world leader in terms of numbers, with an estimated 1.4 billion users worldwide (2014 figures). Since it was launched in 2004 it has grown massively to become something of a social phenomenon. Other SNS include Twitter, MySpace, Friendster, LinkedIn, Google+, Bebo, and Flickr. What these SNS have in common are three things, each of which is vitally important in terms of their use for conducting surveys. First, they are all about *messages*. At the very heart of any SNS lies some form of communication between people. SNS exploit new technologies to make it easier and faster for users to send messages and this can be extremely valuable for social researchers. It provides them with a wealth of data about the people involved which can be of interest to many researchers but, more pertinently, it provides a fast and free method for researchers to make contact with potential participants.

Second, users of SNS are linked via a *communications network*. This opens up access to a potentially vast audience of people. Research populations can be identified on the basis of their interests and the personal information they provide about themselves and contact can be made with these people to invite them to participate in the research.

Third, the communication that takes place tends to be focused on those with some *shared interest* or with some shared identity. The messages are not normally distributed at random nor are they sent to everyone who is signed up to the particular SNS. They are sent to 'friends' or 'groups' or 'followers' – to people who want to be involved with certain others. The clue is in the name: '*social*' networking. This is very useful for researchers because it provides a way of targeting groups of people who have something in common, a thing that the researcher wishes to investigate. There is a ready-made 'research population' (see below) with whom it is relatively easy to make contact. It also helps when it comes to making contact with people who would normally be hard to identify and locate.

Link up with
Snowball
sampling, p. 42.

Using their own personal networks, individuals can open up contact with other potential respondents who would not otherwise have been discovered by the researcher, rapidly expanding access to 'hard-to-find' research populations through a process of 'snowballing'.

> ### ★ Key point
> 'Social networking sites and online questionnaires make it possible to do survey research faster, cheaper, and with less assistance than ever before. The methods are especially well-suited for snowball sampling of elusive sub-populations' (Brickman-Bhutta 2012: 57).

Surveys based on SNS, however, also have their limitations. First, SNS users do not constitute a cross-section of the population in any of the countries in which they exist (Couper 2011; Smith 2013). This means that findings based on surveys using SNS cannot be assumed to apply to the wider population in a simple and straight-forward fashion. As a consequence, SNS are best used when the aim of the survey is to get information from specific kinds of people rather than when trying to get information from people who are representative of the wider population.

The second limitation stems from the *social* nature of such sites and the effect this might have on the honesty of answers that are given to any survey questions. This poses the question: 'Will respondents be more inclined to provide "socially accept-able" answers as they are conscious of the fact that the views they express might be visible to others on the network?' And, for the same reason, might they be more reluctant to divulge personal facts or attitudes that they worry will be regarded as 'bad' by friends or others using the SNS? The answer to this lies in ensuring that SNS users' responses are kept private and are never communicated via a public forum. Although the invitation to participate can legitimately make use of the public areas on the site, any subsequent contact needs to be done on a one-to-one basis as private messaging. And it is vital that potential respondents realize this.

Facebook surveys

Most Facebook users have a lot of 'friends' – estimates vary between 130–230 and significantly more amongst the 12–24 age range. These friends provide a fast and effective way of 'spreading the word' about a topic of interest. Through *personal messaging* researchers can make direct contact with their friends with a request to participate in research. And they can then vastly extend the pool of potential participants by asking those individuals to pass on that request to their 'friends'.

Public messages placed on a 'wall' offer another possibility for 'spreading the word' and distributing an invitation to participate in a survey. Any message sent to an individual user's 'wall' is visible to all 'friends' and obviously this is an effec-tive way of spreading a message to other Facebook users. And as a third option, researchers can use 'groups' as a way of contacting relevant Facebook users. This can either be done by creating a group specifically for the purposes of the research, or it can entail making contact with existing groups that are relevant to the research topic.

An example of how Facebook contacts can be used for surveys is provided by Brickman-Bhutta's (2012) research. Her aim was to make contact with Catho-lics who had ceased to actively practise their faith and who no longer attended church. This research population represented a classic 'hard-to-contact' group. But Facebook provided a means for getting the contact. She set up her own group 'Please Help Me Find Baptized Catholics!' The purpose of the group was explained on the group website and people were invited to sign-up to the group. They were also asked to invite any of their 'friends' who were 'ex-Catholics' to join. After a month, when the group was established, she sent members of the group a link to her online questionnaire and, in this way, obtained a good number of responses from a research population for which there was no obvious list of contacts obtainable through other means. Next, she contacted the administrators of other Catholic groups on Facebook to try to enlist their help. Some adminis-trators were helpful, others less so. And the response rate from these groups was quite low, reflecting the fact that in many cases people sign up to a group on the spur of the moment and never, or hardly ever, return to the site at a later date. So, as a third measure she contacted her own network of 'friends' to cast the net as wide as possible. Overall, her approach worked well. In her words (Brickman-Bhutta 2012: 58):

Link up with Snowball sampling, p. 42.

> Within five days of releasing a 12-minute online survey to a *Facebook* group of potential volunteers, I harvested 2,788 completed questionnaires. Within a month, the total number of respondents increased to about 4,000. Total monetary costs averaged less than one cent (per questionnaire) – vastly less than the cost of surveys obtained through mail, phone, or even email.

Advertising and applications

Separate from making contact with potential respondents with a request to participate in a survey there are two other ways in which social network sites such as Facebook can be used as the basis for collecting survey data. The first of these is *advertising*. Facebook holds data about its users based on the information they provide about themselves and the way they use the social network site, and this allows advertisements to be selectively targeted on Facebook users with particular *demographics* (age, location), particular *attributes* (such as education and job titles), particular *interests* (based on the pages they like or the groups they belong to) and *keywords* to narrow the field and get access to exactly the kind of people they need for the survey. Ramo and Prochaska (2012) used such advertising as a means of recruiting a sample of young smokers aged 18–25 years living in the United States, and their research illustrates the potential of this approach. However, the overall cost of obtaining responses from 1,548 young smokers was $6,628 (£4,100, €4,800) and the cost per completed survey was $4.28 (£2.65, €3.10). While this is certainly cheaper than many alternative modes of survey, it still represents quite a substantial outlay of money and this is likely to put it beyond the pocket of most small-scale project researchers.

A second possibility is to develop an *application* ('app') that can be hosted on Facebook. Apps include games, polls, quizzes and fan pages which appear as sponsored links on the user's home page. It is possible to develop an app specifically for the purposes of a survey – as was done in the case of the myPersonality app (Kosinski et al. 2013). This was an online personality survey that was designed by psychologists and which attracted over 4.5 million users. Developing such apps, though, requires quite a lot of technical skill and the costs can be considerable relative to the resources available for most small-scale research.

The research population

When conducting any kind of survey, researchers need to be clear about the kind of people, events or items that will be relevant for the study and likely to provide valuable data in terms of the topic that is being investigated. It is worth noting that in this context the term 'population' has a specific meaning. Rather than meaning everyone who lives in a country, population refers to all the items in the category of things that are being researched. It means a *research* population. So, if a survey is used to study nurses in Scotland then the survey population refers to all nurses working in Scotland (not all the people who populate Scotland). Likewise, if the research involves a survey of trade union members in the transport industry in Wales then the term 'population' refers to all the transport workers in Wales who belong to a trade union.

Making contact with members of the research population

Whether the researcher wants to include all of the population in the survey or, as discussed in Chapter 2, a sample drawn from the population, the survey cannot begin without having planned some way of making contact with members of the research population. This shifts the emphasis from the question of 'who' to the matter of 'how', as it requires the researcher to think ahead about the practical task of establishing contact with potential participants in the survey or gaining access to suitable events or items. The survey researcher, in effect, needs 'contact points' for the research population. In practice, these tend to come in the form of lists of names, addresses, locations, membership numbers, job titles, schedules of events, inventories of items, etc. that allow the researcher to identify who and where members of the research population can be found. Examples of such information are things like:

- a list of *postal addresses* (e.g. for businesses in a particular industry);
- a list of *names* (e.g. of local residents based on an electoral register);
- *suitable locations* for finding particular kinds of people (e.g. shopping malls to find retail customers);
- a list of *email addresses* (e.g. for employees of a company, or clients for a service);
- *phone numbers* from a directory (e.g. for people or companies in a specific area);
- *online groups* (e.g. for special interest groups or particular kinds of people).

> **Link up with**
> Sampling frame,
> p. 34.

Participation by the research population

The willingness and ability of the research population to participate in the survey are something that can never be taken for granted. When planning a survey, careful thought needs to be given to the matter: What is the likelihood that those people identified as potential participants will agree to co-operate with the research? Much will depend on things like:

- the kind of people involved (e.g. busy or not busy);
- the capacity of the people invited to participate (language, literacy, age, vulnerable groups);
- the topic of the survey;

- the context in which the survey is delivered (when, where);
- the mode of delivery of the survey (face-to-face, Internet, post, phone).

The *consequences* of participation also warrant consideration. At the planning stage for a survey it is essential that thought is given to the question of whether participation in the survey might in any way harm members of the research population, cause them stress, or unduly inconvenience them. Researchers, in other words, must consider the ethics of inviting people to participate in their survey.

> **Link up with**
> Chapter 17
> Research ethics.

Response rates

Rarely do researchers get responses from all the people they invite to participate in their survey. Normally, they can expect to receive replies from only a proportion of those who were originally contacted, and this is a basic fact of doing surveys. The extent to which a survey is successful in getting replies from those who were originally contacted is known as 'the response rate'. It is calculated as a percentage. So, if a researcher distributes 200 questionnaires and receives 110 completed returns then the survey's response rate will be 55 per cent. If 200 questionnaires are distributed and 100 are completed and returned, then this is a 50 per cent response rate.

When planning a survey it is important to anticipate the likely response rate and take this into consideration when deciding on the numbers who will be contacted and asked to collaborate with the research. If you think you might get a 40 per cent response rate and you need 200 completed questionnaires on which to base your analysis, then clearly you will need to distribute 500 questionnaires – a considerably larger number.

How to achieve good response rates

Generally speaking, the aim of a good survey is to achieve a high response rate. The larger the proportion that responds, the better it is for the survey. The design of the survey needs to take this into account and, as far as is possible, survey researchers need to incorporate measures that will encourage people to participate in the survey and, just as importantly, avoid things that are likely to deter people from responding. There is no magic formula that will guarantee a good response rate, but the following factors have been found to have a significant bearing on response rates and they ought to be considered carefully when planning a small-scale survey.

Target appropriate people for the survey: respondent selection

A good response rate depends on using an accurate population list/sampling frame. A scatter-gun approach will cover a large number of potential respondents but many of these will not respond because the topic is not relevant to them. And if they do respond, the data from them might not be pertinent to the topic of the research. The more a survey can identify and locate relevant people (or items), the better the response rate is likely to be.

Follow up non-responses: reminders

The classic way to boost response rates is to 'follow up' non-responses and the standard advice for survey researchers is that they should build into the survey design some tactics for re-contacting anyone who does not respond on the first occasion. Measures should also be taken to repeat the reminder two or three times if needed. There is clear evidence that this boosts response rates in all kinds of surveys (Dillman et al. 2009).

Having said that, there are two issues linked with improving overall response rates through follow-ups which need to be borne in mind. First, there is the time delay caused by the process. When surveys are conducted under strict time constraints, as with much small-scale research, this can pose something of a dilemma. Second, there is the matter of anonymity. If questionnaire responses are completely anonymous and it is not possible to trace the questionnaires back to individual respondents, then it will not be possible to work out who has responded and who has not. Targeting individual non-respondents becomes impossible.

Give prior notification: invitations in advance

Consistently across the range of types of survey it has been found that prior notification is beneficial in terms of response rates. When potential respondents are made aware of the survey in advance there is more chance of them agreeing to participate in the survey. This applies whether the contact is made by post, email or in person. With online surveys, having access to a list of email addresses that can be used to pre-notify people in advance is beneficial in terms of boosting response rates.

Make the topic of interest to respondents: topic salience

Response rates are better when the topic has 'salience'. This means that the topic has to capture the attention of potential respondents. Literally, it has to stand out and be conspicuous. A survey of people belonging to a specific interest group, of course, should have no problem on this score since those involved will have been targeted exactly because of their (known) interest in the topic. In any surveys where such a matching of interests cannot be guaranteed, the onus is on researchers to do all they can to *make* the topic interesting. They need to present the topic in a way that is upbeat, enthusiastic and positive – doing all they can to *get* the respondent interested in the topic.

Show that participation will 'make a difference': response impact

People are more motivated to participate in a survey if they feel that their contribution can have some influence and might actually 'make a difference' – especially when there is some direct, personal benefit to be gained from agreeing to participate. Bearing this in mind, survey researchers should indicate (when it is possible) how taking part in the survey might be in the respondents' interests. If at all possible, they should let potential respondents know how their answers will be valuable, and how their contribution to the survey can have an effect on something in which they have a vested interest. So, for example, potential respondents could be encouraged to participate by knowing that the information they provide will be used to improve the quality of a particular service they receive or product they buy.

Establish the legitimacy of the survey: sponsorship

Response rates are likely to increase to the extent that the survey is regarded as legitimate research. Early in the contact with potential respondents the researcher needs to establish that the survey is for a worthy cause and that it is being conducted under the auspices of a credible organization. There needs to be a basis for *trust*. For small-scale research projects, especially those conducted as part of a university degree, this means that it is important to assure potential respondents that the survey is part of a genuine research project and that it will be properly conducted. The name of the university, assurances of confidentiality, and contact details for the researcher are the kind of thing that give the potential respondent some confidence that the survey is legitimate and, therefore, something that deserves attention.

Minimize the response burden: keep things simple and easy

Asking someone to take part in a survey involves asking for their time and effort. The amount of this 'response burden' can be a major deterrent to participating in a survey. If too much is asked of respondents then response rates will plummet as people fail to finish the questionnaire, put down the phone or delete the message in frustration and annoyance. Recognizing this point, the task for the survey researcher is to *minimize the response burden* by including only those items that are absolutely essential and taking care to ask the questions in a way that keeps things as easy and straightforward as possible.

Provide information about progress towards completion

Many people who start an interview or questionnaire fail to complete it. They stop through frustration and exasperation at the amount of time and effort being asked of them. Such drop-outs obviously reduce the response rate and survey researchers need to do what they can to prevent this happening. One way of tackling the problem is to be clear and open at the outset about the amount of time that participation is likely to take. When considering whether to become involved in the research, people quite reasonably will want to know: How long will the interview take? How many pages are there in the questionnaire? It is good practice, therefore, to *let people know in advance how much of their time will be needed*.

During the process of completing the interview or questionnaire people might also want to know: How much *more*? With a paper questionnaire people can see what needs to be done and can easily monitor their progress through the questionnaire. With online questionnaires, however, the 'finishing line' might not be so obvious and *using a 'progress bar' has been shown to be an effective way of improving response rates* – letting people know how far they have got, and how far they still have to go before completing the questionnaire. In the course of an interview, similarly, it might be wise to verbally reassure the respondent about how far they have progressed and how much is still left to do.

Provide incentives: rewards or feedback

Material incentives can increase response rates. Quite separate from any motivation stemming from the topic itself or the impact that the findings might have, the prospect of material rewards can serve to encourage people to take part in a survey. Market research companies using postal surveys might include a small amount of money as a 'token of thanks'. Online surveys can reward respondents with shopping tokens and vouchers of various kinds. And the promise of inclusion in a prize draw for a large cash prize or a free holiday can be effective with most kinds of survey. But, of course, such *material* incentives cost money – lots of it. Consequently they tend to be used with large-scale commercial research projects where sponsors and clients pick up the bill. *Small-scale researchers, however, cannot normally call on the funding necessary to use this as an effective method of increasing response rates.*

What small-scale low-budget research *can* offer by way of incentives is *feedback*. Respondents can be motivated by offering them copies of the final report or summaries of the findings arising from the investigation. In essence, they can be offered information rather than material rewards – information which stems directly from their participation in the project and which they may find useful and/or interesting. The offer of such feedback, whether it is taken up or not, is a nice gesture and one which signals that the researcher would like to offer something in return to the respondent.

Good practice: Plan ahead to minimize non-response rates

Remember, response rates are affected by:

- the amount of spare time people have;
- the extent to which the survey caters for respondents' abilities;
- social sensitivities around the topic being investigated;
- prejudices and preferences of potential respondents;
- the social climate and freedom to express views.

Response rates and Internet surveys

Fears have been voiced about low response rates from Internet surveys, caused through people feeling ill at ease using computers or not having ready access to the Internet. As time progresses, though, the evidence would suggest that such anxieties are largely unfounded (Sue and Ritter 2012). Indeed, direct comparisons between different survey modes (postal, email, web-based) indicates that, generally speaking, there is now little difference in response rates between postal mail surveys and web-based surveys (Hoonakker and Carayon 2009).

Acceptable levels of response

There is no benchmark figure for judging what is an acceptable response rate and what is not. There is simply no hard and fast rule on the matter. It all depends on the circumstances. A large postal survey sent 'cold' without prior notification to households will get a low response rate – in all likelihood it would be far less that 10 per cent. A survey sent on behalf of a club or association to its members using a membership list is likely to achieve a far higher response rate – possibly over 70 per cent. A survey using face-to-face interviews arranged by personal contact between the researcher and the interviewees is likely to get a very high response rate – possibly up to 100 per cent. So much depends on who is contacted, how they are contacted and what they are contacted about.

Bearing these things in mind, rather than look for a universal benchmark figure for surveys above which response rates are acceptable and below which the results become suspect, it is more productive to gauge whether the response rate is acceptable by making a comparison with *similar* surveys. It is the response rates achieved by surveys that are similar in terms of their methods, their size, their target group, their topic of research, their use of prior contact and other relevant factors that provide an indication of what can be treated as an acceptable response rate.

Good practice

Look at the response rates achieved by similar types of survey. Use these as your target.

Non-response bias

Response rates are important because if a survey has a low response rate, then its findings will miss data from those who have chosen not to respond. At one level this will be disappointing for the survey researcher since fewer responses means less data. But it is not simply the sheer *amount* of potential data that is lost which worries researchers: it is the fear that a (low) response rate can lead to a thing called *non-response bias*. This bias occurs when there is a pattern to the responses in which it becomes clear that those who have not completed the survey tend to be different from those who have. If this happens, the findings from the survey will systematically over-represent data collected from the people who are more likely to respond and, by the same token, systematically under-represent data for those who are less likely to respond. This is likely to have a direct bearing on how fair and objective the survey's findings will be.

Basically, there are two sources of non-response bias. The first of these is *non-contact* bias. If the survey is designed in such a way that it *systematically* favours the inclusion of some types of people (or items) at the expense of others, then a bias will result. An example of this would be if a survey involved researchers calling at home addresses to conduct interviews with residents, and the researchers made their visits between 9 a.m. and 5 p.m. This would tend to miss contact with households where everyone is at work during the day. To avoid this, they would need to make contact in the evenings as well as during the day.

A second cause of bias is *non-response through refusal*. In this case if the design of the survey serves to discourage people from responding and does so in a way that systematically deters certain types of people rather than others, then a non-response bias will occur. The social factors that affect response rates, identified above, are significant in this context because different types of people will be more likely to opt out of a survey depending on things like the nature of the topic, the burden of participating in the survey, and the amount of time they have to spare.

Non-response bias and Internet surveys

Non-response bias through 'non-contact' occurs with Internet surveys to the extent that only those people who have access to the Internet can take part in the survey. Put another way, Internet surveys systematically exclude those who do not have Internet access. Now, although a large and increasing proportion of the population in developed countries is online, it is worth remembering that there are still demographic differences that persist in relation to:

- social class, with wealthier groups being more likely to have access than poorer groups;
- age, with the elderly being less likely to have access to the Internet than other groups.

Internet access also varies across different countries in the world: the vast majority of Internet users live in the USA, Europe or the Asia Pacific rim countries, with those living in poorer parts of the world being less likely to be able to participate in Internet research.

Another potential source of non-response bias occurs when Internet surveys rely on responses from visitors to websites. The problem here is that those who visit the site are *not* likely to constitute a cross-section of the population. The issue relates to the use of chat rooms, news groups and online interviews as well. In such instances the concern is that those who end up participating in the survey might be representative not of the general public but just of those who are online and interested in a particular subject.

This danger is illustrated by the case of the BBC's 'Great British Class Survey'. The British Broadcasting Corporation initiated a survey of social class in Britain. It used a web survey which, following substantial publicity on national TV and radio, produced a large response. Between January and July 2011 the survey achieved 161,400 completed online questionnaires. However, the eventual 'sample' was far from representative of the population as a whole. As Savage et al. (2013: 224) note:

The survey suffered from a strong selection bias, with respondents being predominantly drawn from the well-educated social groups. As one BBC journalist told us when we reported this problem, 'Yes, you seem to have got a typical BBC news audience there.'

Although the number or respondents was large, the online survey proved to be so unrepresentative of the population that the BBC had to get more data from a separate survey. This time they outsourced the work to a survey firm who used quota-sampling and face-to-face contact with 1026 respondents in order to get a nationally representative sample.

Checking for non-response bias

When conducting a survey the researcher needs to ask an important question: *Do the non-respondents differ in any systematic and relevant fashion from those who have responded?* Of course, to answer this question the researcher needs to have some information about those who have been targeted but not responded. This may prove difficult. None the less, it is good practice to endeavour to get some data about the non-respondents and to assess whether they are different from the respondents in any way that will have a bearing on the findings. For instance, are they different in terms of the following:

- who they are? (e.g. age, sex, gender, social class, religion, opinions)
- what they believe? (e.g. opinions, political views)
- what they do? (e.g. activities, lifestyles, purchasing behaviour)

> **Good practice**
>
> Researchers should take what practical measures are possible to find out if respondents are different from non-respondents in some way that is relevant to the survey and which might result in a non-response bias.

Weighting the findings

If it appears that the survey has an imbalance in terms of the kind of people who have responded and those who have not responded, there is a solution: that is to 'weight' the findings. It is worth stressing that this mathematical technique tends to be associated with large-scale surveys and is not normally a technique that should be applied to small-scale research. It is used where the researchers have some firm evidence about the proportions of respondents they would *expect* to find included in their survey. So, for example, if an omnibus survey of consumer attitudes obtains 5000 responses, of which 20 per cent come from the under-25 age range, and if national figures for the population indicate that this age group actually make up 30 per cent of the population, researchers can mathematically boost this group's impact on the overall findings from 20 per cent to 30 per cent – reflecting what would have been the case had the survey been representative of the population. Of course the other age-ranges would also have their impact brought in line with the proportions known to exist in the wider population.

Advantages of surveys

Costs and time

Surveys can be an efficient and relatively inexpensive means of collecting data. In the case of small-scale surveys the researcher's time might be the only significant cost involved and, although large-scale surveys can involve substantial costs, compared with strategies such as experiments and ethnography, they can produce a mountain of data in a short time for a relatively low cost. Results can be obtained over a fairly short period of time and the researcher can set a finite time-span for this, which is very useful when it comes to planning the research and delivering the end-product.

'Real-world' data

As an approach to social research, the emphasis tends to be on producing data based on real-world observations. The very notion of a survey suggests that the research has involved an active attempt by the researcher to go out and look and to search. Surveys are associated with getting information 'straight from the horse's mouth'.

Can be used with large-scale and small-scale research

In the case of large-scale surveys the breadth of coverage is an advantage in getting representative data from which generalizations can be made about the wider population. In the case of small-scale interview surveys researchers can build up a picture based on data that includes the full range of relevant items or people, perhaps selectively including the unusual or extreme 'outliers' that are seen as likely to provide particularly useful information.

Can collect both quantitative and qualitative data

The survey approach lends itself to being used with particular methods, such as the self-completion questionnaire, which can generate large volumes of quantitative data that can be subject to statistical analysis. However, surveys can just as easily produce qualitative data, particularly when used in conjunction with methods such as an interview.

Disadvantages of surveys

Tendency to focus on data accumulation and data description more than theory

With its emphasis on collecting empirical data there is a danger that the 'data are left to speak for themselves' without an adequate account of the implications of those data for relevant issues, problems or theories. There is nothing inevitable about this, however, and *good* survey research certainly does devote attention to the analysis of data.

Depth or detail

The data produced through large-scale surveys are likely to lack depth and detail on the topic being investigated. This is almost inevitable. Such surveys tend to forfeit depth in favour of breadth when it comes to the data that are produced, especially where quantitative data are used. This is not true, however, of small-scale qualitative surveys using interview methods. Where the survey uses interview methods, it can produce data that are rich and detailed, although in this case the trade-off is that the number of people taking part in the survey will be much smaller.

Low response rates

Response rates from surveys are often quite low and getting a reasonable response rate can be quite a challenge for the researcher. This is particularly the case with large-scale surveys where potential participants are selected at random and where the researcher has no personal contact with the potential participants. It is easy to ignore a researcher's request for help that comes through the post or via email. Where selection to a survey involves personal contact the response rates tend to be higher. Low response rates can lead to non-response bias in the survey.

Contact with 'hard-to-reach' research populations

Surveys are easier to use when the research population can be identified and contacted through some pre-existing listing or directory. Where the research population cannot be located through such means – when they are 'hard-to-reach' – survey researchers need to use more time-consuming and possibly innovative means for contacting potential participants.

Further reading

De Vaus, D. (2014) *Surveys in Social Research*, 6th edn. London: Routledge.
Dillman, D. A., Smyth, J. D. and Christian, L. M. (2009) *Internet, Mail, and Mixed-mode Surveys: The Tailored Design Method*. Hoboken, NJ: Wiley.
Schonlau, M., Fricker, R. and Elliot, M. (2002) *Conducting Research Surveys via E-mail and the Web*. Rand Monograph MR-1480-RC. Available at: http://www.rand.org/pubs/monograph_reports/MR1480.html.
Sue, V. M. and Ritter, L. A. (2012) *Conducting Online Surveys*. Thousand Oaks, CA: Sage.
Tourangeau, R., Conrad, F. and Couper, M. (2013) *The Science of Web Surveys*. Oxford: Oxford University Press.

Checklist for the use of surveys

When conducting a survey you should feel confident about answering 'yes' to the following questions: ☑

1 Does the type of survey match the style of research (large-scale/ small-scale, quantitative/qualitative, explanatory/descriptive/ exploratory)? ☐

2 Has a research population been clearly identified? ☐

3 Does a population list/sampling frame exist for the research population and can it be used to make contact with potential participants? (If appropriate.) ☐

4 Have the costs of the survey been estimated and are these 'within budget' for the research? ☐

5 Will a pilot survey be conducted to check for potential problems? ☐

6 Are suitable measures in place to minimize non-responses and to achieve the best possible response rate? ☐

7 Will potential participants receive prior notification about the survey? ☐

8 Will follow-ups be used to bolster the response rate? ☐

9 Have efforts been made to avoid response bias and, where possible, have checks been made to see if there are significant differences between the respondents and the non-respondents? ☐

10 Ethics – has due consideration been given to the possible consequences of the survey for participants? ☐

2 Sampling

Representative samples and exploratory samples • Probability sampling and non-probability sampling • Sampling frames • Probability sampling techniques • Non-probability sampling techniques • Which sampling technique should be used? • Size of the sample • Advantages of sampling • Disadvantages of sampling • Further reading • Checklist for the use of sampling

The basic principle of sampling is that it is possible to produce reasonably accurate findings without the need to collect data from each and every member of a research population. For survey researchers, in particular, this can be an attractive proposition. It means that they might be able to save time and money by reducing the amount of data they need to collect without sacrificing much in terms of the accuracy of their findings.

Representative samples and exploratory samples

When survey researchers select a sample from a population they will be doing one of two things. They will either be trying to get a *representative* sample or they will be trying to get an *exploratory* sample. Each involves a different approach and they tend to be associated with different kinds of social research.

Representative samples tend to be associated with larger surveys and with the use of quantitative data. A representative sample involves a cross-section of the population. It matches the population in terms of its mix of ingredients, and relies on using a selection procedure that:

- includes all relevant factors/variables/events;
- matches the proportions in the overall population.

Information gathered from a representative sample allows the researcher to draw valid conclusions about how things are in the overall research population.

Exploratory samples are often used in small-scale research and tend to lend themselves to the use of qualitative data. An exploratory sample is used as a way of probing relatively unexplored topics and as a route to the discovery of new ideas or theories. The point of the sample is to provide the researcher with a means for generating insights and information. For this purpose it is not always necessary to get an accurate cross-section of the population. There are times when this might be the case, but selection to an exploratory sample is more likely to include interesting, extreme and unusual examples that can illuminate the thing being studied.

Good practice

Researchers need to be very clear and explicit about whether their intention is to use a *representative* sample or an *exploratory* sample.

Probability sampling and non-probability sampling

Echoing in many respects the alternative purposes for which social researchers might use sampling, there are two distinct approaches which can be used for the *selection* of samples. Researchers can either choose *probability sampling* as the basis for selecting their sample from the research population, or they can use *non-probability sampling*.

Probability sampling relies on the use of random selection from the research population. It is known as probability sampling because it is based on statistical theory relating to the 'normal distribution' of events. The theory behind its use is that the best way to get a *representative sample* is to ensure that the researcher has absolutely no influence on the selection of people/items to be included in the sample. The sample, instead, should be based on completely *random* selection from among the population being studied. Probability sampling works best with large numbers, where there is a known population (number, characteristics) and it tends to be associated with large-scale surveys using quantitative data.

Non-probability sampling involves an element of discretion or choice on the part of the researcher at some point in the selection process and it is used when researchers find it difficult or undesirable to rely on random selection to the sample. The reasons for this are varied but, in the main, they will be because:

- The researcher feels it is not feasible to include a sufficiently large number of examples in the study.
- The researcher does not have sufficient information about the *research population* to undertake probability sampling. The researcher may not know who, or how many people or events, make up the research population.
- It may prove exceedingly difficult to contact a sample selected through conventional probability sampling techniques. For example, research on drug addicts or the homeless would not lend itself to normal forms of probability sampling.

Table 2.1 Approaches to sampling

Probability	Random selection	Representative sample	large numbers
Non-probability	Researcher-influenced selection	Representative sample or Exploratory sample	small numbers

> **Link up with**
> Research popula-
> tions, p. 21.

Non-probability sampling can still retain the aim of generating a *representative sample*. In the interests of saving costs, however, the selection of the sample involves an element of expediency and established good practice rather than strict adherence to the principles of random selection. Equally, non-probability sampling can be used where the aim is to produce *an exploratory sample* rather than a representative cross-section of the population. Such approaches involve non-probability sampling because people or items are selected for the sample on the basis of things like their expertise, their experience or the fact that they might be unusual or different from the norm (Table 2.1).

Sampling frames

A sampling frame provides a basis for selecting a sample. It is particularly important when researchers intend to use probability sampling, but can also be valuable for non-probability sampling as well. A sampling frame contains information about the *research population*. Generally it takes the form of a list of names or addresses that includes all of the members of the population from which the sample is to be selected. Sometimes a suitable sampling frame can be easy to find. Research that involves formal organizations can often draw on things like membership lists, email addresses, and employee records to provide a suitable sampling frame that includes all members of the population to be researched. The information is already kept for other administrative purposes. Research involving particular industries and occupations can find that things like trade directories, commercial listings and memberships of professional associations provide suitable sampling frames. And, surveys targeting the general public might be able to use electoral registers or the Postcode Address File (PAF) – a list of postcodes and postal addresses produced by the Post Office which contains about 99 per cent of all private residential addresses. There can be costs associated with some listings. Commercial companies will supply lists of businesses, schools, hospitals, charities and other organizations, but will charge for the service. However, it is possible to be quite specific about which types of organization and which areas are to be included in the list. This suits the needs of small-scale research projects because the lists can be fairly small and supplied at relatively low cost.

> **Link up with**
> Research popula-
> tions, p. 21.

Bias in sampling frames

There is a danger with the use of any sampling frame that it might be incomplete. A list of private addresses will not lead the researcher to those who are homeless and live on the streets. An electoral register will not include those under 18 years of age or those who, for whatever reason, have not registered to vote. Things omitted might well be different in some important respects from the things which actually exist on the list, and overlooking them as part of the research can lead to a biased sample. Just as damaging for the purposes of research, registers can include certain items that should not be there. They can contain names of people who have passed on – in either a geographical or a mortal sense. People move home, people die, and unless the register is regularly and carefully updated on a routine basis there is the likelihood that it will be out of date and include items it should not. Either way, the impact can be significant. If the sampling frame systematically excludes things that should be in, or systematically includes things which should be out, the sample will almost inevitably be biased.

Internet surveys and sampling frames

In general, the nature of the Internet makes good sampling frames relatively more difficult to find. This is because addresses, identities and contact points on the Internet are very different from postal addresses and phone numbers in the 'real' world. In cyberspace, an address and an identity can be very temporary and provide no background information of value to the researcher. People often have more than one email address, use more than one Internet Service Provider (ISP) and there is no guarantee that any address will be used by just one individual. Having said this, there are certain types of email lists that are well suited to being used as a sampling frame when conducting Internet surveys. Primarily, this is when the research is focused on populations who exist in some sort of formal organization because the administration of organizations almost invariably requires the maintenance of good records of the membership, e.g. employees at work, pupils in schools, members of clubs, volunteers with charities. Such email lists tend to serve known populations and can therefore prove to be a valuable basis for a sampling frame.

Link up with Internet surveys, p. 13.

 Key point

A good sampling frame should be:

- *relevant:* it should contain things directly linked to the research topic;
- *complete:* it should cover all relevant items;
- *precise:* it should exclude all the items that are not relevant;
- *up-to-date:* it should incorporate recent additions and changes, and have redundant items cleansed from the list.

Probability sampling techniques

Random sampling: each person/item has an equal chance of being selected

Random sampling is often portrayed as the ideal basis for generating a representative sample. This is because with random sampling the inclusion of a person/item in the sample is based entirely on chance. Random selection ensures that there is no scope for the researcher to influence the sample in some way that will introduce bias.

It is important to appreciate that the term 'random', as used in this context, does not mean that selection can be haphazard or based on an 'any one will do' approach. And it is a dangerous mistake for the project researcher to use the term 'random' in a loose or colloquial way when dealing with sampling techniques. For research purposes the term 'random' actually involves quite specific constraints on the way that persons/items get selected. From a statistical point of view randomness means that 'each unit should have an equal and known probability of inclusion in the sample'.

To get a random sample there needs to be:

1 *a known population* from which the sample is to be taken. The researcher needs to know something about the make-up of the overall population from which the sample is to be extracted (such as the total number, who they are or where they exist).

2 a *sampling frame* that provides a list of all the items in the population and which allows them to be picked via some unique identifier (such as a name, an address, an employee number or a birth date).

3 a process of random selection which provides the basis for including specific units in the sample. For research purposes this can involve the use of a *random number generator* – a utility available free online or through appropriate computer software packages.

 Key point

A random sample is like a lottery draw. The underlying principle is that no person can influence which items get picked. The selection is based on just one factor – *pure chance*.

Systematic sampling: every *n*th case is included

Systematic sampling adheres closely to the principle of random selection but, in this case, the researcher selects items in a systematic way – picking every *n*th item from an appropriate list. For a sample of 50 from a population of 250 it will be every 5th item, for a sample of 70 from a population of 490 it will be every 7th item – *n*th depending on the size of the required sample relative to the number in the research population. It should not matter where on the list the selection starts. The researcher, however, will want to feel sure that there is no order or pattern in the list that might be related to the topic being investigated because this could undermine the principle of random selection and cause some bias to creep into the sample as a result of the system of selection.

Cluster sampling: clusters within the population

Rather than using random sampling to select individual people or items, cluster sampling uses random sampling to select specific clusters or groups. Within each of the clusters all people/items are included in the sample. The advantage of this sampling technique is that the clusters, as the name suggests, contain items that are closely grouped together – normally in one location or in one geographical area. By focusing on such clusters, the researcher can save a great deal of time and money that would otherwise have been spent on travelling to and fro visiting research sites scattered throughout the length and breadth of the land. For this reason cluster sampling is often used by market researchers and others who need to conduct surveys on a limited budget.

There are, however, two important conditions that need to be met for the use of cluster sampling. First, the clusters must be pre-existing, naturally occurring groups. Second, each cluster should reflect the heterogeneity of the total population. The idea is that within each cluster the researcher might expect to find a mini-version of the total population and that by including all members of the cluster within the sample, the researcher will be able to get a representative sample that will produce findings that accurately match the situation in the total research population.

Multi-stage sampling: samples drawn from samples

Multi-stage sampling involves selecting samples in a sequence of stages, each sample being drawn from within the previously selected sample. The underlying principle is still one of random selection, only in this case it involves sampling at multiple stages rather than all at once. In principle, multi-stage sampling can go on through any number of levels, each level involving a sample drawn from the previous level.

The distinction between multi-stage sampling and cluster sampling is that cluster sampling uses all the items or people that exist within each cluster whereas multi-stage sampling selects a sample from within the cluster. This is particularly useful if: (1) the researcher suspects that the population within the chosen clusters will not provide a cross-section of the wider population or (2) if resources dictate that it is too expensive to include everyone in the cluster.

Stratified sampling: sampling based on subgroups in the population

Stratified sampling continues to adhere to the underlying principle of random selection. However, it introduces some element of researcher influence into the selection process and, to this extent, moves away slightly from pure random sampling. Stratified sampling subdivides the research population into different subgroups (strata) and then chooses the required number of items or people from within each subgroup using random sampling techniques. The reason for introducing stratification into the selection process is to ensure that crucial parts of the population are appropriately represented in the overall sample. It allows the researcher to select a sample which he/she knows will include, for instance, equal number of men and women, or perhaps an appropriate balance of different age groups within the sample. There are two important conditions that apply to the use of stratified sampling. First, the subgroups must be fairly homogeneous in the sense that they share something in common which can be used to separate them into clearly identifiable subgroups. Second, this factor must be relevant and significant in terms of what is already known about the topic.

Example 2.1: Probability sampling techniques

Table 2.2 illustrates how different probability sampling techniques can operate. The numbers involved are small which, for the purposes of an illustration, is actually quite useful because it highlights some of the problems that can arise when probability sampling is used with small sample sizes. In practice, however, the size of the samples would need to be considerably larger to allow the probability samples to produce sufficiently accurate results.

In this illustration the population consists of 27 people. Let us presume that they are members of a football supporters' club and that we wish to select a sample of 9 people to take part in our research (and bear in mind that, in reality, the numbers might be one hundred times greater than this miniature illustration). The *sampling frame* consists of a list of members' names. These are ordered alphabetically, and each name has been assigned a number. In principle, this is sufficient for us to produce either a pure random sample or a systematic random sample. The sampling frame contains two further bits of information about the members – location and sex. These permit the use of cluster sampling and stratified sampling.

A *random sample* can be selected using random number generating software. Simple utilities for this can be found on the Internet, or they come as part of standard data analysis software. We use the software to generate a list of 9 numbers between values 1 and 27. Those whose names are matched with these numbers on the list are then selected to form the random sample. Note that in this particular list there are 7 males and 2 females. Running the random number generator again will produce different figures and, in all probability, a different balance of males to females. This effect is exaggerated by the very small numbers involved but as the sample size increases towards 1,000 or more the difference caused by using different random numbers would vastly diminish.

A *systematic sample* can be produced simply by selecting every third person on the list. This will provide the researcher with 9 people who have been selected simply by chance in terms of where they happen to appear on the list. This presumes, of course, that there is nothing in the order of the list that could bias the sample. Note that in this particular systematic sample there are 9 males and

Table 2.2 Illustration of four probability sampling techniques

Sampling frame								Segregated sampling frame		
list no.	name	location	sex	Random	Systematic	Cluster	Stratified	list no.	sex	name
001	Ahmed	A	M	•			•	001	M	Ahmed
002	Ashton	F	M	•				002	M	Ashton
003	Bernbaum	C	M					003	M	Bernbaum
004	Bradford	E	F	•				005	M	Chang
005	Chang	B	M		•		•	006	M	Davies
006	Davies	A	M					009	M	Ewusie
007	Diego	H	F			•	•	012	M	Goldberg
008	Duval	E	F		•	•	•	013	M	Gupta
009	Ewusie	I	M			•	•	015	M	Jones
010	Fleur	A	F				•	017	M	Mars
011	Gerhardt	I	F		•	•		018	M	Merton
012	Goldberg	D	M		•			019	M	O'Reilly
013	Gupta	B	M					020	M	Overton
014	Johnson	G	F	•	•	•	•	021	M	Rahman
015	Jones	B	M	•		•		023	M	Silva
016	Kheidr	I	F			•		024	M	Tunstall
017	Marsh	D	M		•		•	026	M	Webber
018	Merton	G	M					027	M	Williams
019	O'Reilly	H	M	•		•	•	004	F	Bradford
020	Overton	C	M	•	•			007	F	Diego
021	Rahman	G	M					008	F	Duval
022	Robinson	C	F					010	F	Fleur
023	Silva	E	M		•			011	F	Gerhardt
024	Tunstall	F	M	•				014	F	Johnson
025	Waterman	F	F				•	016	F	Kheidr
026	Webber	H	M		•	•		022	F	Robinson
027	Williams	D	M	•			•	025	F	Waterman

0 females. However, if the start point is changed the proportions change dramatically. Check how the balance changes when we start the systematic selection at number 001 (3 males, 6 females) or number 002 (6 males, 3 females) instead.

For a *cluster sample* the selection is based on the random selection of 3 clusters and the inclusion of all those within the cluster as part of the sample. In this illustration the cluster is based on location. If locations B, H and I happen to be randomly selected, the sample will incorporate the 9 people who exist in these locations. The assumption here is that location itself is not a significant factor that could bias the sample.

A *stratified sample* is designed to ensure that there is an appropriate representation of the population within the overall sample. In this illustration a stratified sample could be used to ensure that males and females are represented proportionately in the sample. We know from our sampling frame that there is a ratio of 2:1 of males to females in our population (the football supporters' club members). To get a stratified sample we need to segregate the membership list according to sex. This is how the sampling frame is reorganized on the right of the table – males separated from females. Then, 6 random numbers can be generated for selecting from the list of males and 3 random numbers likewise for selecting from the list of females. In this way the researcher guarantees to get a sample where appropriate proportions have been randomly selected from within specific strata of the membership of the football supporters' club.

Non-probability sampling techniques

Quota sampling: selected to meet specific criteria

Quota sampling is widely used in market research. It operates on very similar principles to stratified sampling. It establishes certain categories (or strata) which are considered to be vital for inclusion in the sample, and also seeks to fill these categories in proportion to their existence in the population. There is, though, one distinctive difference between stratified and quota sampling. With quota sampling, the method of choosing the people or events that make up the required number within each category is not a matter of strict random selection. In effect, it is left up to the researcher to choose who fills the quota. It might be on a 'first to hand' basis – as when market researchers stop people in the street. The people might be appropriate but were chosen because they just happened to be there, not as part of a random selection from a known population. The technical difference here excites statisticians but need not trouble the project researcher too much. The crucial point is that, like stratified sampling, it has the advantage of ensuring the representation of all crucial categories in the sample in proportion to their existence in the wider population. It does so without waste. Because the quotas are set in advance, no people or events that subsequently become 'surplus to requirements' are incorporated into the research. Quota sampling, then, has particular advantages when it comes to costs – especially when used with face-to-face interviewing.

Example 2.2

Quota sampling

Stores in a shopping mall might want to know what their customers think about the facilities that are available (e.g. parking, toilets, restaurants) and whether there are any particular features of the mall that attract them to visit it. A quota sample for face-to-face interviews in the mall could be devised on the basis of including 200 males and 200 females, and within each group there could be a quota of 40 in each of five age categories 12–18, 19–30, 31–45, 46–64, 65+. The quotas for interview, then, would be 40 males aged 12–18, 40 females aged 12–18, 40 males aged 19–30, 40 females aged 19–30, and so on. Interviewers would approach appropriate shoppers and continue to conduct interviews until they had filled the quota for each subgroup.

Purposive sampling: hand-picked for the topic

Purposive sampling operates on the principle that we can get the best information through focusing on a relatively small number of instances deliberately selected on the basis of their known attributes (i.e. not through random selection). With purposive sampling the sample is 'hand-picked' for the research on the basis of:

- *relevance:* to the issue/theory being investigated;
- *knowledge:* privileged knowledge or experience about the topic.

Purposive sampling works where the researcher already knows something about the specific people or events and deliberately selects particular ones because they are seen as instances that are likely to produce the most valuable data. They are selected with a specific purpose in mind, and that purpose reflects the particular qualities of the people or events chosen and their relevance to the topic of the investigation.

A purposive sample can be used in order to ensure that a wide cross-section of items or people are included in the sample. When used in this way purposive sampling is, to a degree, emulating a 'representative sample'. Based on prior knowledge, the researcher can deliberately select the sample in order to ensure that the full range of items or people is included (e.g. all age groups, all ethnic groups). This can be useful with small-scale surveys where random sampling of itself might not be likely enough to include groups that occur in relatively small numbers in the population.

Purposive sampling is particularly well suited for creating an 'exploratory sample'. It provides a way of getting the best information by selecting people most likely to have the experience or expertise to provide quality information and valuable insights on the research topic. It allows the researcher to home in on people or events which there are good grounds for believing will be critical for the research. These might be extreme cases, rare cases or critical cases rather than ordinary ones. Miles and Huberman (2014) call such special instances 'outliers', and commend their inclusion in the process of discovery as a check which explores rival possible explanations and tests any explanation based on mainstream findings, by seeing if they can work with instances which are distinctly *not* mainstream.

Example 2.3

Purposive sampling for key informants

A study of online banking fraud might start by identifying some individuals who play key roles in the detection and prevention of such fraud. Major high street banks have specialist teams dedicated to online security and the researcher could make contact with these teams to arrange interviews. Victims of online banking fraud could be sought to provide their particular perspective, and the researcher might even try to include fraudsters themselves to get even more insight to the topic.

Theoretical sampling: selected to help generate theories

With theoretical sampling the selection of instances follows a route of discovery based on the development of a theory which is 'grounded' in evidence. At each stage, new evidence is used to modify or confirm a 'theory', which then points to an appropriate choice of instances for research in the next phase. The sample evolves, and it continues to grow until such time as the researcher has sufficient information in relation to the theory that is being developed.

Link up with
Chapter 7
Grounded theory.

Example 2.4

Theoretical sampling

A study of teachers' control of classrooms in secondary schools might involve observation in classrooms and in-depth interviews with teachers. From early fieldwork the researcher could be alerted to the particular significance of noise emanating from classrooms as an indicator of (lack of) control. Building on this, theoretical sampling would involve choosing further observations and interviews deliberately to make comparisons and to check the initial 'theory' – perhaps looking for instances where noise might not be likely to signify a lack of control (e.g. music lessons or PE lessons).

Snowball sampling: participants refer the researcher on to other potential participants

With snowball sampling the sample emerges through a process of reference from one person to the next. At the start, the research is likely to involve just one or a few people. Each can be asked to nominate some other people who would be relevant for the purposes of the research. These nominations are then contacted and, it is hoped, included in the sample. The sample thus snowballs in size as each of the nominees is asked, in turn, to nominate further persons who might be included in the sample.

Snowball sampling is an effective technique for building up a reasonable-sized sample, especially when used as part of a small-scale research project. One advantage is that the accumulation of numbers is quite quick, using the multiplier effect of one person nominating two or more others. Added to this, the researcher can approach each new person, having been, in a sense, sponsored by the person who had named him or her. The researcher can use the nominator as some kind of reference to enhance his or her bona fides and credibility, rather than approach the new person cold. Snowball sampling is particularly useful where there is no sampling frame of any kind which can allow the researcher to identify and make contact with appropriate participants. For this reason, it is often used in conjunction with qualitative research based on small-scale exploratory samples, and its use is perfectly compatible with purposive sampling and theoretical sampling. People can be asked to nominate others who meet certain criteria for choice, certain conditions related to the research project and certain characteristics such as age, sex, ethnicity, qualifications, residence, state of health or leisure pursuits.

Link up with Facebook surveys, p. 19.

Example 2.5

Snowball sampling

A study of smoking cessation among 'under-age' smokers could use snowball sampling to good advantage. There is no sampling frame for such people and there is no obvious or simple way to identify such people. So, the researcher could make enquiries until one such person is found. This person is likely to know of others his/her age who have started smoking and subsequently quit before they reached the age of 16. Assuming the young person is willing to co-operate, he/she could be asked to identify two others who have quit smoking. In turn, these two could be asked to identify others who fit the needs of the sample, and so on. This process builds a sample that snowballs in size.

Convenience sampling: first to hand

Convenience sampling is built upon selections which suit the convenience of the researcher and which are 'first to hand'. An element of convenience is likely to enter into sampling procedures of most research. Because researchers have limited money and limited time at their disposal, it is quite reasonable that where there is scope for choice between two or more equally valid possibilities for inclusion in the sample, the researcher should choose the most convenient. If, for example, two or more clusters are equally suitable as research sites, it would be crazy to opt for ones that were the furthest away without some good reason to do so. Convenience sampling, however, takes this to an extreme by using convenience as the main basis for selecting the sample, not a subsidiary one. The criterion for selection to the sample is that items are convenient and the key advantage of convenience sampling is that it is quick, cheap and easy.

Example 2.6

Convenience sampling

A student who wishes to conduct a survey into consumer preferences in relation to soft drinks might choose all the fellow students on the course to be the 'sample'. They are easy to find and can probably be persuaded fairly easily to complete a questionnaire on the subject. Alternatively, using face-to-face interviews, the student could collect data from students using the canteen. Those who are interviewed will constitute a 'convenience sample'.

> **Caution**
>
> *Convenience* itself offers nothing by way of justification for the inclusion of people or events in the sample. It might be a reasonable practical criterion to apply when faced with equally viable alternatives but, in its own right, is not a factor that should be used by researchers to select the sample. Choosing things on the basis of convenience runs counter to the rigour of scientific research. It suggests a lazy approach to the work. Good research selects its items for study not on the basis that they are the *easiest* to obtain but for specific reasons linked to the subject matter of the research and the requirements of the investigation. For this reason, *the practice of convenience sampling is hard to equate with good research.*

Which sampling technique should be used?

From the outline of sampling techniques above we can see that the survey researcher has 10 basic options from which to choose, each characterized by a different method of selecting the people or items to be included in the sample. As Figure 2.1 shows, the sampling techniques sit somewhere on a continuum with, at one extreme, a selection technique which eliminates altogether the influence of the researcher (random selection) and at the other extreme a selection technique where selection of the sample is left entirely to the discretion of the researcher (convenience sampling). In between, there are a range of techniques which differ in the extent to which they adhere to the principle of random selection. But not only do the techniques sit on a sliding scale in terms of the basis for selecting the sample, they also have corresponding positions in terms of the purpose of the sample, the kind of data to be collected, the size of the sample and the amount of resources they are liable to consume. The choice of sampling technique depends, therefore, on how the various techniques fit the needs of the researcher and the kind of research he/she proposes to undertake. When deciding which technique to use the researcher needs to consider five core questions:

1 Is my purpose to produce a representative sample or an exploratory sample?
2 To what extent is this purpose better served by selecting the sample on the basis of random selection or deliberate choice?
3 Will qualitative data or quantitative data be more appropriate for addressing my research questions?
4 Does a suitable sampling frame exist and can I gain access to it?
5 In terms of the resources available for the research (time and money) which sampling technique is both feasible and likely to produce relevant information?

Size of the sample

There are basically three approaches to the calculation of the sample size: statistical, pragmatic and cumulative. The statistical approach is usually presented as the proper approach. As we shall see, however, it is best suited to large-scale

Figure 2.1 Sampling strategies

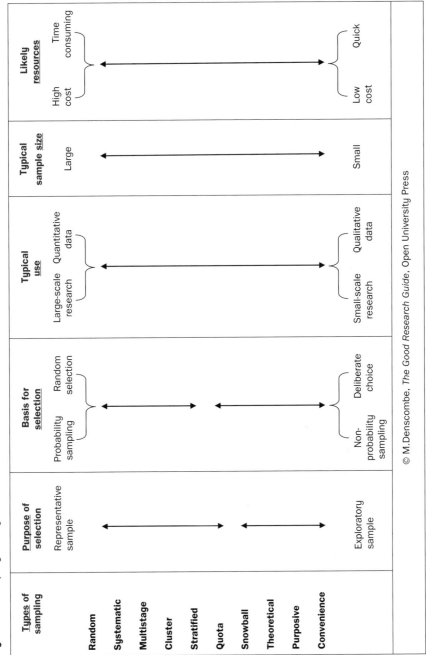

surveys and probability sampling techniques. It is the kind of approach that works well for things like opinion polls and government surveys which involve very large populations and which cost a lot of money. Smaller-scale surveys tend to use a more pragmatic approach. This is partly to do with the costs and partly to do with the difficulties in meeting all the conditions needed for the statistical approach to sample-size calculation. Market researchers often use a pragmatic approach, estimating the sample size on the basis of years of practical experience and on what works well enough within given resource constraints. The third approach is normally associated with small-scale, qualitative research. The cumulative approach is one in which the researcher continues to add to the size of the sample until a point is reached where there is sufficient information and where no benefit is derived from adding any more to the sample.

The purpose of the sample: representative or exploratory?

When deciding which approach to take the researcher needs to bear in mind the kind of sample that is required. Where the aim is to get a representative sample then the numbers involved will tend to be relatively large and where the aim is to produce an exploratory sample the numbers involved will be relatively small. There are different considerations for either kind of sample and any discussion of sample size needs to reflect the different premises on which they operate.

In the case of representative samples there is something of a 'big is beautiful' stance on survey size. This is based on the principle that the more instances that are covered the less likely it is that the sample will be biased. With a large sample, the researcher is more assured that:

- all aspects of relevance to the research question will have been covered and included in the findings;
- there will be some balance between the proportions within the sample and the proportions which occur in the overall population being investigated.

Both factors enhance the representativeness of the sample and, in turn, this allows greater confidence about making generalizations based on findings from the sample.

With exploratory samples the scale of the research tends to be smaller. There are two main reasons for this. First, it is likely that each item or person to be included in the sample will be studied in greater depth and more detail than will be the case with a representative sample. There is no absolute rule on this, but the size of exploratory samples generally reflects the fact that researchers want to probe deeper than they would do with representative samples. Second, the size of exploratory samples is not governed by matters of accuracy but by considerations of how *informative* the sample is. This means that the sample only needs to be sufficient in size to enable the researcher to feel that enough information has been collected.

Caution: The anticipated response rate

There is an important distinction to be made between sample size in the sense of the number of people initially contacted and sample size in the sense of the eventual number who respond. It is the eventual sample size that is crucial for the research. The researcher needs to predict the kind of response rate he or she is likely to achieve and build in an allowance for non-responses. If data are needed from a sample of 100 people and a response rate of 30 per cent is anticipated, the size of the sample that needs to be initially contacted will be 334.

The statistical approach: large-scale surveys using probability sampling for a representative sample

If the survey is large-scale and it uses probability sampling there is a precise way of calculating the required sample size. This is based on statistical theory and the *normal curve* distribution of events. Without getting involved too heavily in statistical theory the calculation of an appropriate sample size will depend on four things:

- The *size* of the research population. It is important to appreciate, though, that population size is significant where smaller numbers are concerned but, as Table 2.3 indicates, when the population moves beyond 5,000, changes in the size of the population cease to have much impact on the sample size.
- The *accuracy* of the estimates. Social researchers need to feel confident that their estimates lie close to the real (i.e. population) figure and they will normally

Table 2.3 Sample size and population size (probability sampling)

Number in the population	Required sample size[1] (at 95% confidence level)		
	5% margin of error	3% margin of error	1% margin of error
50	44	48	50
100	80	92	99
250	152	203	244
500	217	341	475
1,000	278	516	906
5,000	357	879	3288
10,000	370	964	4899
100,000	383	1056	8763
1 million	384	1066	9513
10 million	384	1067	9595

Note: [1]Refers to final usable responses.

tolerate a margin of error of 3 per cent or 5 per cent. More accurate results such as the 1 per cent margin of error require sample sizes that do not offer much saving until the population size exceeds 5,000. The margin of error that is deemed acceptable for a specific project is known as the *confidence interval*.

- *Confidence* that the sample will produce results that are representative of the population. This is the *level of confidence*. Social researchers know that there is always a chance that the sample might be extreme and unusual, and they want to feel very confident that their findings are not the product of any such extreme or unusual sample. In practice, they tend to want a 95 per cent confidence level. They want to know that there would be a less than one in twenty chance of this occurring.

- *Variation* in the population: less variation requires a bigger sample size. In terms of the particular attribute being measured (e.g. voting intention) it matters whether the population is evenly matched (nearing a 50:50 split) or is widely divided (e.g. 70:30 split). Researchers can get some idea of this in advance (i.e. before they actually conduct their survey) either from a review of existing research or by using a pilot survey. If this factor cannot be estimated it should be assumed that the population is evenly matched because this is a 'worst case scenario' as far as things are concerned when it comes to the size of the required sample. By default, the software plays on the safe side.

Taking these four factors into consideration it is possible to calculate the required sample size. There is a formula for this calculation but the maths do not need to concern the project researcher because there are plenty of software utilities freely available on the Internet that do the calculations at the press of a button. A web search on 'sample size calculator' will identify plenty of these (Figure 2.2). Some of these ask for variation (or 'response distribution') figures while others do not.

If in doubt, enter 50% in this box. Where they do not ask the user for the variation, they make the worst case scenario assumption outlined above. What all the sample size calculators do, however, is demonstrate very clearly how the required sample size varies according to what the researcher wants in terms of

Figure 2.2 A sample size calculator

levels of confidence and margins of error. The greater the level of confidence and the greater the level of accuracy, the bigger the size of the sample.

Accuracy and sample size

There is an interesting point that springs from statistical estimates and sample size. It is that there is relatively little advantage to be gained in terms of accuracy once a sample has reached a given size. There are diminishing returns to increases in the size of samples. This runs contrary to common sense, which would probably say to us that the degree of accuracy of results would depend on what proportion of the population is included in the sample. Common sense might say that a sample of 25 per cent of cases will produce better results than a sample of 10 per cent. Statistics would say that where the population size is large, there is hardly any increase in accuracy to be obtained by incorporating another 15 per cent (see Table 2.3).

The pragmatic approach: smaller-scale surveys using non-probability sampling for a representative sample

In practice, social research frequently involves surveys with relatively small numbers – *between 30 and 250* – and when estimating the required sample size such surveys tend to depend on non-probability sampling techniques. There are three pragmatic reasons for this. First, there is the matter of resources. In the real world of research the availability of resources is one factor that always affects the researcher's decision on sample size. The fact is that research does not take place with infinite time and money. In practice, it has to be tailored to meet the constraints imposed by the amount of time and money which can be spent on the investigation, and there are not too many individuals or organizations who can actually afford the scale of investigation that involves samples of 1,000 or more. Project researchers such as those conducting a survey as part of an academic degree are very unlikely to have the time or money to work with large populations and large samples.

Second, there is the nature of research populations and the fact that many of the populations that social researchers might like to investigate are relatively small. Work organizations in the UK, for example, are predominantly small and medium-sized enterprises involving workforces of less than 250 people and any survey of individual work-places might well be obliged to operate with relatively small numbers. And this is true of so many of the groups, events and locations the social researcher might want to study. Project researchers, in particular, are likely to want to focus on localized units involving smallish numbers of people or items.

Third, the pragmatic approach subscribes to the argument that, used properly, non-probability sampling techniques can produce data that is *sufficiently* accurate for the purposes of research. Within the statistical approach, it should be noted, there are ways of accommodating the need for small samples and coping with the likely impact of such small samples on the accuracy of the data they produce. The pragmatic approach, however, tends to rely on non-probability sampling instead. This is because it is less expensive to undertake research using things like quota sampling techniques rather than random sampling techniques. There is, however, an ongoing debate about whether the use of non-random sampling techniques with smaller sample sizes jeopardizes the accuracy of the data. The pragmatic approach takes the position that the level of accuracy needs to be weighed against the additional costs involved and that *the aim is to get accuracy that is good enough for the purposes of research within the resources available for research.* Commercial research companies actually advise potential customers that for a given sum of money they can be supplied with results within a given level of accuracy; a greater level of accuracy will cost more. As a consequence, the customer and the commercial research company need to agree about whether results will be accurate *enough* in relation to the resources available.

 Key point: A pragmatic approach to sample size

'In practice, the complexity of the competing factors of resources and accuracy means that the decision on sample size tends to be based on experience and good judgement rather than relying on a strict mathematical formula' (Hoinville et al. 1985: 73).

The good judgement behind the pragmatic approach to sample size is based on four important factors. These do not provide the exact figure as would be the case with the statistical approach, but they do provide guidelines that can help the researcher decide what sample size might be appropriate and acceptable.

- *Comparison with other similar surveys.* The researcher's literature review should identify instances where other researchers have conducted surveys under comparable conditions, and the sample sizes used in such surveys can provide some starting point for deciding what numbers to include in the sample.
- *Samples should not involve fewer than 30 people or items.* Certainly, it is a mistake to use statistical analyses on samples of fewer than 30 without using great care about the procedures involved.
- *Allowance for the number of subdivisions likely to be made within the data.* A sample size which initially looks quite large might produce only very small returns in relation to specific sub-categories that will be used for analysis of the data. So, for example, a sample of 100 people used to investigate earnings and occupational status might need to be subdivided according to the age, sex, ethnicity, marital status and qualifications of the people, and according to whether they are full-time, part-time, unemployed, child-rearing or retired. This simple investigation would need a cross-tabulation of five personal factors by five occupational factors, i.e. 25 subdivisions of the data. If the data were equally distributed, this means that there would be only four cases in each of the subdivisions, which is hardly an adequate basis for making generalizations. In practice, of course, we know that the data would not be evenly distributed and that many of the subdivisions would end up with no cases in them at all. The researcher therefore needs to think ahead when planning the size of the sample to ensure that the subdivisions entailed in the analysis are adequately catered for. The smaller the sample, the simpler the analysis should be, in the sense that the data should be subjected to fewer subdivisions.
- *Awareness of the limitations.* Special caution is needed about the extent to which generalizations can be made on the basis of the research findings.

Provided that the limitations are acknowledged and taken into account, the limited size of the sample need not invalidate the findings.

The cumulative approach: small-scale surveys using non-probability sampling for an exploratory sample

There are some approaches to social research where the size of the sample cannot be estimated with certainty at the start of the investigation. The sample size grows during the course of the research and continues to grow until the researcher has accumulated sufficient information for the purposes of the research. This cumulative approach relies on non-probability techniques such as purposive, theoretical or snowball sampling and is normally associated with research that:

• is relatively small-scale (with sample sizes in the region of 5–30);
• uses qualitative data;
• cannot identify the research population in advance;
• aims to produce an exploratory sample, not a representative one.

The cumulative approach to sample size is illustrated perhaps most neatly in the grounded theory approach and its use of theoretical sampling. Here the process is one of 'discovery'. Almost like a detective, the researcher follows a trail of clues. As each clue is followed up, it points the researcher in a particular direction and throws up new questions that need to be answered. Sometimes the clues can lead the researcher up blind alleys. Ultimately, though, the researcher needs to pursue his or her investigation until the questions have been answered and things can be explained. A consequence of this is that *the size and composition of the sample are not completely predictable at the outset.*

> **Link up with**
> Chapter 7
> Grounded theory.

Good practice: The cumulative approach and sample size estimates

The fact that the exact size of the sample cannot be stated with certainty at the start of research does not mean that the researcher should start with no idea of the final numbers to be included in the sample. Indeed, it makes good practical sense for researchers using a cumulative approach to have some broad idea of the likely size of their accumulated sample despite their desire to pursue threads of inquiry through to a point where they are satisfied they have enough information. A shrewd look at the time and resources available, and some reading of similar studies, will help to give a reasonable indication before the research starts.

Advantages of sampling

Savings in time and costs

The principal advantage of sampling is that it reduces the time and costs of collecting data when compared with a strategy of including all people or items within the research population.

Provides sufficient accuracy

Sampling need not involve a significant loss of accuracy in terms of its findings. Although there might need to be some compromise in terms of the level of accuracy and level of confidence in the findings, this should be within the bounds of tolerance for most social research projects.

Different techniques for different purposes

There is a range of sampling techniques which cover the requirements of most social researchers. While certain techniques will suit the needs of positivistic styles of research with a focus on quantitative data, other sampling techniques have evolved to suit the needs of interpretive styles of research with a preference for qualitative data. Some techniques are good for getting representative samples, others are good for getting exploratory samples.

Disadvantages of sampling

Sampling error

There is always the possibility of sampling error which needs to be taken into account. Reliance on findings from a sub-section of the total research population inevitably opens up the prospect that another sample from that same research population might produce slightly different findings. Statistically, it is possible to accommodate this fact, but the underlying point is that the use of sampling brings with it a level of uncertainty. It always becomes a matter of how *likely* it is that the findings are correct, and within what margins of error.

Sample bias

Sample bias is a constant source of concern. Researchers need to be vigilant to avoid bias stemming from the choice of people to include (the sampling frame) or the kind of people who participate (response bias).

Availability of sampling frames

Finding suitable sampling frames can pose a challenge, especially for the use of probability sampling.

Further reading

Barnett, V. (2002) *Sample Survey Principles and Methods*, 3rd edn. Chichester: Wiley.
Daniel, J. (2012) *Sampling Essentials: Practical Guidelines for Making Sampling Choices.* Thousand Oaks, CA: Sage.
Emmel, N. (2013) *Sampling and Choosing Cases in Qualitative Research: A Realist Approach.* London: Sage.
Fowler, F. J. (2009) *Survey Research Methods*, 4th edn. Thousand Oaks, CA: Sage.

Checklist for the use of sampling

When undertaking sampling you should feel confident about answering 'yes' to the following questions: ☑

1 Has a clear decision been made about whether the sample selection should be based on *probability or non-probability* sampling? ☐

2 Has a specific sampling *technique* been chosen for use in the research, and has it been explicitly named in any account of the research methodology? ☐

3 Does the selected sampling technique fit comfortably with the *purpose* for which the sample is being used (representative sample or exploratory sample)? ☐

4 Has a suitable *sampling frame* been identified (if the aim is to use a probability sampling technique)? ☐

5 Can the *sample size* be justified on the basis of criteria relevant to the type of sampling technique being used? ☐

6 If the sample size is less than 30, have the implications of this for *statistical analysis* been recognized in the research? ☐

© M. Denscombe, *The Good Research Guide*. Open University Press.

3 Case studies

What is a 'case'? • The case study approach • The purpose of a case study • Selecting a case • Can you generalize from a case study? • Advantages of the case study approach • Disadvantages of the case study approach • Further reading • Checklist for the use of case studies

Case studies focus on one (or just a few) instances of a particular phenomenon with a view to providing an in-depth account of events, relationships, experiences or processes occurring in that particular instance. *The aim is to illuminate the general by looking at the particular.* The case study approach is widely used in social research, particularly with small-scale projects, and in practice it has become aligned with qualitative research rather than quantitative research.

What is a 'case'?

To qualify as something suitable for case study research it is crucial that the thing to be studied has some distinctive identity that allows it to be studied in isolation from its context. If the case has no end-point, no outside, no limits, then it blends into other social phenomena and cannot be viewed as 'a case'. Fundamentally:

- a 'case' needs to be a fairly *self-contained entity*;
- a 'case' needs to have fairly *distinct boundaries*.

As Table 3.1 shows, there are a wide range of social phenomena that meet these criteria and which can be studied using the case study approach.

The case study approach

Spotlight on one instance or a few instances

The main characteristic of the case study approach is its *focus on just one instance of the thing that is to be investigated.* Occasionally, researchers use two or more instances but, in principle, the idea of a case study is that the spotlight

Table 3.1 Types of cases

Type	Examples
Event	strike, street riot, ceremony, music festival
Organization	commercial business, hospital, school
Policy	new health intervention, change to pension schemes
Location	shopping mall, nightclub, accident hotspot
Process	in-service training, recruitment procedure

is focused very narrowly. The case study approach, then, is quite the opposite of any mass study. The logic behind concentrating efforts on one case rather than many is that there may be insights to be gained from looking at the individual case that can have wider implications and, importantly, that would not have come to light through the use of a research strategy that tried to cover a large number of instances.

In-depth study

The prospect of getting some valuable insight depends on being able to investigate things in depth. When a researcher takes the strategic decision to devote all his or her efforts to researching just one instance, there is obviously far greater opportunity to delve into things in more detail and discover things that might not have become apparent through more superficial research.

Focus on relationships and processes

Case studies pay attention to the detailed workings of the relationships and social processes within social settings. They do so because they are not only interested in *what* goes on in the setting, they are also interested in explaining *why* those things occur. End-products, outcomes and results all remain of interest, but the real value of a case study is that it offers the opportunity to go into sufficient detail to unravel the complexities of a given situation. A case study conducted in Company A, for example, might reveal that it has a high turnover of labour. To an extent this fact is interesting in its own right, but the strength of a case study approach is that it allows the researcher to investigate the relationships and processes that explain the actual level of turnover – the interplay between things like the recruitment policy, staff development programme, nature of the work, levels of pay and the social background of the workforce.

 Key point

'The case study is a research strategy which focuses on understanding the dynamics present within single settings' (Eisenhardt 1989: 534).

A holistic view

Relationships and processes within social settings are interconnected and to explain why things happen as they do within a particular case study setting it is necessary to understand how the various facets of the setting are linked together. The case study approach works well here because rather than deal with 'isolated factors' it takes a 'holistic' view of what is going on. It views the case as a whole, in its entirety, and is thus able to discover how the many parts affect one another.

Multiple methods

The case study approach allows the researcher to use a variety of types of data (qualitative or quantitative) and a combination of research methods (observation, interviews, documents, questionnaires) as part of the investi-

Link up with
Chapter 10
Mixed methods.

gation. It not only allows this, it actually invites and encourages the researcher to do so in order to get a holistic view. Whatever methods are appropriate can be used for investigating the relationships and processes that are of interest.

 Key point: The case study strategy
The decision to use a case study approach is a *strategic* decision that relates to the scale and scope of an investigation, and it does not dictate which method(s) must be used. Indeed, one strength of the case study approach is that it allows the use of a variety of methods depending on the circumstances and the specific needs of the situation.

Natural setting

'The case' that forms the basis of the investigation is normally something that already exists. It is not a situation that is artificially generated specifically for the purposes of the research. It is not like an experiment where the research design is dedicated to imposing controls on variables so that the impact of a specific ingredient can be measured. The case is a 'naturally occurring' phenomenon. It exists prior to the research project and continues to exist once the research has finished. Table 3.2 details the characteristics of a case study.

The purpose of a case study

Case studies can be used for a number of purposes. Predominantly, they have been used in relation to the discovery of information (following an inductive logic). The case study approach enables the research to delve deep into the intricacies of the situation in order to describe things in detail, compare alternatives or, perhaps, provide an account that explores particular aspects of the situation.

Table 3.2 The characteristics of case study research

One setting	rather than	Many instances
Depth of study	rather than	Breadth of study
The particular	rather than	The general
Relationships/processes	rather than	Outcomes and end-products
Holistic view	rather than	Isolated factors
Multiple sources of data	rather than	One research method
Natural settings	rather than	Artificial situations

The information can also be used to fathom the underlying causes of the things that have been observed to occur in the case study setting. Used in such ways, case studies provide new information which is valuable: (1) in its own right for what it *says*; (2) for what it *suggests* by way of new avenues to explore; or (3) for what it *explains* in terms of how aspects of the case are interlinked.

Case studies have been used, though less commonly, in relation to the testing of theory (following a deductive logic). The purpose of the case, here, is to allow the researcher to see whether things that a theory predicts will take place will actually be found in practice in real-world settings. Used in this way, the case study either: (1) tries to reinforce the value of a theory by demonstrating how it works in reality; or (2) sets out to test whether a particular theory might work under the specific conditions to be found in the case setting.

It is quite possible for case studies to have more than one purpose. Table 3.3 outlines the possible ways in which case studies might be used, but should not be seen as implying that any particular case study must be restricted to just one type of purpose.

Table 3.3 The purpose of a case study: six possibilities

Discovery-led	
Description	Describes what is happening in a case study setting (e.g. events, processes and relationships)
Exploration	Explores the key issues affecting those in a case study setting (e.g. problems or opportunities)
Comparison	Compares settings to learn from the similarities and differences between them
Explanation	Explains the causes of events, processes or relationships within a setting
Theory-led	
Illustration	Uses a case study as an illustration of how a particular theory applies in a real-life setting
Experiment	Uses a case study as a test-bed for experimenting with changes to specific factors (or variables)

Selecting a case

The case study approach generally calls for the researcher to make choices from among a number of possible events, people, organizations, etc. The researcher needs to pick out one example (or just a few) from a wider range of examples of the class of thing that is being investigated: the choice of one school for a case study from among the thousands that could have been chosen; the choice of one eye injury clinic from among the many in hospitals across the country; the focus on one bus company from among the hundreds throughout the nation which provide local public transport services. Whatever the subject matter, the case study normally depends on a conscious and deliberate choice about which case to select from among a large number of possibilities.

An important point to realize about this is that cases are not randomly selected: they are selected on the basis of known attributes. As a distinct alternative to the randomization principle associated with classic experiments and large-scale surveys, instances selected for a case study are deliberately chosen on the basis of their distinctive features.

Relevance to the topic

A suitable case will be one with features that are relevant in terms of the practical problem or theoretical issue that the researcher wants to investigate. This criterion for selection is crucial for the success of the case study and the researcher's decisions on this point need to be explicit and justified as an essential part of the case study methodology. For example, if the area of interest is 'small firms in the automotive industry' the criterion for the selection of any particular organization as the basis for a case study would be 'size'. If size is defined in terms of the number of employees, then details would need to be given about the number of employees in the selected firm and how this compares with (1) definitions of small firms (the theory), and (2) a profile of the size of other firms throughout the automotive industry. Such details are vital because they justify the choice of the particular firm as a suitable example of the broader category of the thing being studied (small firms) and they form the basis for any generalizations that can be made from the case study findings.

Type of case study

Typical instance

The selection of a particular case can be based on the argument that it is typical. The logic being invoked here is that the particular case is similar to others that might have been chosen, and that the findings from the case study are therefore likely to apply elsewhere. Because the case study is like most of the rest, the findings can be generalized to the whole class of thing.

Extreme instance

A case might be selected on the grounds that, far from being typical, it provides something of a contrast with the norm. An illustration of this would be the selection of an organization which is notably smaller or notably larger than usual. Among local authorities in the country, a very small one might be chosen for a case study, and the logic for doing so would be that this would allow the influence of the factor (size) to be more easily seen than it would be in the average size authority. In an extreme instance, a specified factor is seen in relief – highlighted in its effect.

Test-site for theory

The logic for the selection of a particular case can be based on the relevance of the case for previous theory. This is a point Yin (2014) stresses. Case studies can be used for the purposes of 'theory-testing' as well as 'theory-building', to use Layder's (1993) distinction. The rationale for choosing a specific case, then, can be that it contains crucial elements that are especially significant, and that the researcher should be able to predict certain outcomes if the theory holds true.

Least likely instance

Following the idea of test-sites for theory, a case might be selected to test the validity of 'theory' by seeing if it occurs in an instance where it might be least expected. So, for example, a researcher who wants to test the 'theory' that school teachers place a high value on their autonomy could deliberately select a situation where such autonomy would seem to be least valued: a school with team teaching in open plan classrooms. If there is evidence supporting the 'theory' even under such 'least likely' conditions, then the 'theory' has all the more credibility.

Practical considerations

Although researchers should never rely on practical reasons as the principal or the sole criterion for selecting a case, it would be naïve to ignore the fact that, in the real world of research, such factors do have a bearing on the selection of cases.

A matter of convenience

In the practical world of research, with its limits to time and resources, the selection of cases is quite likely to include a consideration of convenience. Faced with alternatives which are equally suitable, it is reasonable for the researcher to select the one which involves the least travel, the least expense and the least difficulty when it comes to gaining access. The crucial point here, though, is that convenience should only come into play when deciding between equally suitable alternatives. Selection on the basis of 'the first to hand', 'the easiest' or 'the cheapest' is not a criterion in its own right which can be used to justify the selection of cases. If used on its own, in fact, it would almost certainly be a symptom of poor social research. Used properly, it is subordinate to the other criteria.

Intrinsically interesting

If a case is intrinsically interesting, then it can prove an attractive proposition. The findings are likely to reach a wider audience and the research itself is likely to be a more exciting experience. There are even some experts in the field who would go as far as to argue that selection on the basis of being intrinsically interesting is a sufficient justification in its own right (Stake 1995). This goes right to the heart of the debate about whether cases are studied 'in their own right', as Stake would maintain, or for what they reveal about others of the kind, and, in light of its controversial nature, it would be rather foolhardy for the newcomer or project researcher to use this as the sole criterion for selecting a case. The vast majority of social researchers would not see it as a justification for selection in its own right. It might work for journalism, but social research by most definitions calls for more than just this (Ragin and Amoroso 2011). It is far wiser, therefore, to regard any intrinsic interest of the case as a criterion to be used when deciding between instances that in all other crucial respects are equally suitable, and as a bonus.

No real choice

On some occasions, researchers do not really have a great deal of choice when it comes to the selection of suitable cases for inclusion in the investigation. The choice is more or less dictated by circumstances beyond their control. This happens in the following two circumstances.

The study is part of commissioned research

Commissioned research might leave the researcher with little leeway in the selection of cases. The funder will quite likely stipulate that the research must be linked to a specified organization or activity, leaving no discretion on the matter to the researchers themselves. Under such circumstances, there is no real choice in the selection of cases.

There are unique opportunities

There are times when events occur which provide the researcher with unique opportunities. The events themselves, of course, will not be unique; they will be instances of a class of such events. The opportunity to study such events, however, may be unique. Situations which could not be planned or created present themselves as 'one-off chances'. At one level, this could take the form of social catastrophes, such as war, famine or natural disaster. At a more mundane level, the unique opportunities could reflect the unpredictable or rare nature of the events. Strikes, for example, might be the kind of class of events that could be illuminated through the depth study of individual cases. Researchers, though, will have little choice over which instances they select as their cases and will necessarily find themselves homing in on such events as and when they occur. As a consequence, there is no real element of choice in the selection of the cases.

Can you generalize from a case study?

When opting for a case study approach researchers are likely to confront scepticism about how far it is reasonable to generalize from the findings of one case. The researcher will probably find people asking questions such as:

- How *representative* is the case?
- Isn't it possible that the findings, though interesting, are *unique* to the particular circumstances of the case?
- How can you *generalize* on the basis of research into one instance?

These are reasonable questions. They reflect the key issue of generalization in social research (Denscombe 2010) and should not be ignored in the hope that readers of the research report will overlook the point. Indeed, it is good practice for any researcher who decides to choose a case study approach to pre-empt possible criticism by addressing the issue head-on.

Analytic generalizations

One way to address the matter is to emphasize the point that individual case studies should not be regarded as though they form part of a survey sample. They are not a 'slice of the cake' whose function is to reveal the contents of the whole cake. Instead, the findings from a case study are used for the *development of theory*. The point of a case study is to analyse the situation and to arrive at certain concepts, propositions or hypotheses that might explain what is happening, and why, in the particular setting that has been investigated. Viewed in this way, each case study is like an individual experiment and, as Yin (2009: 15) argues:

> Case studies, like experiments, are generalizable to theoretical propositions and not to populations or universes. In this sense, the case study, like the experiment, does not represent a 'sample', and in doing a case study, your goal will be to expand and generalize theories (analytic generalization) and not to enumerate frequencies (statistical generalization).

From this perspective, the findings from case studies are not to be regarded as final or absolute. As with experiments, the findings should be understood as being provisional and in need of corroboration through other research which can check their validity. Or, looked at another way, the findings might be regarded as part of an ongoing process in which initial findings are not only checked for accuracy, they are used to refine the ideas and theories developed in the earlier pieces of research – in the spirit of grounded theory (Eisenhardt and Graebner 2007). Either way, though, case studies tend to be seen as a *starting point* for research, serving as a descriptive or exploratory foundation that helps with the development of theory, and it is in this *analytic* respect that the findings from case studies can be generalized.

Link up with
Chapter 7 Grounded theory.

Transferable findings

Analytic generalizations implicitly treat case studies as part of a broader research programme where the value of any individual case study depends on its link with alternative types of research or further case studies. Within small-scale research projects, however, case studies do not normally occur as part of an ongoing programme of research. In all probability they take place as 'one-offs'. And this calls for a slightly different kind of rationale when it comes to generalizing from case study findings. Rather than treating case studies as a starting point for research they need to be regarded as ends in themselves, finished products whose findings have some value in their own right.

The rationale for generalizing, in this instance, depends *how far the findings are 'transferable' to other settings*. What is crucial is the extent to which those who read the case study findings are able to infer things from them that apply to other settings.

The possibility of transferable findings stems from the fact that although each case is in some respects unique, it is also a single example of a broader class of things. It is one of a type (Hammersley 1992; Ragin and Becker 1992). And the extent to which findings from the case study can be generalized to other examples in the class depends on how far the case study example compares with others of its type. To make some assessment of how far the findings have implications across the board for all others of the type, or how far they are restricted to just the case study example, readers must be provided with the necessary information on which to make an informed judgement on this matter. It is vital, therefore, that reports based on the case study include sufficient detail about how the case compares with others in the class for the reader to make an informed judgement about how far the findings have relevance to other instances. Details should be given about:

- the type of thing (organization, event, process);
- particulars about the case (detailed facts and figures);
- how it compares with others of its type (e.g. factors like size, location, frequency).

Comparison might call for the inclusion of details on factors such as:

Physical location	geographical area, town, building, room, furniture, decor
Historical location	developments and changes
Social location	catchment area, ethnic grouping, social class, age, sex and other background information about the participants
Institutional location	type of organization, size of organization, official policies and procedures

Example 3.1

Transferable findings

In a case study involving a small primary school the 'case' is one of a broader type of other schools which are small and which are in the primary sector. ▶

▶ | The transferability of the findings from the case study to other small primary schools will depend on how far the case study example shares with other schools of the type (small size, primary sector) features which are significant with respect to the findings. This could include things like its catchment area, the ethnic origins of the pupils and the rate of staff turnover. The transferability of the findings from the particular case study school to other small primary schools will depend on the extent to which its profile on these factors is to be found in other examples of this type of school. This means that the researcher must obtain data on the significant features (catchment area, the ethnic origins of the pupils and the rate of staff turnover) for primary schools in general (likely to be based on regional or national figures), and then demonstrate where the case study example fits in relation to the broader picture.

Advantages of the case study approach

Suitable for small-scale research

The case study approach can fit in well with the needs of small-scale research through concentrating effort on one research site (or just a few sites).

Takes a holistic view

The focus on particular instances allows the researcher to take a holistic view (rather than one based on isolated factors) and to look in depth at the subtleties and intricacies of complex social phenomena.

Facilitates the use of multiple methods

The case study approach allows the use of a variety of research methods. More than this, it more or less encourages the use of multiple methods and multiple sources of data in order to capture the complex reality under scrutiny.

Makes use of naturally occurring settings

The case study approach is particularly suitable in circumstances where it is not possible to manipulate features of the setting for the purposes of the research. Because the approach is concerned with investigating phenomena as they naturally occur there is no necessity for the researcher to impose controls or implement changes to key factors or variables.

Flexible approach

Theory-building and theory-testing research can both use the case study approach to good effect.

Disadvantages of the case study approach

Producing generalizable findings

The point at which the case study approach is most vulnerable to criticism is in relation to the *credibility of generalizations* made from its findings. The case study researcher needs to be particularly careful to allay suspicions and to demonstrate the extent to which the case is similar to, or contrasts with, others of its type.

Defining boundaries to the case

On the technical side, the *boundaries* of the case can prove difficult to define in an absolute and clear-cut fashion. This poses difficulties in terms of deciding which sources of data to incorporate in the case study and which to exclude.

Gaining access to case study settings

Negotiating access to case study settings can be a demanding part of the research process. Research can flounder if permission is withheld or withdrawn. In case studies, access to documents, people and settings can generate ethical problems in terms of things like confidentiality.

Focus on process rather than outcomes

Case study research tends to focus on processes rather than measurable end-products. To this extent the approach is sometimes seen as producing 'soft' data because it uses qualitative data and interpretive methods rather than quantitative data and statistical procedures. In line with this, case studies are sometimes regarded as acceptable in terms of providing descriptive accounts of the situation but rather ill-suited to analyses or evaluations. None of this is necessarily justified, but it is a preconception which the case study researcher needs to be aware of, and one which needs to be challenged by careful attention to detail and rigour in the use of the approach.

Further reading

Simons, H. (2009) *Case Study Research in Practice*. London: Sage.
Stake, R. (1995) *The Art of Case Study Research*. Thousand Oaks, CA: Sage.
Swanborn, P. (2010) *Case Study Research: What, Why and How?* London: Sage.
Thomas, G. (2011) *How to Do Your Case Study: A Guide for Students and Researchers*. London: Sage.
Yin, R. (2014) *Case Study Research: Design and Methods*, 5th edn. Thousand Oaks, CA: Sage.

Checklist for the use of case studies

When undertaking research which involves the case study approach you should feel confident about answering 'yes' to the following questions: ☑

1 Is the research based on a 'naturally occurring' situation? ☐

2 Have the criteria for selection of the case (or cases) been described and justified? ☐

3 Has the case been identified as a particular instance of a type of social phenomenon (e.g. kind of event, type of organization)? ☐

4 Have the significant features of the case been described and have they been compared with those to be found elsewhere among the type of thing being studied? ☐

5 Is the case a fairly self-contained entity? ☐

6 Have the boundaries to the case been described and their implications considered? ☐

7 Has careful consideration been given to the issue of generalizations stemming from research? ☐

8 Does the research make suitable use of multiple methods and multiple sources of data? ☐

9 Does the research give due attention to relationships and processes, and provide a 'holistic' perspective? ☐

© M. Denscombe, *The Good Research Guide*. Open University Press.

4 | Experiments

What is an experiment?

An experiment is an empirical investigation under controlled conditions designed to examine the properties of, and relationships between, specific factors. The point of conducting an experiment is to isolate individual factors and observe their effect in detail. The purpose is to discover new relationships or properties associated with the thing that is being investigated, or to test existing theories.

This definition draws on a rather idealized image of the way experiments are conducted but it captures the essence of the notion and incorporates the three things that lie at the heart of conducting experiments in social research:

- *Controls.* Experiments involve the manipulation of variables. The researcher needs to identify factors that are significant and then introduce them to or exclude them from the situation so that their effect can be observed.
- *Empirical observation and measurement.* Experiments rely on detailed empirical observation of changes that occur following the introduction of potentially relevant factors. They also involve the precise measurement of the changes that are observed.
- *The identification of causal factors.* The introduction or exclusion of factors to or from the situation enables the researcher to pinpoint which factor actually causes the observed outcome to occur.

When to use an experiment

There are five conditions that need to be met in order for experiments to be selected as a suitable research approach. The first of these is that they should be used as part of explanatory research rather than exploratory research. This means that the focus should be on questions about 'why' things happen and 'how' they are linked, with the research being designed to explain the link between two or more factors.

Second, the research should be able to draw on a fairly well-established body of knowledge about the topic to be investigated. The factors that are looked at must not be plucked out of thin air but chosen, instead, on the basis of existing knowledge about the topic. They should be selected deliberately because they are known to be relevant and significant. As a corollary to this, experiments are not so well suited to descriptive research or to exploratory research where the point of the research is to discover which factors are significant.

Third, and following on from the previous point, existing knowledge about the topic for the research should allow research questions to take the form of hypotheses. As Brown et al. (1975: 10) point out:

> The formation of a hypothesis has two useful functions. Firstly, it serves to synthesize the experimenter's knowledge of previous research into a predication which can be handled experimentally and, second, it gives direction to his subsequent investigations . . . it provides the means by which the variables are chosen.

Fourth, the kinds of observations and measurement techniques used in experiments mean that they are usually associated with quantitative data rather than qualitative data. Because experiments depend on controlling variables and upon the careful measurement of changes that occur during the experiment, they produce data that are numerical and which lend themselves to statistical analysis.

Fifth, the design of experiments requires the ability to implement controls over factors that are to be studied in the experiment. In 'natural experiments' (described below) this is *not* the case but in other kinds of experiments the researcher needs to have the capability, authority and resources to manipulate relevant variables.

 Key point

Experiments are suitable for *explanatory research* drawing on *well-established theory* to identify relevant variables that allow research questions in the form of *hypotheses* and research designs that produce *quantitative data* in circumstances where the researcher can *manipulate variables* and implement controls.

Types of experiment

Laboratory experiments

Laboratories are purpose-built contexts for the research. They are normally enclosed spaces (buildings or locations) which are set out purposefully to aid the collection of data on specific factors linked to the experiment. They often make use of specialized equipment or facilities to help the researchers obtain detailed data about the phenomenon they are studying.

Laboratory experiments, by their nature, are located *on site* rather than 'in the field'. People or items come to the laboratory in order for the research to take place, rather than things being studied *in situ*. This is necessary, of course, in order to take advantage of the purpose-built nature of the setting and the benefits this has for: (1) *close control* of variables to isolate causal factors; and (2) *precision and consistency of the observations* and measurements that are made. However, the benefits in terms of precision and consistency need to be weighed against the fact that laboratory experiments are conducted under conditions that are artificially created. The artificial setting of an experiment can affect the way people react and the quality of a laboratory experiment always needs to be judged on how well it replicates conditions that would naturally occur outside the laboratory – in 'real' life.

Field experiments

Field experiments are experiments that take place outside the laboratory. They are conducted 'in the field' in places like factories, offices, schools and hospitals. Such settings are not artificially created for the purposes of the research, but they do allow researchers to manipulate certain key variables and focus on measuring the impact of a specific new factor that is introduced into the setting. This new factor often takes the form of a new procedure, a new rule or some other kind of specific new initiative that has been put in place following the adoption of a new policy or introduction of a new programme. The field experiment involves a systematic evaluation of the new factor with the purpose of finding out whether the introduction of the new variable has caused changes to occur as had been anticipated. A classic example of such a field experiment is the Hawthorne experiments where changes to the working environment were introduced in a factory setting in order to find out if things like changes to the level of lighting caused changes in the level of productivity.

Link up with Hawthorne studies, p. 148.

Randomized controlled trials

Randomized controlled trials (RCTs) are a type of field experiment in which the effect of specific 'treatments' is measured in trials involving comparisons between experimental groups and control groups. Random allocation to the groups is used to ensure that there is no difference between the groups. RCTs are regarded as the gold standard for research design in the realms of medical and health research concerned with clinical trials of drugs and other health interventions, and are the preferred approach of the 'evidence-based movement' for whom it represents the most scientific way of conducting research (Higgins and Green 2011).

Natural experiments

Natural experiments make use of events and circumstances that occur naturally in everyday life which provide researchers with the opportunity to observe the effects of particular variables and explain the causes of particular phenomena.

When researchers move outside the laboratory in order to gather data in more natural settings, they are likely to pay a high price in terms of their ability to control the variables. Much like weather forecasters, they rely on observing events which occur in circumstances over which they have no control. Sociologists cannot control levels of incomes in order to conduct experiments on things like poverty. Nor can health educators manipulate levels of smoking among adolescent girls in order to study them. Economists cannot generate a recession in order to investigate its consequences. It is simply not possible to manipulate circumstances like these. So, rather than trying to manipulate the situation, researchers take advantage of 'naturally occurring' experiments – situations in which they can see the possibility of observing and measuring the impact of isolated variables through circumstances as they happen, without creating artificial environments or imposing artificial controls.

Retrospective experiments

Retrospective experiments begin with the 'effect' and the researcher sets out to deduce what factor(s) could possibly be the cause of this outcome. The idea is to work backwards from the effect to find the cause. For example, the researcher might ask, 'Does imprisonment affect earnings after release from detention?' The research design here would be to identify a number of people who had been to prison. This independent variable – imprisonment – is not something the research can or should manipulate. It is a *fait accompli*, existing prior to and quite separate from the research. However, by comparing ex-prisoners with people who in most other respects match them, it is possible to deduce whether or not that factor has had a direct effect on the earnings.

Experiments involving people – the observer effect

When experiments involve people there are three issues that arise which would not apply if the experiment was conducted on plants, chemicals or natural materials. When humans are the thing that is being studied, the nature of the experiment needs to take into account the fact that:

- people react to the knowledge that they are being observed;
- participation in experiments can potentially harm people;
- experiments might involve artificial settings that are different from the real world.

Humans have self-awareness and this makes them very different from plants, chemicals or natural materials. When humans become aware that they are the focus of attention for research, there is the very real possibility that they will act differently from normal. They might become self-conscious or anxious about having their behaviour scrutinized by the researcher and consequently alter their behaviour in some way. This is known as the *observer effect*. They might, on the other hand, enjoy being in the limelight and respond accordingly with enthusiasm and motivation that would not have existed if they had not realized they were the subject of special attention. This is known as the *halo effect*. And if the participants know the true purpose of the research there is, in addition, the prospect that they will alter their behaviour directly to take this into account. They might try to help the researcher by doing what they think is expected of them, or they might try to do the opposite. These are *self-fulfilling prophecies* that can result from the knowledge which participants have (or believe they have) about what the experiment is trying to achieve.

Link up with the Hawthorne studies, p. 14.8.

 Key point: The observer effect

People are likely to alter their behaviour when they become aware that they are being observed. Unlike atoms, people can become aware of being studied – conscious of it – and then react in a way that is not usual.

Experimenters can take steps to overcome the observer effect. They can, for instance, make hidden observations from behind a one-way mirror. If people do not realize they are being observed, then their behaviour should not be affected. Or researchers can disguise the real purpose of the research to avoid altering behaviour in relation to the factor being investigated. They can deceive participants into thinking that the research is about one thing when it is actually about another quite separate topic. But both solutions to the observer effect – secret observations and disguised purpose – raise ethical problems and need very careful consideration before being used.

A series of experiments conducted by Stanley Milgram at Yale University between 1961 and 1962 illustrates the point (Milgram 1974). These experiments were cleverly designed to make participants believe they were administering progressively stronger electric shocks to a fellow participant as part of an experiment which they were told was about 'learning'. In fact, the person apparently receiving the electric shocks was part of the research team and actually received no shocks at all – but the research 'subjects' did not know this. During the experiment the subjects were led to believe that, in the name of science, they needed to administer dangerously high electric shocks to the other participant as part of the experiment on learning. The experiments involved deception about the nature of what was being studied – it was actually about obedience to authority – and involved the subjects being covertly observed from behind a one-way mirror. These alone raise ethical questions. What made the experiments notorious, however, was their impact on the participants. For some people the experience of taking part in the research turned out to be very stressful and perturbing – they believed they had been giving potentially fatal electric shocks to the other person (Perry 2013). The point these experiments highlight is that research involving humans must never lose sight of the fact that it is dealing with real people who have emotions and feelings, and that the well-being of participants must never be sacrificed in the pursuit of findings, no matter how 'useful' those findings might be.

> **Link up with**
> Chapter 17
> Research ethics.

 Key point

A researcher can do things to chemicals and plants that cannot be contemplated with fellow human beings. People have feelings, people have rights.

A final point about experiments involving people is the question of whether the responses and reactions observed under experimental conditions will be replicated under real world conditions. This concerns the *ecological validity* of the experiment. Obviously this is a question that applies mainly to laboratory experiments where the environment and the tasks involved are purpose-built and, in this sense, artificial rather than natural. When it comes to the value of an experiment and the quality of its findings, however, it is a criterion that applies to all types of experiment. The question it poses is this: *is the experiment looking at the right things in order to draw conclusions that apply to people's behaviour in normal, everyday life?*

Causal relationships and variables

Experiments are generally concerned with determining the *cause* of any changes that occur to the thing being studied. It is not normally enough to show that two things that occur are linked; that they always occur at the same time or they always happen in sequence. Useful though it is to know about such a relationship, experiments usually aim to discover which of the factors is the cause. This requires a distinction to be made between *dependent and independent variables*. It is vital that the researcher has a clear idea of which is which, and sets up the experiment in a way which produces results that show the distinction between the two:

- The *independent variable* is the one that has the impact on the dependent variable. Its size, number, structure, volume or whatever exist autonomously, owing nothing to the other variable. A change in the independent variable affects the dependent variable.
- The *dependent variable* is the factor that alters as a result of changes to the independent variable. It literally 'depends' on the independent variable. Any change in the dependent variable does not affect the independent variable.

<hr>

Example 4.1

Tobacco smoking

Tobacco smoking is related to the incidence of lung cancer. Both are variables and both appear to be linked to each other: more smoking, higher incidence of lung cancer; less smoking, lower incidence. Smoking increases the likelihood of lung cancer. Lung cancer does not increase the likelihood of smoking. In this example, there is clearly a dependent variable and an independent variable. Smoking tobacco is the independent variable, and lung cancer is the dependent variable.

<hr>

The use of controls

When conducting an experiment the aim is to show that the dependent factor (for example, the incidence of lung cancer in the population) responds to changes in the independent factor (prevalence of smoking in the society). To do this, the researcher needs to be sure it was definitely the prevalence of smoking that was responsible for the observed levels of lung cancer and not some other factor (e.g. diet or amount of exercise) that actually caused it. This requires the experimenter to control variables like smoking, diet, exercise and other factors that could perhaps affect the incidence of lung cancer to ensure that, of all of them, it is only the one factor, smoking, that could possibly be linked to the level of lung cancer in the population. There are a number of ways in which experiments can be designed to achieve this, each of which involves the use of controls.

Introduce a new factor

The most straightforward way to isolate the impact of a variable is to introduce it while keeping all other relevant factors unchanged. Under these circumstances – 'all things being equal' – it is possible to pinpoint the impact of the new factor and to deduce that any observed changes that occur can be attributed to the new factor. Since the introduction of the new factor is the only thing that has changed, it alone can be held responsible for any subsequent changes that occur. In practice, however, social researchers face two particular difficulties in this regard. First, it can be extremely difficult to ensure that none of the other variables change. Second, variables are often linked so that a change in one variable might cause changes across a range of other variables.

Eliminate the factor from the experiment

Rather than introduce a new factor to the situation, the researcher might find it easier to eliminate one factor. So, for instance, a study of the link between hyperactivity and diet in children might see the researcher deliberately excluding all artificial colourings from the subjects' diets and then observing any change in behaviour. If other factors remain unaltered, it would be logical to deduce that any observed change was due to the absence of this factor.

Hold the factor constant

In social science, a large number of the key relevant variables come in the form of attributes that cannot be written out of the equation through eliminating them from the situation altogether. Things like income, weight and age are attributes that cannot be eliminated. However, they can be controlled for by 'holding the factor constant'. To prevent the factor from having an unwanted intrusion on the outcome of the experiment, the researcher can devise a situation in which the participants are all of the same income or of the same weight. Observed outcomes from the experiment, as a result, can be deduced to stem from some factor other than income or weight.

Control groups

A standard method of introducing controls involves the use of control groups. These are:

> A group of subjects as similar as possible to the experimental group and treated in exactly the same way except that they are not given the experimental treatment. The control group provides a base line against which the effects of this treatment may be measured.
>
> (Brown et al. 1975: 235)

The use of control groups follows a fairly straightforward logic. It reasons that if the control group and the experimental group are identical at the start of the experiment, and a specific variable is introduced to the experimental group but not to the control group, then at the end of the experiment any difference between the experimental group and the control group must have been caused by the variable that was introduced. This was, after all, the only factor that differentiated between the groups.

The starting point for the experiment, then, is *two matched groups* (or samples). The experiment involves introducing a factor to the experimental group and leaving the other group with no artificially induced changes. Having added the new factor, the experimenter can then look at the two groups again with the belief that any *difference* between the groups can be attributed to the factor which was artificially induced. Note here that it is not the *change* in the experimental group as such which is important. Certain changes over time are likely to happen, irrespective of whether an experiment had taken place. Time moves on for all of us. But, if the two groups were as identical as possible at the outset, any change of this kind in one group will also occur in the other group. So, instead of measuring the change from time 1 to time 2, we measure the difference between the control group and the experimental group at the end of the experiment at time 2. Any differences we observe can be logically deduced to come from the factor which was artificially induced in the experiment (see Figure 4.1).

Figure 4.1 Experiments and the use of control groups

Experimental group and control group are matched groups or samples.
Factor E causes a change in the experimental group of (C – A) – (D – B).

Allocation to groups

The use of control groups eliminates alternative possible explanations for any observed differences between groups after the treatment. But this is only true if we can be sure that there is no difference between those who are allocated to the control group and those allocated to the experimental group; that at the start of the experiment the groups are the same. One way to ensure this is on the basis of *random allocation to groups*. If the research subjects are chosen on a random basis, there should be a tendency for those factors which are not crucial to cancel themselves out. The principle here is that by the choice of a large enough group of participants on a random basis, any interference with the results through 'confounding' factors would cancel themselves out in terms of the results for the whole research group.

Link up with
Random sampling, p. 36.

An alternative way of making sure that control groups and experimental groups are the same is by *matching the groups* in terms of factors that are known to be relevant. A social researcher, in this respect, might want to ensure that groups are balanced in terms of things like age, sex, occupation and ethnicity in an effort to establish equivalent groups. Of course, this would involve allocation on the basis of quotas rather than random allocation, but it is likely to prove a method better suited to small-scale research. Whatever way it is achieved, though, the crucial thing is that the researcher creates groups that have no difference on anything relating to the variable that will be introduced.

Blind trials

A factor that is not eliminated by the use of control groups is the participants' knowledge that they have been allocated to one group or the other. The *observer effect* comes into play raising the prospect that those who know they are in the experimental group will *expect* to experience something new whereas those in the control group may not. To overcome this, the design of the experiment needs to include ploys to prevent participants being aware of which group they are in, and whether they are actually receiving a new 'treatment' or not.

One way of doing this is the use of a 'blind trial'. In medical research this involves the use of placebos – a treatment that looks real but which in fact has no healing effect. Everyone appears to be treated the same and through this deception participants do not know whether they are part of the experimental group or the control group. Only the experimenters know which people receive the treatment (in the experimental group) and which receive the placebo (in the control group). This effectively eliminates any possibility that participants' *expectations* could account for any observed changes following the introduction of the treatment.

True experiments and quasi-experiments

To qualify as a 'true' experiment the research design needs to allow the researcher to identify the cause of changes that are observed during the experiment and, crucially, to do so in a way that eliminates any alternative possible explanations for the results. It needs to be able to rule out all other factors that might possibly explain what caused the event or the changes that were observed. A true experiment achieves this through a combination of four things. The design should include:

1 both a *pre-test* and a *post-test* to get measurements before and after the introduction of the variable being investigated;
2 the use of a *control group* for comparisons;
3 the *random allocation* of people or items to the 'control' group and the 'experimental' group;
4 the *introduction (or control) of a variable* whose impact the experiment wishes to observe.

This basic experimental design is known as a *pre-test-post-test control group design* and is often portrayed in the following way:

Group A   R--------O_1---------X---------O_2
Group B   R--------O_1------------------O_2

Notation

- R stands for random allocation to groups
- X stands for introduction of new factor or treatment
- O stands for observation
- Subscripts 1 and 2 refer to the sequential observations.

There are a multitude of experimental research designs that build upon these basic building blocks. Essentially they consist of various combinations of five basic ingredients:

- the times when measurements/observations are made (pre-test/post-test);
- the number of comparison groups used (two-group designs, multiple-group designs);

- whether the control group receives no 'treatment' or it receives an alternative treatment to that received by the 'experimental' group.
- the allocation to groups and whether this is random or not;
- the number of new factors introduced.

The use of pre- and post-test observations acts as a baseline against which to measure any changes that occur, and the use of control groups similarly provides a basis on which the researcher can make comparisons between the experimental group and the control group. Coupled with the allocation to groups on a purely random basis, these allow the researcher to eliminate a host of potential alternative explanations and logically deduce the specific cause of the changes that are observed.

Quasi-experiment is a term used to describe a research design that follows the spirit of the experimental approach but which, for practical reasons, cannot meet one or other of the essential conditions. This situation is most likely to occur when experiments are conducted outside the laboratory 'in the field' where circumstances dictate that it is not possible to implement controls on all the relevant variables. Outside the laboratory researchers might find that:

- they cannot allocate people to groups on a random basis. This will necessitate conducting the experiment using 'non-equivalent' groups; or
- they cannot use a control group for comparisons; or
- they cannot conduct both a pre-test and a post-test to get measurements before and after the introduction of the variable being investigated.

Cook and Campbell (1979) argue that a quasi-experimental design should include no more than one of these three shortcomings. It can use non-equivalent groups *or* it can lack a control group *or* it can lack pre-test measurements – but it cannot incorporate more than one of these without severely jeopardizing its power to identify causal factors. Provided it lacks no more than one of these conditions, however, a quasi-experiment can still be useful. It is an option that can be used prudently as a fall-back position if it proves impossible to meet all the conditions for a true experiment. Its limitations, of course, should always be acknowledged and it should be used cautiously when it comes to identifying causal factors. Cook and Campbell specifically warn against the dangers of making unwarranted causal inferences on the basis of quasi-experimental research designs, especially those where assignment to groups is not based on random selection: 'While they are often useful for suggesting new ideas, they are normally not sufficient for permitting strong tests of causal hypotheses because they fail to rule out a number of plausible alternative interpretations' (1979: 95).

Advantages of experiments

Credibility

The use of experiments is regarded by many people, including some social scientists, as the most scientific and, therefore, the most credible approach to research.

It has a status that trades off an association with 'hard' science, and carries with it a sense of objectivity and impartiality in terms of its findings.

Repeatable

In the case of laboratory experiments, randomized controlled trials and retrospective experiments, the research should lend itself to being checked by other researchers by being repeated using identical procedures. With field experiments and natural experiments, however, there is only a limited possibility of repeating the experiment.

Precision

The nature of experimental research permits a high level of precision and consistency when it comes to the measurements that form the basis of the data.

Causes and explanations

Experiments take place under conditions which involve controls on relevant variables and which allow the researcher to identify the exact cause of things that are observed.

Disadvantages of experiments

Artificial settings

With laboratory experiments there are questions about whether the experimental situation creates conditions comparable with the 'real-world' situations in which the behaviour/decisions would be made, or whether it encourages artificial responses in line with the artificial setting.

Deception and ethics

There are two ethical considerations that need to be borne in mind when considering the use of experiments. First, will the experiment's success depend on keeping its true purpose secret from the research subjects? If so, this raises a question about the ethics of deception when used in social research. Second, if the research design employs the use of control groups, which is likely, will there be any advantage or disadvantage experienced by those in the respective groups? Is it possible that adverse comparisons might result through different treatments of experimental and control groups? If there is a significant difference, this could pose both ethical and practical/political problems for the researcher.

Control of the relevant variables

Being able to control the relevant variables lies at the heart of the experimental method. However, this can be hard to accomplish. And, even when it is possible in a practical sense, there can be ethical issues that arise which need to be taken into account.

Cause and effect

The experimental approach tends to focus on observable effects and works better with relatively straightforward matters. It can miss indirect causes (de Vaus 2001) and is not really well suited to dealing with the more complex underlying causes of many social phenomena (Pawson and Tilley 1997).

Random allocation to groups

When random allocation to the experimental group and the control group is not possible questions will arise about whether the groups genuinely constitute a 'matched pair'. Researchers need to be sure that there is no element of self-selection to the groups and that the groups are 'equivalent'.

Further reading

de Vaus, D. (2001) *Research Design in Social Research*. London: Sage, Chapters 4–6.

Dunning, T. (2012) *Natural Experiments in the Social Science: A Design-Based Approach*. Cambridge: Cambridge University Press.

Milgram, S. (1974) *Obedience to Authority: An Experimental View*. New York: HarperCollins.

Thyer, B. A. (2012) *Quasi-Experimental Research Designs*. New York: Oxford University Press.

Webster, M. and Sell, J. (2007) *Laboratory Experiments in the Social Sciences*. Burlington, MA: Amsterdam Press.

Checklist for the experimental approach

When undertaking research which involves experiments you should feel confident about answering 'yes' to the following questions: ☑

1 Have the key variables been clearly identified? ☐

2 Has a clear distinction been drawn between dependent and independent variables? ☐

3 Can the relevant variables be controlled for the purposes of designing the experiment? ☐

4 Is there a clear hypothesis or proposition that can be tested? ☐

5 Have detailed records been kept of the procedures and the results (in order to evaluate the design and replicate the experiment)? ☐

6 If a control group is used, is it closely matched in all key respects with the experimental group? ☐

7 If the research subjects are fully aware of the nature of the experiment in which they are taking part, has 'the observer' effect been taken into account? ☐

8 If the research subjects are not fully aware of the nature of the experiment in which they are participating, will they be fully informed after the experiment has taken place? ☐

9 Does the experimental situation create conditions comparable to the 'real-world' situations in which the behaviour/decisions would be made? ☐

10 Is the research ethical in terms of its treatment of those involved in the experiment? ☐

© M. Denscombe, *The Good Research Guide*. Open University Press.

5 Ethnography

What is ethnography?

The term *ethnography* literally means a description of peoples or cultures. It has
its origins as a research strategy in the works of the early social anthropologists
whose aim was to provide a detailed and permanent account of the cultures and
lives of small, isolated tribes. Such tribes were seen, with some justification, as
'endangered species', and the social anthropologists saw the need to map out
those cultures before they became contaminated by contact with the industrial
world or withered away to extinction.

The image of the pith-helmeted outsider dressed in khaki shorts arriving
on the shores of some remote and exotic palm tree island to set up camp
and study the lives of the 'native' has become legendary – largely through
the works of people like Bronislaw Malinowski (1922) and Margaret Mead
(1943). The concerns of such social anthropologists and the research strategy
they employed set the scene for much of what is undertaken as 'ethnography'
today.

Ethnography, based on the early anthropological origins of the term and on
subsequent developments by influential classics in the field (e.g. Whyte [1943]
1993), has the following characteristics:

- It requires the researcher to spend considerable *time in the field* among the
  people whose lives and culture are being studied. The ethnographer needs to
  share in the lives rather than observe from a position of detachment. Extended
  fieldwork allows for a *journey of discovery* in which the explanations for
  what is being witnessed emerge over a period of time.

- Routine and normal aspects of *everyday life* are regarded as worthy of consideration as research data. The mundane and the ordinary parts of social life are just as valid as the special events and ceremonies which can all too easily capture our attention.
- There is special attention given to the way the people being studied see their world. Quite distinct from the researcher's analysis of the situation, the ethnographer is generally concerned to find out *how the members of the group/culture being studied understand things*, the meanings *they* attach to happenings, the way *they* perceive their reality.
- There is an emphasis on the need to look at the interlinkages between the various features of the culture and to avoid isolating facets of the culture from the wider context within which it exists. Ethnography generally prefers a *holistic approach* which stresses processes, relationships, connections and interdependency among the component parts.
- There is some acknowledgement that the ethnographer's final account of the culture or group being studied is more than just a description – it is a *construction*. It is not a direct 'reproduction', a literal photograph of the situation. It is, rather, a crafted construction which employs particular writing skills (rhetoric) and which inevitably owes something to the ethnographer's own experiences.

 Key point: The holistic perspective of ethnography

'One of the first conditions of acceptable Ethnographic work certainly is that it should deal with the totality of all social, cultural and psychological aspects of the community, for they are so interwoven that not one can be understood without taking into consideration all the others' (Malinowski 1922: xvi).

The alien, the exotic and the routine

Early anthropologists studied groups in societies that were *different* from their own. Their aim was to explain the culture and lifestyles they found in the 'primitive' society where their fieldwork was based and, through a process of *comparison and contrast*, to cast fresh light on aspects of their own society as well. Ethnography, in this respect, resembles an anthropological approach. However, it does not restrict its attention to remote tribes in distant lands. Indeed, the most popular development of ethnography has been its application to lifestyles, understandings and beliefs within 'our own' society.

In its early days, ethnography 'within our own society' tended to focus on groups who were relatively small in number and who tended to be somewhat alien to the mainstream of society. The 'anthropological stance' was applied to oddball cultures that stood out as different from the norm. And, just as with the study of 'natives' in far-off lands, there was an immediate attraction for studying such groups. They offered something intrinsically interesting in the way their lifestyles seemed quaint, crazy, even exotic, compared with the everyday experience of those who studied the groups and those who read the resulting books. The focus was on 'deviant' groups, such as hobos, alcoholics, drug users, religious sects, street gangs, and the like. And ethnography retains today an interest in the exotic and the special, with ceremonies and the unusual features of social life. A recent ethnography, for example, focused on Wall Street investment bankers, exploring their everyday experiences, beliefs and the culture surrounding their lives as financial high-flyers (Ho 2009). However, the routine and the mundane, the normal and the unspectacular facets of social life have become recognized as equally valid topics for ethnographic enquiry. In recent times, attention has been refocused on to more routine, mainstream aspects of social life, for example, life in classrooms (Woods 2012) or life on a building site (Riemer 1979).

Life on the Internet

The Internet is more than a physical network and electronic technology. It enables a cyberworld populated by particular kinds of people. And this has attracted the attention of some ethnographers. For them, the Internet gives rise to a social phenomenon that needs to be investigated and explained. In this vein, research has emerged on:

- the cultural, social and technological conditions giving rise to the Internet and its widespread use;
- the personal attributes of those who use the Internet and the particular facilities it provides.

For others, the Internet is of particular interest because it is seen as a whole new aspect of social existence inhabited by communities with their own distinctive cultures, styles of interaction and modes of personal communication. The interest in 'online cultures' and 'online communities' has given rise to what Hine (2000) has called 'virtual ethnography' and Kozinets (2010) has termed 'netnography'. Ethnography, in such cases, focuses on the culture of cyberspace.

Life history

A life history approach, in a sense, is like a 'personal ethnography'. It involves the in-depth study of individuals or members of social groups. The aim of the approach is to portray the lives of specific people, to map how their experiences change over time, and to link these experiences with the cultural, social or historical context in which they occur. The approach came to prominence through the work of sociologists at the University of Chicago during the 1920s to 1940s who paved the way by conducting detailed empirical studies of individuals, groups and communities (Denzin 1970; Bulmer 1984). These ethnographies traced the changes and developments that took place over a period of time and paid particular attention to experiences of those whose lives were being studied. More recently the approach has been associated with feminist research (Devault 1990) and studies of individuals in relation to occupations (Woods 1993) and health (Haglund 2004).

Like biographies, life histories can be based on the whole of a person's lifespan from beginning to end, but can also be used to cover portions of lives – extended and substantial parts of people's lives but not the whole of the life.

There are two themes running through most life history research, both of which fit closely with ethnography. The first is that the research provides a 'thick' description of the life of the person. It includes the kind of fine detail that allows the reader to see the complex and multi-layered facets of the person's life. The second is that the individual's understanding of things is treated as a crucial part of the life history. As Marshall and Rossman (2011: 151) put it, the life history approach 'understands a culture through the history of one person's development of life within it, told in ways that capture the person's own feelings, views, and perspectives'.

Contrasting slightly with this, some life histories are used *descriptively*, their main aim being to use the personal biography as a means to reveal new things about the cultural, historical and social circumstances within which the person lives (or lived). The research, in this instance, attempts to provide insights into the lifestyle and beliefs of a particular culture or group. The idea is that we can learn what things were like from someone who had first-hand experience of being there or who had lived during that period.

Other researchers approach life histories in a more *analytic* fashion. They are more inclined to treat the life history as something that should be interpreted in terms of the wider social structure within which it occurs. There is an issue, here, about whether the life history entails recounting the story of a person's life in the way that they see it, or whether there is a need to bring alternative sources to bear by way of corroborating or challenging the person's version of their own life. Denzin argues that:

> The life history must contain reports from persons other than the subject. Not only must users of life histories triangulate methodologies, but they must also triangulate perspectives . . . Unless the perspectives of others are brought to bear upon the subject's statements, observers have no way of assessing the idiosyncrasies of those interpretations.
>
> (Denzin 1970: 238)

Despite these differences in emphasis, what life histories share is an approach that uses the in-depth study of an individual's life in order to get a grasp on their experiences and thinking in a way that links these to the cultural, social and historical circumstances in which they occur.

Life histories generally make use of in-depth interviews to collect the data. They can also make use of secondary source data such as public archive material, private archive material, diaries, letters and other forms of documentary data to build the life history. As with most ethnographic research, a distinctive feature of the data collection is that it takes place over a relatively long period and a life history is not something that can be completed quickly.

Link up with
Narrative analysis, p. 291.

> Usually, it will be gathered over a number of years with gentle guidance from the social scientist, the subject either writing down episodes of life or tape recording them. At its best, it will be backed up with intensive observation of the subject's life, interviews with friends and perusals of letters and photographs.
>
> (Plummer 2001: 14)

Perhaps the most interesting question of methods in relation to the life history approach is not how the data are collected, but how the informants are chosen. As Plummer (2001: 133) puts it so well: 'Who from the teeming millions of the world population is to be selected for such intensive study and social science immortality?' Obviously, it will be people who are 'information rich' – people with poignant experiences, fascinating insights and stories to tell. The way the researcher finds such people, people who are willing to open up their lives to the inquisitive gaze of the researcher, can follow a process of 'selective sampling'. The researcher will be looking in certain appropriate places and will have in mind some kind of person who might have the kind of life history that will be revealing and informative. However, when it comes to finding the 'right' person – the one who turns out to have the treasure trove of life experiences – famous instances of life history research show that luck has a large part to play.

Access to fieldwork settings

Gaining access to people, places and events is a crucial part of successful ethnographic research. For field researchers this access cannot be taken for granted. Researchers need to set about gaining access, and to do this they need to engage in negotiations that have political, ethical and practical implications.

Naturalism

In order to produce a pure and detailed description ethnographers will wish to avoid disrupting the situation by their very presence as observers in the field. They will wish to preserve the natural state of affairs. And this is why *naturalism* is a key concern of ethnography. The ethnographer's concern with naturalism derives from the wish to study things in their natural

> **Link up with**
> Participant obser-
> vation, p. 215.

state – undisturbed by the intrusion of research tools or the disruption of experimental designs. Going 'into the field' to witness events at first hand in their natural habitat lies at the very heart of what it means to do ethnography.

Covert research

It is sometimes possible for an ethnographer to conduct fieldwork without people knowing that they have a researcher in their midst. The researcher can blend into the background by adopting a role that fits in with the normal situation. The researcher can go *undercover* and carry out the research in a clandestine manner. This has benefits as far as ethnography is concerned because: (1) it preserves the naturalness of the setting; and (2) it generally side-steps any need to get authorization to conduct the research. However, it gives rise to a different type of problem. The decision to undertake covert research means that the researcher cannot also have 'informed consent' on the part of the subjects of his or her research, and this raises substantial ethical problems (see Humphreys 1975).

Gatekeepers

Ethnographers do not always work in a covert manner. Indeed, it is fair to say that most ethnographies actually involve some degree of openness about the role of the researcher; that is, *overt* research. When this is the case, the ethical problems cease to be the sole concern. Added to this, ethnographers are faced with the possibility that their explicit research role might disrupt the naturalness of the situation. Most of all, though, an overt research role will most probably bring with it a call for the researcher to make contact with 'gatekeepers' who can help the researcher with the vital business of gaining access to the necessary fieldwork settings.

Identifying key people who can grant permission, and successfully negotiating with them for access to people, places and events, is often a prerequisite without which the fieldwork cannot begin. In informal settings, such sponsors act as guarantors who vouch for the *bona fide* status of researcher. They use their informal status and relationship with subjects as a currency facilitating both contact and trust between researcher and subject or group (e.g. Whyte [1943] 1993; Polsky 2006).

Sponsors and gatekeepers, however, cannot be disregarded once their initial approval has been obtained. In reality, they exercise *continued* influence over the nature of the research. Their influence persists in terms of both:

- the kind of initial agreement established about access (influencing the nature of eventual research findings); and
- the need for access to people and places that were not foreseen at the start of the research.

The influence of such gatekeepers, then, goes beyond a simple granting or denial of contact with research subjects. As Burgess (1984) argues, access is a continual *process* in fieldwork research. It is a process because research is generally conducted over a period of time and it is a process, perhaps more importantly, because access needs to be sought to new people, places and events as new lines of enquiry become incorporated in the research. Since field research, especially ethnographic work, tends to evolve and develop in terms of its focus of enquiry, it is unlikely that the researcher could state at the outset of research the precise nature and extent of access that will be required. Access, in the sense of permission from a gatekeeper, is necessarily renewable and renegotiable, and should be viewed as an 'access relationship' rather than a one-off event.

Gatekeepers' authority to grant or withhold access varies, of course, depending on the degree to which the people, places and events being studied are part of a formal environment. Whereas in the educational context headteachers have formal jurisdiction over entry to school premises and can withhold or grant access to teachers and pupils, in less formal settings the role of the gatekeeper is different. As Whyte illustrated so graphically in his research (Whyte [1943] 1993), the role of gatekeeper can become more akin to a guarantor for the *bona fide* status of the researcher. Whyte's gatekeeper, 'Doc', had no formal authority to grant or deny access; he used his status with the group to open up the possibility of Whyte making contact with the young men in question, and acted as a sponsor/guarantor to enable some trust relationship to develop. This is an important point. As Hammersley and Atkinson (2007) argue, access is not simply a matter of physical presence or absence. It is far more than a matter of granting or withholding of permission for research to be conducted. Worthwhile access to people, places and events involves, as well, an opening up to allow the researcher into the world of the persons involved. Being present is one hurdle, but 'access' also involves being trusted with insights and insider knowledge.

Description and theory

Thick description

Ethnography involves the description of things witnessed first-hand in the field by the researcher. Such descriptions, however, if they are to prove useful from an ethnographic perspective, must go beyond a superficial glance. It is vital that they contain sufficient depth and detail to allow real insights into the situation being studied. The term 'thick description' is often referred to in this context. A 'thick description' (Geertz 1973) aims to describe particular acts or events in relation to their cultural context. The emphasis is not just on describing what 'is' but on explaining how the nature of this phenomenon is closely linked to other aspects of its social context. To illustrate what this means, Geertz himself draws on the example of 'winking'. Simply describing the action itself is 'thin description'. It is important to include as part of the description, but if we want to understand the meaning of the action we need a 'thick description' which supplies information about the intentions of the person doing the winking and the symbolic significance of the gesture in different settings. Only then can we understand whether the action is to be construed as a twitch, as a friendly gesture, as flirting, as a subtle conspiracy or whatever.

Idiographic and nomothetic approaches

Detailed descriptions can stand in their own right as a valuable contribution to knowledge or, alternatively, they can be treated as building blocks towards the creation of more general theories about the kind of culture, lifestyle, beliefs or events being researched. An *idiographic* approach aligns with the first of these two positions. It sees the purpose of ethnographic research as being to produce detailed pictures of events or cultures – descriptions which stand in their own right. From this standpoint there is no need to worry about how representative the situation is or what the broader implications might be in terms of other events or cultures of the type, or of contributing to wider theories. Any ethnographic description is to be regarded as a stand-alone 'one-off' that is to be judged by the depth of its portrayal and the intricacy of its description. There is no attempt to derive something from the description that goes beyond the specifics of the situation and which can, in some way or other, link to broader issues.

Link up with Chapter 6 Phenomenology.

A *nomothetic* approach, however, challenges the value of producing numerous stand-alone descriptions. It argues that if each ethnographic study produces a one-off, isolated piece of information, then there is little prospect of building up any generalized knowledge about human societies. The nomothetic approach takes the position that ethnographic research should be undertaken quite deliberately to develop more generalized and 'theoretical' conclusions that will apply outside the confines of the individual ethnographic study: it should help to generate theories. Or it might even be used to test theories. Porter (1993), for example, argues that ethnographic research should be used as a way of checking whether a theory really does hold true in 'real life'.

So, at one end of the spectrum there are those who regard the main purpose of ethnography as providing rich and detailed descriptions of real-life situations as they really are. At the other end of the spectrum there are those who see the role of ethnographic fieldwork as a means of developing theories by checking them out in small-scale scenarios. And somewhere towards the middle of the spectrum lies the pragmatic view 'that "idiographic" and "nomothetic" approaches are not mutually exclusive, and that we can have both rich and intensive description *and* generalizability' (Woods 2012: 268). Advocates of the middle position are keen to hold on to the idiographic aspect of ethnographic research in as much as it provides a valuable and distinct kind of data – the detailed descriptions of specifics based on first-hand observation in naturally occurring situations. But they also recognize the need for conclusions to be drawn from the research which have implications beyond the bounds of the particular events, customs or people studied. In the words of Hammersley (1990: 598), the 'descriptions must remain close to the concrete reality of particular events but at the same time reveal general features of human social life'.

Good practice: Generalizing from ethnographies

To accommodate the need for ethnographies to combine detailed description of particular settings with the need to produce findings that have some general implications beyond the specifics of the situation studied, ethnographies should:

- compare their findings with those of other similar ethnographies;
- consider how their findings tie in with, or contradict, existing relevant theories and understanding about human social behaviour;
- explain the significance of the topic in relation to the beliefs and priorities of the researcher's own culture.

Reflexivity: ethnographers as part of the world they seek to describe

Ethnographers tend to be very sensitive to the matter of reflexivity and the way it affects their perception of the culture or events they wish to describe. What concerns them is that the conceptual tools they use to understand the cultures or events being studied are not, and can never be, neutral and passive instruments of discovery.

As researchers, the meanings we attach to things that happen and the language we use to describe them are the product of our own culture, social background and personal experiences. Making sense of what is observed during fieldwork observation is a process that relies on what the researcher already knows and already believes, and it is not a voyage of discovery which starts with a clean sheet. We can only make sense of the world in a way that we have learnt to do using conceptual tools which are based on our own culture and our own experiences. We have no way of standing outside these to reach some objective and neutral vantage point from which to view things 'as they really are'. To an extent, we can describe them only 'as we see them', and this is shaped by *our* culture, not theirs.

The question that taxes ethnographers is this: 'How far can my description of the culture or event depict things from the point of view of those involved when I can only use my own way of seeing things, my own conceptual tools, to make sense of what is happening?' Broadly, ethnographers are conscious of the way in which their account of any particular lifestyle or beliefs is a construction based upon the researcher's interpretation of events. Even when it comes to writing up the ethnography, there are deep-rooted doubts about claims to objectivity. The outcome of ethnographic research is generally recognized by those who write it as being a creative work in its own right – the outcome of interpretation, editing and skilful writing techniques as well as a reflection of the reality of the situation they set out to study (Woods 2006). Inescapably, the account is partial – an edited and abridged version – which owes something to the ethnographer as well as the culture or events observed. There is nothing new to this. Malinowski appreciated the point many years ago:

> **Link up with**
> Producing accounts of research, p. 335.

> In ethnography, the distance is often enormous between the brute material of information – as it is presented to the student in his own observations, in native statement, in the kaleidoscope of tribal life – and the final authoritative presentations of the results. The ethnographer has to traverse this distance in the laborious years between the moment when he sets foot upon a native beach, and makes his first attempts to get into touch with the natives, and the time when he writes down the final version of his results.
>
> (Malinowski 1922: 4)

Putting the researcher's 'self' into ethnographic research

One of the characteristic features of ethnography is the significance it attaches to the role of the researcher's 'self' in the process of research. The researcher's identity, values and beliefs become part of the equation – a built-in component that cannot be eliminated as an influence on the end-product findings of the project.

Ethnographic research, therefore, calls for a certain degree of introspection on the part of the researcher. He or she needs to reflect upon the way that background factors associated with personal experiences, personal beliefs and social values may have shaped the way that events and cultures were interpreted.

However, the ethnographic researcher needs to go beyond mere reflection. This is, in a sense, a private activity. Necessary though it is, it needs to be portrayed more publicly if it is to support the research outcomes. Researchers need to supply their readers with some insights into the possible influence of the researcher's self on the interpretation of events or cultures. There needs to be a public account of the self which explores the role of the researcher's self. This account of the self will vary in the amount of detail it provides, depending on the nature of the research topic, the kind of methods used and the audience for whom the ethnography is written. It is obviously a matter of judgement here about the extent to which the account should delve to the depths of detail about researchers' personal matters, and the amount of detail that the readership needs to know in order to arrive at a reasonable evaluation of the likely impact of the 'self' on the research.

Good practice: Reflecting on the researcher's 'self'

Ethnographies require some reflection by the researcher on how his/her biography, values and experiences might have a bearing on the nature of the study. This 'public account of the role of the self' can be included in the methodology section and possibly in the Preface or Introduction to reports of the findings. As a broad guideline, the following factors might be considered:

- personal beliefs relating to the topic (politics, values, standpoint);
- personal interests in the area of investigation (vested interest, history of events);
- personal experience linked to the research topic (incidents affecting self or others close to researchers);
- personal expertise in relation to the topic (qualification, experience).

To give an account of the way personal beliefs, interests, experience and expertise might have a bearing on findings, the researcher is likely to need to draw upon personal details about his or her:

- age
- sex
- ethnicity
- social background (class, family, environment)

- education and qualifications
- work experience and skills.

Advantages of ethnography

Detailed data based on direct observation

As a research strategy ethnography is based on direct observation via fieldwork, rather than relying on second-hand data or statements made by research subjects. It is grounded in empirical research involving direct contact with relevant people and places, and it provides data rich in depth and detail. Potentially, it can deal with intricate and subtle realities.

Links with theory

It can be used as a means for developing theory, and it can also be used for testing theories.

Holistic

Ethnography aspires to holistic explanations which focus on processes and relationships that lie behind the surface events. It puts things in context rather than abstracting specific aspects in isolation.

A fresh view on things

There is an element of contrast and comparison built into ethnographic research which encourages the researcher to look beyond 'the obvious' and to see things relative to other cultures and lifestyles. Cultures and lifestyles are viewed as 'anthropologically strange'.

Actors' perceptions

Ethnographic research is particularly well suited to dealing with the way members of a culture see events – as seen through their eyes. It describes and explores the 'actors' perceptions'.

Self-awareness

It has an open and explicit awareness of the role of the researcher's *self* in the choice of topic, process of research and construction of the findings/conclusions. It acknowledges the inherent reflexivity of social knowledge.

Ecological validity

It is strong in terms of ecological validity, to the extent that the act of researching should have relatively little impact on the setting – retaining things in their 'natural' form.

Disadvantages of ethnography

Tensions within the approach

There is a tension within the realms of ethnography stemming from its twin concerns with naturalism and reflexivity. Ethnographies generally attempt to accommodate an internal contradiction between (1) 'realist' aspirations to provide full and detailed *descriptions* of events or cultures as they naturally exist, and (2) a 'relativist' awareness of the reflexive nature of social knowledge and the inevitable influence of the researcher's 'self' on the whole research endeavour.

Stand-alone descriptions

Ethnographic research has the potential to produce an array of 'pictures' which coexist, but which tend to remain as separate, isolated stories. There is arguably an in-built tendency to scatter these building-block pictures at random, rather than erecting a structure where each is a brick which serves as a base for further bricks to be laid upon, moving it ever upwards. To avoid this, ethnographies need to be guided by (or towards) a coherent theoretical framework.

Story-telling

There is the potential to provide detailed descriptive accounts at the expense of developing an analytic insight or contributing to a theoretical position. The story-telling can become the sole purpose, leaving a research product which is a-theoretical, non-analytic and non-critical.

Reliability

Ethnographic studies, because of their nature, are hard to replicate in order to check the findings. Accounts of the situation often depend on records kept by a single researcher and they tend to rely heavily on the researcher's interpretation of events.

Ethics

There is also a greater potential than with most other approaches to face ethical problems associated with intrusions upon privacy and with gaining informed consent from research subjects.

Access

Ethnographic research can pose particularly acute difficulties of gaining access to settings, access which avoids disrupting the naturalness of the setting.

Further reading

Boellstorff, T., Nardi, B., Pearce, C. and Taylor, T. (2012) *Ethnography and Virtual Worlds: A Handbook of Method*. Princeton, NJ: Princeton University Press.

Brewer, J. (2000) *Ethnography*. Buckingham: Open University Press.

Hammersley, M. and Atkinson, P. (2007) *Ethnography: Principles in Practice*, 3rd edn. London: Tavistock.

Madden, R. (2010) *Being Ethnographic: A Guide to the Theory and Practice of Ethnography*. London: Sage.

Murchison, J. (2010) *Ethnography Essentials: Designing, Conducting, and Presenting Your Research*. San Francisco, CA: Jossey-Bass.

O'Reilly, K. (2012) *Ethnographic Methods*, 2nd edn. London: Routledge.

Checklist for ethnographic research

When undertaking ethnographic research you should feel confident about answering 'yes' to the following questions: ☑

1 Have cultures, lifestyles, customs and beliefs been treated as the main interest of the research? ☐

2 Has a holistic approach been adopted, linking all significant contributing factors? ☐

3 Has the research involved a substantial time 'in the field' collecting empirical data? ☐

4 Has access to the fieldwork settings been negotiated through relevant 'gatekeepers'? ☐

5 Has the research been conducted ethically with due respect to the rights of those being studied? ☐

6 Has the research managed to avoid disrupting the naturalness of the settings? ☐

7 Does the research include an account of the role of the researcher's 'self'? ☐

8 Is there a description of how the ethnography builds on (or contradicts) existing explanations of the phenomenon? ☐

9 Are the findings compared and contrasted with other ethnographies on similar topics? ☐

10 Has due acknowledgement been given to the fact that the ethnography is a researcher's construction rather than a literal description of the situation? ☐

© M. Denscombe, *The Good Research Guide*. Open University Press.

6 Phenomenology

What is the phenomenological approach?

As an approach to social research, phenomenology is sometimes presented as an alternative to positivism. When a simple dichotomy is called for, phenomenology has been useful for some writers as an umbrella term covering styles of research that do not rely on measurement, statistics or other things generally associated with the scientific method. In direct contrast to positivism, it is seen as an approach that emphasizes:

- subjectivity (rather than objectivity);
- description (more than analysis);
- interpretation (rather than measurement);
- agency (rather than structure).

Its credentials as an alternative to positivism are further reinforced by the fact that phenomenological research generally deals with:

- people's perceptions or meanings;
- people's attitudes and beliefs;
- people's feelings and emotions.

Such a thumbnail portrait of phenomenology serves to set the scene and provide an initial view of its direction as a research strategy. It helps to explain why a phenomenological approach has proved useful for researchers in areas such as health, education and business who want to understand the thinking of patients, pupils and employees (van Manen 1990; Crotty 1996). And it gives a clue to why phenomenology is associated with humanistic research using qualitative methodologies – approaches that place special emphasis on the individual's views and personal experiences.

Experience

Phenomenology is concerned, first and foremost, with human experience – something denoted by the term 'phenomenology' itself. A phenomenon is something that stands in need of explanation; something of which we are aware but something that, as yet, remains known to us only in terms of how it appears to us directly through our senses. A phenomenological approach to research, following from this, concentrates its efforts on the kind of human experiences that are pure, basic and raw in the sense that they have not (yet) been subjected to processes of analysis and theorizing. In contrast to other approaches to research that rely on processes of categorizing things, abstracting them, quantifying them and theorizing about them, phenomenology prefers to concentrate its efforts on getting a clear picture of the 'things in themselves' – the things as directly experienced by people.

 Key point: Phenomenology is an approach that focuses on how life is experienced

It is not primarily concerned with explaining the causes of things but tries, instead, to provide a description of how things are experienced first-hand by those involved. The phenomenological investigation of something like 'homelessness', for instance, would focus on the experience of being homeless. It might be interested in trying to get at the essence of what it means to be homeless. It might try to understand homelessness from the point of view of those who are themselves homeless and try to describe how they see things, how they understand the situation, how they interpret events. What it would not try to do is measure the extent of homelessness, or explain the causes of homelessness. Though both might be worthwhile endeavours, neither would be at the heart of phenomenological research.

The everyday world

Phenomenology is also characterized by a particular interest in the basics of social existence. This stems from a philosophical concern with the nature of 'Being-in-the-world' (Heidegger 1962) and the lived experience of human beings within the 'life-world' (Husserl 1950). In practice, this translates into special importance being attached to the routine and ordinary features of social life, and to questions about how people manage to 'do' the everyday things on which social life depends. Sometimes this can involve quite fundamental things associated with the way people experience their lives, for example, ageing, sexual orientation, faith, major life transitions and identity changes (e.g. Bettis 1969; Moustakas 1992; Ahmed 2006). On other occasions phenomenological studies have looked at more mundane things such as daydreaming (Morley 1998) and complaining about chronic pain (Kugelmann 1999). Such topics might draw on normal, routine facets of the everyday world around us but, from the phenomenological perspective, this does not make them trivial or inconsequential.

Seeing things through the eyes of others

When dealing with the way people experience facets of their lives, phenomenology stresses the need to present matters as closely as possible to the way that those concerned understand them. The phenomenologist's task, in the first instance, is not to interpret the experiences of those concerned, not to analyse them or repackage them in some form. The task is to present the experiences in a way that is *faithful to the original*. This entails the ability to see things through the eyes of others, to understand things in the way that they understand things and to provide a description of matters that adequately portrays how the group in question experiences the situation.

This has some significant implications for social research. First, it places the ideas and reasoning of the group being studied at the core of the investigation. The research necessarily revolves around people and their lives, rather than systems, aggregates and trends operating at a high level of abstraction. Second, it elevates the importance of people's thinking in terms of the research. Rather than being treated as something that is the crude foundation on which to build more sophisticated explanations and theories about the experiences, that thinking becomes the topic of investigation in its own right. Third, people's everyday thinking is given credibility and respected in its own right as valid. It is not necessarily treated as less rational than or inferior to the 'scientific' thinking of the social researcher, but is considered as rational in its own terms of reference. For these reasons, *phenomenology has an affinity with humanistic perspectives on research that are keen to accord normal people and their own everyday reasoning higher status in research.*

The social construction of reality

Phenomenology is particularly interested in how social life is constructed by those who participate in it, and it makes two points about this. First, it regards people as creative interpreters of events who, through their actions and interpretations, literally make sense of their worlds. From the perspective of the phenomenologist people do not passively obey a set of social rules; nor do they slot into an external social structure; nor do they simply respond to their internal physiological drives or psychological dispositions. They are viewed instead as 'agents' who interpret their experiences and who actively create an order to their existence. As an approach to understanding the social world this sets phenomenology apart from any belief that things are preordained, that there is a reality to social life that exists independently from the way people experience it or that the way we experience and understand things is structured by the way human minds are programmed to perceive things.

Good practice: Making sense of reality

Phenomenological research should focus on the ways in which people interpret events and, literally, make sense of their personal experiences.

Second, it acknowledges that the processes of interpreting sights and sounds into meaningful events are not unique to each individual. Necessarily, they must be shared with others who live in the group or community (Berger and Luckmann 1967). If they were not, people would find it virtually impossible to interact with one another, since they could be operating on quite different understandings about what is going on. They could be living in different worlds, unable to communicate and unable to grasp the implications of other people's actions. Without some shared basis for interpreting their experiences there would be no way of knowing what others were doing or what their intentions were. There would, effectively, be no basis for social life.

Multiple realities

When the social world is seen as 'socially constructed' it opens up the possibility that different groups of people might 'see things differently'. There is the prospect of alternative realities – realities that vary from situation to situation, culture to culture. In this respect phenomenology stands in stark contrast to positivistic approaches to social research that are premised on the assumption of *one* reality. Whereas positivistic approaches look for explanations that fit one universal reality, phenomenological approaches tend to live with, even celebrate, the possibility of *multiple realities*. Reflecting the fact that the world as experienced by living humans is something that is created through the way they interpret and give meaning to their experiences, phenomenology rejects the notion that there is one universal reality and accepts, instead, that things can be seen in different ways by different people at different times in different circumstances, and that each alternative version needs to be recognized as being valid in its own right.

 Caution: Multiple realities

This phenomenological position certainly allows for competing versions of what things are, how they work and what they mean. It implies that there might not be one 'right' explanation and that different theories might be equally valid. It moves researchers away from a mind set where one theory is correct and ▶

▶ others are inadequate or wrong. It does not imply, however, that there are as many social realities as there are individuals – each interpreting his or her world in their own unique way. As has been stressed, phenomenology does not treat interpretations of the social world as totally individual things. Necessarily, they are shared between groups, cultures and societies, and it is only at these levels that phenomenology recognizes the possibility of there being multiple realities.

Description

When it comes to the matter of how phenomenologists actually do their research, a key characteristic of the approach is its emphasis on describing authentic experiences. Rather than directing their attention to explanations and analyses of experiences in an attempt to discover why they occurred, phenomenologists focus instead on trying to depict the relevant experiences in a way that is as faithful to the original as possible.

To provide a description of the *authentic* experience, phenomenological research first and foremost needs to provide a description that adequately covers the complexity of the situation. One of the crucial benefits of a phenomenological approach is that it deals with things in depth and does not try to gloss over the subtleties and complications that are essential parts of many – possibly most – aspects of human experience. The description, therefore, must be fairly detailed.

The phenomenological description should also be prepared to recognize and include aspects of the experience that appear to be self-contradictory, irrational or even bizarre. The researcher's role is not to act as editor for the way people explain their experiences. Nor is it to impose some artificial order on the thoughts of those being studied by trying to remedy any apparent logical inconsistencies. The social world is rarely neat and phenomenology does not involve the attempt to present life experiences as though they are entirely coherent.

Good practice: Dealing with complexities and contradictions

Phenomenological research should involve a detailed description of the experience that is being investigated – one that does not gloss over the complexities and contradictions that inhabit real life.

The suspension of common-sense beliefs

A phenomenological approach not only encourages the researcher to provide a detailed description of experiences, it also advocates the need to do so with a minimum reliance on the researcher's own beliefs, expectations and predispositions about the phenomenon under investigation.

From a phenomenological perspective, researchers are part and parcel of the social world they seek to investigate. Phenomenologists see the social world as existing only through the way it is experienced and interpreted by people – and this includes researchers as much as anyone else. Researchers, like other people, use common-sense assumptions when interpreting events, and this is where phenomenology has an important point to make for researchers. Researchers need to be *aware* of the fact that they rely on such everyday common sense, and make an effort to minimize the impact of these assumptions. They need to stand back from their ordinary, everyday beliefs and question them to see if they are blinkering the researcher's vision of what is happening. As best they can, researchers need temporarily to suspend common-sense beliefs. For the purposes of being able to provide a 'pure' description, researchers need to approach things without predispositions based on events in the past, without suppositions drawn from existing theories about the phenomenon being studied and without using their everyday common-sense assumptions. Such things need to be put to one side for the moment, 'bracketed off' so that researchers are able to describe things not through their own eyes but through the eyes of those whose experiences are being described.

One way of 'bracketing off' presuppositions is to adopt the stance of 'the stranger' (Schutz 1962). The value of this is that it allows the researcher to see things that would otherwise be hidden from view – things that are so normal and obvious that they would not come to the attention of the researcher as something significant. A stranger is naïve about how things work, and needs to figure them out from first principles before he or she can begin to operate as a competent member of the society. A 'stranger' is faced with the prospect of understanding *how* members of the society make sense of events. By adopting the stance of the stranger, then, the researcher is best able to see things for what they are, uncluttered by assumptions that form part of everyday thinking about those things.

Good practice: Suspending common-sense beliefs

Researchers who use a phenomenological approach need to be explicit about their own ways of making sense of the world and, in order to get a clear view of how others see the world, they need to suspend (or bracket off) their own beliefs temporarily for the purposes of research.

Members' accounts

Data collection by phenomenology tends to rely on tape-recorded interviews. The interviews are conducted with members of the particular group whose experiences are being investigated. These members can provide insights into the thinking of the group and, through in-depth interviews, their experiences and their reasoning can be described and explained to the researcher in a way that allows the researcher to see things from the member's point of view (Denscombe 1983).

The process of interviewing is valuable for phenomenologists for a number of reasons. First, it provides the possibility of exploring matters *in depth*. In phenomenological research, interviews tend to be relatively long (in the region of one hour, often more) so that there is plenty of time to delve deeply into issues as they arise. Second, interviews allow the interviewee to raise issues that he or she feels are important. This helps the phenomenologist's investigation by highlighting things that matter to the person being interviewed. It helps to 'see things from the member's point of view'. To encourage this, phenomenological researchers tend to use relatively 'unstructured' interviews. Rather than the interview being conducted using a series of questions devised by the researcher, unstructured interviews allow plenty of scope for interviewees to move the discussion to areas that *they* regard as significant. Third, the interview process gives an opportunity for interviewees to provide an 'account' of their experiences. It is *their* version, spoken in their own words. It allows them both to describe the situation as they see it and to provide some justification or rationale, again from their point of view. Fourth, interviews allow the researcher the opportunity to *check* that he or she is understanding the interviewee correctly. As a normal part of the interview process the researcher can take special care to make sure that what he or she is 'hearing' is really what the interviewee is trying to put across, not a partial or mistaken interpretation resulting from the researcher's common-sense assumptions or presuppositions.

Link up with
Chapter 12
Interviews.

Types of phenomenology: underlying essences or actual experiences

Over time, different versions of phenomenology have developed and there are sometimes disagreements among those who would call themselves 'phenomenologists' about which is the 'true' version. The social researcher who is thinking about adopting a phenomenological approach should be aware that such differences of opinion exist. Although many versions exist, it is probably most straightforward to characterize phenomenology as consisting of two main types. One version derives from the European tradition of thought and the other, the 'new phenomenology', has a North American origin (Crotty 1996).

The European version is more steeped in the discipline of philosophy and can lay claims to being the original version since it owes much to the founding father of phenomenology, Edmund Husserl. His 'transcendental phenomenology' (Husserl 1931) approaches the study of human experience with the aim of discovering underlying, fundamental aspects of experience – features that are universal and that lie at the very heart of human experience. Though differing somewhat, the 'existential phenomenology' of Jean-Paul Sartre (1956) and the 'hermeneutic phenomenology' of Martin Heidegger (1962) draw on similar European philosophical roots and have a crucial thing in common. They share a concern with investigating *the essence of human experience*.

The kinds of experience dealt with by these writers tend to revolve around fundamental philosophical questions about 'being-in-the-world' and similar issues relating to 'the meaning of (everyday) life'. However, this form of phenomenology can operate at a more mundane level. For example, it could address something as topical and down-to-earth as bullying in schools. Based on this tradition of phenomenology the research would be interested in the experience of being bullied and, in particular, it would focus on the essential features of that experience. It would try to identify the core components of the notion of bullying by investigating the experiences of those who have found themselves the victim of bullying. It would not focus on the *extent* of bullying in schools, nor would it try to explain the *causes* of bullying. Its focus would be on the *essence of the experience of being bullied.*

Importantly, though, the European tradition of phenomenology stresses that such essences exist beyond the realms of individual, personal experiences of specific events. While such individual instances might be the starting point for investigation, the purpose is always to use them as a means for getting a clearer picture of the essential qualities of the experience that exist at a general level. In relation to the example of bullying, individual instances of bullying would be of interest only to the extent that they could be used to help the identification of the broader, essential qualities of that experience: they would be valuable as means towards an end, but would not constitute an end in themselves as far as research is concerned.

Contrasting with this tradition there is the North American version of phenomenology which is more commonly linked to the disciplines of sociology, psychology, education, business studies and health studies. It emanates from the 'social phenomenology' of Alfred Schutz (1962, 1967). Schutz was primarily interested in the mental processes through which humans make sense of the many things they experience. His early work focused on the way that, in order to make sense of the social world, people interpret things through seeing them as specific instances of more general categories – a process that involves what he referred to as 'typifications'. Within the realms of phenomenology this shift in focus had important repercussions. Indeed, through his focus on interpretation of the social world, Schutz's work actually spawned a rather different kind of phenomenology. This kind of phenomenology is less concerned with revealing the essence of experience and more concerned with describing the ways in which humans give meaning to their experiences. Here lies the defining characteristic of the North American approach: *its concern with the ways people interpret social phenomena.*

This form of phenomenology retains a concern with things like experience, an interest in everyday life and suspending common-sense assumptions in order to provide a description that is true to the way those involved experience things. However, it also incorporates elements of pragmatism and social interactionism into the approach – things that make it controversial in two ways as far as the European phenomenological tradition is concerned. First, the North American phenomenology is comfortable in describing *what* is being experienced (for example, in relation to something such as homelessness), rather than attempting to uncover the essence of what is meant by the term. Second, and linked with this, it also places some value on describing individuals' experiences for their own sake. The new phenomenology might well investigate homelessness by asking what being homeless means to those who are homeless, what events and emotions they have experienced as a consequence of being homeless and what it means to them. The experiences of the individual are taken as significant data in their own right, not something to be put to one side in order to identify the universal essence of the phenomenon.

Good practice: Clarity of purpose

In practice, it is not always easy to separate the two traditions of phenomenology. Ideas from one area are imported to the other, not always reflecting the original very faithfully. Such blurring of the boundaries complicates life for project researchers. This should not, though, deter a researcher from choosing this approach, since many aspects of social research operate in such contested domains. It does, however, highlight the need for the researcher to be very clear about his/her specific aims when investigating the phenomena of human experience.

Advantages of phenomenology

Suited to small-scale research

Phenomenological research generally relies on in-depth interviews and does not call for technologically sophisticated or expensive equipment for the purposes of data collection and analysis. Coupled with this, it is often undertaken in specific localities such as hospitals, schools or industrial plants. In both respects, it lends itself to small-scale research where the budget is low and the main resource is the researcher himself/herself.

The description of experiences can tell an interesting story

There is an inherent potential within (new) phenomenology to describe experiences in a way that is immediately accessible and interesting to a wide range of readers. By unfolding the events and laying bare the feelings experienced by people, the research is likely to attract a relatively wide readership. It deals with everyday life and people can generally relate to this.

Offers the prospect of authentic accounts of complex phenomena

The social world is complex and rarely straightforward. A phenomenological approach allows the researcher to deal with that complexity. It scratches beneath the superficial aspects of social reality. It calls for the researcher to delve into phenomena in depth and to provide descriptions that are detailed enough to reflect the complexity of the social world.

A humanistic style of research

There is a respect for people built into the phenomenological approach. It carries an aura of humanism and, in its efforts to base its enquiry on the lived experiences of people in the everyday world, it represents a style of research that is far removed from any high-minded, abstract theorizing. In effect, the researcher needs to be close to the objects of study.

Disadvantages of phenomenology

Lacks scientific rigour

The emphasis of phenomenology on subjectivity, description and interpretation contrasts with the scientific emphasis on objectivity, analysis and measurement. Although phenomenology is self-consciously non-positivist – and proud to be so – there is the danger that this can be turned against it and be treated as a weakness rather than a strength by those who do not share its stance.

Associated with description and not analysis

The importance attached to providing a detailed and accurate description of the events and experiences being studied can lead to accusations that phenomenology does nothing but provide descriptions. This might not be warranted, in particular where the phenomenologist goes on to develop explanations based on the descriptive material. There is, none the less, the danger that those who are not sympathetic to phenomenology might seize the opportunity to criticize it for its primary focus on description.

Generalizations from phenomenological studies

Phenomenological research does not normally involve large numbers of the phenomenon being studied. This will always raise questions about the representativeness of the data and how far it is justifiable to generalize from the findings. Phenomenologists, for their part, might not regard such a concern as relevant to their work, but many other kinds of researchers will be concerned with this issue.

Attention to the mundane features of life

For phenomenologists the study of routine aspects of everyday life occurs because it is fundamental for understanding the nature of the social world. For others it might be (mis)interpreted as dealing with things that are mundane, trivial and relatively unimportant compared with the big issues of the day in the spheres of social policy, international relations, economic progress, and the like.

Feasibility of suspending common sense

In principle, suspending presuppositions about the way things work might seem a reasonable way of trying to get a clearer view of them. However, it is doubtful indeed if it is ever possible to rid ourselves entirely of such presuppositions. Socialization and the use of language make it impossible. What can be done, though, is to be reflective and self-conscious about the way perceptions are shaped by things like common sense and then to try to moderate their impact.

Further reading

Gallagher, S. (2012) *Phenomenology.* Basingstoke: Palgrave.

Lewis, M. and Staehler, T. (2010) *Phenomenology: An Introduction.* London: Continuum.

Moustakas, C. (1994) *Phenomenological Research Methods.* Thousand Oaks, CA: Sage.

Smith, J. A., Flowers, P. and Larkin, M. (2009) *Interpretative Phenomenological Analysis: Theory, Method and Research.* London: Sage.

Van Manen, M. (2014) *Phenomenology of Practice: Meaning-Giving Methods in Phenomenological Research and Writing.* Walnut Creek, CA: Left Coast Press.

Checklist for phenomenology

When undertaking phenomenological research you should feel confident about answering 'yes' to the following questions: ✓

1 Is the research concerned with one or more of the following?

- Looking for the essential features of a phenomenon ☐
- Describing the content and nature of lived experiences ☐
- Investigating the everyday rules by which experience is structured ☐

2 Does the research take into consideration:

- the social construction of reality? ☐
- multiple realities? ☐

3 Have efforts been made to bracket off common-sense assumptions and take account of researchers' presuppositions in order to provide a 'pure' description? ☐

4 Does the research provide a description that adequately deals with the complexity, subtlety and contradictions of the phenomenon? ☐

5 Does the description authentically represent the way things are seen by those whose experiences are being studied? ☐

6 Does the research involve the suitable use of interviews and transcripts for checking members' meanings and intentions? ☐

© M. Denscombe, *The Good Research Guide*. Open University Press.

7 Grounded theory

What is the grounded theory approach? • When is the grounded
theory approach useful? • Starting grounded theory research
• Theoretical sampling: the selection of sites for fieldwork • Completing
the research (theoretical saturation) • Methods of data collection
• Analysing the data • Displaying the process • Theories and grounded
research • Developments in grounded theory • Advantages of the
grounded theory approach • Disadvantages of the grounded theory
approach • Further reading • Checklist for the grounded theory
approach

The grounded theory approach has become a popular choice of methodology among social researchers in recent times. In particular, it has been adopted by those engaged in small-scale projects using qualitative data for the study of human interaction, and by those whose research is exploratory and focused on particular settings.

What is the grounded theory approach?

The approach originated with the work of Barney Glaser and Anselm Strauss and, in particular, their book, *The Discovery of Grounded Theory*, which was published in 1967. Since that time the notion of grounded theory has come to mean slightly different things to different people. There has been a tendency for researchers to 'adopt and adapt' grounded theory and to use it selectively for their own purposes. There are, though, certain basic ideas associated with the grounded theory approach that remain fairly constant, and these are outlined in this chapter. They draw principally on the writings of Glaser and Strauss themselves and the main focus is on those components of the grounded theory approach that mark it out as distinctive and constitute its core components as an approach to social research (Figure 7.1).

Theories should be 'grounded' in empirical research

The approach directly challenges the value of theorizing at a high level of abstraction and then, subsequently, doing some empirical work to see if the

Figure 7.1 Grounded theory

Grounded theory is an approach dedicated to generating theories. In this sense it contrasts with approaches concerned with testing theories, and is different from research whose main purpose is to provide descriptive accounts of the subject matter.

Theory

Grounded theory is an approach that emphasizes the importance of empirical fieldwork and the need to link any explanations very closely to what happens in practical situations in 'the real world'. It is different, here, from approaches based on 'armchair theorizing' or explanations that are thought up in the abstract as a neat system of ideas, and then afterwards checked to see if they work in reality.

Grounded

theory actually works. Instead, it sets out to develop the theories on the basis of empirical research and gradually build up general theories that emerge from the data.

The insistence that theories should be 'grounded' brings with it the idea that researchers should be engaged with fieldwork as the fundamental part of the work they do. When adopting the grounded theory approach the researcher should undertake data collection in the field, not only as the starting point of the research but throughout the course of the research as well.

Theories should be generated by a systematic analysis of the data

The emphasis on collecting data in the field does not mean that the researcher should simply amass as much detail as possible about particular situations and then 'let the data speak for themselves'. Always high on the agenda for grounded theory research is a concerted effort to *analyse* the data and to generate theories from the data. And grounded theory is characterized by the specific way in which it approaches the business of analysing the data. Concepts and theories are developed out of the data through a persistent process of comparing the ideas with existing data, and improving the emerging concepts and theories by checking them against new data collected specifically for the purpose – the 'constant comparative method'.

The selection of items to be included in the research reflects the developing nature of the theory

The items to be included follow a trail of discovery – like a detective follows a 'lead'. Each new phase of the investigation reflects what has been discovered so far, with new angles of investigation and new avenues of enquiry to be explored. So, in the spirit of 'grounded theory' it is neither feasible nor desirable for the researcher to identify prior to the start exactly who or what will be included in the sample. This, of course, runs right against the grain as far as conventional social research practice is concerned. Normally, the social researcher would be expected to have a very clear vision of the intended sample, chosen on the basis of criteria linked to the ideas and theories being tested by the research.

Researchers should start out with an 'open mind'

In marked contrast to the researcher who sets out to *test* a theory the researcher who follows the principles of grounded theory needs to approach the topic *without a rigid set of ideas* that shape what they focus upon during the investigation. Rather than basing an investigation upon whether certain theories do or do not work, the researcher embarks on a voyage of discovery.

This should not be seen to imply that a good social researcher starts out with a 'blank' mind.

> To be sure, one goes out and studies an area with a particular . . . perspective, and with a focus, a general question or a problem in mind. But the researcher can (and we believe should) also study an area without any preconceived theory that dictates, prior to the research, 'relevancies' in concepts and hypotheses.
> (Glaser and Strauss 1967: 33)

Theories should be useful at a practical level and meaningful to those 'on the ground'

The grounded theory approach has its roots in *pragmatism* whose guiding philosophy is clearly acknowledged by Glaser and Strauss. Pragmatism places great emphasis on the 'practical' rather than the 'abstract' when it comes to issues of knowledge and truth and it operates on the premise that the value of any theory can only be gauged by how well it works in practice. For grounded theory this means that the theories produced should have practical relevance and *make sense to those whose actions it explains.*

When is the grounded theory approach useful?

The grounded theory approach does not purport to be the only proper way of conducting social research. It is but one approach among many. What it does claim, however, is that it offers an approach that is well suited to the needs of four kinds of research:

- qualitative research;
- exploratory research;
- studies of human interaction;
- small-scale research.

Qualitative research

Although in their original exposition of grounded theory Glaser and Strauss claimed that the approach could be applied to quantitative data as well as qualitative data, and despite subsequent claims that 'It transcends specific data collection methods' (Glaser 1978: 6), the grounded theory approach has become firmly associated over time with qualitative research. The nature of Glaser and Strauss's own research effectively set the tenor for the kind of research that has come to be associated with the grounded theory approach and by far the most common use of the grounded theory approach by other researchers has been with studies using qualitative data.

Exploratory research

Because there is an emphasis on discovery and because there is a stress on the need to approach investigations without being blinkered by the concepts and theories of previous research, the grounded theory approach fits neatly with the needs of researchers who are setting out to explore new territory in terms of either the subject matter of their investigation or the extent to which relevant theories have already been developed.

Studies of human interaction

The grounded theory approach is appropriate for social research that focuses on human interaction, particularly where the researcher wishes to investigate:

* practical activity and routine situations;
* the participants' points of view.

This reflects the roots of grounded theory within an approach called *symbolic interactionism*. This is a form of social research that focuses on the way that participants in social settings make sense of situations and events through the use of symbolic actions.

Small-scale research

Grounded theory's affinity with qualitative research, its desire to generate explanations from the study of particular instances, its need for detailed data about activities and practice and its value for exploratory research, combine to make it an approach that is well suited to small-scale research conducted by individual researchers operating within the constraints of a tight budget.

Starting grounded theory research

Initial ideas and concepts

The grounded theory approach expects the researcher to start research without any *fixed* ideas about the nature of the setting that is about to be investigated. The aim is to approach things with an open mind. An open mind, of course, is not a blank mind and it is inevitable that existing theories and personal experience will have some influence on what the researcher already knows about a topic. However, the crucial point is that pre-existing knowledge and concepts are to be treated as 'provisional' and open to question. They are simply a tentative starting point from which to launch the investigation.

Initial sites for fieldwork

Researchers who adopt the grounded theory approach need to start their investigation by concentrating on a particular situation, event or group. At the beginning, all that is required is that this site is 'relevant'. The criterion for its selection need only be that it might reasonably be expected to provide relevant information on the situation, event or group the researcher is interested in investigating.

The criterion of 'relevance' means that the grounded theory approach takes a distinct position in its choice of the initial site for fieldwork. It differs from the case study approach in the sense that there is no need for researchers using the grounded theory approach to get overly concerned about locating their initial fieldwork in a setting that can be demonstrated as being 'representative', 'typical' or 'extreme'.

Theoretical sampling: the selection of sites for fieldwork

After having selected the initial site for research, subsequent sites are selected according to a process of *theoretical sampling*. This form of sampling is a distinctive feature of the grounded theory approach and it involves six key features:

- Sites to be included in the research are *deliberately selected by the researcher* for what they can contribute to the research. This means that, unlike random sampling, theoretical sampling is a form of non-probability sampling in which the new sites are consciously selected by the researcher because of their particular characteristics.

> **Link up with**
> Purposive sampling, p. 41.

- Theoretical sampling is *cumulative*. There is a sense of building on the previous instances that have been sampled to date, and on building up a strong foundation for the concepts and categories that are being refined through the grounded research approach. Events, instances or people sampled early in the research should be considered as an integral part of the overall sample – a vital component in the path of discovery – and not jettisoned as being obsolete, irrelevant or wrong.

> **Link up with**
> Cumulative sampling, p. 51.

- Theoretical sampling is not random or haphazard. Sites are selected because of their *relevance to emerging categories and concepts*. They are deliberately chosen to allow comparisons and contrast with previous sites and they allow the researcher to test out emerging concepts and verify the developing theory as the research goes along. As Corbin and Strauss (2008: 144) stress:

> In theoretical sampling the researcher is not sampling persons but concepts. The researcher is purposely looking for indicators of those concepts so that he or she might examine the data to discover how concepts vary under different conditions.

- Theoretical sampling involves an increased *depth of focus*. Initially, the researcher's aim is to generate a large number of categories related to the phenomenon being studied – to keep things as 'open' as possible early on. For this purpose it is necessary to spread the net wide and gather data on a wide range of relevant things. As the work progresses, though, certain initial codes and categories will become relegated in importance and not pursued. As things move on, the researcher will find himself or herself able to concentrate on a smaller number of codes and categories – the ones that emerge as being more crucial to the analysis. And, because these ones are more central to the analysis and are fewer in number, he or she will be in a position to probe them more fully and investigate them in more depth.

- Theoretical sampling needs to retain some element of *flexibility*. Partly this is necessary to allow the researcher to respond to opportunities that arise during the course of fieldwork. Equally it is vital to permit the exploration of new avenues of investigation that the researcher could not have anticipated as being relevant.

- Researchers following the principles of grounded theory will not want to, or be able to, specify at the outset exactly what the sample will include. They will not be able to state exactly how large the sample will be or exactly what sites (events or whatever) will be included because the sample *emerges*, reflecting the pursuit of generating theory. The process of research will involve the continued selection of units until the research arrives at the point of '*theoretical saturation*' (see below). It is only when the new data seem to confirm the analysis rather than add anything new that the sampling ceases and the sample size is 'enough'.

Example 6.1

Theoretical sampling

A researcher wishing to investigate 'classroom control' could initiate research by observing a small number of lessons in one school. In the first instance the selection of the particular lessons and the specific school only requires that the sites are relevant for the broad purposes of the research. When some lessons have been observed and various participants interviewed, however, the subsequent sites for research will be selected to follow up ideas prompted by an early review of the data. From this time forward the selection of sites becomes far more critical for the research and far more constrained by the need to fit the lines of enquiry suggested by the codes, concepts and categories developing from the research. Following the example above, sites (schools) might be selected as instances where control problems are acknowledged to be rife, and lessons might be selected for observation that offer a relevant contrast in terms of the way they are routinely organized. History and English lessons in a normal classroom might be compared with art lessons, sports classes and chemistry laboratory sessions. The relevance of such different contexts might not have been realized at the beginning, but their significance is something that emerges as the research progresses and new paths of enquiry emerge.

Completing the research (theoretical saturation)

Grounded theory research will continue until the research arrives at the point of 'theoretical saturation'. It is only when the new data seem to confirm the analysis rather than add anything new that the sampling ceases and the sample size is 'enough'. This, of course, stands in stark contrast to the conventions that expect researchers to be clear at the outset about the size and nature of their intended sample.

 Key point: Theoretical saturation

Theoretical saturation occurs 'when additional analysis no longer contributes to discovering anything new about a category' (Strauss 1987: 21).

Methods of data collection

There is not one particular method of data collection that is claimed to be unique to grounded theory. Indeed, as Strauss (1987: 1) has indicated, 'Very diverse materials (interviews, transcripts of meetings, court proceedings; field observations; other documents, like diaries and letters; questionnaire answers; census statistics; etc.) provide indispensable data for social research.'

Having made this point, there are certain methods that lend themselves better than others to use within a grounded theory approach. These are methods that allow the collection of data in a 'raw' state – not unduly shaped by prior concepts or theories. The point is to generate theories, not to test them, and so there is a preference for unstructured interviews rather than structured interviews, for the use of open-ended questions in a questionnaire rather than fixed-choice answers, and the use of field notes rather than observations based on a tick-box schedule. The preference, quite logically, is for the use of methods that produce qualitative data that are relatively unstructured.

Good practice: The use of unstructured data

Methods should be used that produce unstructured data – normally in the form of text or images. Unstructured interviews, open-ended questions in questionnaires, and field notes based on observations can all produce suitable data.

Analysing the data

Codes, categories and concepts

The first stage of analysis involves the coding and categorizing of the data. This means that the researcher begins to assign bits of the 'raw data' to particular categories. Careful scrutiny of the data (for example, an interview transcript) will allow the researcher to see that certain bits of the data have something in common. Possibly they will refer to the same issue. Possibly they will involve statements about the same emotion. Possibly they will share the use of a similar word or phrase in relation to a specific topic. Whatever it is, the chunks of raw data have something in common that the researcher can identify and that allows those chunks of data to be coded (tagged) as belonging to a broader category.

Link up with Chapter 16 Qualitative data.

Unlike codes used with quantitative data, in grounded theory, the codes are open to change and refinement as research progresses. Initially, the codes will be fairly descriptive and are likely to involve labelling chunks of data in terms of their content. This is referred to as *open coding*. As the codes take shape, the researcher will look for relationships between the codes – links and associations that allow certain codes to be subsumed under broader headings and certain codes to be seen as more crucial than others. This is referred to as *axial coding* since it shifts the analysis towards the identification of key (axial) components. Eventually, the researcher should be in a position to focus attention on just the key components, the most significant categories, and concentrate his or her efforts on these. This *selective coding* focuses attention on just the core codes, the ones that have emerged from open and axial coding as being vital to any explanation of the complex social phenomenon.

The aim of this process is to arrive at *concepts* that help to explain the phenomenon – basic ideas that encapsulate the way that the categories relate to each other in a single notion. These concepts then form the cornerstone for the generation of theories that provide an account of things and, in some sense or other, explain why things happen as they do. In the words of Strauss and Corbin (1990), 'Concepts are the basis of analysis in grounded theory research. All grounded theory procedures are aimed at identifying, developing, and relating concepts.'

Good practice: Use a computer to help with the data analysis

There are a number of commercially available software programs that can help researchers with the analysis of qualitative data. It is good practice to store the data in a suitable program – such as NVivo – right from the beginning of the data collection. Such programs are designed to help researchers to code their qualitative data and to develop categories and concepts based on these codes.

Link up with Computer-assisted qualitative data analysis, p. 280.

The constant comparative method

The grounded theory approach uses the constant comparative method as a means of analysing the data. This entails a commitment to comparing and contrasting new codes, categories and concepts as they emerge – constantly seeking to check them out against existing versions. By comparing each coded instance with others that have been similarly coded, by contrasting instances with those in different categories, even using hypothetical possibilities, the researcher is able to refine and improve the explanatory power of the concepts and theories generated from the data. Such comparison helps the researcher to refine the codes, categories and concepts by doing the following:

- highlighting the similarities and differences that exist (promoting better categories and descriptions);
- allowing researchers to integrate categories and codes under common headings (facilitating the reduction of complex phenomena to simpler elements);
- allowing researchers to check out their developing theories as they emerge (incorporating a way to verify them or refute them at the stage of production rather than after the event).

By using the constant comparative method the researcher can never lose sight of the data, or move the analysis too far away from what is happening on the ground. It ensures that any theory developed by the research remains closely in touch with its origins in the data – that it remains 'grounded' in empirical reality. This, of course, is of vital importance to the whole approach.

Note that an important distinction occurs here between the analysis of qualitative data and that of quantitative data. Following the grounded theory approach, the concepts that form the foundation of the theory/analysis emerge from the process of the research activity itself and are not, as is the case with quantitative data, established *prior* to the investigation itself.

 Key point: Data analysis using the constant comparative method
Analysis should always involve:
- *coding* and categorizing the raw data (e.g. interview tapes);
- constantly *comparing* the emerging codes and categories with the data;
- *checking* them out against new data specifically collected for the purpose;
- generating *concepts* and theories that are thoroughly grounded in the data.

Displaying the process

The process of analysing the data needs to be explained to those who read reports about grounded theory research. The logic and reasoning used to move from open coding through to the eventual concepts and theory should be described along with some justification for the coding decisions made by the researcher. The process of analysis, in other words, needs to be transparent. It is not sufficient to describe the process of collecting the data and then move on to 'these are my findings' or 'this is my interpretation of the data'. This leaves a gap in the account of the research.

The process of analysis, of course, cannot be depicted in every minute detail. Necessarily, any account can only capture the key points of what is likely to be a complex, iterative process of making sense of the data. It is, none the less, vital that some information is provided to the reader about the logic used by the researcher when deciding on how to interpret and re-interpret the data. This information allows readers to decide for themselves whether the decisions of the researcher seem reasonable: they do not simply have to 'take the researcher's word for it' that the concepts and theory really do derive from the data.

Link up with Audit trail, p. 298.

> **Good practice: Displaying the analytic process**
> When software like NVivo is used to aid the coding process, it becomes possible to display aspects of the analytic process visually using diagrams showing the link between categories, codes and concepts.

Theories and grounded research

The grounded theory approach, when it was originally conceived by Glaser and Strauss, was a reaction against the kind of 'grand' theories produced through the *logico-deductive method* of science that Glaser and Strauss encountered during the late 1950s and early 1960s. As Layder (1993: 42) points out:

> Such theories are generally 'speculative' in nature because they have not grown directly out of research, and thus remain ungrounded. As a consequence, these theories very often lack validity because they do not 'fit' the real world and thereby remain irrelevant to the people concerned.

Glaser and Strauss were dissatisfied with this approach and argued that a theory developed through the grounded theory approach would have distinct advantages over those derived from the more traditional 'scientific' methods.

First, it is unlikely that new data will be found that serve to refute the theory. Since the theory has been built upon substantive data extracted from fieldwork, the theory should already take account of all the crucial aspects of the situation it explains so that there should be no 'nasty surprises' waiting to be uncovered that will point to a major weakness in the theory. This contrasts, of course, with theories that have been logically deduced and that are then subjected to test by seeing if they work in practice. The 'scientific' approach certainly is susceptible to such nasty surprises and radical rethinks about the theory when findings do not support the theory. In grounded theory the testing is conducted as an integral part of the development of the theory – as an ongoing process – not as a separate process conducted after the theory has been put together in an abstract form.

Second, the theory has more credibility. Because the theory emerges from the data, there ought to be a comfortable fit between the facts of the situation and the theory used to explain them. Put rather simply, the theory is shaped by the facts and therefore there should be a good fit. There should be a close correspondence between the realities of the situation and the theories used to explain them. On this basis there can be no allegations that researchers are in any sense *forcing* a fit between the data and the theory. By contrast, the process of testing theories can involve a search, more or less consciously, for facts that fit the theory. Without necessarily intending to do so researchers can have their vision of facts shaped by the theory they are setting out to test. They can end up being selective about what they 'see' and what they find, managing to corroborate their theory by a process of selective perception in which facts that do not fit the theory get subtly edited out of the picture as irrelevant or non-existent.

Substantive theory and formal theory

There are two kinds of theory that can be generated using the grounded theory approach. The first is linked closely to the empirical situation that has been the subject of study. It is a fairly localized kind of theory and is known as *substantive theory*. This is by far the most common kind of theory associated with the approach. The other kind of theory is more conceptual, with more general coverage and application to circumstances beyond particular settings. This is known as *formal theory*. Ultimately, the aim is to move from a growing body of good, grounded substantive theories towards the integration of these in higher-level formal theories.

Developments in grounded theory

Since the notion of a grounded theory approach was first conceived subsequent works by the originators have moved in slightly different directions. This divergence reflects two potential stances that coexist within the original grounded theory approach. On the one hand, there is Glaser's version (Glaser 1978, 1995, 1999, 2003). As Charmaz (2000: 510) argues, 'Glaser's position often comes close to traditional positivism, with its assumptions of an objective, external reality [and] a neutral observer who discovers data.' It rests on the belief that the meaning of the data will emerge inductively from the data if studied using a suitably neutral methodology. Put simply, the meaning exists in the data and the grounded theory approach allows the researcher to extract the meaning and develop it into a more abstract theory. By looking closely at the data, concepts will occur to the researcher and these concepts can be developed and refined by continually comparing them and checking them with the original data and with new data collected specifically to verify the concepts.

Contrasting with this there is Strauss's version (Strauss 1987; Strauss and Corbin 1990, 1998), which moves towards a more *post-positivist* stance. This stance sees the researcher as inevitably imposing some shape and sense on to the data. It accepts that researchers cannot be entirely neutral and that the meaning attached to any data involves some kind of *interpretation* by the researcher. The meaning will not, cannot, simply emerge inductively from the data. In practice, the researcher needs to *make* sense of the data; that is, to interpret the data in a systematic way. To this end there is extensive guidance offered by Strauss and Corbin

(1990, 1998) on how researchers should proceed with their analysis, turning the spotlight away from the data and more towards the procedures for analysing the (qualitative) data. Glaser, for his part, has expressed strong reservations about this trend, arguing that there is a potential to 'force' the data to fit researchers' categories rather than let the data speak for themselves (Glaser 2003).

Some writers have wanted still greater emphasis on the role of the researcher as interpreter rather than discoverer of reality. In line with this, Charmaz (2014) has advocated a *constructivist* grounded theory, Clarke (2005) has adapted grounded theory to *postmodernism* in what she calls 'situational analysis', and Corbin (Corbin and Strauss 2008) has developed her earlier Straussian position to reflect the postmodernist critique with its emphasis on the existence of alternative perspectives and constructions of realities. The researcher who wants to use the grounded theory approach needs to be aware that such debates and developments exist under the umbrella term 'grounded theory'. They might even need to delve into the schisms and controversies in order to defend their research as being in line with a particular version of grounded theory (see Bryant and Charmaz 2010). Professional researchers and those using grounded theory as a core feature of a PhD would fall into this category. Project researchers, however, are less likely to need to pursue the methodology to this depth. They should be justified in saying that they have adopted a grounded theory provided their research:

- uses theoretic sampling as the basis for an emergent research design;
- develops codes and concepts through an iterative process involving constant reference to fieldwork data;
- includes some account of how the codes and concepts were developed;
- aims to produce 'theory', at least in the form of modest localized explanations based on the immediate evidence.

 Caution: The use and misuse of the term 'grounded theory'

The term 'grounded theory' is often used in a rather loose way to refer to approaches that accept some of the basic premises but do not adopt the methodological rigour espoused by the originators of the term. All too frequently Glaser and Strauss are cited by way of justification for methodologies that actually bear few of the hallmarks of the strict conception of 'grounded theory'. Worse than this, there is a very real danger that the term 'grounded theory' can be hijacked and cited as justification for what is, in reality, sloppy research. Taken out of context, 'grounded theory' can be misused as a rationale for approaching research:

- without too clear an idea of the topic of research;
- without a clear basis in mind for selecting the sample;
- with a general 'jump in at the deep end', 'try it and see', 'find out as we go' approach.

This is certainly not in tune with the spirit of grounded theory and its clear concern with rigour in the analysis of qualitative data.

Advantages of the grounded theory approach

Suited to small-scale research

From a project researcher's point of view, use of the grounded theory approach can be appealing because it lends itself to being conducted by lone researchers working on a limited budget.

Recognized rationale for qualitative research

The notion of grounded theory has currency in the research community and it has become a recognized rationale for qualitative research. Grounded theory provides a standard justification that can fend off potential criticism from those who might otherwise question the rigour of small-scale qualitative research.

Adaptable

The approach is fairly adaptable, lending itself to use with a variety of qualitative data collection methods (e.g. interviews, observation, documents) and forms of data (interview transcripts, fieldwork, texts).

Systematic way of analysing qualitative data

Especially as developed by Strauss, this can be helpful to the newcomer who might wonder how on earth he or she can make sense of the data and how he or she can move towards developing concepts and ultimately theories.

Theory development

The approach includes the means for developing theoretical propositions from data, and should boost project researchers' confidence in the realms of theorizing. All researchers – not just the venerable experts – are encouraged to arrive at modest theories on the basis of the data that they have collected.

Explanations are grounded in reality

Concepts and theories are developed with constant reference to the empirical data and this means that, unlike speculative, abstract theory, they are built on a sound foundation of evidence. This ensures that grounded theories are kept in touch with reality.

Well suited to exploratory research

The approach permits a degree of flexibility in both the selection of instances for inclusion in the sample and the analysis of the data – both of which are well suited to the exploration of new topics and new ideas.

Disadvantages of the grounded theory approach

Planning

The approach does not lend itself to precise planning. The use of 'theoretical sampling' means that it is not possible to predict in advance the nature of the sample that will be used. And the need to achieve 'theoretical saturation' makes it impossible to state at the outset the eventual size of the sample. The voyage of discovery comes with a price and that price is the ability to plan all aspects of the research in advance and anticipate when the research will be completed.

Context

By focusing research on specific instances of behaviour in particular settings, there is a tendency to divorce the explanation of the situation being studied from broader contextual factors. In particular, there is the danger that the theory generated from the data might ignore the influence of social, economic and political factors (e.g. power, globalization, migration, social class, gender and race inequalities) and the historical background to events, which might be vital to any full and valid theory explaining the phenomenon.

Open-mindedness

An 'open-minded' approach to the data is something that can operate at a variety of levels. The need to approach things with an 'open mind' is a fundamental principle of the grounded theory approach but, in practice, it raises some awkward questions. Researchers are inevitably influenced by prior conceptions based on their own culture and personal experience. The question is: how far can these be put to one side for the purposes of analysing the data? There is also the controversial point about how far previous concepts and theories should be allowed to influence matters. Should grounded theory researchers avoid undertaking a literature review in order to avoid having their minds 'contaminated' by existing concepts and theories? And, if so, does this invite the possibility of 'reinventing the wheel' or failing to learn from what has been researched in the past? Within the grounded theory approach different researchers adopt different positions on such issues.

Complexity

The systematic way of analysing data developed by Strauss and Corbin can be daunting in terms of the complexity of the process. Indeed, Strauss's development of 'guidance' for the analysis of qualitative data actually incensed his former collaborator, Barney Glaser, who saw the template and framework for analysis as unnecessary and going against the spirit of grounded theory by 'forcing' categories and codes on to the data, rather than letting them 'emerge' naturally.

Positivism

Interpretivists will be unhappy with any suggestion that substantive theories provide the one correct explanation of things. Yet in the writings of Glaser (rather than Strauss) there are occasions when this position is taken. There is a positivistic strand of thought in which the 'grounding' of theory means that it is not liable to be refuted by the later discovery of facts that do not fit the theory. If the theory emerges from the data and is meaningful to the participants, then it is a good theory that stands in its own right – not open to alternative interpretation.

Empiricism

The approach can be criticized as being 'empiricist'. By looking to fieldwork data as the source of its theories, and by setting itself against the use of general theories, it opens itself to the criticism that it relies too heavily on the empirical data – expecting an explanation to exist within the accumulated data, waiting to be 'discovered' by the researcher. This inductive approach is rather naïve about the complex relationship between theory and data collection and the way it calls for researchers to approach the data without the use of prior theories and concepts (Layder 1998).

Generalizations

Generalizing from the findings can be misunderstood. It is important for those using the grounded theory approach to be clear that any generalizations derived from the research are *theoretical* generalizations. They are 'abstractions' from the data that are conceptual and which are used to construct theories. They are not generalizations in the sense that many people might think of them, and grounded theory researchers need to be careful to avoid any impression that they are attempting to identify patterns of behaviour in the population on the basis of the small, purposively selected sample that they have studied. The purpose of grounded theory is not to make generalizations from the sample to a wider population as a survey approach might do.

Further reading

Birks, M. and Mills, J. (2011) *Grounded Theory: A Practical Guide*. London: Sage.
Charmaz, K. (2014) *Constructing Grounded Theory*, 2nd edn. Thousand Oaks, CA: Sage.
Gibson, B. and Hartman, J. (2014) *Rediscovering Grounded Theory*. London: Sage.
Oktay, J. (2012) *Grounded Theory*. Oxford: Oxford University Press.
Urquhart, C. (2013) *Grounded Theory for Qualitative Research: A Practical Guide*. London: Sage.

Checklist for the grounded theory approach

When undertaking grounded theory research you should feel confident about answering 'yes' to the following questions: ☑

1 Is the aim of the research to generate concepts and theory geared to 'localized' explanations (substantive theory)? ☐

2 Will empirical data be used as the foundation for generating the concepts and theories? ☐

3 Have measures been taken to adopt an open-minded approach to the meaning of the data? ☐

4 Will the data be analysed through a systematic process of coding and categorization (open coding, etc.)? ☐

5 Will the codes, categories and concepts be developed with constant reference to the fieldwork data (constant comparative method)? ☐

6 Does (or will) any report of the research include a section that demonstrates how the codes and concepts have been developed? ☐

7 Is there, or will there be, an explicit justification for the choice of the initial site for fieldwork in terms of its relevance to the area of research? ☐

8 Have subsequent sites been selected on the basis of theoretical sampling? ☐

9 Did, or will, the research continue until it has reached a point of theoretical saturation? ☐

10 Has the research produced explanations that are recognizable to the subjects of research? ☐

© M. Denscombe, *The Good Research Guide*. Open University Press.

8 Action research

What is action research?

Action research is normally associated with 'hands-on', small-scale research projects. Its origins can be traced back to the work of social scientists in the late 1940s on both sides of the Atlantic who advocated closer ties between social theory and the solving of immediate social problems. More recently, action research has been used in a variety of settings in the social sciences but its growing popularity as a research approach perhaps owes most to its use in areas such as education, organizational development, health and social care. In these areas it has a particular niche among professionals who want to use research to improve their effectiveness as practitioners.

Action research, from the start, was involved with practical issues – the kind of issues and problems, concerns and needs that arose as a routine part of activity 'in the real world'. This specifically practical orientation has remained a defining characteristic of action research. Early on, action research was also seen as research specifically geared to changing matters, and this too has remained a core feature of the notion of action research. The thinking here is that research should not only be used to gain a better understanding of the problems which arise in everyday practice, but actually set out to alter things – to do so as part and parcel of the research process rather than tag it on as an afterthought which follows the conclusion of the research. This, in fact, points towards a third defining characteristic of action research: its commitment to a process of research in which the application of findings and an evaluation of their impact on practice become part of a cycle of research. This process, further, has become associated with a trend towards involving those affected by the research in the design and implementation of the research – to encourage them to participate as collaborators in the research rather than being subjects of it.

Together, these provide the four defining characteristics of action research:

* *Practical nature*. It is aimed at dealing with real-world problems and issues, typically at work and in organizational settings.
* *Change*. Both as a way of dealing with practical problems and as a means of discovering more about phenomena, change is regarded as an integral part of research.
* *Cyclical process*. Research involves a feedback loop in which initial findings generate possibilities for change which are then implemented and evaluated as a prelude to further investigation.
* *Participation*. Practitioners are the crucial people in the research process. Their participation is active, not passive.

 Key point

Action research is a *strategy* for social research, not a method. It is concerned with the aims of research and the design of the research, but does not specify any constraints when it comes to the means for data collection that might be adopted by the action researcher.

The practical nature of action research

Action research is essentially practical and applied. It is driven by the need to solve practical, real-world problems. It operates on the premise, as Kurt Lewin put it, that 'Research that produces nothing but books will not suffice' (Lewin 1946: 35).

But being practical would not be enough to set it apart from other approaches to research. After all, many approaches can lay claim to this territory. Many can claim with justification to offer applied research. While it certainly does embrace this aim, being 'practical' has a second sense as far as action research is concerned, and it is this which helps to give it a unique identity as a research strategy. The research needs to be undertaken *as part of practice* rather than a bolt-on addition to it.

 Key point: Linking research with practice

'Action research [rejects] the concept of a two-stage process in which research is carried out first by researchers and then in a separate second stage the knowledge generated from the research is applied by practitioners. Instead, the two processes of research and action are integrated' (Somekh 1995: 34).

Clearly, if the processes of research and action are integrated, then action research must involve 'the practitioner' very closely. And this provides a further meaning which can be added to the practical nature of action research: *practitioner research*. However, although it may be linked with the notion of practitioner research, it is important to appreciate that action research is not exactly the same thing as practitioner research. Edwards and Talbot stress this point: 'Practitioner research can only be designated action research if it is carried out by professionals who are engaged in researching . . . aspects of their own practice as they engage in that practice' (1999: 62). It is not enough for the research to be undertaken as part of the job because this could include all kinds of data gathering and analysis, the findings from which might have no bearing on the practitioner's own activity. To accord with the spirit of action research the researcher needs to investigate his or her *own* practices with a view to altering these in a beneficial way.

Change and professional self-development

Action research is wedded to the idea that change is good. Initially, this is because studying change is seen as a useful *way of learning more about the way a thing works*. Change, in this sense, is regarded as a valuable enhancer of knowledge in its own right, rather than something that is undertaken after the results of the research have been obtained. But, of course, the scale and the scope of changes introduced through action research will not be grand. The scale of the research is constrained by the need for the action researchers to focus on *aspects of their own practice as they engage in that practice*. So change as envisaged by action research is not likely to be a wide-spread major alteration to an organization. The element of change will not be in the order of a large-scale experiment such as changes in the bonus schemes of production workers at Ford's car assembly plants. No. Because, action research tends to be localized and small-scale, it usually focuses on change at the micro level.

One of the most common kinds of change involved in action research is at the level of *professional self-development*. It is in keeping with the notion of professional self-development that a person should want to improve practices and that this should involve a continual quest for ways in which to change practice for the better. Action research provides a way forward for the professional which, while it entails a certain degree of reflection, adds the systematic and rigorous collection of data to the resources the professional can use to achieve the improvement in practice.

It is important to recognize that reflection may be of itself insufficient to make the professional's endeavour 'action research'. The reflection needs to be systematic if it is to qualify as action *research*. Merely *thinking* about your own practice – though possibly a valuable basis for improving practice – is not the same as researching that action. And here a distinction needs to be made between the 'reflective practitioner' (Schön 1983) as one who strives for professional self-development through a critical consideration of his or her practices, and the action researcher who, while also being a reflective practitioner, adds to this by using research techniques to enhance and systematize that reflection.

Action research as a cyclical process

The vision of action research as a cyclical process fits in nicely with the quest for perpetual development built into the idea of professionalism (see Figure 8.1). The purpose of research, though it might be prompted by a specific problem, is seen as part of a broader enterprise in which the aim is to improve practice through a rolling programme of research.

Figure 8.1 The cyclical process in action research

The crucial points about the cycle of enquiry in action research are: (1) that *research feeds back directly into practice*; and (2) that *the process is ongoing*. The critical reflection of the practitioner is not only directed to the identification of 'problems' worthy of investigation with a view to improving practice, but can also involve an evaluation of changes just instigated, which can, in their own right, prompt further research. It is fair to point out, however, that this is something of an ideal and that, in reality, action research often limits itself to discrete, one-off pieces of research.

Participation in the research process

The participatory nature of action research is probably its most distinctive feature since, in some ways, it goes straight to the heart of conventions associated with formal social research. Conventionally, research is the province of the expert, the outside authority who is a professional. This researcher more often than not initiates the process of research, sets the agenda and designs the collection and analysis of data. After the research is concluded, those involved might receive some feedback in the form of results from the research. They may, or may not, instigate changes on the basis of such findings. Broadly speaking, the act of doing research is separated from the act of making changes. Action research, by contrast, insists that practitioners must be participants, not just in the sense of taking part in the research but in the sense of being *an equal partner in the research*.

With action research it can be the practitioner, not some outside professional researcher, who wants to instigate a change and who consequently initiates the research (Elliott 1991). The research, in this sense, is practitioner-driven, with the practitioner not just an equal partner but a sponsor and director of the research process. And if this sounds radical, there are others who would push the matter further, insisting that the practitioner should be the dominant partner – calling the shots at all stages and in all aspects of the research.

Even in less radical revisions to the conventional relationship between researcher and practitioners, the inclusion of participation as a fundamental feature of action research brings with it a shift in the direction of *democratizing the research process*. Control is transferred away from the professional researcher and towards the practitioner. Power shifts towards the insider who is the practitioner. There is, of course, still a role for the outside expert but that role shifts in the direction of mutual collaboration in the research process, or even to the position where the outside expert has the role of *facilitator* of the practitioner's own project, a resource to be drawn upon as and when the practitioner sees fit.

Behind this shift in the relationship there rests a respect for the practitioner's knowledge. Again, this respect may not be unique to action research but it is an aspect of action research which is distinctive and built into an approach which is broadly sympathetic to democratizing the research process by challenging the separation of expert from lay person in research.

There can be an explicitly political angle to the participatory aspect of action research, with its 'democratization' of the research process and 'respect for practitioner knowledge'. Zuber-Skerritt (1996) refers to this as *'emancipatory'* action research. This type of action research is quite clear about the nature of the change which is brought about through action research; it is change which challenges the existing system. It is change which goes beyond *technical* matters that can have a bearing on the effectiveness or efficiency of the professional's current practice. It is change which goes beyond *practical* matters that can have a bearing on the way practitioners interpret the task at hand. For sure, emancipatory action research incorporates these, but it also challenges the fundamental framework within which the practice occurs.

 Key point: Three approaches to action research

According to Zuber-Skerritt (1996: 4–5):

1 Technical action research aims to improve the effectiveness of educational or managerial practice. The practitioners are co-opted and depend greatly on the researcher as a facilitator.

2 Practical action research, in addition to effectiveness, aims at the practitioners' understanding and professional development. The researcher's role is . . . to encourage practical deliberation and self-reflection on the part of the practitioners.

3 Action research is emancipating when it aims not only at technical and practical improvement and the participant's better understanding, along with transformation and change within the existing boundaries and conditions, but also at changing the system itself of those conditions which impede desired improvement in the system/organization.

Issues connected with the use of action research

'Ownership' of the research

The participatory nature of action research brings with it a question mark concerning who owns the research and its outcomes. With conventional approaches to research this tends to be less complicated. To offer something of a caricature, the outsider researcher initiates the process and approaches practitioners to gain their permission for the research to be conducted (by the outsider). Having obtained authorization from relevant people, research proceeds, with the outsider 'owning' the data collected and having full rights over the analysis and publication of findings. Of course, complications arise with various forms of sponsored research and consultancy where authorization might include certain restrictions on the rights of the two parties over the research and its findings. However, these are likely to be *explicitly* recognized as a result of negotiating access.

In the case of action research the *partnership* nature of work can make matters rather less clear-cut. Who is in charge? Who calls the shots? Who decides on appropriate action? Who owns the data? These and similar issues need to be worked out sensitively and carefully by the partners to *ensure that there are shared expectations about the nature of participation* in action research.

Ethical issues associated with action research

The distinct ethical problem for action research is that, although the research centres on the activity of the practitioner, it is almost inevitable that the activity of colleagues will also come under the microscope at some stage or other as their activity interlinks with that of the practitioner who instigates the research. Practitioners are not 'islands' – isolated from routine contact with colleagues and clients. Their practice and the changes they seek to make can hardly be put in place without some knock-on effect for others who operate close by in organizational terms.

The idea that the action researcher is exempt from the need to gain authorization, as a consequence, evaporates. Because the activity of action research almost inevitably affects others it is important to have a clear idea of when and where the action research necessarily steps outside the bounds of collecting information which is purely personal and relates to the practitioners alone. Where it does so, the usual standards of research ethics must be observed: permissions obtained, confidentiality maintained, identities protected.

Two things follow. First, there is a case for arguing that those who engage in action research should be open about the research aspect of their practice. It should not be hidden or disguised. Second, the need for informed consent from those involved in the research should be recognized.

Good practice: Ethics in action research

Action researchers should respect the rights and sensitivities of colleagues and clients who become involved in the research. In practice, as Winter (1996: 17) suggests, this means:

- Permission must be obtained before making observations or examining documents produced for other purposes.
- The researcher must accept responsibility for maintaining confidentiality.
- The development of the work must remain visible and open to suggestions from others.
- Description of others' work and points of view must be negotiated with those concerned before being published.

Reflexivity and action research

Practitioners who engage in action research have a privileged insight into the way things operate in their particular 'work-sites'. They have 'insider knowledge'. This can be a genuine bonus for research. However, it can also pose problems. The outsider – 'the stranger' – might be better placed to see the kind of thing which, to the insider, is too mundane, too obvious, to register as an important factor. Because the practitioner cannot escape the web of meanings that the 'insider' knows, he or she is constrained by the web of meanings. The outsider 'expert' may not have the 'right' answer, but can possibly offer an alternative perspective which can help the practitioner to gain new insights into the nature of the practical problem.

Link up with
Reflexivity,
p. 88.

So, although action research respects the knowledge of the practitioners, it would be rather naïve to assume that practitioners' knowledge – of itself – provides all the answers. Particularly in relation to *practical* action research and *emancipatory* action research, their aim is to enhance practitioner understanding and this is likely to call upon some modicum of outsider advice.

Resources and action research

The action researcher's investigation is necessarily fairly localized and relatively small-scale. None the less, the action researcher faces the difficulty of trying to combine a probably demanding workload with systematic and rigorous research. Time constraints, alone, make this hard to accomplish. Even if, as should be the case, action research is integrated with practice rather than tagged onto practice, the routine demands of the job are unlikely to be reduced by way of compensation. In the short run, prior to positive benefits emerging, the action researcher is likely to face extra work.

Generalizability and action research

Given the constraints on the scope of action research projects, it might be argued that their findings will rarely contribute to broader insights. Located as they are in the practitioner's work-site, there are not very good prospects for the representativeness of the data in action research. The setting and constituent features are 'givens' rather than factors which can be controlled or varied, and the research is generally focused on the one site rather than spread across a range of examples. Action research, therefore, is vulnerable to the criticism that the findings relate to one instance and should not be generalized beyond this specific 'case'.

In one sense, this reservation needs to be acknowledged. Certainly, practice-driven research in local settings hardly lends itself to conclusions with universal application. New truths and new theories will be unlikely to find foundation in such studies alone. And this caution is worth taking to heart for the action researcher: beware of making

Link up with
Chapter 3,
Case studies.

grandiose claims on the basis of action research projects. However, it can rightly be argued that action research, while practice-driven and small-scale, should not lose anything by way of rigour. Like any other small-scale research it can draw on existing theories, apply and test research propositions, use suitable methods and, importantly, offer some evaluation of existing knowledge (without making unwarranted claims). It is the rigour, rather than the size of the project or its purpose, by which the research should be judged.

Advantages of action research

Participation

It involves participation in the research for practitioners. This can democratize the research process, depending on the nature of the partnership, and generally involves a greater appreciation of, and respect for, practitioner knowledge.

Professional development

It has personal benefits for the practitioner, as it contributes to professional self-development.

Practical

It addresses practical problems in a positive way, feeding the results of research directly back into practice. In the words of Somekh (1995: 340), 'It directly addresses the knotty problem of the persistent failure of research in the social sciences to make a difference in terms of bringing about actual improvements in practice.'

Continuous

It should entail a continuous cycle of development and change via on-site research in the workplace, which has benefits for the organization to the extent that it is geared to improving practice and resolving problems.

Disadvantages of action research

Scope and scale

The necessary involvement of the practitioner limits the scope and scale of research. The 'work-site' approach affects the representativeness of the findings and the extent to which generalizations can be made on the basis of the results.

Control

The integration of research with practice limits the feasibility of exercising controls over factors of relevance to the research. The setting for the research generally does not allow for the variables to be manipulated or for controls to be put in place, because the research is conducted not alongside routine activity but actually as part of that activity.

Ownership

Ownership of the research process becomes contestable within the framework of the partnership relationship between practitioner and researcher.

Work load

Action research tends to involve an extra burden of work for the practitioners, particularly at the early stages before any benefits feed back into improved effectiveness.

Impartiality

The action researcher is unlikely to be detached and impartial in his or her approach to the research. In this respect, action research stands in marked contrast to positivistic approaches. It is clearly geared to resolving problems which confront people in their routine, everyday (work) activity, and these people therefore have a vested interest in the findings. They cannot be entirely detached or impartial in accord with the classic image of science.

Further reading

Coghlan, D. and Brannick, T. (2010) *Doing Action Research in Your Own Organization.* London: Sage.

Kemmis, S., McTaggart, R. and Nixon, R. (2014) *The Action Research Planner: Doing Critical Participatory Action Research.* Singapore: Springer.

McNiff, J. (2013) *Action Research: Principles and Practice*, 3rd edn. London: Routledge.

Reason, P. and Bradbury, H. (eds) (2013) *Handbook of Action Research*, 2nd edn. London: Sage.

Somekh, B. (2006) *Action Research: A Methodology for Change and Development.* Maidenhead: Open University Press.

Checklist for action research

When undertaking action research you should feel confident about answering 'yes' to the following questions: ☑

1 Does the research project address a practical problem?   ☐

2 Is there participation by the practitioner in all stages of the research project?   ☐

3 Have the grounds for the partnership between practitioner and any outside expert been explicitly negotiated and agreed?   ☐

4 Is the research part of a continuous cycle of development (rather than a one-off project)?   ☐

5 Is there a clear view of how the research findings will feed back directly into practice?   ☐

6 Is it clear which kind of action research is being used – 'technical', 'practical' or 'emancipatory'?   ☐

7 Has insider knowledge been acknowledged as having disadvantages as well as advantages for the research?   ☐

8 Is the research sufficiently small-scale to be combined with a routine workload?   ☐

9 Have ethical matters been taken into consideration?   ☐

q Systematic reviews

Systematic reviews are used by a range of social researchers, practitioners and policy-makers who want to get a reliable and objective overview of the evidence that is currently available on a specific topic or the impact of a new intervention. They have been applied to things such as:

* the *effectiveness* of innovations in health service delivery;
* the *dissemination* and *take up* of new practices in organizations;
* the *incidence* of illicit drug use by young people;
* the *consequences* of social policy in relation to old age pensions;
* the *success rates* of motivational interviewing for smoking cessation.

Systematic reviews tend to be associated with '*evidence-based practice*' – an approach that stresses the need for decisions to be based on firm evidence from good quality research – and they came to prominence in connection with medical and pharmaceutical research where they have now become well established as a method for evaluating findings from clinical trials on the effectiveness of specific drugs and particular treatments (e.g. the Cochrane Reviews).

What is a systematic review?

A systematic review is a review of the research literature whose aim is to arrive at a conclusion about the state of knowledge on a topic based on a rigorous and unbiased overview of all the research that has been undertaken on that topic. To do this, systematic reviews entail:

- a *search* for the relevant literature using explicit methods that are both rigorous and systematic;
- a *review* of the findings which compares them and evaluates them using explicit criteria;
- a *conclusion* based on an objective analysis of the existing data.

What is the difference between a systematic review and a traditional literature review?

Systematic reviews are not quite the same as a traditional literature review. There are three main areas of contrast. First, systematic reviews are a self-contained study in their own right – rather than a prelude to some empirical investigation. Second, they focus on a very specific question, usually linked to a policy or practical problem. And third, as the name indicates, they are very systematic in the process that is used to review the literature.

Benefits of a systematic review

What we already know about a particular topic is not always straightforward or clear-cut. There are two main reasons for this. First, research projects investigating specific topics do not always produce the same findings on which everyone can agree. Indeed, in most fields of study there are contested areas where the findings from different research projects are disputed and where people disagree about 'what is true' or 'what works best'. Second, reviews of the evidence can be based on a selection of sources which might not necessarily be the *best* sources. Indeed, there might be an emphasis on certain findings (and disregard for others) on the basis of how far the findings match the preferences of the individual doing the review rather than the quality of the research itself.

A consequence of these two difficulties is that knowledge about the available evidence can be patchy or even biased. But this is where *systematic* reviews come into the picture. Their aim is to reduce the potential for bias by being open and honest about:

- how the search for relevant findings was conducted;
- how decisions were made about which sources to include and which to exclude;
- how judgements were arrived at about the quality of the data reported in the various published findings of research.

 Key point

Systematic reviews are rigorous in the search for data and transparent in the methods of review.

Kinds of research problem suitable for systematic review

Systemic reviews are valuable when tackling specific questions on which there already exists a considerable body of evidence. They are suited to topics where previous research has established some agreement about what needs to be known and how it should be investigated, and in this respect they are more appropriately applied to findings from explanatory research than exploratory research. When the studies share some basic premises about what is to be investigated, and how this should be done, this allows a comparison of like-with-like studies whose evidence can be directly contrasted. Only when this is the case is there a reasonable prospect of using the existing research findings to arrive at some single 'objective' conclusion about what works best, what is right, where the truth lies. In practice, this means that there are five criteria that must be met in order for systematic reviews to work well:

1 the topic or problem being reviewed must be clearly defined and quite narrowly focused;

2 a substantial body of research findings must already exist on the topic;

3 the available evidence must come from studies that use similar methods;

4 the 'evidence' must lend itself to measurement, comparison and evaluation (NHMRC 1999; Gough et al. 2012);

5 the findings are usually based on quantitative data.

Qualitative research and systematic reviews

Although the drive for systematic reviews has come predominantly from 'scientific' research where the findings are based on 'hard, quantitative data', there has been some attention given to the inclusion of qualitative research within systematic reviews. From the perspective of medical and health science research, the interest in qualitative research has tended to focus on the way that it can support and supplement quantitative research. The view is taken that

> qualitative studies can: (a) contribute to the development of a more robust intervention by helping to define an intervention more precisely; (b) assist in the choice of outcome measures and assist in the development of valid research questions; and (c) help to understand heterogeneous results from studies of effect.
>
> (Petticrew and Roberts 2006: 72)

Within the social sciences, by contrast, qualitative research is more likely to be treated as a genuine equal and alternative to quantitative research, offering its own contribution to knowledge (Dixon-Woods et al. 2006; Pawson 2006; Petticrew and Roberts 2006; Pope et al. 2007; Denyer and Tranfield 2009). In either case, the challenge facing those who want to conduct a systematic review of qualitative research is how to compare, evaluate and synthesize findings based on methodologies that do not conform to a standard model such as the randomized controlled trial (RCT). Qualitative research, after all, tends to be conducted in a variety of ways and in differing contexts – things which invariably hinder the prospect of direct comparisons between their findings. The response to this challenge, described in more detail below in relation to Stage 6 in the process of conducting systematic reviews, has been to review the findings through 'narrative analysis', 'thematic analysis' and 'realist synthesis' rather than attempt to aggregate the findings from existing research (see below).

How to conduct a systematic review

There are seven key stages involved in a systematic literature review. These stages reflect both the process of actually doing a review and the requirements for writing up a systematic review. So both aspects – doing and reporting – are dealt with stage by stage in the outline that follows.

Stage 1: The scope of the study

The first task is to decide upon the specific scope of the study. It is important that the area of interest that is chosen for the review is quite specific and *narrowly focused* because this sets the boundaries in terms of the content area for the search. Systematic reviews cannot work with vague or broad topics because this would make it almost impossible to decide what research findings to search for and what evidence to consider.

When writing up the review all significant choices made in connection with the scope of the review need to be described and justified. This is in line with the spirit of transparency which lies at the heart of systematic literature reviews. The review needs to start with a statement which pinpoints the chosen area of interest and explains why that topic warrants attention.

Stage 2: The search process

Initially this involves a careful consideration of the most accurate and appropriate 'key words' and *search terms* to be used. These should be words or short phrases that will best target the relevant research findings: they need to capture the essence of the chosen topic. Next, decisions need to be made about where these search terms will be used. Which databases, which search engines, which archives, which catalogues – what sources will be searched? This might include reference to databases such as PsychINFO, LexisLibrary, Medline (PubMed), Web of Knowledge. Such sources need to be selected strategically in order to produce the best returns from the search. Obviously, the aim here is to conduct as comprehensive a search as possible of the available literature on the topic. Ideally, it should involve not only published works but also any other relevant findings which are available, perhaps in the form of conference papers or unpublished reports, although the extent to which this is possible will depend largely on the resources that are available. Small-scale research is likely to concentrate on finding just published works.

In terms of writing up the review, and again in the spirit of transparency, there needs to be an explicit description of how the search was conducted. As part of the 'audit trail' sufficient details about the search process need to be provided in order to allow other researchers to replicate the search should they wish to do so, and readers of the review need to be told about the reasoning behind the various choices that have been made. The account of the search process, therefore, needs to include:

- a list of the *search terms* used, and an explanation of why they were deemed to be the most appropriate ones on which to base the research;
- a list of the *databases* that were searched, along with some explanation of why these were considered to be the most relevant ones to use;
- information about the *period covered* by the search, plus a justification for focusing on those particular years;
- details about the actual *dates when the search was conducted.*

Stage 3: Evaluation of quality

The sources of information thrown up by the search process will differ in their value for the review. Some are likely to be more closely related to the topic than others, and some are likely to be of a better quality that others in terms of the research on which they are based. So, decisions need to be made about which to include and which to exclude from consideration when it comes to the review. Such decisions need to be made on explicit criteria: not hunch, not convenience, not appeal nor gut-reaction, but explicit and justifiable bench-marks for objective decisions. A crucial task, then, when conducting a systematic literature review is to establish a set of criteria on which to judge:

- the *relevance* of sources to the topic being considered. Findings from previous research that is close to the topic might be treated as more significant than findings that are less directly on the topic.
- the *quality* of the sources. The credibility of the findings might be gauged according to the methods used in the research, with higher significance being attached to findings produced by particular kinds of research design, for instance, or from larger samples.

These criteria need to be systematically applied to each of the studies included in the review, and that is why systematic reviews generally require the researcher to use a *data extraction form* for collecting information about the studies. The data extraction form acts as a kind of checklist with all the important items the researcher needs to record about each study listed, and space for relevant details from each study to be noted alongside each item. It is important to recognize that the specific items included in any data extraction form will be tailored to meet the specific requirements of the particular review. There is no universal form that applies on all occasions. Table 9.1, however, provides some basic starting points for the construction of a data extraction form to be used in connection with small-scale social science projects.

Table 9.1 Data extraction form: some basic items for inclusion

Item	Data extracted	Reviewer notes
Author(s)		
Year of publication		
Title of project		
Period when research was conducted		
Funding source/sponsors		
Location of research		
Objectives of the research		
Type of study		
Underlying tradition/philosophy of the research		
Research design		
Data collection methods		
Research population		
Number of participants		
Sampling techniques		
Factors/variables used for analysis		
Techniques for data analysis		
Quality controls: actions taken to support quality and avoid errors in the data		
Findings		
Recommendations		
Evaluation: Researcher assessment of reliability of methods and validity of findings		

As with the previous stages, when writing up the review it is vital to provide sufficient detail about the decision-making to allow other researchers to understand the reasoning and check the procedures should they wish to do so. This entails the inclusion of an open and explicit explanation for the decisions made with respect to the individual sources identified in the review. This explanation needs to cover:

- a statement of the *rationale for inclusion* or exclusion of studies;
- the specific *criteria of relevance*, and some discussion of their link with the topic of the review;

- the *criteria for quality assessment,* and some account of how these were applied;
- a copy of the *data extraction form.*

Stage 4: List of sources included in the review

A full list of the works that are to be incorporated into the review should be provided. There are two angles to this. First, it is standard practice to produce a flowchart that visually represents the process of inclusion and exclusion of studies in the review. Figure 9.1 indicates a straightforward way of doing this in the context of a small-scale social research project.

Second, there needs to be sufficient bibliographic detail to allow other researchers, should they wish to do so, to find these sources and check their contents. Normally, this is supplied in the form of a table containing the basic information about those studies actually included in the review subsequent to the review of Abstracts stage.

Figure 9.1 Flowchart showing the inclusion and exclusion of studies from the review

Source: Developed from Pettigrew and Roberts (2006: 300).

Good practice

When writing up the systematic review it is necessary to provide:

- *a flowchart indicating the number of studies* included and the numbers excluded at each stage of the review;
- *a table listing basic information* about each of the studies whose findings have been reviewed.

Stage 5: Descriptive summary

Having listed the research findings that will be used, the next stage in a systematic review is to produce a descriptive summary of the works – something that tells the reader about when the research projects were done, where they were done, how they were done (methods) and by whom. This entails categorizing the various studies according to a set of explicit criteria that cover the origins of the work, and counting the numbers that fall into the various categories. Such information is useful because it provides the reader with an overview of the *origins of the information* that will be included in the review.

Writing up this part of a systematic review partly involves stating how many works fall in to specific categories, and partly involves a written 'narrative' that describes the nature of the research that is to be included in the review. Combined, these two aspects of the descriptive summary should capture the key dimensions of the overall body of work that has been selected for review. They should provide the reader with important sign-posts about the available, relevant, good quality research in terms of things like:

- how *recent* the work is;
- *what groups of people* have shown the most interest in conducting the research;
- who has *funded* or sponsored the research;
- which *regions* or *countries* are most commonly represented in the work that has been done;
- which research *methods* have been used in the studies.

Stage 6: Analysis

Meta-analysis

At the heart of the systematic review lies the analysis. What does this involve? Well, for some people the ideal thing to do would be to conduct a *meta-analysis*. For those involved in reviews of health, medical and pharmaceutical research this is often the ultimate goal. As Goldacre (2012: 14) describes it:

> When you've got all the trial data in one place, you can conduct something called a meta-analysis, where you bring all the results together in one giant spreadsheet, pool all the data and get one single, summary figure, the most accurate summary of all the data on one clinical question.

To aggregate the data in this way, however, the findings need to be based on research that shares a similar methodology. In systematic reviews of health, medical and pharmaceutical research, 'clinical trials' are the shared methodology which allows the possibility of pooling all the data together and arriving at the overall result. In the social sciences, however, there is far less prospect of aggregating findings in this way from a variety of research projects on a given topic. In the social sciences the methods used by researchers tend to be more varied and the findings less amenable to being amalgamated in the way that meta-analysis requires. And, for this reason, systematic reviews of research findings in the social sciences are much more likely to be based on some form of narrative analysis (Tranfield et al. 2003; Denyer and Tranfield 2009).

Narrative analysis

A *narrative analysis* provides an account of the findings based on the use of words (rather than figures). It involves an attempt to 'tell the story' behind the findings of the various works that have been reviewed. Now, in the traditional literature review the choice of the works to be reviewed, the order in which they are introduced, and the emphasis that is placed on individual pieces of research are things which depend on the literary skills of the reviewer and the story he/she wishes to tell. A good literature review guides the reader; it takes them on a journey of discovery which ends with a persuasive case being made for the reviewer's conclusion about what the available evidence suggests.

In a *systematic* review, however, any narrative account needs to be based on *all* the research findings that meet explicit quality standards. Also, in a systematic review the persuasiveness of the narrative should stem from the findings themselves rather than the literary skills of the reviewer or any preferences he/she might have in relation to the conclusion to be drawn from the review. The nature of the review, in fact, needs to be more transparent, explicit and structured than would normally be associated with a traditional literature review. Whether identifying themes running through the various research findings (a *thematic* synthesis) or focusing on the reasoning used by the researchers to explain their findings (a *realist* synthesis) the narrative analysis must always endeavour to be highly systematic and objective.

Thematic synthesis: organize findings; look for themes; identify patterns

Thematic synthesis, as the name suggests, depends on identifying themes that emerge in the existing research. At one level, this involves the search for some consensus across the studies being reviewed. Is there agreement about things? Is there a shared opinion emerging from the research about the situation and its causes? Does existing research produce findings that are consistent and which point to causes and consequences upon which there is general agreement? If so, then it becomes quite easy to draw a definitive conclusion about the 'truth' of the situation or what 'works best'. If not (which in the social sciences is quite likely), then the thematic review needs to establish what the disagreements are and what issues underlie these 'contested areas'. Is it a matter of researchers approaching a topic using a similar approach and methods but arriving at different findings and alternative conclusions? Or, perhaps, it might be a matter of researchers adopting markedly different approaches to a topic which produce findings that disagree. Does the source of funding or sponsorship align with the kind of findings emerging from the research, or do findings differ according to the location in which the research took place? Whatever, the role of the thematic review is to establish where the division lines are and explain what lies behind the differences of opinion.

Key point

A thematic synthesis focuses on the substance of the findings and any recommendations arising from the studies included in the review.

Realist synthesis: look for the underlying causes

The analysis does not necessarily have to be based on a review of the *findings* from various studies. Sometimes, it is not so much the findings as the *reasons* for the findings which are the basis for the analysis. From a critical realist perspective the quest for themes running through the literature can be directed at the factors that researchers see as explaining their findings – the *underlying causes*. As Pawson (2006, 2013) argues, a 'realist synthesis' looks across the range of relevant studies to see which underlying factors or mechanisms are being used to explain the findings. The various pieces of research included in the review can be 'regarded as case studies whose purpose is to test, revise and refine the preliminary theory' (Pawson 2006: 74). The aim is to draw on these various explanations to arrive at a conclusion which takes the form of a general proposition or theory. Using existing work, for example evaluating the effectiveness of particular social policies or interventions, the realist synthesis allows conclusions to be drawn about what will work (or not work) for whom under what circumstances.

 Key point

A realist synthesis focuses on explanations for the findings reported by the studies included in the review, and it is concerned with developing theories.

Stage 7: Conclusion

The review provides the platform for a synthesis of the distinct elements of the findings into something new – *an objective, over-arching conclusion based on the various findings from all the published research that is available on a specific topic*.

The importance of the conclusions reflects the point that systematic reviews are intended to have a practical value. They are, as has been noted, associated with 'evidence-based practice' where policy-makers and others look to the systematic review for guidance. What these people want from a systematic review is some definitive statement about the 'state of things', something quite specific and clear-cut, which they can use as the basis for planning a course of action. Conclusions that involve hedging bets, sitting on the fence, or a series of either/or options are not so useful in this respect.

Good practice

Systematic reviews should aim to arrive at clear-cut conclusions.

Limitations to systematic reviews

There are three limitations to the value of systematic literature reviews which need to be borne in mind. The first of these is the general point that such reviews are based on findings that have been published or which, through some other means, are publicly available. As Goldacre (2012) stresses, though, not all findings from research get published. Referring in particular to the development of pharmaceutical drugs, he shows that research producing negative results are simply less likely to hit the light of day. Either researchers do not bother to publish findings about things that don't work (preferring to concentrate on things that do) or there can be a more conscious pressure for commercial reasons to suppress negative results – they might prevent the further development of the drug. Commercial reasons to suppress certain research findings may not apply in the same way to social science research but the underlying point still holds – systematic literature reviews are based on *published* findings, and cannot cover findings from research which, for whatever reason, have not been made publicly available.

The second limitation concerns the premise that a fairly large body of relevant published findings on a specific topic have already been published. This is more likely to be the case when it comes to trials of specific drugs or medicines, underlining the emergence of systematic literature reviews in that area. It may be less the case in relation to the social sciences. In the social sciences there will always be existing research which *relates* to a given topic, but there is less likely to be instances of previous research which is on exactly the same topic and which allows for the direct comparison of the findings. The nature of social science topics means that there is less prospect of comparing and evaluating data from different studies in a direct fashion.

The third limitation continues this theme that systematic literature reviews are more easily applied to (medical) science rather than social science. Evaluating the quality of data from findings and arriving at 'objective' conclusions are things that sit more comfortably with quantitative data produced through research designs such as experiments and randomized controlled trials (Tranfield et al. 2003). Indeed, reflecting this point, it is perhaps not surprising that randomized controlled trials are considered to provide the best kind of evidence when it comes to evaluating the findings from research in the medical world (Higgins and Green 2011). But what about other kinds of research designs? Can the methods of systematic review be applied to alternative research designs such as case studies, action research, grounded theory, ethnography and phenomenology? And, in particular, can they work with studies that have produced qualitative data? Well, as we have seen, the answer is a qualified 'yes'. Instead of trying to combine the data from different research projects (as in 'meta-analysis') we can use some kind of 'narrative analysis'. As Tranfield et al. (2003: 216) argue, a narrative analysis can work, provided that the review adheres to the spirit of 'systematic reviews' by containing clear and explicit statements about:

- the criteria used for evaluating the quality of the qualitative research studies being considered. And there are a number of suggestions available on this score (e.g. Seale 1999; Silverman 2013).
- the reasons for including or excluding particular studies (which, of course, should be related to these criteria).

Advantages of systematic reviews

Systematic reviews have credibility

They aim to provide an impartial review of existing research and, to this end, they adopt a rigorous and transparent approach to the selection and analysis of suitable evidence. This bolsters the credibility of the findings and enhances the scientific standing of the conclusions that are drawn.

Systematic reviews have practical value – they provide answers to questions

Specifically they address questions like 'what works best?' and produce answers that are of direct value to policy-makers and practitioners who need some guidance about 'the truth of the matter' in the midst of large amounts of scientific evidence.

Disadvantages of systematic reviews

Applicability to qualitative research

Despite the possibilities offered by narrative analysis, thematic synthesis and realist synthesis (noted above) there are still some question marks over how neatly the process of systematic review translates from its use with clinical trials to its use with social research – qualitative research in particular. Research in social sciences does not often lend itself to direct comparison in the way that findings from clinical trials of drugs might do.

Reliance on existing body of knowledge

Systematic reviews work best in areas that have already attracted a lot of attention from researchers. They draw on a body of existing research findings – but for areas where there is little work that has already been done, it is not really possible to conduct a systematic review.

Research evidence that has not been published will not be included. Systematic reviews do not cover findings that, for whatever reason, have been kept out of the public eye.

Resources

Systematic reviews can require a level of resourcing and team-work not normally associated with small-scale social research projects.

Further reading

Gough, D., Oliver, S. and Thomas, J. (2012) *An Introduction to Systematic Reviews.* London: Sage.

Higgins, J. and Green, S. (eds) (2011) *Cochrane Handbook for Systematic Reviews of Interventions* Version 5.1.0 (updated March 2011). The Cochrane Collaboration. Available at: www.cochrane-handbook.org.

Pawson, R. (2006) *Evidence-Based Policy: A Realist Perspective*. London: Sage, especially Chapters 1 and 4.

Petticrew, M. and Roberts, H. (2006) *Systematic Reviews in the Social Sciences: A Practical Guide*. Oxford: Blackwell.

Pope, C., Mays, N. and Popay, J. (2007) *Synthesizing Qualitative and Quantitative Health Research: A Guide to Methods*. Maidenhead: Open University Press.

Checklist for the use of systematic reviews

When undertaking a systematic review you should feel confident about answering 'yes' to the following questions: ☑

1 Has a literature *search* been undertaken that confirms there is not already a systematic review available on the topic? ☐

2 Do you have *access to the software* for logging and analysing the numerous studies and their findings? ☐

3 Is the *scope of the review* sufficiently narrow and well-defined? ☐

4 Are the *criteria for inclusion* of studies in the review clear and explicit? ☐

5 Will the *methods* of the review be described in sufficient detail for readers to understand the rationale of the researcher's decisions? ☐

6 Has a *data extraction form* been produced to systematize the data collection? ☐

7 Will a *descriptive summary* of the works be included in the review? ☐

8 Will the *type of analysis* match the nature of the research findings being reviewed? (Meta-analysis, narrative analysis, thematic analysis, realist synthesis?) ☐

9 Is there, or will there be, a clear-cut *conclusion* resulting from the review? ☐

10 Will any limitations to the review be openly acknowledged? ☐

© M. Denscombe, *The Good Research Guide*. Open University Press.

10 Mixed methods

What is the mixed methods approach? • The benefits of using a mixed methods approach • Resources and skills • The design of mixed methods projects • Triangulation in mixed methods research • Non-corroboration of data • Pragmatism and mixed methods • A new research paradigm? • Advantages of the mixed methods approach • Disadvantages of the mixed methods approach • Further reading • Checklist for mixed methods research

A number of different names have been given to mixed methods strategies. 'Mixed research', 'mixed methodology', 'multiple research approaches', 'multi-strategy research', 'integrated methods', 'multi-method research' and 'combined methods' research are just some of the alternatives. The names bear testimony to the variety of ways in which research can be mixed and the many aspects of the research process that can be involved. The most common form of mix, however, involves a mix of methods and, in practice, the term 'mixed methods' is used in a general sense to cover the spectrum of ways in which mixing can occur in the research process.

What is the mixed methods approach?

The mixed methods approach has three characteristic features that set it apart from other strategies for social research. These are:

1 *A preference for viewing research problems from a variety of perspectives.* At the heart of the approach there is a commitment to viewing things from different angles. Rather than rely on findings from a single method or a single approach, the mixed methods approach regards the use of multiple sources as beneficial in terms of the quality and fullness of data it produces. For this reason the idea of *triangulation* plays a major role in mixed methods research.

2 *The combination of different types of research within a single project.* There is a willingness to combine methods from different 'paradigms' – from different

traditions of research with mutually incompatible philosophies. In most cases this means mixing 'qualitative' and 'quantitative' components with researchers variously writing about using both qualitative and quantitative *methods*, qualitative and quantitative *data* or qualitative and quantitative *research*.

3   *The choice of methods based on 'what works best' for tackling a specific problem.* The approach is problem-driven, and the research problem is always considered to be the most important thing when it comes to the choice of methods. It is not a matter of particular methods being intrinsically 'good' or 'bad'; it is a matter of how useful they are in terms of the specific issue that is being investigated. This primacy of the research problem, coupled with the mixing of methods from different paradigms, explains why the mixed methods approach tends to be associated with *pragmatism.*

The benefits of using a mixed methods approach

Accuracy of findings

Researchers can improve their confidence in the accuracy of findings through the use of different methods to investigate the same subject. In line with the principles of triangulation, the mixed methods approach provides the researcher with the opportunity to check the findings from one method against the findings from a different method. Where different methods produce data that are more or less the same, the researcher can feel more confident in assuming that the findings are accurate.

Using the same principle of triangulation researchers can also check on the impact of a particular research method. For example, if a researcher wants to know whether online questionnaires 'distort' the kind of answers that are given by respondents, he/she could compare the findings from this method of data collection with findings from a similar set of respondents completing a conventional paper questionnaire. If there is no marked difference between the methods in terms of the data collected, the researcher can feel confident that the use of the online questionnaires does not have a distorting impact on the data (at least, no impact that is different from the conventional paper questionnaire).

 Key point

This use of the mixed methods approach 'seeks convergence, corroboration, correspondence of results from the different methods' (Greene et al. 1989: 259).

A more complete picture

The use of more than one method can enhance the findings of research by providing a fuller and more complete picture of the thing that is being studied. The benefit of the mixed methods approach in this instance is that the data produced by the different methods can be complementary. They can provide alternative perspectives that, when combined, go further towards an all-embracing vision of the subject than could be produced using a mono-method approach. In terms of the mixed methods approach this tends to involve the use of both qualitative and quantitative methods as a means of seeing things from alternative perspectives and, thereby, getting a more complete overview of the subject.

 Key point

'The use of multiple methods, or triangulation, reflects an attempt to secure an in-depth understanding of the phenomenon in question' (Denzin 2012: 82).

Consider, for example, research that focuses on smoking and the health-related behaviour of young people. A quantitative survey approach would certainly produce evidence of the extent of smoking by under-16s and could provide good demographic details that will help us to understand the social backgrounds of those involved. A series of focus groups involving young smokers could be used to provide qualitative data that would help to explain why the under-age smokers started smoking and what motivates them to continue. In their own right, both the quantitative and the qualitative methods are valuable and can make a worthwhile contribution to what is known on the matter. Combining the methods, however, allows the researcher to produce a fuller account of the situation that covers not only the scale of the issue (e.g. numbers involved, age, sex, ethnic group) but also gives some insight into the motivational factors that give rise to the behaviour (e.g. self-image, stress, peer groups).

Developing the analysis

Within a mixed methods strategy contrasting methods can be used as a means of moving the analysis forward, with one method being used to inform another. In this sense, methods are introduced sequentially as a way of developing the findings obtained from a previous phase of the research.

This can be useful as a means of developing research instruments. For example, researchers who are designing a survey questionnaire can start by conducting focus groups or interviews and use these to discover what kinds of issues are most important to include in the subsequent survey questionnaire. In this way the quantitative data collected using the survey questionnaire are developed *from* the qualitative data that were collected through interviews or focus groups.

Mixed methods can also be used to develop *on* the findings from other parts of a research project. In this case, a new method is introduced specifically to address a research issue arising through findings produced by a previous method. A classic study illustrates how this can work. Between 1924 and 1933 research was conducted at the Western Electric company's Hawthorne Plant in Chicago. The aim of these *Hawthorne studies* was to discover which factors affected worker productivity. Initially, management at the plant conducted a sequence of quasi-experiments in which they altered the level of lighting to see if this was linked with productivity. Subsequently, researchers from the Harvard Business School joined the investigation and conducted a further series of studies designed to investigate the link between fatigue, monotony and worker productivity (Mayo [1933] 2003; Roethlisberger and Dickson [1939] 2003). All these controlled, quasi-experimental studies produced rather puzzling and inconclusive results and this prompted the researchers to introduce an alternative approach. Instead of trying to *measure* the factors that affected productivity they decided to *ask* the workers what motivated them. The researchers embarked on a huge programme of interviews with the workforce. What they found out about workers' motivation through the interviews helped the researchers to make sense of the findings from the initial experimental approaches used for the research. The interviews revealed that the workers were motivated by factors other than just money; there were personal and social rewards from work that affected their productivity as well. Once the researchers understood this, they could make sense of the results from the earlier phase. Finally, to confirm their findings from the interview phase the researchers embarked on a third phase of research which involved *observing* the informal group behaviour of workers. In this way they progressively developed the analysis of the factors influencing the productivity of the workers at the plant.

 Key point: The main benefits of using a mixed methods approach
- Check accuracy of findings.
- Provide a more complete picture.
- Help to develop the analysis.

Resources and skills

The benefits of using a mixed methods approach need to be weighed against the extra demands this approach can place upon the researcher. The most obvious extra demand on the research comes in the form of the multi-skilling that is required. If the researcher is to use more than one method, he/she must become proficient in the use of the alternative methods – and this takes time. Added to this, data analysis becomes more complex when using mixed methods. Not only does the researcher need to use more than one kind of analysis, there is also the need to compare, contrast and integrate the findings in a way that is likely to be more challenging than sticking with just one method.

 Caution
The additional demands of using a mixed methods approach need to be taken into account when deciding how long the research will take and what it will cover.

The design of mixed methods projects

A lot of attention is given to the *design* of mixed methods projects. This is because the research design explains the rationale for mixing the various components: it indicates which methods are considered to be appropriate for the research question being investigated and it shows how the various methods can be interlinked to best advantage (Creswell 2013; Morgan 2014).

A large number of design possibilities have been suggested. There have been numerous typologies produced which catalogue alternative designs for mixed methods research (Onwuegbuzie and Combs 2010; Natasi et al. 2010) and there are ongoing efforts to refine and extend the underlying premises of mixed methods research (see, for example, Leech and Onwuegbuzie 2009; Onwuegbuzie and Frels 2013). However, the first thing to note about the various typologies for mixed methods research is the way they tend to be based on a clear distinction between qualitative and quantitative forms of enquiry. Reflecting this, the design of mixed methods research tends to follow a conventional notation in which:

- QUAL stands for qualitative data in the form of text or pictures that provide the basis for interpretations of the meaning they convey;
- QUAN stands for quantitative data in the form of numbers that provide objective measurements of observed events.

The labels QUAL and QUAN actually represent a simplified view of a complex reality. In practice the dividing line between qualitative and quantitative approaches is not always clear-cut or simple (Reichardt and Rallis 1994; Hammersley 1996; Bergman 2008; Onwuegbuzie 2012). But the labels QUAL and QUAN are easy to understand and they provide a convenient short-hand notation that signals the amount of *emphasis* specific methods put on interpretation (QUAL) or measurement (QUAN). For this reason, if no other, the distinction between QUAL and QUAN remains in widespread use in relation to mixed methods research designs

The second point to note about the many mixed methods typologies is that they really boil down to some fairly simple and straightforward issues (Guest 2013). In fact, the basic things a mixed methods researcher needs to explain about his/her research design can be reduced to just three things:

- the *sequence* of the QUAL and QUAN components;
- the relative *importance* attached to the QUAL and QUAN components;
- the *purpose* of linking the QUAL and QUAN components.

Sequence

When a research design involves the use of methods or strategies drawn from different paradigms, the order in which the methods/strategies are used is significant. Given that they are used as part of the same investigation of the same research question, the sequencing reflects the researcher's beliefs about how the combination of methods and strategies works best. For some purposes it might be better to have QUAN followed by QUAL; for other purposes the opposite might

Table 10.1 Sequence in mixed methods research designs

Sequential studies	e.g. QUAL → QUAN
(two phases)	QUAN → QUAL
(possibly '*multi-phase*')	QUAN → QUAL → QUAN
Simultaneous studies	e.g. QUAN ⎫
(sometimes called '*parallel*' studies)	QUAL ⎬ →

be true. Possibly, more phases within a research project might be most useful, in this case calling for a sequence of three or more QUAL/QUAN components. There might also be occasions when the research is best served by conducting the contrasting alternatives alongside each other at the same time. This would involve the 'simultaneous' use of QUAL and QUAN. These basic design options relating to sequence and timing are shown, using the conventional notation, in Table 10.1.

Relative importance

Research designs that incorporate aspects of both QUAL and QUAN need not necessarily attach equal weight to the two. Indeed, there is a strong likelihood that researchers will tend to regard one as the 'main' and the other as the 'subsidiary' counterbalance or check. For example, the researchers might start by collecting and analysing a relatively small amount of qualitative data as an exploratory phase of the investigation. They might use interviews or focus groups to get a feel for the relevant issues and to explore the way things are perceived. Armed with this knowledge, the researchers can then produce a questionnaire (or other quantitative research instrument) that can build on information obtained in advance. Some psychology and marketing research adopts this approach, using the QUAL as a preliminary checking device to ensure the validity of a QUAN research instrument. In this approach, it is the QUAN data that are treated as the most important material for the investigation.

In contrast to this, the design might treat QUAL as the dominant, perhaps preceding the QUAN subsidiary. An example of this would be the use of a detailed case study that is followed up with small-scale questionnaire survey to check the case study findings. The research design, in this instance, centres on the collection and analysis of qualitative data. It might, for example, consist of interview data collected from employees within a particular business. From these interviews the researchers might reach certain conclusions. At this point, they might choose to conduct a survey of other businesses to check if these conclusions tend to be borne out in other situations. The key points might be included in a questionnaire distributed to a representative sample of businesses nationwide, with the hope that the responses they receive will corroborate the conclusions based on the detailed case study. The main thrust of the investigation, in this example, is the QUAL (interviews) with the QUAN (questionnaire survey) being used in a supporting role.

In a simplified depiction of the range of possibilities, the sequencing and dominance of methods from different research paradigms might take one of the following forms (Table 10.2).

Table 10.2 Relative importance of components in mixed methods research designs

Equivalent status	e.g. QUAL $\rightarrow$ QUAN
	QUAN $\rightarrow$ QUAL $\rightarrow$ QUAN
Dominant/less dominant status*	e.g. qual $\rightarrow$ QUAN
	QUAL $\rightarrow$ quan

*Note: use of lower case letters to denote less importance

Purpose of the link

Mixed methods research involves more than simply having bits of QUAL and QUAN research coexisting within a project. The key to good mixed methods research is to link these components in a way that is beneficial for the research and what it is trying to achieve. So, one of the crucial things that need to be addressed within any mixed methods research design is the matter of what each component contributes to the others. Some key possibilities here are:

- *comparison of findings:* The link might involve comparing and contrasting the findings from various (QUAL and QUAN) components as a means of cross-checking the results and confirming the validity of the findings.
- *building up findings*: The link involves one component adding to the findings of another. Each extra bit of the research provides a new dimension to what is known about the topic, adding an alternative perspective and producing different kinds of information.
- *developing on the findings*: This can involve specific parts of the research being used to shape the issues looked at by subsequent components and to *inform the direction* the research should take. Or the link can be based upon the use of findings from particular components to explain findings from another part of the research. The point in this case is to *take the analysis further* (as, for example, occurred in the Hawthorne studies described above).

These three options map closely onto the three main benefits associated with mixed methods research. Comparison is useful for checking the accuracy of findings. Building helps to provide a fuller picture. And developing the findings is valuable for taking the analysis forward. When taken together with the options for sequencing and the relative importance attributed to the components, these provide a basic list of 10 mixed methods design options for the project researcher. These design options are outlined in Table 10.3.

Some typologies of mixed methods design incorporate a further element. Creswell and Plano Clark (2010: 69–70), for example, refer to 'Explanatory sequential designs' and 'Exploratory sequential designs' among their list of design options. Terms like 'explanatory' and 'exploratory', though, do not relate exclusively to mixed methods research. They tell us about the overall nature of the research and what it is trying to achieve and, as such, can be applied to any research design in the social sciences (rather than describing how the mixed methods elements within the project are linked).

Table 10.3   Ten basic design options for mixed methods research

Benefit	Link	Notation	Description
Improved accuracy	Comparison of findings	QUAL + QUANT	*Convergent findings.* Alternative methods address the same question and are given equal status in terms of cross-validating the findings. The findings from each method are used as a check on the accuracy of findings from the other(s).
More complete picture	Build up findings	QUAL + QUANT Qual + QUANT QUAL + quant	*Additional coverage* Different methods are used to investigate separate components of the overall question. When brought together these add new dimensions to what is known about the topic.
Developing the analysis	Inform the direction Explain the findings	QUAL → QUAN QUAN → QUAL qual → QUAN quan → QUAL QUAL → quan QUAN → qual	*Sequential contributions* Findings from one method are used to inform research in the next phase within the project. There is a clear development that plays to the strengths of different methods. Emphasis can be placed on one component rather than treating them equally.

 Key point: The mix can involve more than just 'methods'

There is no absolute reason why the mix must be a mix of methods. A 'mixed methods' approach can be based on the mixing of research *designs*, research *strategies* and modes of *analysis*. Furthermore, the mix does not have to involve qualitative and quantitative components. It is possible to combine different quantitative methods together and equally to combine different qualitative methods within one study (Denzin 2012; Flick et al. 2012).

Triangulation in mixed methods research

One of the defining characteristics of mixed methods research, as noted at the beginning of the chapter, is a preference for viewing research problems from a variety of perspectives. As we have seen this can be achieved by combining different components of a research project in different ways. What each of the design options share, however, is the aim of getting a better 'fix' on the thing that is being investigated by using more than one method to see it from more than one angle. The rationale for this owes much to the notion of 'triangulation' and in the sphere of mixed methods research triangulation has assumed a particular significance as a foundation for the premise that a research topic can be better understood if it is viewed from more than one perspective.

The idea of triangulation derives from trigonometry and the geometric laws associated with triangles. These laws make it possible to find the exact location of an item if it is viewed from two other known positions (provided there is information about the angles and distances from these two other positions). In practice, triangulation is used by geologists, surveyors, navigators and others to measure exact locations of things in the physical world.

Social researchers have adapted and developed triangulation for use in the social world. Usually drawing on Denzin's (1970) early work in this area, they point to five distinct ways in which triangulation can be used in the social sciences. These are:

1 *methodological triangulation (between-methods)*. This is the most common form of triangulation adopted by mixed methods researchers. The use of alternative methods allows the findings from one method to be contrasted with the findings from another. The key to this form of triangulation is the use of approaches that are markedly different and which allow the researcher to see things from as *widely different perspectives* as possible.

2 *methodological triangulation (within-methods)*. Comparisons can be made using *similar kinds of methods* rather than ones that are markedly different. This is the form of triangulation used by Campbell and Fiske (1959) and Webb et al. (1966) in their pioneering work on triangulation. The reasoning here is that if similar methods produce the same results, it would seem reasonable to conclude that the findings are accurate and that they are authentic (rather than being some artificial by-product of the methods used).

3 *data triangulation (use of contrasting sources of information)*. The validity of findings can be checked by using different *sources of information*. This can mean comparing data from different informants (informant triangulation) or using data collected at different times (time triangulation). The notion also incorporates the idea of space triangulation (the use of more than one cultural, social or geographical context).

4 *investigator triangulation (use of different researchers)*. As a check against bias arising from the influence of any specific *researcher*, the findings from different investigators can be compared for consistency. Do the researchers 'see' things in the same way? Do they interpret events similarly? Do they attach the same codes to the same source of data (e.g. interview transcript,

observed event)? To the extent that they do, the findings can be accepted with more confidence.

5   *theory triangulation.* This involves the use of more than one *theoretical position* in relation to the data. Different theories can shape the kind of data that are collected and the way the data are interpreted. These different perspectives can be based on the approaches of different disciplines. So, for example, researchers might choose to contrast a sociological with a psychological approach to the particular topic being investigated.

 Caution: The use of triangulation in social science

The social world is different from the physical world and social researchers are not usually able to make use of fixed/objective positions, universally agreed, from which to make their observations. The use of triangulation by social researchers, therefore, is not literal. It is not the same as that used by geologists, surveyors or navigators. It generally refers more loosely to the broader underlying principle that viewing something from more than one viewpoint allows you to get more worthwhile findings from the research.

 Key point: Mixed methods and triangulation: the benefits

* Improved accuracy:
  * *validation of findings* in terms of their accuracy and authenticity
  * *checking for bias* in research methods
  * *development of research instruments.*

This involves the use of methods, data, etc. that are relatively *similar.*

* Fuller picture and more complete findings:
  * production of *complementary data* (different but related)
  * production of *further data* (developing out of previous findings).

This involves the use of methods, data, etc. that are contrasting and relatively *dissimilar.*

The use of triangulation in mixed methods research can be illustrated through a research project on classroom control (Denscombe 2012). This research primarily made use of between-methods triangulation and information triangulation. The starting point for the research was the problem of disruptive behaviour by students in secondary school classrooms. Such behaviour has a serious impact on lessons. It is stressful and challenging for teachers, and it detracts from the learning environment for students. The circumstances giving rise to such behaviour, and the techniques used by teachers to control it are, therefore, of practical concern and typical of the kind of *research problem* that can be tackled using a mixed methods approach.

The first phase of the study involved classroom *observation.* The researcher began by sitting in classrooms making field notes about events and focusing, of course, on incidents of disruptive behaviour. This use of observation as the initial data collection method produced both quantitative data relating to the frequency of such behaviour and qualitative data relating to the circumstances surrounding the events.

These data were useful in their own right. However, when used as part of a mixed methods research design there was more to be gained from them. As part of a mixed methods study they could provide:

- *insights* about the problem and suggested further avenues of enquiry to be pursued in connection with disruptive behaviour;
- a particular *perspective* on disruptive behaviour (based on classroom observation);
- *information* that could subsequently be checked in terms of (a) accuracy and (b) interpretation against findings from alternative sources of information and different research methods.

Such benefits, though, required the data from classroom observation to be used alongside other methods and other sources of information about disruptive behaviour. To exploit the benefits of between-methods triangulation these other methods needed to be quite different from observation, allowing disruptive behaviour to be viewed from a distinctly different angle. So the research went on to include a series of one-to-one interviews. In these interviews teachers and students were asked to reflect back on actual incidents of disruptive behaviour observed by the researcher during lessons. Used in this way, the interviews served two purposes. First, they added background information helping to explain why the events occurred. Second, they produced depth information shedding light on the meaning of the events for those involved and how the situations were negotiated.

To add yet another perspective the research also made use of written, documentary sources of data on disruptive behaviour. This involved an element of data triangulation. School records and school rules provided an 'official' standpoint on the matter, one which offered an interesting contrast to the findings emerging from observation and interviews. Finally, a questionnaire survey of teachers and students was used as a means of verifying the analysis and seeing how far the findings could be applied more generally to a wider population.

The research, then, used different types of methods and alternative sources of information to look at disruptive behaviour in classrooms from different angles. In an effort to get a better overall understanding of the phenomenon it used between-methods triangulation and data triangulation. There were, though, two aspects to this better understanding. As Figure 10.1 illustrates, triangulation was used to check the accuracy of the findings (e.g. about the frequency of disruptive behaviour), and it was used to provide a fuller picture (e.g. of the significance of disruptive behaviour in terms of its meaning for teachers and students).

Note than in the case of accurate measurement it should not be inferred that the use of triangulation will pinpoint a precise, correct 'truth' about the situation. It will not 'prove' that the researcher 'has got it right'. It can only help to corroborate findings and give the researcher more confidence about the conclusions.

Likewise with the use of triangulation to get a more complete picture, it should never be suggested that the use of triangulation will have covered all the angles and allowed the researcher to say all there is to say on a topic. What it can do, more modestly, is help to provide a fuller understanding and produce alternative kinds of information which move things *towards* the complete picture.

Figure 10.1 Mixed methods and triangulation

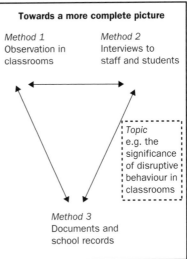

Non-corroboration of data

The mixed methods approach tends to operate on the *assumption* that findings will coincide or be complementary and that this will be a positive contribution to the research project. There is, however, an inherent risk that the findings from the various components might not point in the same direction.

In principle, the non-alignment of results should not be regarded as a setback or failure of some kind. It should spur further research to investigate the difference in findings. The contradictions could be very interesting – revealing limitations to the methods of data collection or teasing out fascinating complications within the phenomenon being studied.

In practice, though, non-corroboration can have challenging consequences. Project researchers and contract researchers can be under pressure to arrive at conclusions within a given time-frame. They can be expected to produce reports that have to be delivered by a given deadline. But, at the end of the project they could be left with contradictory findings from the alternative methods (or data sources) and no firm conclusion. Where people look to research to provide concrete findings or practical solutions to a pressing problem, they might not be very receptive to conclusions that are based on conflicting data from different methods. The audience for the research (e.g. funders, examiners) might feel dissatisfied that the completion of the project does not provide a clear-cut finding. They might even interpret things to mean that one or other of the methods (or data sources) employed was 'wrong' and should not have been used within the project. Under circumstances such as these the fact is that the non-corroboration of data can become a challenging and possibly unwelcome occurrence for the mixed methods researcher.

Pragmatism and mixed methods

Pragmatism is generally regarded as the philosophical partner of the mixed methods approach. This means that there is some broad agreement among mixed methods researchers that social research should not be judged by how neatly it fits with the quantitative paradigm (positivism) or with the premises of the competing camp – the qualitative paradigm (interpretivism). Decisions about which methods to use should, instead, be based on how *useful* the methods are for addressing a particular question, issue or problem that is being investigated. The crucial consideration is how well the research tools *work* rather than how well they fit within a specific research philosophy.

Pragmatism

In the context of research, pragmatism tends to revolve around the following core ideas:

- Knowledge is based on practical outcomes and 'what works'. The key criterion for judging knowledge is how useful it is perceived to be and how well it works when applied to some practical problem.
- Research should test what works through empirical enquiry.
- There is no single, best 'scientific' method that can lead the way to indisputable knowledge.
- Knowledge is provisional. What we understand as truth today may not be seen as such in the future. Knowledge is seen as a product of our times. It can never be absolute or perfect because it is inevitably a product of the historical era and the cultural context within which it is produced. The quest for absolute 'Truth' is consequently seen as a hopeless cause.

Traditional dualisms in the field of philosophy and science are regarded as not helpful. In particular, there is scepticism about the distinction between quantitative and qualitative research, but there is also a rejection of distinctions like facts/values, objectivism/subjectivism and rationalism/empiricism.

Mixed methods as an alternative option

The link between pragmatism and mixed methods research can be interpreted in more than one way. For some mixed methods researchers the tenets of pragmatism leave the door open for the use of purely quantitative research or purely qualitative research – providing the use of either in isolation can produce the kind of findings that work sufficiently well to answer a research problem. Pragmatism leads them to regard the use of mixed methods as a third *alternative* – another option open to social researchers if they decide that neither quantitative nor qualitative research alone will provide adequate findings for the particular piece of research they have in mind. Rather than see positivism and interpretivism as having become obsolete, these researchers regard the mixed methods approach as simply an alternative research strategy that can be used if, and when, necessary. As Morgan (2014: 4, emphasis added) makes the point:

> Simply having more results or different kinds of results does not inherently improve your work; in addition, you must bring those results together in a way that demonstrates the value of your additional effort. Hence, research projects that use multiple methods are not *automatically* preferable to studies that use just one method.

Mixed methods as a better option

There are others who see pragmatism as representing an advance in thinking about social research – the basis for a new research paradigm that should replace the earlier paradigms based on positivism and interpretivism (e.g. Tashakkori and Teddlie 1998, 2003; Johnson and Onwuegbuzie 2004; Teddlie and Tashakkori 2009; Creswell and Plano Clarke 2010). This paves the way for a subtly different stance in which the combination of quantitative and qualitative research is seen as a good thing in its own right. From this position it is not only allowable to mix methods from alternative and incompatible paradigms of research but it is also *desirable* to do so in order to provide answers that work – or, at least, that work better than those based on the use of just quantitative or just qualitative research.

A new research paradigm?

The image of mixed methods as a new paradigm has been useful for promoting it as the new breakthrough approach that cuts through the stand-off between two old-style narrow-visioned paradigms. It creates an identity for the approach and it literally 'makes sense' of a complex area in a way that is particularly useful for newcomers to social research who will find it easy to understand. It is useful, therefore, to *introduce* the approach along lines forged by the 'mixed methods movement' (as has been done in this chapter).

It would be wrong, however, to suggest that the use of mixed methods is entirely new to social research. The idea of combining different kinds of research methods within a single research project has been around for a long time (Johnson and Gray 2010). Numerous examples of classic studies, including the Hawthorne studies referred to earlier in this chapter, have brought together methods and data from contrasting paradigms using different underlying philosophies. What *is* relatively new is the identification of something called the *mixed methods approach*. As an approach, with a recognized name and research credibility, it has only come to the fore in recent years championed by writers such as Tashakkori and Teddlie (1998, 2003), Johnson and Onwuegbuzie (2004), Greene (2007), Teddlie and Tashakkori (2009), Creswell and Plano Clark (2010), Creswell (2013) and Morgan (2014)..

It would also be wrong to infer that pragmatism is the only research philosophy that can be linked with the use of mixed methods. Researchers from other philosophical positions have argued for the benefits of using mixed methods. Notably, mixed methods has been linked with critical realism (Layder 1993, 1998; Pawson and Tilley 1997; Lipscomb 2008; Harrits 2011), constructivism (Denzin 2012), and transformative/emancipatory styles of research (Mertens 2009; Onwuegbuzie and Frels 2013). The use of mixed methods, then, is not *exclusively* tied to pragmatism.

Advantages of the mixed methods approach

A better understanding of the thing that is being studied

Using a form of triangulation the mixed methods approach can be used: (1) to validate findings and improve accuracy or (2) to produce a more comprehensive account of the thing being researched.

A practical, problem-driven approach to research

As a movement, the mixed methods approach is problem-driven rather than theory-driven. Its underlying philosophy is that of pragmatism. As such, it gives voice to the general practice of a large proportion of social researchers who have, for years, used methods from different research paradigms because it has been practical to do so.

Clearer links between different methods and the different kinds of data

The mixed methods approach places emphasis on the integration of alternative approaches and encourages the researcher to provide an explicit account of how and why the different methods and data complement each other. Good mixed methods research avoids an arbitrary 'mix-and-match' approach.

Compensating strengths and weaknesses

Research strategies and methods each have their own strengths and their own weaknesses and a shrewd combination of strategies and methods allows the researcher to exploit the strengths of a particular method without leaving himself/herself vulnerable to criticism in connection with that method's weakness.

Disadvantages of the mixed methods approach

The time and costs of the research project can increase

The combination of phases can extend the time-frame for research design and data collection.

The researcher needs to develop skills in more than one method

The researcher needs to develop and exercise skills covering both qualitative and quantitative approaches. This adds demands on the researcher and opens up the possibility of 'missing the mark' for experts in either camp.

Findings from different methods might not corroborate one another

If findings from the different methods do not corroborate one another, the researcher can be faced with the need to extend the research to unravel the reasons for this.

The QUAL/QUAN distinction tends to oversimplify matters

When making the QUAL/QUAN distinction mixed methods researchers need to be aware that the clarity and simplicity of the terms mask a more complicated reality.

The underlying philosophy of the mixed methods approach – pragmatism – is open to misinterpretation

There is a common-sense use of the word pragmatic which implies expediency and a certain lack of principles underlying a course of action. There is the danger, then, that the mixed methods approach is associated with this understanding of the word and thus becomes regarded as an approach in which 'anything goes'. It should be stressed that this is not the philosophical meaning of pragmatism and it is not a meaning that should be associated with the mixed methods approach.

Further reading

Cresswell, J. W. (2013) *Research Design: Qualitative, Quantitative and Mixed Methods Approaches*, 4th edn. Thousand Oaks, CA: Sage, especially Chapters 1 and 10.

Creswell, J. W. and Plano Clark, V. (2010) *Designing and Conducting Mixed Methods Research*, 2nd edn. Thousand Oaks, CA: Sage.

Morgan, D. L. (2014) *Integrating Qualitative and Quantitative Methods: A Pragmatic Approach*. Thousand Oaks, CA: Sage.

Teddlie, C. and Tashakkori, A. (2009) *Foundations of Mixed Methods Research: Integrating Quantitative and Qualitative Approaches in the Social and Behavioral Sciences*. Thousand Oaks, CA: Sage.

Checklist for mixed methods research

When undertaking mixed methods research you should feel
confident about answering 'yes' to the following questions: ☑

1 Does the research project do one or more of the following things?
   • make use of more than one research method ☐
   • combine more than one kind of research data ☐
   • ask questions based on different models (exploratory/ ☐
     explanatory)

2 Has a clear statement been made about the *benefits* of using a
   mixed methods strategy compared with using just one method? ☐

3 Is the *justification* for using a mixed methods strategy based on
   one or more of the following criteria? ☐
   • the needs of the particular research question
   • checking the accuracy of findings
   • providing a more complete picture
   • developing the analysis
   • a means of compensating the strengths and weaknesses of
     particular methods

4 Does the research have a clear *design* showing the sequence,
   dominance, and link between the QUAL and QUAN parts? ☐

5 Are details provided about how *triangulation* is used in relation to:
   • the different methods of data collection? ☐
   • the use of qualitative and quantitative data? ☐
   • the kinds of data analysis? ☐

6 Has consideration been given to the additional *skills and resources*
   that might be required in order to conduct mixed methods research? ☐

© M. Denscombe, *The Good Research Guide*. Open University Press.

Part 2

Methods of data collection

There are four main methods of data collection that social researchers can use: questionnaires, interviews, observation and documents. In many ways these are the social scientist's equivalent of the microscope, the scales and the micrometer that natural scientists might use in relation to material objects in the physical world. They are tools that help the researcher to gain:

- a clearer picture of things;
- an accurate measurement of things;
- facts and evidence about the subject matter.

Selecting methods: a matter of 'horses for courses'

In the following chapters there is guidance about the key features of each method. However, before choosing and using any of them it is important to consider three things. First, research methods are often associated with specific research strategies. Questionnaires tend to be linked with surveys, for example, while participant observation tends to be used with ethnography. And there are some sound theoretical reasons that explain the tendency of particular methods to be linked to particular strategies. The linkage, however, is not watertight and it is important for the project researcher to recognize that there is likely to be some *element of choice* when selecting which method to use.

Second, each of the methods has its particular strengths and weaknesses. These are listed at the end of each chapter. Bearing this in mind, rather than trying to look for a method that is superior to all others in any absolute sense, it is better to look for a method that works best in practice for the specific purposes of the investigation. When it comes to choosing a method, in other words, researchers should base their decision on the criterion of 'usefulness'. Researchers should ask themselves which method is best suited to the task at hand and operate on the premise that, when *choosing a method for the collection of data, it is a matter of 'horses for courses'*.

Third, research methods do not need to be seen as mutually exclusive. If no method is intrinsically better than others, and if methods are to be chosen pragmatically, then this opens up the possibility of combining methods and using a *mixed methods approach* (see Chapter 10). More than one method can be used for the research with the clear intention that weaknesses in one method can be compensated for by strengths in another method.

Authorization for the research

Having selected the most appropriate method(s) there might be a strong temptation to get things started and forge ahead with the data collection. However, before any data collection occurs it is essential that the planned research has been approved and authorized. This involves two things: ethics approval and authorization.

- *Ethics approval*. Ethics approval is required for the vast majority of social research projects. It involves making an application to a Research Ethics Committee or its equivalent. Ethics approval must be obtained *before* embarking on data collection – this is absolutely essential. See Chapter 17 Research Ethics for further guidance on this point.
- *Authorization*. Permission should be obtained from those 'in authority' who control access to the people and settings involved in the research. This might mean getting written approval, for example, from senior managers within an organization or from 'guardians' who have responsibility for protecting the interests of vulnerable people. It is vital that such authorization is obtained *before* the data collection begins.

Good practice: Approval for research
Always get approval in advance. Never start data collection without having already had the proposed research formally approved.

Preparation, planning and project management

In general, researchers do not have the time or resources to repeat pieces of research nor do they have the opportunity to make amendments and corrections to the method of data collection once it has been put in place. And the vast majority of respondents are likely to be less than sympathetic to a plea from the researcher to repeat the research a second time in order to overcome a mistake in the first version. There is, therefore, a lot of pressure to *get it right first time*. This involves suitable preparation, planning and project management. Three things worth considering in this respect are:

- *The timescale and schedule*. Researchers need to consider what timescale is likely to be involved, and it is good practice here to work out a suitable schedule for the data collection using a Gantt chart or similar wall-chart planner.

- *Resources*. Provision should be made for the costs involved in the process of data collection (transport, equipment, etc.) and the amount of researcher's time that will be needed in order to complete the data collection successfully and on time.
- *Research design*. The researcher should not be running around frantically trying to gather whatever information comes to hand: data collection should be conducted as part of a clear pathway for research. It should form part of a research design in which the purpose of doing the research is clear and the means for accomplishing it are mapped out in advance.

Record keeping

Whichever research method is used written records should be kept as a matter of good practice during the course of the project. There are two facets to this:

- *Diary of events and decisions*. There should be a record of the collection process. This is like a diary of events that occur and decisions made during the research project. Such records provide a documented history that can be referred back to for information at a later stage.
- *Organization of the data*. Careful record keeping needs to be done in connection with the actual data that are collected. The data need to be logged and catalogued, filed and indexed in ways that allow the researcher to know exactly what data have been collected and to locate specific aspects of the data when this is necessary.

Such records of the research must be kept secure: either under lock and key or by password protection of computer files – ideally both.

> **Link up with**
> Data protection,
> p. 317.

Pilot study

Finally, another matter of good practice that applies to any data collection method. The method should always be tested out in advance to check how well it works in practice. No matter how much time and effort a researcher puts into devising a good data collection tool, there is no real substitute for trying it out 'in the field' with real participants. If all goes well the researcher can feel reassured that there should be no nasty surprises when the data collection proper begins. If the pilot study reveals areas for improvement, then these can be incorporated before the research goes 'live' – avoiding what might otherwise have been damaging problems for the research.

11 Questionnaires

What is a questionnaire? • When is it appropriate to use a questionnaire? • Self-completion questionnaires • Successful questionnaires • Vital elements of a research questionnaire • The length of the questionnaire • Questionnaire fatigue • Devising the questions • Check questions • 'Open' and 'closed' questions • Types of questions • Web-based questionnaires • Advantages of questionnaires • Disadvantages of questionnaires • Further reading • Checklist for the use of questionnaires

What is a questionnaire?

There are many types of questionnaires. They can vary enormously in terms of their purpose, their size and their appearance. To qualify as a research questionnaire, however, they should meet the following three criteria.

First, they should be designed to *collect information which can be used subsequently as data for analysis*. As a research tool, questionnaires do not set out to change people's attitudes or provide them with information. Though questionnaires are sometimes used for this purpose – for instance, as a way of marketing a product – it is not strictly in keeping with the spirit of a *research* questionnaire, whose purpose is to discover things.

Second, they should consist of *a written list of questions*. The important point here is that each person who answers the particular questionnaire reads an identical set of questions. This allows for consistency and precision in terms of the wording of the questions, and makes the processing of the answers easier. (Occasionally, pictures might be used instead of written questions.)

Third, they should *gather information by asking people directly* about the points concerned with the research. Questionnaires work on the premise that if you want to find out something about people and their attitudes, you simply go and ask them what it is you want to know, and get the information 'straight from the horse's mouth'.

When is it appropriate to use a questionnaire?

Different methods are suited to different circumstances, and questionnaires are no exception. Although they can be used, perhaps ingeniously, across a wide spectrum of research situations, questionnaires are at their most productive:

* when the information required tends to be fairly *straightforward information* – relatively brief and uncontroversial;
* when there is a need for *standardized data* from identical questions – without requiring personal, face-to-face interaction;
* when the respondents can be expected to be *able to read and understand the questions* – the implications of age, intellect, language, and eyesight need to be considered;
* when the *social climate is open* enough to allow full and honest answers.

Self-completion questionnaires

The main focus of this chapter is on *self-completion* questionnaires. Self-completion questionnaires rely on respondents working independently from the researcher, providing written answers at their own pace, in their own time. The researcher, even if present when the respondent completes the questionnaire, does not get involved with the process of filling in the answers. When researchers do have some direct involvement, however, things are a bit different. When questionnaires are delivered over the phone, or when a researcher stops someone in the street and asks them to complete a questionnaire that is read to them from a clipboard or mobile device, then it is more like using a 'structured interview'. The direct interaction between the researcher and the respondent brings into play a range of additional issues linked with the 'interviewer effect'. These issues are covered in Chapter 12 on interviews.

Successful questionnaires

The success of a research questionnaire depends on three things:

i)	response rate	*(how many are returned)*
ii)	completion rate	*(how fully completed)*
iii)	validity of responses	*(how honest and accurate)*

Unless questionnaires are completed and returned to the researcher, they have no value at all. It does not matter how technically correct they might be or how beautifully designed they are, the simple fact is that research questionnaires are worthless unless and until those who receive them bother to provide answers and deliver the completed questionnaire to the researcher. Returned questionnaires that have lots of questions left unanswered, of course, are not likely to be of much use: if questionnaires are to be of any value, they must also have a sufficient proportion of questions filled-in. And, of course, the value of any questionnaire will depend on the extent to which respondents provide answers that are 'real' in the sense that the information is both honest and accurate. Bogus answers or mistaken answers are perhaps worse than no answers at all.

The challenge facing the researcher is how to design and distribute the questionnaire in a way that will achieve a good response rate, with most items in the questionnaire filled in, and where there are reasonable grounds for supposing that the answers are honest and accurate. There are few absolute rules and no absolute guarantees on this score but, in essence, when designing and distributing a questionnaire, researchers need to take into consideration four things.

Capabilities of respondents

The questionnaire design needs to take into account the particular capabilities of those who receive the questionnaire. Different target groups might have different abilities and disabilities which have to be taken into consideration not just as an ethical point but as a practical point as well. Where people are not able to answer, or find it hard to complete a questionnaire, the response rate will suffer. Factors to be taken into account here are things like:

- literacy (reading ability, proficiency with the language);
- sight capacity (blindness, vision disorders, age);
- vulnerability (young people, the elderly, learning disabilities);
- memory (ability of recall, amount of detail, time since event).

Respondent motivation

Co-operation with the research will depend on the respondent's motivation to spend time and effort filling-in the questionnaire. Researchers should never take this for granted. Faced with respondents who might be weary of requests for help, they need to think carefully about what they can do to motivate people, taking the following factors into account:

- interest, enthusiasm, goodwill (topic, money, prize draw);
- circumstances of distribution (convenience, time).

Sensitivity of the topic

Researchers need to be aware that questions on certain topics can be awkward for respondents to answer and, for this reason, might be likely to produce answers that are not totally honest, or lead to items being missed altogether as respondents simply avoid them. This is not just a matter of the topic itself, it can also reflect the context within which the question is posed and the respondents' understanding of who will get to see the answers, so researchers need to take into account the potential effect of:

- asking about sensitive or embarrassing subjects (personal, emotional);
- context of the research (climate of trust and openness, or fear of reprisal).

Questionnaire design

The design of a questionnaire can make it attractive. It can also include clever features that are useful for the researcher. However, probably the most significant aspect of questionnaire design concerns the 'response burden' – the time and effort it takes for the respondent to complete the questionnaire. As a rule of thumb a good research design should minimize the response burden in order to bolster the prospects of a good response rate. This means that researchers need to consider two key factors:

- the amount of time needed to complete the questionnaire (number of questions);
- the ease of answering questions (no ambiguity, suitable format for question).

Bearing these points in mind, Table 11.1 provides a summary of the key criteria researchers need to be aware of when producing or evaluating a questionnaire.

Table 11.1   Criteria for the production and evaluation of a research questionnaire

Criterion	Research issue	Factors to be considered
Feasibility What are the prospects of contacting suitable respondents?	Practicality and Resource constraints	• available means for contacting relevant people and distributing the questionnaire • time and money to cover the preparation and distribution of the questionnaire
Response rate Will a sufficient proportion of questionnaires be returned to avoid bias in the information collected?	Reliability	• good design of questionnaire • motivation of respondents • follow-ups used
Full information Does the questionnaire gather information on all the crucial areas necessary for the research?	Completeness	• inclusion of all vital topics • all sections of the questionnaire answered
Accurate information Is the information free from errors arising (intentionally or accidentally) from the nature of the questions being asked?	Validity	• appropriate questions for the topic/concepts being investigated • clear, precise and unambiguous questions • honest answers
Ethical stance Has due consideration been given to the rights of those supplying the information?	Professional integrity	• voluntary co-operation • information given about the way data will be used • respondents' identities not disclosed • protection of sensitive data

---

Good practice: The mindset for success

1 Start from the assumption that people will be reluctant to complete the questionnaire, and then think how you can entice them to make the effort to fill it in.

2 Put yourself in their shoes and ask, 'Why should I bother to help the researcher?'

3 Anticipate low response rates: don't be over-optimistic on this matter.

Vital elements of a research questionnaire

All research questionnaires should include some background information about the research, some instructions to the respondent to help them with the task of filling in the answers, and some means of giving each completed questionnaire a unique identifying code or number. These are three features whose inclusion is considered to be 'good practice' in relation to any research questionnaire.

Background information

From both an ethical and a practical point of view the researcher needs to provide some background information about the research and the questionnaire. Each questionnaire should have information about:

- *The sponsor.* Under whose auspices is the research being undertaken? Is it individual research or does the research originate from an institution? Headed notepaper is an obvious way to indicate the nature of the institution from which the questionnaire comes.
- *The purpose.* What is the questionnaire for, and how will the information be used? It is important here to reveal sufficient information to explain the purpose of the research without going too far and 'leading' the respondent into a line of answering. A brief paragraph should suffice.
- *Return address and date.* It is vital that the questionnaire contains in it somewhere quite visibly the name and contact address (postal or email) of the person(s) to whom the completed questionnaire is to be returned.
- *Confidentiality.* Respondents should be reassured that the information they provide will not be disclosed to others (assuming that the research is operating according to a conventional code of ethics for social researchers).
- *Voluntary responses.* Respondents are under no obligation to answer the questions, and reassurances about the voluntary nature of their participation should be given.
- *Thanks.* Courtesy suggests that some word of thanks from the researcher should appear either as part of the introduction or right at the end of the questionnaire.

Instructions to the respondent

It is very important that respondents are instructed on how to go about answering the questions. Assuming that this is obvious will likely prove to be a big mistake. It is useful, therefore, to provide:

- *An example.* An example at the start of the questionnaire can set the respondent's mind at rest and indicate exactly what is expected of him or her.
- *Instructions.* Specific instructions should be given for each question where the style of question varies throughout the questionnaire.

The allocation of serial numbers

With web-based questionnaires the serial numbers are added automatically. Other forms of questionnaire might need serial numbers to be added manually. In this case, each questionnaire should be numbered so that it can be distinguished from others and located if necessary. The serial number can be used to identify the date of distribution, the place and possibly the person. But note: if the questionnaires are anonymous, such serial numbers should only allow general factors such as the date and location to be identified – not the identity of any individual person.

The length of the questionnaire

There is no hard and fast rule about the number of questions that can be included in a questionnaire. This will depend on factors such as the topic under investigation, how complex the questions are, the nature of the respondents who have been targeted and the time it takes to complete the questionnaire. Decisions about the size of a questionnaire are ultimately a matter of judgement: the researcher needs to gauge how many questions can be included before the respondent is likely to run out of patience and consign the questionnaire to the waste bin.

In most cases, researchers do not get a second chance to follow up issues they might have missed in the initial questionnaire. Conscious of this 'one-shot' constraint, there may be the temptation to ask about everything that might possibly be of relevance. It is, after all, vital to cover all key matters if the questionnaire is to supply data which permit a reasonable analysis by the researcher. But the shrewd researcher realizes that it is counter-productive to include everything that might *feasibly* have some relevance to the research issues. Every effort should be made to keep the questionnaire as brief as possible by avoiding any superfluous detail or non-essential topics. When designing a questionnaire, then, the researcher has to walk a tightrope between ensuring coverage of all the vital issues and ensuring the questionnaire is brief enough to encourage people to bother answering it.

To accomplish this balancing act there are certain rules to bear in mind.

1 *Only ask those questions which are absolutely vital for the research.* The better the research is planned, the easier it will be to identify the absolutely crucial questions and discard the 'just in case I need this information later' questions.

2 *Be rigorous in weeding out any duplication of questions.* For example, if a questionnaire contains as separate questions, 'What is your date of birth?' and 'How old are you?' we need to ask just how vital it is that both are included.

3 *Pilot the questionnaire to see how long it takes to answer* and then consider whether it is reasonable to expect the specific target group to spare this amount of time supplying the answers.

Questionnaire fatigue

Good practice: Keep questionnaires as short as possible

A questionnaire needs to be crisp and concise, asking just those questions which are crucial to the research. It is worth remembering that there is, perhaps, no more effective deterrent to answering a questionnaire than its sheer size.

Answering a survey questionnaire takes *mental effort.* Even though someone has agreed to complete a questionnaire, they can lose enthusiasm as they progress through the answers. One obvious result of this is that the respondent will 'drop out' and not complete the questionnaire. Another consequence is that they might not complete all of the questions. And a third consequence is that their effort tails off during the process of answering the questionnaire. They don't withdraw (which of course they are perfectly entitled to do) but their answers are progressively based on *minimizing the effort* taken to provide an answer. As Krosnick (1991) points out, the mental burden of answering the questionnaire can lead to 'satisficing' answers. These are answers which might appear to the researcher to be genuine but which are actually based on the respondent going through the routine of ticking boxes but doing so with minimum effort and not a lot of regard for the truth of the matter. This can involve taking the 'easy option' (e.g. agreeing with all statements), opting for 'don't know' answers, sticking to the same point on scale (following a pattern) or even resorting to random answers simply to put something in the box. The danger here is that the questionnaire will appear to have been completed, and the various questions within the questionnaire will have answers recorded against them, but those answers might not be the most accurate or most thought-through responses. At worst, they could simply be anything the respondent can find to fill the box.

The question is, 'How can this danger be minimized?' What can be done to offset the prospect of questionnaire fatigue and encourage respondents to complete questionnaires thoughtfully and honestly? Well, there are a number of things that help when it comes to the way the researcher designs and delivers the questionnaire, the main ones being:

- *Make the task of answering questions as straightforward and easy as possible.* Everything should be clear and succinct in terms of what is being asked of the respondent, and the layout of the questionnaire should enable respondents to work their way through the questions without difficulty. They should not need to fathom what is expected of them – it should be obvious.

- *Let respondents know the extent of the burden they are facing.* At the beginning of the questionnaire the respondents should be given an honest indication of how long it will take to complete the questionnaire and how many questions are involved. With web-based questionnaires the inclusion of a 'progress indicator' is really helpful in this respect, allowing respondents to see how far they have gone and how much remains to be done.

- *Don't make unrealistic demands in terms of the questions that are asked.* Respondents are likely to become demoralized and frustrated if they are confronted with questions that are overly complex or hard to answer. The questions should take into account the ability of respondents to recall things and make judgements about things, and recognize that hard questions take mental effort to answer.

There are two other factors that will have a bearing on the extent of response fatigue experienced by respondents. These are things that the researcher might not be in a strong position to influence directly, but they can be addressed in the covering letter/statement that is given to respondents as a way of attempting to motivate respondents and encourage them to feel enthusiastic about the task of completing the questionnaire.

- *Subject salience.* The covering letter/statement should do what it can to point out how the topic might be of interest. If the respondent can see that the topic of the questions is interesting and relevant for them personally, then there is an increased prospect that they will complete the questionnaire and put the effort into answering all questions openly and honestly.

- *Respondent accountability.* To the extent that respondents believe that their answers will 'make a difference' then they are more likely to engage more fully with the questionnaire and provide thoughtful and genuine answers. Again, the covering letter/statement provides an opportunity to put across the message that respondents have some stake in the findings and that their answers could contribute to some real outcome that affects them personally.

Link up with
Response rates, p. 22.

Devising the questions

Suitable topics

The willingness of respondents to co-operate with research by filling in a questionnaire can easily be undermined by the nature of the topics in the questionnaire. To avoid this possibility researchers need to ensure that the questions are on topics that respondents will:

- *be willing to answer.* When constructing the questions the researcher needs to think about whether the respondent will *want to* answer the kind of questions that are being asked. This point applies, in particular, to questions touching on personal matters or sensitive areas linked with political and religious beliefs.

- *have some information, knowledge, experience or opinions on.* It is no good constructing questions where the responses are likely to be a series of 'don't knows' or 'not applicable'.

Direct or indirect questions

Researchers need to consider whether the information being sought from the respondent is amenable to direct questions, or whether it will need to be measured by indirect means. Where the information being sought is of an overt, factual nature, there is not normally a problem on this point. The questions will take the form of 'How many times . . .?' or 'When did you last . . .?' However, questionnaires are frequently geared to less straightforward matters where a direct question would be inappropriate. If, for example, the researcher wishes to know what social class the respondent comes from, it would not be wise to ask the straightforward question, 'What is your social class?' Apart from the fact that some people might find this offensive, the term 'social class' has different meanings for different people, and the question will produce inconsistent answers. In this case, the researcher needs to pinpoint exactly what he or she defines as social class and then devise questions that will supply the type of information which will allow the respondent's social class to be deduced. For this purpose, indirect questions will be used about occupation, income, education, etc.

The wording of the questions

Questions should not be irritating or annoying for the respondents to answer. The success of the questionnaire, after all, depends on the willingness of the respondents to spend their time completing the answers and they should not be deterred from this task by any sense of frustration arising from the manner in which the questions are worded. There are some specific things that researchers can do to help avoid this possibility:

- *Make sure the wording is completely unambiguous.*
- *Avoid vague questions.* The more specific and concrete the question, the easier it is to give a precise answer. And, in all probability, the answer will prove to be of more value to the researcher.
- *Use only the minimum amount of technical jargon.* In terms of a questionnaire, the aim is not to see how clever people are.
- *Use wording that is suited to the specific target group.* Questions geared to 14-year-olds will need to be different in terms of conceptual complexity and wording from ones aimed at, for example, members of a professional association.
- *Keep the questions as short and straightforward as possible.* This will avoid unnecessary confusion and wasted time re-reading questions or trying to decipher the meaning of the question.
- *Avoid asking the same question twice in a different fashion* (except as 'check' questions).
- *Avoid the use of 'leading' questions.* These are questions which suggest an answer or which prompt the respondent to give a particular kind of answer

(e.g. Would you agree that there should be controls on the emission of carbon dioxide from cars?).

- *Be sure to include sufficient options in the answer.* If the list might prove too long, selecting the main possibilities and then tagging on the 'Other (please specify)' option is a good strategy.
- *Pay attention to the way the questions are numbered.* Obviously they should be sequential, but there are clever ways of using sub-questions (e.g. 4a, 4b and so on) which can help the respondent to map his or her way through the series of questions.
- *Avoid words or phrases which might cause offence.* If, for example, the questionnaire involves ethnic minority issues, it is prudent to use the 'politically correct' terms.

Good practice: Questions should be worded with clarity and precision

There is little room for vagueness or imprecision. This means that the researcher must have a clear vision of exactly what issues are at the heart of the research and what kind of information would enlighten those issues.

The order of the questions

The ordering of the questions in a questionnaire is important for two reasons. First and foremost, it can entice or deter the respondent from continuing with the exercise of providing answers. If the respondent is immediately faced with the most complex of the questions at the start of the questionnaire this might deter him or her from going any further. However, if the questionnaire starts with straightforward questions and then gradually moves towards such questions at a later stage, there is a greater likelihood that the respondent will persevere. This same point is true for those questions which might be perceived as more personal and on sensitive issues. There will be a greater chance of success if such questions appear later in the questionnaire than if they appear right at the start.

The second way in which the ordering of questions can be important is that questions asked at an earlier point in the questionnaire can affect the answers supplied at a later stage. This is evident in many commercial 'marketing/sales questionnaires' where there is a conscious attempt to make use of this feature of questionnaires.

Good practice: The order of the questions

It is usually best to ensure that:

- the most straightforward questions come at the start;
- the least contentious questions and least sensitive issues are dealt with at the beginning of the questionnaire;
- the sequence of questions does not lead the respondents towards 'inevitable' answers, where the answers to later questions are effectively predicated on the answers to earlier ones.

Check questions

'Check questions' are questions embedded in a questionnaire whose specific purpose is to check the respondent's answers for *consistency*. A check question is not a simple duplication of a question: it is a question that appears in a different guise but whose answer should be the same as an alternatively worded question that is placed elsewhere in the questionnaire. To the extent that check questions do provide answers that match, the researcher can feel some confidence that the questionnaire is a reliable research instrument and that the findings are valid. Where there is not a match, then it raises questions about whether the other responses on the questionnaire can be treated as honest and accurate.

'Open' and 'closed' questions

Open questions are those that leave the respondent to decide the wording of the answer, the length of the answer and the kind of matters to be raised in the answer. The questions tend to be short and the answers tend to be long. For example, the questionnaire might ask, 'How do you feel about the inclusion of nuclear arms as part of Britain's defence capability?' and then provide a number of empty lines which invite the respondent to enter his or her thoughts on the matter.

The advantage of 'open' questions is that the information gathered by way of the responses is more likely to reflect the full richness and complexity of the views held by the respondent. Respondents are allowed space to express themselves in their own words. Weighed against this, however, there are two disadvantages which are built into the use of open questions. First, they demand more effort on the part of the respondents (which might well reduce their willingness to take part in the research). Second, they leave the researcher with data which are quite 'raw' and require a lot of time-consuming analysis before they can be used.

Closed questions structure the answers by allowing only answers which fit into categories that have been established in advance by the researcher. The researcher, in this case, instructs the respondent to answer by selecting from a range of two or more options supplied on the questionnaire. The options can be restricted to as few as two (e.g. 'Yes' or 'No'; 'Male' or 'Female') or can include quite complex lists of alternatives from which the respondent can choose.

The advantages and disadvantages of the 'closed' question are more or less a mirror image of those connected with the open, unstructured approach. In a nutshell, the structure imposed on the respondents' answers provides the researcher with information that lends itself nicely to being quantified and compared. The answers, in fact, provide pre-coded data that can easily be analysed. Weighed against this, however, closed questions allow less scope for respondents to supply answers which reflect the exact facts or true feelings on a topic if the facts or opinions happen to be complicated or do not exactly fit into the range of options supplied in the questionnaire. As a result, respondents might get frustrated by not being allowed to express their views fully in a way that accounts for any sophistication, intricacy or even inconsistencies in their views.

Types of questions

There are a variety of ways in which questions can be put in a questionnaire, and these are listed in Example 11.1. However, from the outset it is worth giving some thought to whether the overall questionnaire will benefit from using a variety of kinds of questions, or whether it is better to aim for a consistent style throughout. Variety has two potential advantages. First, it stops the respondent becoming bored. Second, it stops the respondent falling into a 'pattern' of answers where, for example, on a scale of 1–5 he or she begins to put 4 down as the answer to all questions. Aiming for a consistent style of question, for its part, has the advantage of allowing the respondent to get used to the kind of questions so that they can be answered quickly and with less likelihood of confusion or misunderstanding. There is no hard and fast rule on this point: it is down to a judgement call on the part of the researcher.

Example 11.1

Ten types of question

1 An amount
Example:
How many times have you travelled from the UK to another European Union country in the past 5 years? _____

2 A 'yes/no' answer
Example:
Have you travelled from the UK to another European Union country in the past 12 months? Yes/No

3 Choose from a list of options
Example:
Which ONE of the following list of European countries do you feel has the strongest economy?

Spain	UK	Belgium	Poland
Ireland	France	Germany	Italy

4 Rank order
Example:
From the following list of European countries choose the THREE which you feel have the strongest economies and put them in rank order: 1 = strongest, 2 = second strongest, 3 = third strongest.

Spain	UK	Belgium	Poland
Ireland	France	Germany	Italy

5 Agree/disagree with a statement
Example:
Would you agree or disagree with the following statement?
European unity carries economic advantages which outweigh the political disadvantages. Agree/Disagree

6 Degree of agreement and disagreement: *the Likert Scale*
Example:
Membership of the European Union is a good thing for the UK.

Strongly agree	Agree	Neutral	Disagree	Strongly disagree

▶

▶ **7 Rate items**
Example:
How significant would you rate the following factors in affecting further
European integration?

	Not significant						Very significant
political sovereignty	1	2	3	4	5	6	7
national identities	1	2	3	4	5	6	7
past history	1	2	3	4	5	6	7
religious differences	1	2	3	4	5	6	7
language barriers	1	2	3	4	5	6	7

8 Feelings about a topic: *the semantic differential*
Example:
Progress towards European unity is:

Important	1	2	3	4	5	Unimportant
Difficult	1	2	3	4	5	Easy
Risky	1	2	3	4	5	Safe
Unlikely	1	2	3	4	5	Likely
Boring	1	2	3	4	5	Interesting

9 A list
Example:
Please list the issues you feel are most important in relation to the UK's
membership of the European Union:

_____

_____

_____

_____

10 A statement
Example:
What do you think about the UK's membership of the European Union?

_____

_____

_____

Web-based questionnaires

Web-based questionnaires are well suited to the needs of small-scale social
research. Generally, such questionnaires are designed using software provided
by an organization that 'hosts' the questionnaire and makes
it available to respondents online. The commercial companies are ones like SurveyMonkey, QuestionPro, KwikSur-
veys, Survs, and many others that are easily located by
doing an online search for 'web questionnaires'.

Link up with
Internet
surveys, p. 13.

There are some distinct advantages to using the design facilities provided by
such organizations because, as Bhaskaran and LeClaire (2010) point out:

- *They help with good practice*: There are plenty of templates and examples that are freely available which can be used as a starting point for designing the questionnaire. No need to start from scratch – help is always at hand. And the software, in any case, tends to have built-in assistance that guides you towards good practice when setting up the questions.
- *They encourage completion*: The options available for the design and layout of the questionnaire can be used to make it appealing. Colourful images and graphs are easy to incorporate within a web-based questionnaire and these can provide a means for sparking interest in the topic and encouraging the respondent to spend time completing the questionnaire.
- *They reduce potential errors*: The questionnaire can incorporate a range of features which reduce the possibility of errors creeping in during the process of completing the questionnaire. These features boost the prospects of getting questionnaires returned that have been completed fully and clearly, and which have a minimum amount of 'missing data'.
- *They help with data processing*: The respondents' answers are automatically transferred from the questionnaire into a data file. The software does not do the analysis for the researcher, but it does transfer the data from the questionnaires and puts them into a data file which is in a format that can be entered straight into an Excel spreadsheet or some equivalent. This automated process saves the researcher an awful lot of time but, perhaps even more importantly, it also removes an element of the survey process where human error can occur.

Design options for web-based questionnaires: what features are available?

The software for designing web-based questionnaires offers a large array of options. Some of them are available when you sign up for the basic 'trial' version; others come at a price when you upgrade from the free introductory package. Table 11.2 gives an overview of the main options available. Schonlau et al. (2006), however, warn against getting carried away with the design options. The emphasis should be on keeping things clean and simple, they argue, and it is for this reason that graphics and matrix questions should be used sparingly. They also advise that making questions *mandatory* can deter people from completing a questionnaire. Such forced answers should only be used when really necessary.

> **Link up with**
> Web-based questionnaire surveys, p. 14.

Table 11.2 Design options for web-based questionnaires

Templates	A range of established designs is normally available to copy or adapt
Appearance	Options for background colour, fonts and layout are available
Logos	Logos, images and other personalizing features can be inserted
Progress bar	To show respondent how far they are through the questionnaire
Identifier	Unique number; web address of sender; timestamp

(continued)

Table 11.2 Design options for web-based questionnaires (*Continued*)

Question types	Single option answer: radio buttons Multiple choice answer: check box/drop down menu Matrix questions: used for rating and scaling Rank order questions Open-ended text
Order of questions	Randomize the order of questions Question branching: respondent's answer determines subsequent series of questions Skip logic: to allow certain questions to be missed Question numbering: automatic
Response options	Mandatory answer: Respondents will not be able to submit their questionnaire unless they have answered these questions

Radio buttons and check boxes

When preparing questions for an online questionnaire it is important to distinguish between *radio buttons* and *check boxes*. Radio buttons are used when respondents need to select a single option from a list: they do not permit the respondent to enter more than one choice from the list. Check boxes (or tick boxes) allow respondents to make multiple choices from a list: they permit respondents to choose two or more choices from the list of possible answers provided by the researcher.

 [Select one from] [Check all that apply]

If the appropriate choice is not made at the design stage there will be big trouble ahead when it comes to the analysis of the data. Think: 'Do I want respondents to provide one single answer to the question I am asking, or do I want to allow them to select two or possibly more options?' If you want to allow multiple responses you need to work out in advance how you plan to analyse the data. Note that the *safer* thing to do is to stick to the radio buttons, keeping things simple and straightforward by permitting just one response to be chosen from a list of alternatives presented to respondents in the question: one answer to one question.

Advantages of questionnaires

Questionnaires are economical

They can supply a considerable amount of research data for a relatively low cost in terms of materials, money and time.

Relatively easy to arrange

Self-completion questionnaires are easier to arrange than, for example, personal interviews. Respondents are free to choose when and where they fill-in the questionnaire.

The delivery of questions is standardized

All respondents are posed exactly the same questions. And with self-completion questionnaires there is little scope for the data to be affected by *interpersonal factors* or the manner in which the questions are asked.

Data accuracy

The answers to web-based questionnaires can be fed directly into a data file, thus automating the process of data entry. This effectively eliminates the human error factor that inevitably arises when people need to read the responses to a paper questionnaire and then enter the data manually via the computer keyboard.

Online questionnaires facilitate 'accessibility'

They can be configured so that people with sight impairment or learning difficulties can have the same opportunity as others to respond to the questionnaire. This is very important in terms of equal opportunities.

Disadvantages of questionnaires

In many respects the potential disadvantages of questionnaires go hand in hand with the potential advantages.

Pre-coded questions can be frustrating

While the respondents might find it less demanding merely to tick appropriate boxes they might, equally, find this restricting and frustrating – and it could even deter respondents from completing the questionnaire.

Pre-coded questions impose a structure on the answers

This can bias the findings towards the researcher's, rather than the respondent's, way of seeing things. Questionnaires, by their very nature, start to impose a structure on the answers and shape the nature of the responses in a way that reflects the researcher's thinking rather than the respondent's. Good research practice will minimize the prospect of this, but there is always the danger that the options open to the respondent when answering the questions will channel responses away from the respondent's perception of matters to fit in with a line of thinking established by the researcher.

Checks on truthfulness

Self-completion questionnaires offer little opportunity for the researcher to check the truthfulness of the answers given by the respondents. Because the research does not take place face-to-face and because the answers are given 'at a distance' the researcher cannot rely on a number of clues that an interviewer might have about whether the answers are genuine or not.

Further reading

Brace, I. (2013) *Questionnaire Design*, 3rd edn. London: Kogan Page.
Bradburn, N. M., Sudman, S. and Wansink, B. (2004) *Asking Questions: The Definitive Guide to Questionnaire Design*, 2nd edn. San Francisco, CA: Jossey-Bass.
Gillham, B. (2007) *Developing a Questionnaire*, 2nd edn. London: Continuum.
Oppenheim, A.N. (2000) *Questionnaire Design, Interviewing and Attitude Measurement*, 2nd edn. London: Continuum.

Checklist for the use of questionnaires

When using a questionnaire for research you should feel confident about answering 'yes' to the following questions: ☑

1 Has an explanation of the purpose of the questionnaire been provided? ☐

2 Has information about the researchers (including contact details) been included? ☐

3 Are there assurances about anonymity and the confidentiality of data? ☐

4 When necessary, are instructions given on how to complete the questions? ☐

5 Have thanks been expressed to the respondents? ☐

6 Has a progress indicator been included or some alternative information about the time needed for completion of the questionnaire? ☐

7 Have the design of the questionnaire and the wording of the questions been tailored to suit the particular kind of respondents? ☐

8 Have all non-essential questions been excluded? ☐

9 Does the layout of the questionnaire make it easy to follow? ☐

10 Are the questions clear and unambiguous? ☐

11 Are the questions in a suitable order? ☐

12 Has the questionnaire been piloted? ☐

© M. Denscombe, *The Good Research Guide*. Open University Press.

12 Interviews

What is a research interview?

Research interviews are a method of data collection that uses people's answers to researchers' questions as their source of data. In this respect they have something in common with questionnaires – the data comes from what people tell the researcher. This contrasts with observational methods (which look at what people *do*) and the use of documents (where attention is given to what has been *written and recorded*). Research interviews, for their part, focus on *self-reports* – what people say they do, what they say they believe, what opinions they say they have.

Interviews and conversations

Research interviews involve a set of implicit assumptions about the situation that are not associated with a normal conversation (Denscombe 1983; Silverman 1985, 2013). When someone agrees to take part in a research interview they recognize that they are taking part in a formal piece of research and, through their agreement to be interviewed, they tacitly acknowledge that:

- *They give their consent to participation in the research.* It is explicitly a meeting intended to produce material that will be used for research purposes – and the interviewee understands this and agrees to it. From the researcher's point of view this is particularly important in relation to research ethics.
- *Interviewees' words can be used as research data.* Unless interviewees specify to the contrary, what is said during the interview can be taken as material that is both 'on record' and 'for the record'.

- *The agenda for the discussion is set by the researcher.* Although the degree of control exercised by the researcher will vary according to the style of interviewing, there is a tacit agreement built into the notion of being interviewed that the proceedings and the agenda for the discussion will be controlled by the researcher.

 Caution: Consent to be interviewed

Although agreeing to be interviewed carries an *implicit* understanding about what the interview situation entails, it is generally good practice to put these things in writing, for example as part of the 'consent form'.

Link up with
Chapter 17
Research ethics.

When is it appropriate to use interviews?

The decision to use interviews for a research project needs to take account of their feasibility as a data collection method. The first thing to be considered in this respect is the possibility of gaining *access* to potential interviewees. There is obviously no point in pursuing the idea of conducting interviews unless there are good grounds for believing that the necessary people can be accessed. Two factors come into play here. Important people are likely to be busy and might well have secretaries devoted to protecting their boss's diary. Getting a time-slot in the diary of such people might not be easy or, indeed, it might prove impossible. There is also the matter of authorization. Even if an individual agrees to be interviewed, access might depend on gaining approval for the interview from some relevant authority. This can be important in the case of people working in a formal organization, and it is absolutely vital in the case of interviewing anyone considered 'vulnerable' (e.g. children).

The next thing to consider is the *cost*. Research interviews can prove to be a relatively expensive way of collecting data. They can involve considerable travel costs if interviewees are scattered widely, and they are fairly time-consuming in terms of travel time, the time of the interview itself and the analysis of the data (see Transcribing audio recordings of interviews, p. 277). Online interviews (see below) can eliminate many of the costs but when contemplating the use of *face-to-face interviews* it is important to consider whether interviews are viable in terms of the costs in time and travel involved. Particularly with low-budget, small-scale research projects, the researcher needs to ensure that the people are not distributed too widely across a large geographical area and that conducting the interviews will not incur prohibitive costs.

The third thing to be considered is the kind of data that is required for the research project. If the aim is to collect information on simple and uncontroversial facts, or if the aim is to accumulate quantitative data, then that kind of data can be collected just as effectively but more cheaply using an alternative method. Distributing a questionnaire is likely to prove to be a more cost-effective method to use. Particularly in the context of low-budget small-scale research, the time and effort put into conducting interviews are best rewarded when the research wants to explore complex and subtle phenomena – things such as:

- *Opinions, feelings, emotions and experiences*, where the aim of the research is to understand them in depth rather than report them in a simple word or two.
- *Complex issues*, where the research focuses on complicated matters that call for a detailed understanding of how things work, how factors are inter-connected or how systems operate.
- *Privileged information*, where the opportunity arises to speak with key players in the field who can give particularly valuable insights and wisdom based on their experience or position.

 Key point

The use of interviews in small-scale research tends to involve the use of semi-structured interviews to investigate attitudes and issues in detail, and is generally used as part of qualitative research.

The structure of interviews

Interview data are collected at a meeting, or series of meetings, which are normally pre-arranged and where the interviewer and the interviewee engage in a sequence of questions and answers on a specific topic of interest to the researcher. The extent to which the sequence of questions and answers stick rigidly to an agenda can vary and it is conventional to classify interviews as being 'structured', 'semi-structured' or 'unstructured' to signify how much flexibility there is in the format of the meeting.

- *Structured interviews* involve tight control over the format of the questions and answers. In essence, the structured interview is like a questionnaire which is administered face-to-face with a respondent. The researcher has a predetermined list of questions, to which the respondent is invited to offer limited-option responses. This standardizes the process of data collection, something that is particularly useful with large-scale projects involving 'computer-assisted personal interviewing' (CAPI) with many interviewers inputting responses direct into mobile devices (tablets, smart phones, laptop computers).
- With *semi-structured interviews* the interviewer still has a clear list of issues to be addressed and questions to be answered. However, the interviewer is prepared to be flexible in terms of the order in which the topics are considered, and, perhaps more significantly, to let the interviewee develop ideas and speak more widely on the issues raised by the researcher. The answers are open-ended, and there is more emphasis on the interviewee elaborating points of interest.

- *Unstructured interviews* go further in the extent to which emphasis is placed on the interviewee's thoughts. The interviewer's role is to start the ball rolling by introducing a theme or topic, but then to be as non-directive as possible. The idea is to let interviewees develop their own ideas and pursue their own train of thought rather than have the discussion shaped by questions which the researcher already has in mind.

With semi-structured and unstructured interviews it is the possible for the interview to develop and change through the course of the project – to be used *developmentally*. Rather than keeping each interview the same, the questions asked can change from one interview to the next as a result of information given in previous interviews and a desire to follow up new lines of enquiry. Such interviews take place consecutively and are normally associated with qualitative research and approaches such as grounded theory (see Chapter 7).

Good practice

It is crucial from the start to have a clear idea about whether the research project needs a standardized interview procedure (structured) or whether it needs to develop ideas through a more flexible approach (semi- or unstructured).

One-to-one interviews

The most common form of interview is the one-to-one variety which involves a meeting between one researcher and one informant. One reason for its popularity is that it is relatively easy to arrange. Only two people's diaries need to coincide. Another advantage is that the opinions and views expressed throughout the interview stem from one source: the interviewee. This makes it fairly straightforward for the researcher to locate specific ideas with specific people. A third advantage is that the one-to-one interview is relatively easy to control. The researcher only has one person's ideas to grasp and interrogate, and one person to guide through the interview agenda. And a fourth advantage of conducting one-to-one interviews becomes evident when the researcher embarks on transcribing the interview tape: it is far easier to transcribe a recorded interview when the talk involves just one interviewee. There is only one voice to recognize and only one person talking at a time.

Group interviews

A disadvantage of the one-to-one interview is that it limits the number of views and opinions available to the researcher. Listening to one person at a time effectively restricts the number of voices that can be heard and the range of views that can be included within a research project. Group interviews, however, provide a practical solution to this. By interviewing more than one person at a time the researcher is able to dramatically increase the number and range of participants involved in the research.

Increasing the numbers involved can have benefits in terms of the representativeness of the data. The inclusion of more participants is likely to mean that a broader spectrum of people are covered by the research and that there might be a greater variety of experiences and opinions emerging from the investigation. Indeed, under certain circumstances researchers can deliberately select participants who are very different in order to gather widely differing views and experiences on the topic of the interview.

A group interview can be conducted very much like a one-to-one interview in the sense that the interviewer remains the focal point of the interaction that takes place. The questions and answers are channelled through the interviewer. The difference is that instead of each question prompting a response from just one interviewee the researcher can get perhaps four responses from four people during the interview.

An alternative vision of the group interview is one that stresses the 'group' characteristics of the interaction during an interview. It sees the group interview as distinctive in the way that it can get the participants to respond as part of a group, rather than as individuals. The researcher's incentive for using a group interview, in this case, is not a quantitative one concerned with increased numbers and improved representativeness. It is, instead, a qualitative one concerned with the way that group discussions can be more illuminating. The group discussion allows participants to listen to alternative points of view. It allows members to express support for certain views and to challenge views with which they disagree. The group interview, in this sense, trades on group dynamics. It uses the social and psychological aspects of group behaviour to foster the ability of participants to get involved, speak their minds and reflect on the views of others.

Focus groups

Focus groups consist of small groups of people who are brought together by a 'moderator' (the researcher) to explore attitudes and perceptions, feelings and ideas about a specific topic. Typically they last for 1½ to 2 hours and are useful for gauging the extent to which there are shared views among a group of people in relation to a specific topic. Ideally, focus groups have six to nine people in them. This is a large enough number to allow a range of views and opinions to be present among the group but not too large as to be unmanageable in terms of the discussion. In small-scale research projects the numbers are often smaller. The reason for this is that focus groups can be costly and time-consuming to arrange. It is not easy to organize a venue for the meeting and get six or more people to turn up on time. And it can prove to be quite expensive if the researcher needs to fund participants' travel and pay for the room.

Focus groups have three distinctive features which mark them out as different from other kinds of interview:

- there is a *focus* to the session, with the group discussion being based on an item or experience about which all participants have similar knowledge;

- the moderator's role is to *facilitate* the group interaction rather than lead the discussion;
- particular emphasis is placed on *group dynamics* and interaction within the group as means of eliciting information.

During a focus group session participants are encouraged to discuss the topic among themselves. This interaction helps the researcher to understand the reasoning behind the views and opinions that are expressed by group members. It provides the researcher with a method of investigating the participants' reasoning and a means for exploring underlying factors that might explain why people hold the opinions and feelings they do. As Morgan (2006: 121) puts it:

> [Focus group members] share their experiences and thoughts, while also comparing their own contributions to what others have said. This process of sharing and comparing is especially useful for hearing and understanding a range of responses on a research topic. The best focus groups thus not only provide data on *what* the participants think but also *why* they think the way they do.

Such sharing and comparing of personally held points of view can lead in either of two directions – both of which can be of value to the researcher. The group discussion can lead to some consensus with members of the group largely agreeing and arriving at some shared viewpoint. Alternatively, the group discussion might serve to expose significant differences among group members in which case the researcher is presented with data about a range of opinions and feelings relating to the topic. Either way, the benefit of the discussion and interaction, questioning and reflection, is that it reveals the reasoning and underlying logic used by participants. It thus gives the researcher an insight into not only what people think, but also *why* they hold those views.

The success of a focus group, however, depends on establishing a climate of trust within the group, and it is a key part of the role of the moderator to foster a situation in which participants feel at ease and sufficiently comfortable in the company of the other group members to express themselves freely. A crucial factor here is *confidentiality*. Group members need to feel assured that if they express a personal feeling or reveal some aspect of their personal life during the discussion that such information will be treated as confidential by the group. What is said by individuals during the focus group session ought to remain private and not be disclosed publicly by other members of the group.

The interviewer effect

Personal identity

People respond differently depending on how they perceive the person asking the questions. In particular, the *sex*, the *age* and the *ethnic origins* of the interviewer have a bearing on the amount of information people are willing to divulge and their honesty about what they reveal. The data, in other words, are affected by the personal identity of the researcher.

The impact of the researcher's personal identity, of course, will depend on who is being interviewed. It is not, strictly speaking, the identity in its own right that affects the data, but what the researcher's identity means as far as the person being interviewed is concerned. And, of course, the effect of the researcher's identity will also depend on the nature of the topic being discussed. On sensitive issues or on matters regarded as rather personal, the interviewer's identity assumes particular importance. If the research is dealing with religious beliefs, with earnings, with sexual relationships, with personal health or any of a host of similar issues, the sex, age and ethnicity of the interviewer in relation to the sex, age and ethnicity of the interviewee are very likely to influence the nature of the data that emerge – their fullness and their honesty. On some questions people can be embarrassed. They can feel awkward or defensive. Whenever this is the case, there is the possibility that interviewees might supply answers which they feel fit in with what the researcher expects from them – fulfilling the perceived expectations of the researcher. Or the answers might tend to be tailored to match what the interviewee suspects is the researcher's point of view, keeping the researcher happy. Either way, the quality of the data suffers.

From the perspective of the small-scale project researcher there is a limit to what can be done about this. Although interviews conducted over the Internet, and to a lesser extent interviews conducted by phone, do provide some possibilities for disguising who we are, there are definite limits to the extent that researchers can disguise their 'self' during face-to-face interviews. We bring to such interviews certain personal attributes which are 'givens' and which cannot be altered on a whim to suit the needs of the research interview. *Our sex, our age, our ethnic origin, our accent, even our occupational status, all are aspects of our 'self' which, for practical purposes, cannot be changed.* We can make efforts to be polite and punctual, receptive and neutral, in order to encourage the right climate for an interviewee to feel comfortable and provide honest answers. What we cannot do is change these biographical attributes.

Good practice: Be aware of the interviewer effect

Social researchers should consider the following questions:

- What are the social status, educational qualifications and professional expertise of the people to be interviewed, and how do these compare with my own? Is this likely to affect the interviewer–interviewee relationship in a positive or negative manner?
- Is there likely to be an age gap between myself and the interviewee(s) and, if so, how might this affect the interview?
- In relation to the topic being researched, will interviewing someone of the opposite sex or a different ethnic group have an impact on their willingness to answer questions openly and honestly?

Self-presentation

Conventional advice to researchers has been geared to minimizing the impact of researchers on the outcome of the research by having them adopt a passive and neutral stance. The idea is that the researcher:

- presents himself or herself in a light which is designed not to antagonize or upset the interviewee (conventional clothes, courtesy, etc.);
- remains neutral and non-committal on the statements made during the interview by the interviewee.

Passivity and neutrality are the order of the day. The researcher's 'self', adopting this approach, is kept firmly hidden beneath a cloak of cordiality and receptiveness to the words of the interviewee. To a certain degree, this is sound advice. The researcher, after all, is there to listen and learn, not to preach. The point is to get the interviewee to open up, not to provoke hostility or put the interviewee on the defensive.

Personal involvement

One line of reasoning argues that a cold and calculating style of interviewing reinforces a gulf between the researcher and the informant, and does little to help or empower the informant. Now, if the aims of the research are specifically to help or empower the people being researched, rather than dispassionately learn from them, then the approach of the interviewer will need to alter accordingly (Oakley 1981). Under these circumstances, the researcher will be inclined to show emotion, to respond with feeling and to engage in a true dialogue with the interviewee. The researcher will become fully involved as a person with feelings, with experiences and with knowledge that can be shared with the interviewee. A word of warning, though. This style of interviewing remains 'unconventional', and the researcher needs to be confident and committed to make it work. The researcher also needs to feel sure that his or her audience understand and share the underlying logic of the approach rather than expecting the researcher to adopt the cool and dispassionate stance.

Skills for face-to-face interviewing

A good research interview is not simply a casual conversation. This point has already been made. Unlike casual conversations, research interviews require a good deal of concentrated effort if they are to be successful. The researcher needs to think about how to get the best response from the interviewee and how to make the interview as productive as possible in terms of the aims of the research. This is particularly the case with face-to-face interviews. In this context:

- *The good interviewer needs to be attentive.* This may sound obvious, but it is all too easy to lose the thread of the discussion because the researcher needs to be monitoring a few other things while listening closely to what the informant has to say: writing the field notes, looking for relevant non-verbal communication, checking that the recorder is working.

- *The good interviewer is sensitive to the feelings of the informant.* This is not just a matter of social courtesy, though that is certainly a worthy aspect of it. It is also a skill which is necessary for getting the best out of an interview. Where interviewers are able to empathize with the informant and to gauge the feelings of the informant, they will be in a better position to coax out the most relevant information.

- *The good interviewer is able to tolerate silences* during the talk, and knows when to shut up and say nothing. Anxiety is the main danger. Fearing that the interview might be on the verge of breaking down, the researcher can feel the need to say something quickly to kick-start the discussion. Worrying about cramming in every possible gem of wisdom in the allotted time, the interviewer can be inclined to rush the informant on quickly to the next point. But, most of all, feeling uncomfortable when the conversation lapses into silence, the interviewer can be all too quick to say something when a more experienced interviewer would know that the silence can be used as a wonderful resource during interviews.

- *The good interviewer is adept at using prompts.* Although silences can be productive, the interviewer needs to exercise judgement on this. There are times during an interview when the researcher might feel that it is necessary to spur the informant to speak. Listed below are some examples of how this can be done. What the examples share is a degree of subtlety. It is not normally acceptable for research interviewers to *demand* that the informant answers the questions. Research interviews are not police interviews. The idea is to nudge the informant gently into revealing their knowledge or thoughts on a specific point.

- *The good interviewer is adept at using probes.* There are occasions during an interview when the researcher might want to delve deeper into a topic rather than let the discussion flow on to the next point. An informant might make a point in passing which the researcher thinks should be explored in more detail. Some explanation might be called for, or some justification for a comment. Some apparent inconsistency in the informant's line of reasoning might be detected, an inconsistency which needs unravelling. Without being aggressive the good interviewer knows how to probe points further when it is required.

- *The good interviewer is adept at using checks.* One of the major advantages of interviews is that they offer the researcher the opportunity to check that he or she has understood the informant correctly. As an ongoing part of the normal talk during interviews, the researcher can present a summary of what they think the informant has said, which the informant can then confirm as an accurate understanding, or can correct if it is felt to be a misunderstanding of what has been said. Such checks can be used at strategic points during the interview as a way of concluding discussion on one aspect of the topic.

- *The good interviewer is non-judgemental.* As far as possible interviewers should suspend personal values and *adopt a non-judgemental stance* in relation to the topics covered during the interview. This means not only biting your lip on occasion, but also taking care not to reveal disgust, surprise or pleasure through facial gestures. The good interviewer must also *respect the rights of the interviewee*. This means accepting if a person simply does not wish to tell you something and knowing when to back off if the discussion is beginning to cause the interviewee particular embarrassment or stress. This is a point of personal sensitivity and research ethics.

* *With group interviews and focus groups, the good interviewer/facilitator manages to let everyone have a say.* It is vital to avoid the situation where a dominant personality hogs the discussion and bullies others in the group to agree with his or her opinion.

Good practice: Tactics for interviews – prompts, probes and checks

Prompts: Offer some examples (to help with answering the question)
Repeat the last few words spoken by the interviewee (to invite them to continue)
Repeat the question (to clarify and allow more time for a response)
Remain silent (to allow a pause that encourages them to pursue their thoughts)

Probes: Ask for an example
Ask for clarification
Ask for more details

Check: Summarize their thoughts, e.g. So, if I understand you correctly . . .
What this means, then, is that . . .

Conducting a face-to-face interview

Planning the interview

In the case of face-to-face interviews, securing an agreement to be interviewed is normally easier if the prospective interviewee is *contacted in advance*. This allows both parties to arrange a mutually convenient time for the interview. At this point, of course, the researcher will probably be asked how long the interview will take, and should therefore be in a position to respond. It is most unlikely that busy people will feel comfortable with a suggestion that the interview will 'take as long as it takes'. The researcher needs to make a bid for an *agreed length of time* whether it be 15 minutes, half an hour, 45 minutes or an hour.

Where a face-to-face interview takes place 'on site', events are sometimes beyond the control of the researcher. This means there is an added danger that things can go wrong. Through whatever means, though, the researcher needs to try to get a *location for the interview* which will not be disturbed, which offers privacy, which has fairly good acoustics and which is reasonably quiet. This can prove to be a pretty tall order in places like busy organizations, schools, hospitals, and so on. But at least the desirability of such a venue should be conveyed to the person arranging the interview room.

Within the interview room, it is important to be able to set up the *seating arrangements* in a way that allows comfortable interaction between the researcher and the interviewee(s). In a one-to-one interview the researcher should try to arrange seating so that the two parties are at a 90 degree angle to each other. This allows for eye contact without the confrontational feeling arising from sitting directly opposite the other person. With group interviews, it is important to arrange the seating to allow contact between all parties without hiding individuals at the back of the group or outside the group.

Introduction and formalities

At the beginning of a research interview there should be the opportunity to say 'Hello', to do some introductions, to talk about the aims of the research and to say something about the origins of the researcher's own interest in the topic. During the initial phase, there should also be confirmation that you have permission to record the discussion and reassurances about the confidentiality of comments made during the interview. The aim is to set the tone for the rest of the interview – normally a relaxed atmosphere in which the interviewee feels free to open up on the topic under consideration. *Trust* and *rapport* are the keywords.

During the pre-interview phase, the interviewer should do two other things:

- prepare the recording equipment;
- as far as possible, arrange the seating positions to best advantage.

Starting the interview

The first question takes on a particular significance for the interview. It should offer the interviewee the chance to settle down and relax. For this reason it is normally good practice to *kick off with an 'easy' question*: something on which the interviewee might be expected to have well-formulated views and something that is quite near the forefront of their mind. Two tactics might help here.

- Ask respondents, in a general way, about themselves and their role as it relates to the overall area of the interview. This allows the researcher to collect valuable *background information about informants* while, at the same time, letting informants start off by covering familiar territory.
- *Use some 'trigger' or 'stimulus' material*, so that the discussion can relate to something concrete, rather than launch straight into abstract ideas.

Monitoring progress

During the interview the researcher should keep a discreet eye on the time. The good researcher needs to wind things up within the allotted time and will have covered most of the key issues during that time. While doing this the good interviewer also needs to attend to the following things during the progress of the interview itself:

- *Identify the main points being stated by the interviewee* and the priorities as expressed by the interviewee. With focus groups, what consensus is emerging about the key points?
- Look for the underlying logic of what is being said by the informant. *The interviewer needs to 'read between the lines'* to decipher the rationale lying beneath the surface of what is being said. The interviewer should ask 'What are they really telling me here?' and, perhaps more significantly, 'What are they *not* mentioning?'
- *Look for inconsistencies* in the position being outlined by the interviewee. If such inconsistencies exist, this does not invalidate their position. Most people have inconsistencies in their opinions and feelings on many topics. However, such inconsistencies will be worth probing as the interview progresses to see what they reveal.
- Pick up clues about whether the informant's answers involve an element of *boasting* or are answers intended to *please the interviewer*.
- Be constantly on the look-out for the kind of answer that is a *'fob-off'*.
- *Get a feel for the context* in which the discussion is taking place. The priorities expressed by the interviewee might reflect events immediately prior to the interview, or things about to happen in the near future. They might be 'issues of the moment', which would not assume such importance were the interview to be conducted a few weeks later. The researcher needs to be sensitive to this possibility and find out from the interviewee if there are events which are influencing priorities in this way.
- Keep a suitable level of eye contact throughout the interview and *make a note of non-verbal communication* which might help a later interpretation of the interview talk.

Finishing the interview

Having kept an eye on the time, and having ensured that most of the required areas for discussion have been covered, the interviewer should draw events to a close making sure that:

- the interviewee is invited to raise any points that they think still need to be covered and have not been covered so far;
- the interviewee is thanked for having given up the time to participate in the interview.

 Caution: Interviews are more than a conversation

The superficial similarity between an interview and a conversation should not lead the researcher into thinking that interviewing is an easy option when it comes to data collection. The research interview, like any other method, requires proper planning and the use of appropriate techniques and skills.

Recording the interview

Memory is a rather unreliable way of capturing the discussion that happens during a face-to-face interview. As psychologists tell us, human memory is prone to partial recall, bias and error. Interviewers, instead, should rely on other more permanent records of what was said.

Audio and video recordings

In practice, most face-to-face interviewers rely on *audio recordings*. Initially, interviewees can feel rather inhibited by the process of recording but most participants become more relaxed after a short while. When used sensitively, audio recording does not pose too much of a disturbance to interview situations, and it has certain clear benefits. Audio recordings offer a *permanent record* and one that is fairly complete in terms of the speech that occurs. They also lend themselves to being checked by other researchers. However, the downside is that they capture only speech, and miss non-verbal communication and other contextual factors. Video recordings, for their part, capture non-verbal as well as verbal communications and offer a more complete record of events during the interview. And, as with audio recordings, they provide a permanent record that can be checked by other researchers. The use of video recordings, however, tends to be the exception rather than the rule. It is not the cost factor that explains this because video equipment is not particularly expensive. Generally, it is the intrusiveness of video recordings that deters researchers from using them. For practical purposes most interviewers would consider that audio recordings provide data that are good enough for the purpose of the research, and that the benefits gained through the video recording of an interview are outweighed by the extra disruption that video recording brings to the setting.

> **Link up with**
> Transcribing
> audio recordings
> of interviews,
> p. 277.

Good practice: Recording equipment

Use equipment that is good enough to supply adequate sound (or visual) reproduction.

- Be certain that the equipment is functioning well before the interview.
- Have a reliable power source plus back-up in case of emergency.
- Choose storage devices that have enough memory, or last long enough, to cover the planned duration of the interview.

Field notes

Under certain circumstances interviewers will need to rely on field notes. Most commonly this occurs when interviewees decline to be recorded. When this happens it raises the prospect of there being no record of the actual discussion that takes place. This means that the words spoken during the interview will always remain a matter of recollection and interpretation. Of course, where the discussion touches on sensitive issues, commercially, politically or even personally, this might well suit the needs of certain interviewees. Field notes, however, offer a compromise in such situations. Provided that they are written during the interview or, if this is not feasible, as soon afterwards as possible while events remain fresh in the mind, they provide the interviewer with some permanent record of the event which can be referred to at various later stages in the research in order to refresh the memory about what was said.

Field notes, however, can play another role in relation to interviews: they can be used as a *complement to audio recording*. They can be used to fill in some of the relevant information that a recording alone might miss. Field notes can cover information relating to the context of the location, the climate and atmosphere under which the interview was conducted, clues about the intent behind the statements and comments on aspects of non-verbal communication as they were deemed relevant to the interview.

Good practice: Write field notes as a complement to audio recordings

When conducting face-to-face interviews it is valuable to combine the use of audio recording with field notes that provide important supplementary information.

Online interviews

Online interviews can be conducted with anyone who has access to a computer and the Internet. The costs are negligible and this mode of conducting interviews allows the researcher to interview people across the world without worrying about the time and costs of travel. This is obviously an attractive proposition.

Real time with visual contact

Online interviews can take place in real time and include visual contact between the interviewer and the interviewee. Using a webcam and communication software like Skype the interview can be conducted very much like a face-to-face interview – only at a distance. Such Skype interviews share the benefits and the drawbacks associated with the personal interaction involved in face-to-face interviews but avoid the costs and inconvenience associated with travel.

Without direct visual contact

Online interviews can be conducted in ways that do not include real-time visual interaction between the interviewer and the interviewee. An online interview can be based on straightforward email correspondence with a sequence of written questions prompting follow-up answers from the respondents. Or it can take place using social networking sites, discussion forums or even SMS text messaging. Basically, interviews can be conducted online using any of the available communication platforms. Like face-to-face interviews these kinds of interview retain a basic question and answer sequence. There are, however, some significant differences that need to be taken into account, and these are outlined below.

Recording online data

One distinct advantage to conducting online interviews is that the responses are provided in *written format*. There is, therefore, no need to transcribe verbal statements which, in turn, means there are no transcription errors, nor are there any indecipherable parts of the interview which are unusable. Added to that, the responses are already in a digital format that can be downloaded directly into a word processor or qualitative data analysis software (e.g. NVivo).

Private contact with interviewees

The use of social networking sites, discussion forums and, indeed, any online technology for interviews depends crucially on one thing: it must allow *private exchanges* between the interviewer and the interviewees. When conducting one-to-one interviews online it is essential that the exchanges are private and that care is taken to avoid the messages getting distributed to other users. With group interviews and focus groups online the same proviso operates: the communication must be restricted to just those people directly involved.

 Caution: Online interviews

Care needs to be taken to ensure that questions and especially the answers are not broadcast to everyone using the network or forum.

Remoteness

In contrast with face-to-face interviews there is *no direct visual contact* involved. The effect of this is that the respondent is more 'remote' and distant not just in a physical sense but in a psychological sense as well. And this can have some interesting consequences. On the downside, it means that the researcher has less opportunity to confirm the identity of the interviewee or verify the information given by that person. It can be difficult to know for certain who the respondent is or that their answers are genuine and honest.

Weighed against this, the remoteness can have its benefits. The most significant of these is that it can reduce the 'interviewer effect' through the way it does the following:

- *Reduces the culture and gender effects of interaction.* The absence of visual clues means that what is stated by the interviewees is less likely to be affected by status factors linked to the respective age, sex, ethnicity, accent and social class of the interviewer and the interviewee. It acts as an 'equalizer' in terms of the communication.

- *Overcomes embarrassment on some topics.* The lack of face-to-face contact can help to reduce any sense of discomfort when responding to questions on sensitive topics. The contact, being less 'personal', is less likely to cause embarrassment because there is no direct interaction with the researcher. There is no need to feel awkward in the presence of a researcher whose age, sex, social class or ethnic origin could inhibit the interviewee from giving a candid and honest answer. A cautionary note, however, is needed on this point. As so often happens with research methods there can be exceptions to the rule. Sometimes the personal element of face-to-face interviews might actually be a crucial factor encouraging people to talk openly about intimate issues, more so than they would have done in an email interview (Gillham 2005). This is more likely to happen with depth, unstructured interviews where a good rapport and climate of trust are developed between the interviewer and the interviewee.

Time delay

Another difference from conventional face-to-face interviews is that, depending on the particular online platform being used, there can be a time-delay between the questions and answers. Again, this can have an impact on the information provided by the respondent. Specifically it allows interviewees *time to reflect on the question* and provide a response that they have had time to think about carefully. Now this could be a good thing from the researcher's point of view, or it might not be if the researcher is hoping to get a fast reaction to the question rather than a cautiously considered answer.

Written responses to interview questions

Online interviews generally require the respondents to *write* their answers rather than speak them. An important thing to bear in mind here is that there can be a significant difference in the way people express themselves verbally compared with the way they express themselves in writing. At one level this could affect the *style* of language. In the context of an online interview people might use the kind of informal 'text talk' and abbreviations associated with online media and social networks, whereas in the context of a face-to-face interview a more formal style might be adopted. At another level it can affect the *quantity* of data gathered through the interview. A likely consequence of needing to write answers is that interviewees will use fewer words than they would have done if they were talking to an interviewer face-to-face. As is so often the case with social research methods, however, there is not a hard and fast rule on this. With interviewing a lot depends on how confident and articulate the person is in face-to-face situations. Someone who is shy could well prefer to write a response and perhaps go into greater depth and detail using a keyboard than talking directly to a researcher in a face-to-face interviewer situation.

Key point: Online interviews

If the online interview does not make use of software like Skype to conduct the equivalent of a face-to-face interview, then researchers need to weigh up the likely consequences of collecting interview data in terms of:

- the remoteness and loss of visual contact
- the time-delay between interactions
- the reliance on written answers rather than spoken words.

How do you know the informant is telling the truth?

This is a crucial question facing research interviews. When the interview is concerned with gathering information of a factual nature the researcher can make some checks to see if the information is broadly corroborated by other people and other sources. When the interview concerns matters such as the emotions, feelings and experiences of the interviewee, it is a lot more difficult to make such checks. Ultimately, there is no absolute way of verifying what someone tells you about their thoughts and feelings. Researchers are not 'mind readers'. But there are still some practical checks researchers can make to gauge the credibility of what they have been told. It should be stressed, though, that these are not watertight methods of detecting false statements given during interviews. They are practical ways of helping the researcher to avoid being a gullible dupe who accepts all that he or she is told at face value. They help the researcher to 'smell a rat'. By the same token, if the following checks are used, the researcher can have greater confidence in the interview data, knowing that some effort has been made to ensure the validity of the data.

Check the data with other sources

The researcher should make efforts to corroborate the interview data with other sources of information on the topic. *Triangulation* should be used. Documents and observations can provide some back-up for the content of the interview, or can cast some doubt on how seriously the interview data should be taken. Interview content can even be checked against other interviews to see if there is some level of consistency. The point is that interview data should not be taken at face value if it is at all possible to confirm or dispute the statements using alternative sources.

Link up with Triangulation, p. 154.

Check the transcript with the informant

Where possible, the researcher should go back to the interviewee with the transcript to check with that person that it is an accurate record. This is known as 'respondent validation'. If the researcher is solely concerned with gathering facts from the interview, this is an opportunity to ensure that the facts are correct and that the interviewer has got the correct information. That is a nice safeguard. If, alternatively, the interview is concerned with a person's emotions, opinions and experiences, the exercise invites the interviewee to confirm that the views expressed during the interview were meant, and not something given 'in the heat of the moment'. Either way, there is an initial check on the accuracy of the data.

Check the plausibility of the data

Some people are interviewed specifically because they are in a position to know about the things that interest the researcher. The 'key players' are picked out precisely because they are specialists, experts, highly experienced – and their testimony carries with it a high degree of credibility. This is not necessarily the case with those chosen for interview on some other grounds. When assessing the credibility of information contained in an interview, the researcher needs to gauge how far an informant might be expected to be in possession of the facts and to know about the topic being discussed. The researcher should ask if it is reasonable to suppose that such a person would be in a position to comment authoritatively on the topic – or is there a chance that they are talking about something of which they have little knowledge?

Look for themes

Where possible, interview research should avoid basing its findings on one interview. It is safer to look for themes emerging from a number of interviews. Where themes emerge across a number of interviews, the researcher does not have to rely on any one person's statements as the sole source of what is 'real' or 'correct'. A recurrent theme in interviews indicates that the idea/issue is something that is shared among a wider group, and therefore the researcher can refer to it with rather more confidence than any idea/issue that stems from the words of one individual.

| Link up with |
| Chapter 16 |
| Qualitative data. |

Advantages of interviews

Depth of information

Interviews are particularly good at producing data which deal with topics in depth and in detail. Subjects can be probed, issues pursued and lines of investigation followed over a relatively lengthy period.

Insights

The researcher is likely to gain valuable insights based on the depth of the information gathered and the wisdom of 'key informants'.

Equipment

Interviews require only simple equipment (digital recorder, computer, online connection).

Informants' priorities

Interviews are a good method for producing data based on informants' priorities, opinions and ideas. Informants have the opportunity to expand their ideas, explain their views and identify what *they* regard as the crucial factors.

Flexibility

With semi-structured and unstructured interviews adjustments to the lines of enquiry can be made during the interview itself. Interviewing allows for a developing line of enquiry.

High response rate

Interviews are generally prearranged and scheduled for a convenient time and location. This ensures a relatively high response rate.

Validity of the data

In the case of face-to-face interviews, direct contact at the point of the interview means that data can be checked for accuracy and relevance as they are collected. In the case of online interviews there is also the elimination of errors at the data entry stage. The researcher is no longer faced with passages in an audio-recorded interview where voices cannot be heard clearly and where there is consequently some doubt about what was actually said.

Therapeutic

Interviews can be a rewarding experience for the informant. Compared with questionnaires, observation and experiments, there is a more personal element to the method, and people tend to enjoy the rather rare chance to talk about their ideas at length to a person whose purpose is to listen and note the ideas without being critical.

Disadvantages of interviews

Validity of the data

The data from interviews are based on what people say rather than what they do. The two may not tally. What people say they do, what they say they prefer and what they say they think cannot automatically be assumed to reflect the truth.

Interviewer effect

Interviewee statements can be affected by the identity of the researcher. However, online interviews can go a long way towards avoiding this problem.

Reliability

With semi-structured and unstructured interviews consistency is hard to achieve. The data collected are, to an extent, affected by the specific context and the specific individuals involved.

Time-consuming

Semi-structured and unstructured interviews produce data that are not pre-coded and have a relatively open format. This means that data preparation and analysis are generally 'end-loaded'. The transcribing and coding of interview data are a major task for the researcher which occurs *after* the data have been collected.

Resources

With face-to-face interviews the costs of the interviewer's time and travel can be relatively high, particularly if the informants are geographically dispersed.

Inhibitions

In the case of face-to-face interviews, the audio recorder (or video recorder) can inhibit the informant. Although the impact of the recording device tends to wear off quite quickly, this is not always the case. Online interviews, of course, do not have this problem.

Invasion of privacy

Tactless interviewing can be an invasion of privacy and/or upsetting for the informant. While interviews can be enjoyable, the other side of the coin is that the personal element of being interviewed carries its own kinds of dangers as well.

Further reading

Diamante, T. (2013) *Effective Interviewing and Information Gathering: Proven Tactics to Increase the Power of Your Questioning Skills*. New York: McGraw-Hill/Business Expert Press.

Gillham, B. (2005) *Research Interviewing: The Range of Techniques*. Maidenhead: Open University Press.

Kamberelis, G. and Dimitriadis, G. (2013) *Focus Groups: From Structured Interviews to Collective Conversations*. London: Routledge.

Keats, D. M. (2000) *Interviewing: A Practical Guide for Students and Professionals*. Maidenhead: Open University Press.

Checklist for the use of interviews

When conducting interviews you should feel confident about answering 'yes' to the following questions: ☑

1 Is it clear which type of interview is being used and why (one-to-one, group, online, focus group)? ☐

2 Does the format of the interview match the aims of the research in terms of the kind of data that is required (structured, semi-structured, unstructured) ☐

3 Have field notes been written to provide supplementary information about the interaction during the interview? ☐

4 Have relevant details been collected about the context within which the interviews took place (location, prior events, ambience, etc.)? ☐

5 Has consideration been given to the effect of the recording equipment on the openness with which informants replied? ☐

6 Where possible, have attempts been made to check the accuracy and honesty of statements made by interviewees (triangulation, respondent validation)? ☐

7 With semi-structured and unstructured interviews have prompts, probes and checks been used to gain worthwhile, detailed insights? ☐

8 Has consideration been given to the interviewer effect and the way the researcher's self-identity might have affected:
   • the interaction during the interview? ☐
   • the interpretation of the data? ☐

9 With online interviews has consideration been given to the effects of:
   • the loss of visual clues during the interaction? ☐
   • the use of non-real-time communication? ☐

© M. Denscombe, *The Good Research Guide*. Open University Press.

13 Observation

What is observational research?

There are essentially two kinds of observational research used in the social sciences. The first of these is *systematic observation* (also known as 'structured observation'). Systematic observation has its origins in social psychology – in particular, the study of interaction in settings such as school classrooms. It is normally linked with the production of quantitative data and the use of statistical analysis. The second is *participant observation*. This is mainly associated with sociology and anthropology, and is used by researchers to investigate the lifestyles, cultures and beliefs of particular social groups. It is normally associated with qualitative data and ethnographic approaches to research.

These two methods might seem poles apart in terms of their origins and their use in current social research, but they share some vital characteristics:

- *Direct observation.* They both rely on direct evidence of the eye to witness events at first hand. In this respect they stand together, in contrast to methods such as questionnaires and interviews, which base their data on what informants tell the researcher, and in contrast to documents where the researcher tends to be one step removed from the action.
- *Fieldwork in natural settings.* They both rely on collecting data in real-life situations, out there 'in the field'. Fieldwork observation occurs in situations

which would have occurred whether or not the research had taken place. The whole point is to observe things as they normally happen, rather than as they happen under artificially created conditions such as laboratory experiments. There is a major concern to avoid disrupting the *naturalness of the setting* when undertaking the research. In this approach to social research, it becomes very important to minimize the extent to which the presence of the researcher might alter the situation being researched.

- *The issue of perception.* Systematic observation and participant observation both recognize that the process of observing is far from straightforward. Both are acutely sensitive to the possibility that researchers' perceptions of situations might be influenced by personal factors and that the data collected could thus be unreliable. They offer very different ways of overcoming this, but both see it as a problem that needs to be addressed.

Perception and memory

On the basis of common sense it might seem fairly obvious that two researchers looking at the same event will record precisely the same things as having happened. Their records of the events – the data – should be identical. Yet in practice this might not be the case. It is quite possible that the two researchers will produce different records of the thing they jointly witnessed. Why should this be the case? Obviously, the competence of each individual researcher is a factor which has to be taken into consideration. The powers of observation, the powers of recall and the level of commitment of individual researchers will vary, and this will have an effect on the observational data that are produced. However, the variation in records also reflects more general psychological factors connected to memory and perception, and there are three things which are particularly important that emerge from the work of psychologists in this area.

First, psychologists point to the frailties of human memory and the way that we cannot possibly remember each and every detail of the events and situations we observe. Basically, we forget most of what we see. But what we forget and what we recall are not decided at random. There is a pattern to the way the mind manages to recall certain things and forget others. There is *selective recall*.

Second, they point to the way the mind filters the information it receives through the senses. It not only acts to reduce the amount of information, it also operates certain 'filters' which let some kinds of information through to be experienced as 'what happened', while simultaneously putting up barriers to many others. There is *selective perception*.

Third, they point to experiments which show how these filters not only let in some information while excluding the rest, but also boost our sensitivity to certain signals depending on our emotional and physical state, and our past experiences. What we experience can be influenced to some extent by whether we are, for instance, very hungry, angry, anxious, frustrated, prejudiced, etc. What we experience is shaped by our feelings at the moment and by the emotional baggage we carry around with us as a result of significant things that have happened to us during our lifetime. These things account for *accentuated perception*.

Without delving too deeply into the psychology of perception, it is easy to appreciate that, as human beings, researchers do not simply observe and record the events they witness in some mechanical and straightforward fashion. In practice, there is *an element of interpretation* with the mind acting as an intermediary between 'the world out there' and the way it is experienced by the individual.

Systematic observation

The possibility that different observers might produce different records of the situation is rather worrying when it comes to the use of observation as a method for collecting data. It suggests that the data could vary depending on the particular observer rather than the event being researched. But it is precisely this problem which is addressed by *systematic* observation. Systematic observation, as the name suggests, is a research method that introduces a system to the process of observation, a system that aims to produce data that are consistent between observers – eliminating variations arising from the psychological factors that influence individual researchers' perceptions of events and situations.

Observation schedules

To achieve this aim, systematic observation makes use of *observation schedules*. These schedules contain a list of items that act much like a checklist. All observers involved with a project use identical schedules and thus have their attention directed to the same things. This helps to make the record of the events consistent between researchers because *what* is being observed is dictated by the items contained in the schedule.

Observation schedules not only specify *what* is to be observed, they also specify *how* those things are to be measured. This is important. The data collected by different observers are hardly likely to be consistent and standardized simply by directing attention to key items of interest and then leaving it up to individual observers to decide how they record the item. Individuals could choose different terms to describe what they see and produce collections of data that, while focused on the same event or behaviour, might vary widely in format and detail. To be *systematic* the observation needs to include some way of ensuring that that the events or behaviour are recorded in an objective and consistent manner. This is done by collecting *quantitative* data based on counts, amounts and frequencies relating to the item of interest. Rather than portray the events or behaviour in words, the purpose of the observation schedule is to produce data using things like:

- the *frequency of events*: making a numerical count of the frequency with which the items on the observation schedule occur.
- the *duration of events*: quantifying the amount of time covered by an event or taken by a specific behaviour. When instances of the item occur they are timed, start to finish, so that the researcher gets information on the total time

for each item and the points at which it occurred during the overall time-block for the period of observation.

When researchers are properly trained and experienced there should be a good *inter-observer reliability* with different researchers producing almost identical data when observing the same social setting. The influence of the individual researcher and factors affecting his/her perception and memory should be minimal.

Good practice

Observation schedules should:

- ensure that all researchers are alert to the same activities and looking out for the same things;
- get researchers to record data systematically and in a standardized fashion

---

Selection of specific items for inclusion in the observation schedule

Events and behaviour that occur within social settings tend to be complex and multi-faceted. This creates a challenge for researchers wishing to use systematic observation. In settings where they might want to use an observation schedule it is likely that there will be many things going on at the same time – so many, indeed, that it would be impossible for any observation schedule to cover every aspect of what happens in the setting. Inevitably, then, researchers need to exercise some *selectivity* in terms of the items they include in the schedule and the ones they leave off the list.

When selecting which events or behaviours to include in the observation schedule there are four basic things that need to be taken into consideration. First and foremost, the items to be included should be valid indicators of the topic that is being investigated. Obviously, the findings from an observation schedule will only be of value if the items listed in the schedule are the most *relevant* for the purposes of the investigation. Precise records of something that is irrelevant will not advance the research at all. Previous research and previous theories provide the key to deciding what things warrant attention and, initially, a *literature review* should be used to identify significant things to be included in the observation schedule.

Second, the items that are included should cover all possibilities: they should be *complete*. Care needs to be taken to ensure, as far as is possible, that the categories on the observation schedule cover the full range of possibilities and that there are not gaps which will become glaringly evident once the observation schedule is used in the field.

Third, the items should be *clear-cut and self-evident*. Observers should not need to decipher the action or wonder whether an action fits one or another category – it should be fairly obvious. This means that items on the schedule should only include *overt behaviours and events* that are observable in a direct manner. Things like attitudes and thoughts that need to be inferred by the researcher are not suitable because they are not visible in a direct manner. It also means that the items need to be *precise*. There should be no ambiguity and no overlap between the items on the observation schedule.

Last, but not least, the choice of items for inclusion in the schedule needs to be conscious of practical issues relating to the *frequency and sequencing* of events to be observed. On the one hand the items should occur with *sufficient regularity* for the observer to be able to collect a reasonable amount of data. If the event is something that occurs infrequently and is relatively rare, it will prove frustrating and wasteful of time to have a researcher poised – waiting, waiting, waiting for something to happen. On the other hand if the actions or events are too frequent it might be impossible for the observer to keep up to speed. If the events are bunched and all come at once the observer might well find it impossible to log all instances.

 Key point: Suitability of events or behaviour for observation

The events or behaviour selected for inclusion in an observation schedule should be:

- relevant – the best indicators of the thing being investigated;
- complete – include the full range of possibilities for the item;
- overt – observable and measurable in a direct manner;
- obvious – require a minimum of interpretation by the researcher;
- precise – there should be no ambiguity about the categories;
- easy to record – occur with sufficient regularity and sequence for the observer to be able to log the occurrences accurately.

Sampling and observation

Researchers using systematic observation generally organize their research around set time-blocks of observation in the field. For example, these might be one-hour chunks of time *in situ*. These time-blocks themselves need to be chosen so as to avoid any bias and to incorporate a representative sample of the thing in question. So, if the research were to involve observations of interaction in school classrooms the researcher would need to ensure that the research occurred across the full school week, the full school day and a cross-section of subjects. To confine observations to Friday afternoons, or to one subject such as history, would not provide an accurate picture across the board.

The same applies to the selection of people or events for inclusion in the study. To get a representative picture of the situation, systematic observation can involve a deliberate selection of people or events to be observed so that the data cover a cross-section of the whole research population. This can take the form of:

- *time-sampling* to ensure a sequence of snap-shot observations at set intervals. Every 30 seconds, for instance, the observer could record the relevant events or behaviour that are happening at that instant.

> **Link up with**
> Chapter 2
> Sampling.

- *tracking the activities of specific individuals one after another.* Individuals can be observed for predetermined periods of time, after which the observer's attention is switched to another person in a rota designed eventually to produce a reasonable profile covering all those involved.

Good practice: Use field notes to complement systematic observation data

Quantitative data produced by systematic observation schedules should be complemented by field notes (qualitative data) in which the researcher (1) describes the *context* and (2) records his/her impressions about the *circumstances* surrounding the events or behaviour being observed (Galton et al. 1980). Such background information helps to explain the events that are observed and should be logged with the schedule results to help the observer understand the data he or she has collected.

Retaining the naturalness of the setting

With systematic observation, the issue of retaining the naturalness of the setting hinges on the prospect of the researcher fading into the background and becoming, to all intents and purposes, invisible. At first this might seem an implausible thing. Armed with some kind of equipment for keeping a record of what is observed (such as a laptop, tablet or clipboard), and looking like a 'time and motion' researcher, it would seem unlikely that such systematic observation could avoid disrupting the events it seeks to measure. However, those who engage in this style of research report that it is indeed possible to 'merge into the wallpaper' and have no discernible impact. They stress that to minimize the likelihood of disruption researchers should pay attention to three things:

- *Positioning.* Unobtrusive positioning is vital. But the researcher still needs to be able to view the whole arena of action.
- *Avoiding interaction.* The advice here is to be 'socially invisible', not engaging with the participants in the setting if at all possible.

> **Link up with**
> the Observer
> effect, p. 70.

- *Time on site.* The experience of systematic observers assures them that the longer they are 'on site' the more their presence is taken for granted and the less they have any significant effect on proceedings.

Example of an observation schedule

If systematic observation was used for the study of art classes in a primary school, it might use an observation schedule specifically designed to collect data about pupils' activity during the lessons. The motive for doing the research might be to provide quantitative, objective data in support of the art teacher's bid for resources to have a second sink installed in the art classroom, and to do so by measuring the amount of lesson time wasted by students queuing to clean their paint brushes in the one sink that is currently available in the classroom. A simple observation schedule that could be used for this purpose might be as shown in Figure 13.1.

Figure 13.1 Observation schedule

Location: School A   Teacher: Chris Jones   Art lesson
Observation #4
Date: 28 April
Time: 11 a.m. to 12 noon

Name	Time starts queuing	Time arrives at sink	Queuing time
Asha	11.15	11.15	0
Sami	11.15	11.18	3
Douglas	11.15	11.20	5
Olivia	11.16	11.23	7
Jack	11.17	11.24	7
Jing	11.19	11.26	7
Max	11.22	11.28	6
Olga	11.23		

In this example, a decision has been made to record the amount of time spent queuing. It would have been possible to record the number of occasions that students in the class queued, or to have noted at intervals of, say, 30 seconds over a one-hour period how many students were queuing at that moment. These would have provided three slightly different kinds of results. If we were concerned with how queuing interrupted the concentration of students on a task it would have been more appropriate to record the *frequency*. Had the aim been to look at bottlenecks in the queuing then *time sampling* would have allowed the ebb and flow of students to the sink to be shown quite clearly. In this example, however, the aim is to support the claim that students' time is wasted in queues for the sink and it is therefore appropriate to record the *amount* of time spent in the queue.

The item to be observed in this example is suitably straightforward. It is reasonable to presume that standing in line is an obvious and observable form of behaviour and that, despite some occasions when students might not be solely concerned with getting their paint brushes clean when they join the queue (they might be socializing or wasting time deliberately), standing in line offers a fairly valid indicator of the thing that is of interest to the researcher: time wasted queuing.

Advantages of systematic observation

Direct data collection

It directly records what people do, as distinct from what they say they do.

Systematic and rigorous

The use of an observation schedule provides an answer to the problems associated with the selective perception of observers, and it appears to produce *objective* observations. The schedule effectively eliminates any bias from the current emotions or personal background of the observer.

Efficient

It provides a means for collecting substantial amounts of data in a relatively short time-span.

Pre-coded data

It produces quantitative data which are pre-coded and ready for analysis.

Reliability

When properly established it should achieve high levels of inter-observer reliability in the sense that two or more observers using a schedule should record very similar data.

Disadvantages of systematic observation

Behaviour, not intentions

This method of data collection focuses on overt behaviour and manifest events. It therefore describes what happens, but not why it happens. It does not deal with the intentions that motivated the behaviour or factors that caused the events.

Oversimplifies

Systematic observation assumes that overt behaviours can be measured in terms of categories that are fairly straightforward and unproblematic. This is premised on the idea that the observer and the observed share an understanding of the overt behaviour, and that the behaviour has no double meaning, hidden meaning or confusion associated with it. As such, systematic observation has the inbuilt potential to oversimplify; to ignore or distort the subtleties of the situation.

Contextual information

Observation schedules, by themselves, tend to miss contextual information which has a bearing on the behaviours recorded.

Naturalness of the setting

Although researchers who use systematic observation express confidence that their presence does not actually disrupt the naturalness of the setting to any significant extent, some question mark must surely remain about the observer's ability to fade into the background. Can a researcher using an observation schedule really avoid disrupting the naturalness of the setting?

Further reading

Bakeman, R. and Gottman, J. M. (1997) *Observing Interaction: An Introduction to Sequential Analysis*, 2nd edn. Cambridge: Cambridge University Press.

Croll, P. (1986) *Systematic Classroom Observation*. London: Falmer Press.

Gillham, B. (2008) *Observation Techniques: Structured and Unstructured Approaches*. London: Continuum.

O'Leary, M. (2014) *Classroom Observation*. London: Routledge.

Yoder, P. and Symons, F. (2010) *Observational Measurement of Behavior*. New York: Springer Publishing.

Checklist for the use of observation schedules

When using an observation schedule you should feel confident about answering 'yes' to the following questions: ☑

1 Are the events/behaviour to be observed:
   • sufficiently clear-cut and unambiguous to allow reliable coding? ☐
   • the most relevant indicators for the purposes of the research? ☐

2 Is the schedule complete (incorporating all likely categories of events/behaviour)? ☐

3 Do the events/behaviour occur regularly enough to provide sufficient data? ☐

4 Does the schedule avoid multiple simultaneous occurrences of the event/behaviour which might prevent accurate coding? ☐

5 Is the kind of sampling (event/point/time) the most appropriate? ☐

6 Do the planned periods for observation provide a representative sample (time, place, context)? ☐

7 Have efforts been made to minimize any disturbance to the naturalness of the setting caused by the presence of the observer? ☐

8 Is there provision for the collection of contextual information to accompany the schedule data? ☐

© M. Denscombe, *The Good Research Guide*. Open University Press.

Participant observation

Participant observation is an unobtrusive method of data collection that allows the researcher to gather information about lifestyles, cultures and beliefs as they exist in their natural setting. A classic definition of participant observation spells out the crucial characteristics of this approach and the things which distinguish it from systematic observation:

> By participant observation we mean the method in which the observer participates in the daily life of the people under study, either openly in the role of researcher or covertly in some disguised role, observing things that happen, listening to what is said, and questioning people, over some length of time.
>
> (Becker and Geer 1957: 28)

There are two main reasons for such participation. First, lifestyles, cultures and beliefs can be very intricate and complex things – difficult to understand and hard to explain. There is more likelihood of producing a good account of such things using a method that puts the researcher 'on site' and in the thick of the action for a reasonable period of time. Second, there are aspects of lifestyles, cultures and beliefs that people might feel inhibited about revealing to an outsider – particularly a researcher wishing to conduct an interview or distribute a questionnaire. Becoming a participant in the setting provides a way of sidestepping such inhibitions.

 Key point: Participant observation has three elements

An insider's perspective
The *experience* of participating in everyday life situations gives researchers a 'feel' for the situation which can generate *insights* into particular cultures, lifestyles or beliefs. These insights come specifically from the experience of things as *an insider*.

Link up with Chapter 6 Phenomenology.

Naturalness of the setting
A concern for seeing things 'as they really are' without disturbing the *naturalness of the setting* makes preserving the naturalness of the setting a key priority.

Link up with the Observer effect, p. 70.

Depth and detail
Participant observation helps researchers to deal with the detail, the subtleties, the complexity and the interconnectedness of the cultures, lifestyles and beliefs being investigated.

Link up with Chapter 5 Ethnography.

Types of participation

The participant observer can operate in a completely covert fashion – like an undercover agent whose success depends on remaining undetected, whose purpose remains top secret. If no one knows about the research except the researcher, the logic is that no one will act in anything but a normal way.

There are versions of participant observation, however, in which participation means something slightly different. It can, for instance, mean operating within a setting but not actually taking part in the particular actions that are the focus of concern for the research. For example, in Humphreys' (1975) study of impersonal sexual encounters in public toilets, he adopted a 'lookout' role which allowed him to be accepted as part of the general scene without actually taking part in the sexual encounters. And when O'Connell Davidson (1995) was studying the working practices of Madame Desirée – a prosperous independent prostitute – she occasionally posed as Madame Desirée's receptionist working from a desk outside the rooms used by clients. This allowed her to be part of the normal scene but also allowed her a judicious distance from the heart of the action. Obviously, in this instance the researcher's role was not totally secret. Madame Desirée knew that O'Connell Davidson was a researcher, but the clients did not.

Another possibility involves hanging out with a group rather than becoming a member of that group. This can allow researchers to be open about their purpose – to get consent for the research – in a way that is denied to the covert version of participant observation. Of course, the downside of this is that the presence of the researcher can serve to disrupt the naturalness of the setting.

There are numerous variations to the extent of total participation and the extent of open observation that can be used, but broadly speaking these boil down to three basic alternatives:

- *Total participation,* where the researcher's role is kept secret. The researcher assumes the role of someone who normally participates in the setting. Consent cannot be gained for the research, which poses ethical problems.
- *Participation in the normal setting,* where the researcher's role may be known to certain 'gatekeepers', but may be hidden from most of those in the setting. The role adopted in this type of participant observation is chosen deliberately to permit observation without affecting the naturalness of the setting, but it also allows the researcher to keep a distance from the key group under study. This distance might be warranted on the grounds of propriety, or the researcher lacks the personal credentials to take on the role in question.
- *Participation as observer,* where the researcher's identity as a researcher is openly recognized – thus having the advantage of gaining informed consent from those involved – and takes the form of 'shadowing' a person or group through normal life, witnessing at first hand and in intimate detail the culture/ events of interest.

Fieldwork

The researcher enters the field to learn about the situation. The longer the researcher is able to spend 'on site' the better because the longer he or she is part of the action, the more can be learnt about the situation. Good participant observation demands that the researcher devotes considerable time to the fieldwork. This is not a hit-and-run research method. Time on site is needed to gain trust, to establish rapport and foster insights, insights that are the trademark of participant observation as a research method.

What to observe

Participant observers usually start out being fairly non-selective in terms of what they observe. Before anything else they aim to get an 'overall feel' for the situation, and to do this they tend to begin by engaging in what can be termed 'holistic observation'. This is valuable as a background scene-setting device but, in practice, getting a general feel for the setting normally acts as a prelude to more *focused observations*. As things emerge which appear to have particular significance or interest, observation will shift from the broad canvas of activity in the setting towards specific areas. Things which emerge as important, strange or unusual invite closer scrutiny. Following from focused observations the researcher might be able to undertake special observations which concentrate on aspects of the setting in which there appear to be things which are unexpected or contradictory. Attention can be focused upon things that, according to the observer's common sense, ought not to happen. Finally, observations can try to *identify issues and problems* which participants themselves regard as crucial. The point is to observe instances which indicate how members of the setting see things – their views, beliefs and experiences.

Making field notes

The fieldwork researcher needs to translate the observations into some permanent record at the very earliest opportunity. This might be 'field notes' in the form of written records or tape-recorded memos. Whatever the form, the researcher doing fieldwork needs to develop a strategy for writing up field notes as soon as possible after the observation.

The need to do so stems from two things. First, the human memory is not only selective, but also frail. It is so easy to forget things, particularly the minor incidents and passing thoughts, if field notes are delayed for a matter of days, let alone weeks. *Field notes are urgent business*. The researcher needs to build into the research some provision to make the field notes on a regular and prompt basis. The second factor involved here is the general need to take field notes outside the arena of action. To take field notes while engaging in the action as a participant, to state the obvious, would be (1) to disrupt the naturalness of the setting, and (2) to disclose the researcher's role as observer. As a general rule, then, participant observers need to establish occasions during fieldwork, or very soon afterwards, when they can make field notes in private and unknown to those being observed. The simplest strategy is to write up the field notes as soon as you get home – assuming that home is separate from the field being studied.

> **Good practice: Making field notes with participant observation**
> Detailed field notes should be made to accompany participant observation. These notes should be made as soon as possible following each episode of observation.

Research ethics

Participant observation can pose particular ethical problems for the researcher. If 'total' participation is used, then those being studied will not be aware of the research or their role in it. They can hardly give 'informed consent'. The justification for such covert research cannot depend on consent, but draws instead on two other arguments. First, if it can be demonstrated that none of those who were studied suffered as a result of being observed, the researcher can argue that certain ethical standards were maintained. Second, and linked, if the researcher can show that the identities of those involved were never disclosed, again there is a reasonable case for saying that the participant observation was conducted in an ethical manner.

Whichever variant of participant observation is used there is the possibility that confidential material might 'fall into the hands' of the researcher. Now, while this is true of most research methods its prospects are exacerbated with the use of participant observation owing to the closeness and intimacy of the researcher's role vis-à-vis those being researched. Confidential material might be disclosed inadvertently by someone who does not know the research interest of the participant. Or, possibly even more problematic, things might get revealed as a result of the trust and rapport developed between the researcher and those being observed. This could be true for any of the variants of participant observation. The ethical problem is whether to use such material and how to use it. And here the guidelines are quite clear: (1) any use of the material should ensure that no one suffers as a result; and (2) any use of the material should avoid disclosing the identities of those involved. Any departure from these guidelines would need very special consideration and justification.

Link up with
Chapter 17
Research ethics.

Self, identity and participant observation

Equipment for research: the 'self'

One of the attractions of participant observation is that it hinges on the researcher's 'self', and does not call on much by the way of technical back-up in the form of gadgets or software. Nor does it tend to produce data that call for statistical analysis. *The key instrument of participant observation methods is the researcher as a person.*

This suggests that there is little in the way of 'entry costs' to act as a deterrent. Equipment costs are very low. There might appear to be no need for training (though this, of course, would be a fallacy). The researcher, it might seem, can jump right into the fieldwork and get on with it. However, as we see in the next sections, this dependence on the 'self' is not altogether a straightforward advantage.

Access to settings

From the participant observer's point of view gaining access to a setting might involve something more than getting approval from relevant authorities or getting a 'gatekeeper' to help open doors to the necessary contacts and settings. When engaging in the total version of participant observation there is a further issue affecting access. If the researcher is to adopt a role in the setting then he or she needs to have the *necessary credentials.*

To operate 'under cover' in a setting it is obvious that the researcher should not stand out like a sore thumb. Depending on the situation this can effectively exclude many researchers from many roles. The age factor will bar most (all?) researchers from using participant observation to investigate student cultures in schools. Observing the setting as a teacher is a more likely prospect. Sex will offer other barriers. Male researchers will be hard pushed to use total participant observation for the study of, for example, cocktail waitresses. Observing as a barman in the setting is a more likely prospect. Black researchers will find it exceptionally difficult to infiltrate the Ku Klux Klan. The biological factors place severe constraints on access to situations. Skills and qualifications provide another barrier. To participate in the sense of adopting a role it is necessary to have the necessary skills and qualifications associated with that group. As Polsky (2006) points out, his study of pool hall hustling was only possible as a participant observer because – through a 'misspent youth' – he was already something of an accomplished pool player himself. The would-be researcher, however, might be reluctant or unable to achieve such a skill specifically for the purpose of a piece of research. Following the logic here, there are many, many roles which the researcher will be unable to adopt – from brain surgeon to tree surgeon – because of a lack of personal credentials.

Selecting a topic

In view of the constraints on access as a full participant, there are two things which emerge that have a direct bearing on the selection of a topic.

- To a large extent researchers who do participant observation have their topic selected for them on the basis of their pre-existing personal attributes. The 'choice' is rarely much of a free choice. The researcher's self – age, sex, ethnicity, qualifications, skills, social background and lifestyle – tends to direct the possibilities and provide *major constraints on the roles that can be adopted.*

- While it is arguably the most revealing and sensitive of research methods in the social sciences, it is also very demanding. *It is not a soft option.* The level of commitment needed for full participant observation can be far more than that demanded by other methods – commitment in terms of researcher's time and the degree to which the act of research invades the routine life of the researcher.

It is not surprising, then, that many of the fascinating studies emerge as 'one-offs' in which researchers have explored an area of social life for which they are uniquely qualified to participate through their own past experience. It is far more unusual to find examples where researchers have been deliberately employed to infiltrate a group (e.g. Festinger et al. 1956) or where researchers have consciously adopted a role which is alien to them and which involves danger and discomfort (e.g. Griffin 1962).

Another consequence of the restrictions to full participation is the decision of many social researchers to opt for the version of participant observation which is not 'total participation'. Participation in the setting and participation as observer offer approaches which side-step some of the dangers of total participation and offer a more palatable experience for the researcher on many occasions (e.g. Whyte [1943] 1981; Humphreys 1975; O'Connell Davidson 1995).

 Key point: Choosing a topic to suit your 'self'

Researchers using participant observation generally choose a topic about which they have some insider knowledge and personal experience. The setting is normally one where the researcher can fit in easily and comfortably without disturbing the naturalness of the setting. In both senses, then, the choice of topic tends to suit the researcher's 'self'.

Dangers of fieldwork

Doing participant observation can be dangerous. First, there is *physical danger.* As Lee (1995) points out, being physically injured while doing fieldwork is fairly unlikely but, depending on the circumstances, cannot be ignored as a possibility. It is a potential built into some forms of fieldwork. Danger lurks for anthropologists who travel in remote regions with inhospitable climates and treacherous terrains. In the early years of the century, evidently, there were instances where anthropologists were actually killed by the people they were studying (Howell 1990). Danger lurks for political scientists who operate in unstable societies where the rule of law is tenuous and civilians can get caught up in factional disputes. Danger lurks for sociologists and ethnographers when they make contact with groups whose activities are on the margins of, or even outside, the law. As they tap into the underworlds of drugs, prostitution, football hooligans, bikers, religious sects and the like, they are taking a risk. This is not just a reference to the prospect of getting mugged or assaulted, or of retribution if the cover is blown at some stage. There is also the danger posed by the lifestyle itself and the impact on health of a changed diet and changed accommodation. Changing lifestyle carries its own hazards. Of course, if the researcher were to become dependent on the use of hard drugs, the health consequences could be far more dramatic.

The fieldwork could involve a second danger: *legal prosecution*. Being 'part of the scene' when hard drugs are around immediately puts the researcher at risk of prosecution. There are no special immunities afforded to social researchers.

The researcher who chooses to engage in such fieldwork might also jeopardize his or her social well-being. The 'other' life he or she is called upon to live for the purposes of the research can have an adverse effect on domestic life, on relationships with others and on commitments to do with work and leisure which make up the 'normal' life of the researcher. *The researcher, in effect, needs to sustain two lifestyles*, and these may not be compatible. Being away from home, being out late and doing fieldwork at 'unsocial' hours can tax the patience of the nearest and dearest. And then there is the psychological danger resulting from the dual existence demanded of fieldwork such as this. The lifestyle, at its worst, can have something of a traumatic effect on the researcher, or can have a lasting or permanent effect on the researcher's personality.

Going native

When it requires some form of 'dual existence' the success of participant observation depends on the researcher being able to draw a line between the two roles. There is a danger, though, that the researcher might become unable to draw a clear distinction between themselves as a researcher and themselves as a participant. At its most extreme it can involve *joining the group that you set out to study*. If the researcher's 'self' gets lost in this way this is rather like an anthropologist forgetting all about the research and settling down to live out their days as a member of the 'tribe' that they had originally set out to study. This is known as 'going native'. As Delamont (1992: 34) points out:

> Going native is an objectionable term, deservedly, for an objectionable phenomenon. It means over-identifying with the respondents, and losing the researcher's twin perspective of her own culture and, more importantly, of her 'research' and outlook.

Good practice: Avoid dangerous fieldwork

A risk assessment of the fieldwork setting should be conducted and potential dangers identified. Although experienced researchers might venture into dangerous contexts to conduct their participant observation, this should not be done by project researchers.

Advantages of participant observation

Basic equipment

Participant observation uses the researcher's 'self' as the main instrument of research, and therefore requires little by way of technical/statistical support.

Non-interference

It stands a better chance of retaining the naturalness of the setting than other social research methods.

Subjects' points of view

As a method of social research, participant observation is good for getting at actors' meanings as they see them.

Insights

It provides a good platform for gaining rich insights into social processes and is suited to dealing with complex realities.

Ecological validity

The data produced by participant observation have the potential to be particularly context-sensitive and ecologically valid.

Disadvantages of participant observation

Access

There are limited options open to the researcher about which roles to adopt or settings to participate in.

Commitment

Participant observation can be a very demanding method in terms of personal commitment and personal resources.

Danger

Participant observation can be potentially hazardous for the researcher; physically, legally, socially and psychologically risky.

Reliability

Dependence on the 'self' of the researcher and on the use of field notes as data leads to a lack of verifiable data. Reliability is open to doubt. Because participant observation relies so crucially on the researcher's 'self' as the instrument of research, it becomes exceedingly difficult to repeat a study to check for reliability. The dependence on field notes for data, constructed (soon) after fieldwork and based on the researcher's recollections of events, does little to encourage those who would want to apply conventional criteria for reliability to this method.

Representativeness of the data

There are problems of generalizing from the research. The focal role of the researcher's 'self' and the emphasis on detailed research of the particular setting open participant observation to the criticism that it is difficult to generalize from the findings. In one sense, this might hold water as a valid criticism. After all, the situations for research using participant observation are not selected on the grounds of being representative. As we have seen, they tend to be chosen on the basis of a mixture of availability and convenience. However, it might be argued that it is inappropriate to apply standard criteria of reliability and generalizability to this method.

Deception

When researchers opt to conduct full participation, keeping their true identity and purpose secret from others in the setting, there are ethical problems arising from the absence of consent on the part of those being observed, and of deception by the researcher.

Further reading

DeWalt, K. M. and DeWalt, B. R. (2011) *Participant Observation: A Guide for Fieldworkers*, 2nd edn. Lanham, MD: AltaMira Press.

Gillham, B. (2008) *Observation Techniques: Structured and Unstructured Approaches*. London: Continuum.

Jorgensen, D. L. (1989) *Participant Observation: A Methodology for Human Studies*. Thousand Oaks, CA: Sage.

Sanger, J. (1996) *The Compleat Observer?: A Field Research Guide to Observation*. London: Falmer Press.

Checklist for participant observation

When undertaking participant observation you should feel confident about answering 'yes' to the following questions: ✔

1 Does the participant observation research allow insights to events, cultures and lifestyles that would not be possible using other methods? ☐

2 Are there good grounds for believing that participant observation will not, or did not, disturb the naturalness of the setting? ☐

3 Is it clear which type of participant observation will be, or has been, used (total participation, participation in normal setting, participation as observer)? ☐

4 Has consideration been given to the ethics of the fieldwork (secrecy, consent, confidentiality)? ☐

5 Has the influence of the researcher's self-identity been examined in terms of:
   • the choice of fieldwork situation? ☐
   • access to the setting? ☐
   • the perception of events and cultures? ☐

6 Has sufficient time been spent in the field:
   • to allow trust and rapport to develop? ☐
   • to allow detailed observations and an in-depth understanding of the situation (detail, context, interconnections)? ☐

7 Have field notes been made at the time or soon after participating in the field? ☐

8 Has a risk assessment been conducted which shows that there are no specific dangers linked with the fieldwork? ☐

14 Documents

What is documentary research?

Documentary research, as the name implies, is a kind of social enquiry that uses documents as its source of data. More specifically, it treats documents as a source of *primary* data and, in this respect, it contrasts with the use of questionnaires, interviews or observation in social research. Documents can exist as:

- *written text* (e.g. books, articles, reports);
- *digital communication* (e.g. web pages, SMS texts, blogs, social network sites);
- *visual sources* (e.g. pictures, video, artefacts).

Whatever form they take, documents have two features that are useful when it comes to social research. First, they contain information that can be *used as evidence* of something. Built into the concept of a 'document' is the idea that the information it contains is of value beyond its literal contents. It stands for something and it conveys something that is significant and useful. This feature is obvious in documents such as contracts, charters, deeds, registers, reports, forms and certificates. For social researchers, though, this suggests that documents can serve as a source of data that can be used to reveal things that are not immediately apparent. Rather than take the contents at face value there are things to be learnt from a deeper reading of the document. Documentary research, for this

> **Link up with**
> Chapter 16
> Qualitative data.

reason, generally goes beyond the straightforward collection of facts from documents: it tends to involve *interpreting* the document as well, looking for hidden meanings or
structures in the work.

Second, the notion of a document carries with it the idea
of a *permanent record*. Documents provide some record whose existence, if not
permanent for all of time, does at least persist in a stable form well beyond the
moment in which it was produced. The information documents contain is neither
fleeting nor transitory: it is captured in some format or other, and saved. This
feature, again, is useful in the context of social research.

Sources of documentary data

Government publications and official statistics

Government publications and official statistics would appear to provide a documentary source of information that is:

- *Authoritative.* Since the data have been produced by the state, employing
  large resources and expert professionals, they tend to have *credibility.*
- *Objective.* Since the data have been produced by officials, they might be
  regarded as *impartial.*
- *Factual.* In the case of the statistics, they take the form of numbers that are
  amenable to computer storage/analysis, and constitute 'hard facts' over which
  there can be no ambiguity.

It is not surprising, then, that in the Western world government publications and
official statistics have come to provide a key source of documentary information
for social scientists. However, the extent to which such documents can live up to
the image of being authoritative, objective and factual depends very much on the
data they contain (see below).

Newspapers and magazines

The 'Press' provides a potentially valuable source of information for research
purposes. One reason for this is that newspapers and magazines can supply good,
up-to-date information. In this case, the value of the newspaper or magazine for
the research will stem from one or a combination of:

- the expertise of the journalists;
- the specialism of the publication;
- the insider information which the correspondents can uncover.

So, for example, in the UK, business researchers might use *The Economist* or
the *Financial Times* for these reasons. Of course, the discerning researcher will
also realize that there are plenty of newspapers and magazines whose contents

should not be relied upon to reflect anything approaching an objective account of real events!

Records of meetings

The bureaucratization of industrial society has created a wealth of documentation in relation to administration, policy, management, finance and commerce. These provide an abundant source of data for social researchers in whatever field they operate.

The purpose of most such documentation is to enhance accountability. The records kept of meetings (minutes), the records kept of transactions, the records kept of finances, etc. are kept in principle so that people and institutions can be held accountable for their actions. This means that the records need to have two qualities, both of which happen to be of particular value for research.

- *Systematic picture of things that have happened.* These might be decisions of a committee or transfers of money between accounts. Whatever the records, though, the principle behind them is that they provide a detailed and accurate picture of what took place. They have got to make events sufficiently transparent for the readers to comprehend what took place and why.
- *Publicly available.* The records only serve the function of accountability to the extent that they are made available to relevant people to scrutinize.

Letters and memos

Private correspondence between people can be used for research purposes. This can take the form of memos sent between people at work or even personal letters exchanged between people. The more private the correspondence, of course, the more difficult it is for the researcher to gain access to the documents.

These are really at the other end of the spectrum from the publicly available reports, and pose far more of a challenge for the researcher when it comes to getting hold of such documents and, especially, when it comes to getting permission to use them as research data.

Letters and memos also differ from reports in terms of the extent to which there is any formal obligation on the writer to give a full and accurate portrayal of events. Because they are written to specific people, rather than for a broader public, their contents are likely to rely far more on assumptions about what the other person already knows or what that person feels. They are more likely to 'fill in the bits' rather than paint the whole picture. They can be expected to be from a personal point of view rather than be impartial. When contemplating the use of letters or memos as data for research, then, you need to recognize that they are not very reliable as accounts which depict objective reality, but they are extremely valuable as a source which reveals the writer's own perceptions and views of events.

Diaries

As a source of documentary data, diaries are written by people whose thoughts and behaviour the researcher wishes to study. For research purposes such diaries are important in terms of recording things that have already happened. We are not talking about the kind of diaries which act as a planner, noting commitments in the future that need to be scheduled. For research purposes, the diary is normally a retrospective account of things that have happened.

There are three crucial elements to this kind of diary – three elements which, incidentally, are shared with the literary diary and the statesman's diary:

- *factual data*: a log of things that happened, decisions made and people involved;
- *significant incidents*: the identification of things seen as particularly important and a description of the diary-writer's priorities;
- *personal interpretation*: a personal reflection and interpretation of happenings, plus an account of the personal feelings and emotions surrounding the events described.

Each of these three things has the potential to provide a rich source of data for the researcher. However, the accounts they provide should not be used by the researcher as a statement of objective fact. That would be very naïve. As a retrospective account, diaries must always be seen as a *version* of things as seen by the writer, filtered through the writer's past experiences, own identity, own aspirations and own personality.

It is also worth noting that diaries, as a form of documentary data, lend themselves to being analysed in a variety of ways. As a method of data collection they do not prescribe such matters and, as Alaszewski (2006) argues, they can be analysed using approaches as widely different as content analysis, grounded theory and discourse analysis.

Link up with
Chapter 16
Qualitative data.

Website pages and the Internet

Documents, as a form of data, include material obtained via the Internet. In a sense, the medium through which the document is obtained is not the issue. We can read newspapers in their original paper form, or we can read them on microfiche or via a CD-ROM. Equally, we can obtain documents through website pages, apps on mobile devices or email, and this does not, of itself, have a bearing on the use of the output as a document for research. Websites, though, can be treated as documents in their own right. Home pages, etc. can be treated as a form of document, and their content analysed in terms of the text and images they contain. In effect, they can be treated like *online documents*.

Access to documentary sources

Probably the greatest attraction of using documentary sources is their accessibility. To get hold of the material the researcher needs only to visit the library or go online via a computer. The Internet provides the researcher with access to a host of government sites that provide a wide range of information on social and economic factors. In the UK a list of government websites can be found at https://www.gov.uk, and in the USA there are sites like http://www.gpo.gov and http://fedworld.ntis.gov that offer entry points to search for official data and government publications. This means that vast amounts of information are conveniently available without much cost, without much delay, without prior appointment, without the need for authorization and without any likelihood of ethical problems. Documents, in other words, pose considerably fewer problems than people as a source of data for social researchers. Table 14.1 presents examples of access to documents.

Table 14.1 Access to documents for research

Type of document	Examples	Access via	Typical use
Public domain	Books, journals, official statistics, some company records	Internet, libraries	Academic research and consultancy
Restricted access	Medical records, police files, internal memos, personal papers/diaries, some tax accounts	Negotiations with gatekeepers, sponsors	Consultancy and academic research
Secret	Military plans, Cabinet minutes, corporate plans, records of illegal trade	Insider knowledge, participation, deception	Investigative journalism, fraud detection, undercover work

There are times, however, when the use of documents does not completely side-step the kind of problems that face researchers using other sources. While access to documents in the public domain is certainly straightforward, researchers can sometimes need to use materials whose availability is deliberately restricted. When this is the case, access becomes a crucial part of the research method – more than something that can be taken for granted. When documents are not available, researchers need to enter negotiations with those who hold the data in order to persuade them to allow the researcher the privilege of access to the material. Documents such as police files and medical records, and certain kinds of company reports and memos, might rightly be considered sensitive and confidential by those who 'own' them, and they are only likely to grant access when they are convinced that the researcher will honour the confidentiality of the material and use it in a way that will not harm the interests of anyone concerned.

Good practice: Gaining access to documentary sources of data

Researchers should check in advance whether their access to documentary data sources will need authorization or require payment. The feasibility of using documentary research should then be assessed bearing in mind any restrictions these factors might impose on full access to the documents.

Access to information on the Internet can be controlled by the actions of certain strategic 'gatekeepers' who can influence what information is made available and who is allowed access to that information. Some information, such as academic articles and market research data, will only be accessible on condition of payment of money. Separate from this, Internet researchers need to be sensitive to the role of 'moderators' and 'webmasters' in filtering the information. Some sites, but by no means all, are controlled by people whose role it is to monitor the content of the site and the conduct of those who use it. Moderators (mailing lists, chat rooms) and webmasters (email servers) acting in this capacity are effectively 'gatekeepers'. They have the power to deny access to the site and might need to be persuaded of the relevance and worthiness of a proposed piece of research before they will grant access.

In the case of documents considered to be secret, of course, the holders will seek to deny any access to outsiders. Companies may have secret strategic plans regarded as too sensitive for even a bona fide researcher. The government wishes to keep many documents secret 'in the national interest'. Records of illegal activities, whether a drug smuggler's diary or a second set of books for VAT returns, are extremely unlikely to be opened to the researcher. To get access to such secret documents requires the approach of investigative journalism or participant observation with a degree of deception and covert infiltration being used.

The validity of documentary data

For the purposes of research, documentary sources should never be accepted at face value. Their validity is something that needs to be established and it is important that any documents used as sources of data are evaluated in relation to four basic criteria.

Authenticity. Is it the genuine article? Is it the real thing? Can we be satisfied that the document is what it purports to be – not a fake or a forgery?

Representativeness. Is the document typical of its type? Does it represent a typical instance of the thing it portrays? Is the document complete? Has it been edited? Is the extract treated 'in context'?

Meaning. Is the meaning of the words clear and unambiguous? Are there hidden meanings? Does the document contain argot and subtle codes? Are there meanings which involve 'what's left unsaid' or 'reading between the lines'?

Credibility. Is it accurate? Is it free from bias and errors? This will depend on factors like:

- What *purpose* was the document written for?
- Who produced the document? What was the status of the author and did he or she have a particular belief or persuasion that would colour the version of things?
- If it reports on events, was it a first-hand report directly witnessed by the author? How long after the event was the document written?
- *When was the document produced?* In what social context and climate?

The credibility of articles, journals and books

Academic journals and commercial publishers generally have their material reviewed by experts in the field before the work is published, so the researcher has some assurance about the quality of their content. However, this offers no absolute guarantee. And how does the reader find out which journals use 'peer review' and which publishers are reputable? Some rules of thumb might help here. For journals:

- How long has the journal existed? Generally, a journal which has existed for a long time will be OK. Less confidence can be held about new journals. However, this does not mean old equals good, new equals bad: that would be far too simplistic.
- Does the title involve a national title (e.g. *British Medical Journal, American Journal of Sociology*)? Again, there is nothing cast iron about this, but it offers some clue as to the standing of the journal.
- Is the journal published by, or on behalf of, a professional association or some authority?
- Does the journal website provide a list of its editorial board and editorial advisers, and do these people strike you as 'of high standing' in the field?
- Is there a clear statement that articles are peer reviewed?

For books and their publishers, the following questions might help with the evaluation of the sources.

- Is the publisher a university press (e.g. Cambridge University Press)? If so, again this offers some confidence about the academic quality of the work being published.
- Is the book in a second or subsequent edition? If so, there has been sufficient demand for the book to warrant new editions, and this would suggest that it has something worthwhile to say. The same applies to a lesser extent where a book has been reprinted several times. Look for the details, usually contained on the imprint page between the title and contents pages.

The evaluation of Internet documents and web pages

The evaluation of the documents downloaded from the Internet centres around one issue more than others. Because there are few restrictions on what is placed on the Internet any documents to be used for research need to be considered very carefully in terms of their authorship, their credibility and their authenticity. The documents need to be subjected to the researcher's own quality audit along the lines of those recommended in relation to books and journals – but with even more vigour and rigour.

When it comes to the evaluation of the websites a similar point applies. For research purposes, judgements need to be made about the credibility of the site where the pages are located. Judgements about this can be made on the basis of four criteria:

- The *authoritativeness* of the site. A university or government site might add some credibility to the source, whereas a private web page might need to be viewed with caution.
- The *trustworthiness* of the site. Does the site convey a sense of serious and legitimate purpose? Does it contain suitable disclaimers and explicit statements about its purpose?
- How *up-to-date* the site is. Attention should be given to how regularly the pages are updated. Is the date of last updating visible and, crucially, is it recent?
- The *popularity* of the site. The extent of interest in a website and the size of its audience can suggest something about the site's recognition and popularity. These can be gauged by the number of times people have logged on to that site – the number of 'hits' on the site.

The credibility of official statistics

Certain types of official statistics will, to all intents and purposes, provide an objective picture of reality. Unfortunately, the same cannot be said for certain other types of official statistics. When politicians debate the accuracy of unemployment figures or the significance of particular national economic figures there is clearly room for some doubt and controversy about the objectivity, the accuracy, the completeness and the relevance of some official statistics. This should alert us to the point that official statistics cannot always be taken as 'objective facts'.

To say this is not to reject the use of all official statistics as a source of data for social research. But what it *does* mean is that before treating a set of official statistics as accurate and objective the researcher should consider the following factors:

- *The extent to which the event or thing being measured is clear-cut and straightforward.* Basically, the more clear-cut the event, the more confidence we can have in the data. The official statistics on things like births, deaths, marriages and divorce are likely to be virtually complete. Whether or not someone is born or dies, whether a marriage or divorce occurs, does not require much in the way of interpretation by the registrars involved. The events themselves happen or don't happen, with little scope for 'creative accounting' or biased interpretation. Alright, a very small number of births and deaths might go unrecorded and slip through the net of the tight official procedures for collecting such data. But the numbers will be sufficiently low not to present any serious challenge to the idea that these official statistics are a full and accurate record. Things like unemployment, homelessness and ill health, though, are far less clear-cut. There are a number of ways of defining these things and this opens up the possibility of disputes about whether the statistics depict real levels of unemployment, etc., or whether they offer a picture biased by the nature of the definition that has been used.

- *Whether there are vested interests behind the statistics that are produced.* When those who produce the statistics stand to gain or lose on the basis of what the figures reveal, the astute researcher should treat them with some caution. Trade figures, hospital waiting lists, sales figures: all have consequences for people who want or need the statistics to reveal a particular trend. And official statistics are not immune to the point. Governments can have a vested interest in a variety of statistics, from trade to inflation, from unemployment to health.

- *The extent to which the statistics are the outcome of a series of decisions and judgements made by people.* The more the statistics rely on decisions and choices by those who produce them, the more the eventual official statistics become open to being challenged. The more the statistics are the end-product of a series of choices made by people – choices that involve judgement and discretion – the more the official statistics can be regarded as a 'social construction' rather than a detached, impartial picture of the real world.

Crime statistics provide a good illustration of the *construction* of official statistics. Crime statistics are based on those crimes that people decide to report to the police. A large proportion of crime, however, never gets reported. Petty crimes may go unreported. Theft is frequently not reported, particularly when people see no chance of recovering their property and when the property is not insured. (If a claim is to be made through insurance, a 'crime number' is needed from the police and this motivates people to report the crime.) Many crimes are not discovered and so obviously do not get reported (e.g. embezzlement). There are the 'crimes with no victims' where, unless someone is caught by the police no record of the offence will ever appear (e.g. recreational drug use). In the case of some crimes there may be an unwillingness of the victim to complain because of the accruing stigma (e.g. rape) or fear of retribution.

Even when a crime is reported to the police there is a level of discretion open to them about how they interpret things and whether to formalize the matter. A lot of 'crime' is sorted out informally, without ever entering the system as a recorded crime. Even when it is in the system, the nature of the offence is open to some degree of interpretation. From the police officer receiving the report onwards, there is some scope for leeway and interpretation about (1) whether to prosecute; (2) what kind of offence gets noted; (3) whether a caution is given; (4) whether the matter proceeds to court; and (5) whether the prosecution is successful or not. At each stage, people are taking decisions, using discretion and making judgements. Overall, these can have a marked impact on the end-product: the official statistics. It means that there will be a huge difference (in the case of crime) between the real level of crime in society and the figures that get published by the government as 'the crime rate'. It is estimated that recorded crime may be as little as one-fifth of 'actual' crime.

The credibility of records of meetings

Records of meetings, whether publicly available or on restricted access, purport to depict things that have happened in a full and accurate manner. However, there is ample evidence that such records tend to be partial – in both senses of the word. They will tend to be selective in terms of what they report, emphasizing some things and ignoring others, and thus recording only part of the overall event. They will also tend to reflect a particular interpretation of what happened, recording events from a particular angle. We should remember that when such records are produced as part of public accountability there will be a tendency to be cautious about what is recorded. Things might have been said 'off the record' or following 'Don't minute this but . . .'. The records, in other words, may be subtly edited to exclude things which might render people vulnerable to criticism when the record is published. *The researcher, therefore, needs to be cautious about accepting such records at face value.* Publicly available records reflect upon matters in a way that is publicly acceptable at a given time and in a given social sphere. They tend to offer a version of reality massaged to meet public expectations.

Good practice: Always assess the credibility of documentary sources

Before being used in research, documents should always be checked in terms of the credibility of their origins, their purpose and their author.

Image-based research

The documents referred to so far have been text-based. There are, however, alternative kinds of documentary data available to social researchers, ones that are based on *visual* images. Central to the idea of image-based research, visual images can be used as data in their own right – distinct from text, numbers or sounds as a potential source of research information. Just like other documents, visual images can prove to be valuable for the purposes of the research in terms of:

- the factual information they contain;
- how they represent things (the symbolism and hidden meanings communicated through the document or image).

Types of image

For practical reasons there has been a tendency to concentrate on two-dimensional 'still' images such as photographs as the source of image-based data. Photographs are relatively inexpensive. They also lend themselves to analysis and reproduction alongside more conventional text-based research, e.g. in printed journals or academic dissertations. Potentially, though, there are a wide variety of visual images that could be used. There have been adventurous attempts on occasion to explore the possibilities of moving images and even three-dimensional objects (Banks 2001, 2007; Emmison et al. 2012) (Table 14.2).

Table 14.2 Potential sources of image-based documentary data

Still	Movie	Object
Photographs, advertisements, drawings, graffiti	Video recording, archive film	Cultural artefacts, clothing and fashion items, built environment and places, body signs/language

The use of 'created' images

Researchers can generate images specifically for the purposes of their investigation – so-called *created* images. The visual images, in this sense, provide primary source data. These images can be valuable as a means of recording things. Researchers can make records of events, people, cultures, and so on by photographing, filming or drawing them. Such visual records provide an alternative to tape recordings (*sound*), an alternative to the use of written documents such as field notes, diaries or minutes (*text*) and an alternative to the use of quantitative data such as figures from questionnaires or statistics based on systematic observation (*numbers*).

Link up with the analysis of image-based data, p. 292.

When contemplating the use of created images there are some practical issues that ought to be borne in mind. The first concerns equipment. Cameras/phones for photographs and camcorders for videos come in a range of technical specifications and prices. The researcher needs to decide what equipment will best suit the purposes of the research and what equipment is actually available. This may well call for some sort of compromise decision that balances the quality and format of the output against the resources that exist. In arriving at the decision the researcher will need to be aware that more sophisticated equipment might call for specific technical skills and expertise and that any additional technical wizardry attached to more expensive equipment might be wasted without the necessary talent to make use of it. Weighed against this, cheap equipment that produces poor quality images might prove to be a poor saving of resources. Forethought needs to be given to the environments in which the images will be collected. Will the lighting be adequate to avoid flash photography that might be intrusive or distracting? Will better quality equipment overcome such a problem? Will a zoom lens be necessary to capture enough detail?

Quite apart from the technical considerations involved with image-based research when researchers set out to capture data by 'creating' the images first hand, they are confronted as well by a range of social and cultural factors that can have a marked impact on their ability to record things 'as they are'. Even when things might seem quite straightforward there can be problems lurking just beneath the surface. For example, filming objects such as buildings, transport facilities and artefacts would appear to be fairly unproblematic as a means of data collection. There are circumstances, however, where filming and photography are not allowed. Some countries might regard it as a security threat depending on the location. There are issues of privacy to be considered, and in galleries and museums there are often restrictions on photography and filming of the artefacts. Forethought needs to be given to the legal and cultural context within which data collection is to take place in order to minimize the risk that the filming or photography of specific objects will be regarded as an offence or as offensive.

When the image-based research involves people, there is all the more need for sensitivity to the social and cultural context. As Prosser and Schwartz (1998: 119) point out, researchers need to appreciate that 'making pictures can be a threatening act (amply demonstrated by the metaphors photography invokes: we "load", "aim" and "shoot").' The act of being 'captured' on film can be perceived as threatening even if the researcher's intention is benign, and this likelihood has two important repercussions for the process of data collection:

- It can *limit access* to research sites. If people feel threatened, if they feel that there is an invasion of privacy, they might well refuse to cooperate with the research.
- It can cause people to *become self-conscious* and to act in a way that they would not do normally.

There is, in effect, an element of reflexivity involved with the collection of 'created' images. Prosser (1998: 104–5) writes of this in terms of 'procedural reactivity' and 'personal reactivity'. Procedural reactivity refers to the way the act of taking the photographs makes the researcher more obviously visible when collecting data for the record and the way that this can alter the natural state of affairs by inhibiting, embarrassing or in some other way altering the behaviour and activities of the person(s) being photographed. Personal reactivity refers to the way the photographer/researcher can have an effect on the situation simply on the basis of their own identity and personal characteristics, and their own judgements in terms of the nature of the photograph that is taken. An example might be a photographer's presence when recording images at the birth of a child and the way the sex and age of the photographer might have a bearing on the types of photograph that are taken and the reaction of the mother, the father and nursing staff to being photographed during this intimate moment.

Bearing the issue of reflexivity in mind, researchers need to be conscious of the way their actions will be perceived. Consideration needs to be given to the impact of things like:

- *The equipment.* Flash photography will be more evident than daylight photography, and a discreet small digital camera will be less visible than bulky, professional camcorder equipment.
- *The situation.* Certain events involve film records more normally than others. Ceremonial events, for instance, might allow the use of created images by the researcher in a way that would not be the case in more personal, intimate circumstances.
- *The people involved.* People who live 'in the public eye', those with high-profile jobs and people like media celebrities, will probably be fairly comfortable

in the knowledge that they are being filmed or photographed because it is a routine part of their working lives. They might, however, reserve the right to privacy on occasions when they are 'off duty', regarding this as their personal and private life.

- *Personalities*. Extroverts and publicity seekers will be likely to adore the attention of the camera in a way that more introverted and camera-shy people will not.

These factors come into play, of course, only when people are aware that they are being filmed. This need not always be the case. The researcher might choose to undertake covert research, in which the process of filming is kept secret from those who are being studied. There are particular ethical issues that arise in this case and to gain approval from any relevant authorizing body (e.g. an ethics committee) a strong case will need to be made for *not* seeking informed consent from those being studied. This pertains, of course, to a range of social research methods but the fullness of the data captured on film can make people all the more defensive and reticent to co-operate – more than would be the case if the research relied on things like interviews or questionnaire data.

| Link up with |
| Chapter 17 |
| Research ethics. |

The use of 'found' images

Documentary research can be based on images that already exist rather than ones produced by the researcher for the specific purposes of the research. They can use '*found* images' that have been produced by other people for reasons not directly connected with the researcher's investigation.

The kind of images used depends largely on the subject discipline of the researcher. Media studies and marketing often use advertisements and newspaper photographs. Anthropologists, historians and sociologists will use images of groups and cultural events portrayed using film, photographs, paintings, graffiti or artefacts. Such items contain a visual record that can be used to provide factual information about groups or events, or the images can be interpreted to provide some better understanding of the ideas and lifestyles that generated the images.

As a source of data, 'found' images sidestep a number of problems associated with the data gathering process for 'created' images. Technical issues about equipment and practical issues of access to locations, for instance, no longer arise since the image already exists. Immediately, this suggests that the use of found images is an attractive proposition for the social researcher because it requires less skill to produce and may well prove less expensive if it saves fieldwork, travel and production costs. Equally attractively, it overcomes the ethical concerns of getting informed consent in those cases where the image involves living people. Added to this, the Internet offers a huge stock of downloadable images that social researchers can potentially use. No fieldwork and no travel are required.

However, the ease with which found images can be obtained should not seduce the researcher into opting for their use without recognizing that there are also some specific issues that need to be weighed against the ease and cost factors – issues surrounding the authenticity of the images and copyright protection.

Authenticity

As with other documentary data, the social researcher who uses visual images will want to feel certain about the authenticity of the image. This is particularly the case with 'found' images that are to be used as a source of factual information. The researcher needs to be wary about whether the image has been tampered with, changed or edited from the original. Computer software, of course, makes this increasingly simple to do. Photographic images, in particular, are relatively easy to alter and the researcher should not take it as a matter of trust that the image is genuine. As Loizos (2000: 95) warns:

> One fallacy is implied by the phrase 'the camera cannot lie'. Humans, the agents who wield cameras, can and do lie: . . . they can distort the evidential recording capacity of visual data just as readily as they can distort written words.

Copyright

Ownership of an image is an important issue particularly if the image is to be reproduced and made publicly available through the process of research. Where the image has been created by the researcher there is generally not too much of a problem. The image is usually owned by the researcher. However, this may not always be the case. In some cases ownership of the image might be claimed on behalf of the person or event portrayed. However, as Banks (2001: 168) notes, this issue is 'relevant largely to representations of celebrities, those deemed likely to have a financial interest in the use of their representations'.

If the image already exists, the chances are that it 'belongs' to some person, company or institution, in which case it is necessary to obtain permission to use the image. At one extreme this might be a fairly informal thing. If, for example, the image to be used is a personal photograph from a family album the necessary permission could involve little more than getting approval (preferably in writing) from the owner for the use of the image for research purposes. At the other extreme images based on advertisements, or works of art, or drawn from news media, entertainment magazines or the Internet, are the kind of thing that will probably require a very formal request to the copyright holder for permission to reproduce the image. If the copyright holder agrees to this it might be conditional on the payment of a fee. The fee can be prohibitively large and it is important to make it clear when requesting permission that the image is to be used for the purposes of small-scale, private research from which there will be no monetary gain. Fees might be waived or reduced under these circumstances, though this will depend on the nature of the image and the policies of the particular copyright holder. If the image to be used has an obscure origin and the copyright holder cannot be traced there is a standard solution to the problem which consists of making a clear statement at the start of any report or dissertation along the lines that 'Efforts have been made to obtain permission from copyright holders of the (photographic images) used. Where the copyright owners have not been traced the author invites further information from anyone concerned and will seek to remedy the situation.' This does presume, of course, that rigorous efforts have indeed been made and the statement should not be used as a way to avoid the work of tracing copyright holders.

 Key point: Copyright and visual images

Special care should be taken to ensure that the use of visual images for research purposes, especially those downloaded from the Internet, do not infringe copyright laws.

 Caution: The use of image-based data

Despite claims that contemporary society has become more of a 'visual culture' than in the past, and despite some signs of a growing interest in visual research, the use of image-based data remains relatively uncommon in the social sciences. Part of the reason for this is that film, video and three-dimensional images do not readily fit the medium within which research data and analyses are normally presented. They may not fit in dissertations, journals or computer documents that favour a two-dimensional, text-based format. Although digital technology now makes it easy to incorporate pictures and video data within such documents it is clear that image-based research remains somewhat marginalized and, as yet, struggles to achieve a parity of status in the social sciences with research whose data take the form of numbers or words. The project researcher undertaking small-scale research might do well to bear this in mind.

Advantages of documentary research

Access to data

Vast amounts of information are held in documents. Depending on the nature of the documents, most researchers will find access to the sources relatively easy and inexpensive.

Cost-effective

Documentary research provides a cost-effective method of getting data, particularly large-scale data such as those provided by official statistics.

Permanence of data

Documents generally provide a source of data which is permanent and available in a form that can be checked by others. The data are open to public scrutiny.

Disadvantages of documentary research

Credibility of the source

Researchers need to be discerning about the information they use. They need to evaluate the authority of the source and the procedures used to produce the original data in order to gauge the credibility of the documents. This is not always easy. Internet documents, in particular, need special scrutiny. Information found on the Internet can be up-to-date and good quality stuff. However, just as easily, it can be out-of-date, poor quality material because there is little control over what is placed on the Internet.

Secondary data

When researchers use documents as a source of data, they generally rely on something which has been produced for other purposes and not for the specific aims of the investigation.

Social constructions

Documents can owe more to the interpretations of those who produce them than to an objective picture of reality.

Further reading

Banks, M. (2007) *Using Visual Data in Qualitative Research*. London: Sage.
Marion, J. S. and Crowder, J. W. (2013) *Visual Research: A Concise Introduction to Thinking Visually*. London: Bloomsbury Academic.
Plummer, K. (2001) *Documents of Life 2: An Invitation to a Critical Humanism*. London: Sage.
Prior, L. (2003) *Using Documents in Social Research*. London: Sage.
Rapley, T. (2007) *Doing Conversation, Discourse and Document Analysis*. London: Sage.
Scott, J. (1990) *A Matter of Record: Documentary Sources in Social Research*. Cambridge: Polity.
Spencer, S. (2011) *Visual Research Methods in the Social Sciences: Awakening Visions*. London: Routledge.

Checklist for the use of documents (text and visual images)

When undertaking documentary research you should feel confident about answering 'yes' to the following questions: ✓

1 Am I satisfied that the documents/images are genuine in terms of what they purport to be (not drafts, forgeries, misleading second versions, etc.)? ☐

2 Have I considered the credibility of the documents or images in terms of:
- their source (published book, journal article, official statistics)? ☐
- their author or creator (status, role, in a position to know)? ☐
- their sponsorship (organization, funding, pressure group)? ☐
- the accessibility of the information they use (public domain, restricted, secret)? ☐

3 Have website sources been evaluated in terms of their accuracy and how recently they have been updated (where applicable)? ☐

4 Am I satisfied that I have taken account of possible bias in the document or image arising from:
- its purpose (description, theory, persuasion)? ☐
- how representative it is (typical, extreme)? ☐
- the editing and selection of extracts used in it? ☐
- its interpretation of facts or theories? ☐
- sensitivity to the information or image it contains? ☐

5 Have I provided full details of the sources of the texts or images used? ☐

6 Has the research avoided contravening copyright laws? ☐

© M. Denscombe, *The Good Research Guide*. Open University Press.

Part 3

Data analysis

The purpose of analysing something is to gain a better understanding of it. Through a detailed examination of the thing that is being studied the analysis aims to do the following:

- *describe* its constituent elements; or
- *explain* how it works; or
- *interpret* what it means.

Description

A description can provide the basis for research in its own right. There are types of social research such as ethnography and phenomenology where the researcher's aim is to portray particular cultures or experiences in depth and in detail, allowing the texture and subtlety of the situation to become visible to the reader. In this case the description is valuable in its own right through the way it allows new insights to be gained. On other occasions descriptions are used as a starting point for research – a platform for a subsequent analysis based on explanation or interpretation. The logic here is that there needs to be a clear vision of what the thing entails before it is possible to give an accurate explanation or interpretation of how it works. Either way, whether the description is to be used in its own right or as a prelude to further investigation, the emphasis is on providing details about:

- *What* the thing looks like: measurements, components, appearance, duration, etc.
- *When* it happened: dates, context of other events, etc.
- *Who* was involved: the individuals, the demographics of the sample/population, etc.
- *How often* it happens: frequency, duration, etc.

Explanation

An explanation looks for rules and regularities that underlie the occurrence of particular social phenomena. The aim is to find out how things work by looking for evidence of cause–effect relationships in the data. Once the researcher has discovered the causes of specific behaviour, events or interactions there is the possibility of predicting how and when things might happen in the future – a prospect which has proved very enticing for disciplines such as economics and psychology but which has also been relished by many researchers in areas of health, education and business studies. What these researchers are trying to discover is:

- *How* things are connected: associations and correlations, etc.
- *Why* things happen: underlying mechanisms, causes, etc.
- *When* things will happen: probability of recurrence, projections for the future, etc.

Interpretation

Interpretation, like explanation, is interested in patterns and regularities that lie behind the occurrence of social phenomena. The difference is that interpretive researchers see their analysis as a matter of providing an understanding rather than providing something that is an objective, universal truth. Interpretivists are still interested in gaining knowledge about how and why things happen, but they are sceptical about the prospects of being able to provide explanations that can ever be purely objective. They argue that, to a greater or lesser extent, theories must inevitably reflect the cultural and historical context within which the research takes place and be shaped by the personal values and experiences of the researcher. Any theories that are produced, it follows, will be 'value-laden' rather than objective. The consequence of such reasoning is that for interpretivists the aim of analysis is to produce a viable account of how things work (rather than discover regularities that exist objectively in the social world). Bearing this in mind, they tend to focus on things like:

- *How* and *why* things happen: in terms of possible mechanisms, potential causes, plausible theories, etc.
- *Who* undertook the research: researcher biography, identity and experiences.
- *When and where* the study took place: cultural and historical context, social values.
- *What* alternative explanations exist: comparisons with competing theories.

Quantitative and qualitative research

There are many kinds of analysis the social researcher can use in order to describe, explain or interpret the data. In practice, though, the options tend to gravitate around the notions of 'quantitative' and 'qualitative' research. These terms are widely used and commonly understood within social research, and they have come to represent contrasting alternatives that signify distinct, some would even say incompatible, stances on a broad range of beliefs and practices relating to social research. Initially, the contrast concerns the different kinds of data that they use and the implications of this are explored in Chapters 15 and 16. In a nutshell, the distinction between the approaches centres on the fact that:

- quantitative research uses *numbers* as the unit of analysis;
- qualitative research uses *words or visual images* as the unit of analysis.

Linked with this the terms have also come to be associated with a particular set of assumptions about the nature of the social world. Quantitative research tends to be linked with *positivism* and qualitative research tends to be associated with *interpretivism*. This division is far from watertight but it continues to work as an initial assumption about the respective stances of quantitative and qualitative research. Quantitative research is associated with the production of numerical data that are 'objective' in the sense that they exist independently of the researcher and are not the result of undue influence on the part of the researcher. Ideally, the numerical data are seen as the product of research instruments that have been tested for validity and reliability to ensure that the data accurately reflect the event itself, not the researcher's preferences. Qualitative research, by contrast, tends to place emphasis on the role of the researcher in the construction of the data. There is typically little use of standardized research instruments in qualitative research. Rather, it is recognized that the researcher is the crucial 'measurement device' and that the researcher's background, values, identity and beliefs might have a significant bearing on the nature of the data collected and the analysis of that data. In essence, this means that:

- quantitative research tends to be associated with researcher *detachment*;
- qualitative research tends to be associated with researcher *involvement.*

The terms are also associated with visions about the size, focus and design of the investigation that is required. Quantitative research tends to favour larger-scale research with larger numbers and greater quantities. The sheer amounts involved, once they have been transformed into numerical data, do not slow down the analysis to any discernible degree. A statistical procedure can be undertaken by a computer on a sample of 1,000 pretty much as quickly as it can on a sample of 100. The results, though, will be more reliable when conducted on 1,000 than on 100. The larger the numbers involved the more the results are likely to be generalizable and reliable, statistically speaking. By contrast, qualitative research tends to involve relatively few people or events. Much of this reflects the preference for depth of study and the associated 'thick description' which only becomes possible in relation to limited numbers. Qualitative researchers like to be 'close to the data' and like to have a detailed familiarity with the data in order to conduct the analysis. Their preference for small-scale studies also reflects the fact that words do not lend themselves to the kind of analysis that can utilize the power of computers in the same way that numbers do. For the qualitative researcher there *is* a vast difference in the time it takes to analyse results from larger amounts of data compared with smaller amounts. For these reasons:

- quantitative research tends to be associated with *large-scale* studies;
- qualitative research tends to be associated with *small-scale* studies.

The terms quantitative and qualitative research also imply a distinction in terms of the breadth of focus of an investigation. In the case of quantitative research there is a tendency to focus on specific variables and to study them, if not in isolation, at least with reference to a limited range of other variables. Qualitative research, on the other hand, generally exhibits a preference for seeing things 'in context' and for stressing the importance of multiple interrelationships between a wide range of factors in operation at any one time in the setting. Qualitative research tends to operate on the assumption that '[social] realities are wholes that cannot be understood in isolation from their contexts, nor can they be fragmented for separate study of their parts' (Lincoln and Guba 1985: 39). As a generalization, then:

- quantitative research tends to be associated with analysing *specific variables*;
- qualitative research tends to be associated with a *holistic perspective*.

Finally, the notions of quantitative and qualitative research carry with them an image of contrasting approaches to research design. Quantitative research tends to be associated with precise research designs in which the process of analysis is clearly separated from the process of data collection. At the beginning the research questions or hypotheses are carefully formulated. After this comes the process of data collection which usually involves a predetermined sample to be collected or experimental procedure to be undertaken. And then there comes the data analysis stage in which the data that have been previously collected are subjected to statistical tests or other quantitative analysis. In contrast with this qualitative research tends to be linked with the idea that research questions should not, and cannot, be specified precisely in advance of the data collection stage. Nor can data analysis be hived off to a period after the data collection has been completed. As exemplified by the grounded theory approach (see Chapter 7) this style of qualitative research sees the formulation of the research question, the collection of data and the analysis of data as an emerging and iterative process. In effect, the analysis commences at the earliest stage of research and continues throughout the whole time of the investigation. The distinction, then, revolves around the way that:

- quantitative research tends to be associated with data analysis *after* data collection;
- qualitative research tends to be associated with data analysis *during* data collection.

 Caution: The distinction between quantitative and qualitative research

In the real world of social research things may not fall neatly into the two categories. There are three main reasons for this:

1 In theory, the distinction is too simplistic. The assumptions associated with the two approaches are sometimes shared and sometimes overlap.

▶

▶
> 2 In practice, many researchers use a mixed methods approach which combines quantitative and qualitative research rather than treating them as incompatible alternatives.
> 3 Strictly speaking, the distinction between 'quantitative' and 'qualitative' should relate to the treatment of *data*, rather than types of research as such.

The process of data analysis

The analysis of research data tends to follow a process involving five stages. The stages can be seen in relation to both quantitative and qualitative data, as Table P3.1 shows. However, it also shows that there are differences between quantitative and qualitative data analysis, with quantitative approaches tending to shape their data more consciously and more explicitly in the earlier stages of the process compared with qualitative approaches. More details on the specific approaches to data analysis are provided in Chapters 15 and 16.

Table P3.1 Five stages of data analysis

	Quantitative data	Qualitative data
1 Data preparation	Coding (which normally takes place before data collection) Categorizing the data Checking the numbers	Cataloguing the text or visual data Transcribing the text Preparation of data and loading to software (if applicable)
2 Initial exploration of the data	Look for obvious trends or correlations	Look for obvious recurrent themes or issues Add notes to the data. Write memos to capture ideas
3 Analysis of the data	Use of statistical tests (e.g. descriptive statistics, factor analysis, cluster analysis) Link to research questions or hypotheses	Code the data Group the codes into categories or themes Comparison of categories and themes Look for concepts (or fewer, more abstract categories) that encapsulate the categories
4 Presentation and display of the data	Tables Figures Written interpretation of the statistical findings	Written interpretation of the findings Illustration of points by quotes and pictures Use of visual models, figures and tables

(continued)

Table P3.1   Five stages of data analysis (*Continued*)

	Quantitative data	Qualitative data
5 Validation of the data	External benchmarks Internal consistency Comparison with alternative explanations	Data and method triangulation Member validation Comparison with alternative explanations

Source: Adapted from Creswell and Plano Clarke (2007: 129), Table 7.1.

15 Quantitative data

Sources of quantitative data • Types of quantitative data • Describing the mid-point or average • Describing the spread of data • Looking for patterns and relationships in the data • Statistical tests for association and difference • Presenting the data: tables and charts • Reliability and validity: quantitative research • Advantages of quantitative data analysis • Disadvantages of quantitative data analysis • Further reading • Checklist for the use of quantitative data

This chapter focuses on basic aspects of the analysis and presentation of quantitative data. There is no attempt to cover more advanced statistical procedures that use quantitative data for testing hypotheses or forecasting outcomes. Such 'inferential' statistics are valuable, but they require a level of familiarity with statistics that project researchers might not have the time or inclination to acquire. For those who want to study the statistical analysis of quantitative data in more depth there are many textbooks and online resources that are readily available, and reference should be made to such sources. The majority of project researchers, however, will prefer to restrict their analysis to the use of basic descriptive statistics. The premise of this chapter is that, properly used, simple 'descriptive' statistics can offer the project researcher a straightforward, yet rigorous way of:

- describing the profile of findings (frequencies, averages, distributions);
- exploring connections between parts of the data (correlations and associations);
- summarizing and displaying the findings.

 Key point: The use of quantitative data in small-scale research
Quantitative data can be used very effectively without the need for complex statistical analysis. 'Every researcher can and should use numbers in their research' (Gorard 2006: 2).

Sources of quantitative data

Quantitative data take the form of numbers. They are associated primarily with strategies of research such as surveys and experiments, and with research methods such as questionnaires and observation. These are not, however, the only sources of quantitative data. As Table 15.1 indicates, quantitative data can be produced by a variety of research methods.

Table 15.1 Sources of quantitative data

Numbers	Research method
Answers to closed-ended questions	Questionnaires
Content analysis of transcripts	Interviews
Measurements from experiments	Observation
Observation schedule used with events	
Official statistics (health, education, trade, etc.)	Documents
Business data (performance, employment, etc.)	
Content analysis of, for example, company reports	

Types of quantitative data

Numbers can represent different types of things, and social researchers who want to use quantitative data need to be absolutely clear about the type of numerical data they are using. This makes a major difference to what can be done with the data, statistically speaking, and the kind of conclusions that can be drawn from the analysis. There are certain statistical techniques that work with some kinds of data that will not work with others. In this respect, numerical data can be considered under six headings. The first four concern the distinction established by Stevens (1946) between four types of measurement. These are called nominal, ordinal, interval and ratio. In addition to this, researchers should also be aware of the difference between 'discrete' and 'continuous' data.

Nominal data

As the name suggests nominal data represent something to which a name has been attached. In social research, an example of this occurs in relation to any numerical data collected about people's sex or their ethnicity. It is useful to collect data that allow us to quantify the population in terms of things like their sex and their ethnicity, but these features of people's identity do not naturally occur as a number. Any numerical data that are collected about them are based on the named categories of sex and ethnicity that we choose to apply (such as male/female or White/South Asian/African Caribbean). Nominal data of this kind are used very widely in social research and they allow us to talk about amounts, proportions and frequencies of a range of categories like locations, religions, diseases, personalities, etc. We can count the numbers in each category and use the figures to good effect. However, nominal data allow little by way of mathematical manipulation compared with the other types of data. It makes no sense, for instance, to think of the average place to live or the average illness to suffer. The numbers are based simply on names of things, and there is no underlying order to what those names signify.

Ordinal data

Like nominal data, ordinal data are based on counts of things assigned to specific categories but, in this case, the categories stand in some clear, ordered relationship. The categories are in rank order. This means that the data in each category can be compared with data in the other categories as being higher or lower than, more or less than, etc., those in the other categories. The most obvious example of ordinal data comes from the use of questionnaires in which respondents are asked to respond on a five-point scale, known as the Likert scale. The responses coded as 2 (agree) can legitimately be seen as more positive than those coded as 3, 4 or 5 (neutral, disagree, strongly disagree), but less positive than those coded 1 (strongly agree).

1	2	3	4	5
Strongly agree	Agree	Neutral	Disagree	Strongly disagree

Interval and ratio data

With interval data the 'distance' between the data points is *proportionate*. This means that the researcher not only can deal with the data in terms of 'more than' or 'less than', but also say how much more or how much less. Calendar years provide a suitable example of such data. Data collected for the years 1974, 1984, 1994, 2004 and 2014 not only differ in terms of being earlier or later than one another, they are also earlier or later by a known timespan interval. This allows the researcher to measure the difference between various periods: the difference between 1984 and 1994 can be directly compared with the difference between 2004 and 2014, and so on. Ratio data are like interval data except that they exist on a scale which has a 'true zero' or an absolute reference point. When the categories concern things like incomes, distances and weights, they give rise to ratio data because the scales have a zero point. Calendar years, in the previous example, do not exist on such a scale, because the year 0 does not denote the beginning of all time and history. The important thing about interval and ratio data, however, is that the researcher can compare and contrast the data for each category in terms of ratios, using multiplication and division. They are the highest level of data in terms of how amenable they are to mathematical manipulation.

Discrete data

Certain data are based on phenomena which naturally come in whole units. Numbers of children per family, in reality, have to be whole numbers. We might aggregate the numbers to arrive at an average figure of 1.9 or whatever, but we do not suppose that there exists anywhere 0.9 of a child belonging to a family. In this example, our measurement of children per family can be exact for each and every household, with no need for approximations or results accurate to the nearest fraction. The *discrete data* come in chunks: 1, 2, 3, 4, and so on.

Continuous data

Contrasted with this there are certain kinds of data which, for practical purposes, are inevitably measured 'to the nearest unit' simply because they do not come in neat, discrete chunks. Such things are measured to the nearest small unit because, as a variable, they are *continuous*. People's height, age and weight are obvious examples here. In principle, there is no end to the precision with which we might try to measure these items. We could measure height in millimetres, weight in grammes, age in seconds. For practical purposes, however, such precision would be counter-productive because it would throw up vast arrays of data which would not lend themselves to analysis. When variables are continuous, the researcher, in practice, needs to categorize the data. The unit of data is not exact height, exact weight, exact age; rather, it is 'height falling within a range of 2 cm', 'weight to the nearest 0.5 kilogrammes' or 'age at last birthday'.

The significance of continuous data lies with the implicit categories which are formed by the researcher to cope with difficulties of measuring points/units on a sliding scale. The researcher needs to be absolutely clear about the boundaries to such categories and exactly where the mid-point of the category resides. The accuracy of statistics based on continuous data depends on knowing the boundaries and mid-point to the categories of the data.

 Key point: Different kinds of numerical data
Researchers wanting to use quantitative data need to understand what kind of data they are working with and appreciate the possibilities and limitations associated with that particular kind of numerical data.

Describing the mid-point or average

One of the basic things that a researcher needs to do with a quantitative data set is to provide a description of the mid-point or the average. There are three ways of doing this and the choice of which *measure of central tendency* is used will depend on the kind of numerical data involved.

The mean (the arithmetic average)

The mean is what most people have in mind when, in common parlance, they think about 'the average'. It is a measure of central tendency based on imagining what would happen if instead of the values in the distribution all varying they were all the same – if there was an *equal distribution of values*. By adding all the values together and dividing by the number of cases it is easy to calculate this arithmetically. To calculate the mean of the values below:

- add together the total of all the values for a variable or category (= 116)
- divide this total by the number of cases (÷ 8)

This gives a mean of 14.5.

| 1 | 4 | 7 | 11 | 12 | 17 | 17 | 47 |

For social researchers, the mean has certain strengths and certain limitations when it comes to describing the data.

- *The mean can be used with interval and ratio data.* In practice, it is often used with ordinal data as well, although this is controversial. Calculations of the mean, however, are definitely not appropriate when working with nominal data. Clearly it makes no sense to think of the average when the researcher is dealing with nominal data such as categories of sex, ethnic group or occupations; how can you calculate the average of two sexes, of four ethnic groups or of ten occupations?
- *The mean is affected by extreme values ('outliers').* Because the mean includes *all* values, it is prone to being affected by the odd one or two values that might be vastly different from the rest. Extreme or unusual values get included in the overall mean, and can shift the figure for the mean towards any such 'outliers'. Two things will minimize the impact of such outliers. First, a large data set will shroud the influence of the odd one or two outliers. An outlier will have less of a distorting impact on a large sample than it will on a small sample, because the extent of its deviation from the rest will get subdivided more and more as the size of the sample gets bigger. Second, and linked to this, calculations of the mean are safest when there are relatively few outliers, and the outliers that do exist have a tendency to balance up and cancel each other out.
- *Use of the mean may lead to strange descriptions.* When we conclude, for example, that the average size of households in Britain has fallen from 2.91 persons in 1979 to 2.1 persons in 2014 we clearly do not mean this as a *literal* description of the situation. What does 0.3 of a person look like? It is a *statistical* description.

The median (the middle point)

The idea of 'average' can sometimes carry with it the idea of 'middle of the range' and this is the sense in which the median operates. The median is the mid-point of a range.

Calculation of the median is really very straightforward. Values in the data are placed in either ascending or descending rank order and the point which lies in the middle of the range is the median. With even numbers of values, it is the mid-point of the two central values. So, in the following set of data, the *median* is 11.5, half-way between the two middle values.

1   4   7   11   12   17   17   47

There are some crucial advantages and limitations connected with the use of the median as a measure of central tendency.

- *It can be used with ordinal data as well as interval and ratio data.* This opens up the scope of uses to many areas which are not suitable for the arithmetic mean.
- Because it is an ordinal operation, *the median is not affected by extreme values*, the 'outliers'. Looking at the values above, it should be clear that the value of 47, an obvious outlier, does not affect the calculation of the median. It does, though, affect the calculation of the mean. As far as the median is concerned, that value could lie anywhere between 18 and infinity because its sole significance is that it exists as a value in the range which is greater than 17. Now this, of course, can cut both ways. While the median is unaffected by outliers, it is equally insensitive to the implications of any such extreme values. It effectively eliminates such data from the picture.
- *The median works well with a low number of values.* In fact, in contrast to the mean, it is better suited to low numbers of values.
- We have the advantage of knowing that *exactly half the values are above the median* and half the values are below the median. It offers a quick and easy-to-grasp measure of the central point of the data.
- The main disadvantage of the median is that it does not allow for further mathematical processing.

The mode (the most common)

As the name suggests, when social researchers use the mode as a measure of central tendency they have in mind the most fashionable or popular figure. But this does not imply that they are looking for the best liked value in the data. It is the value which is *most common* that is the mode. Identification of the modal value simply consists of seeing which value among a set occurs most frequently: this is the mode. In the set below, *the mode is 17*.

1 1 4 4 7 11 12 17 17 17 47

As with the mean and the median, there are certain strengths and weaknesses pertaining to the use of the mode, and these need to be considered:

- *The mode can be used with nominal data*, as well as ordinal, interval and ratio data. It has the widest possible scope for application, then, in relation to social data. As a measure of central tendency it makes sense, for example, to talk about the most commonly watched soap opera on TV, whereas we cannot sensibly talk about the mean or median soap opera.
- Like the median, it is *unaffected by outliers* or extreme values. It focuses only on the most common value and ignores all others.
- It shares with the median the limitation that the mode *does not allow any further mathematical processing* to be undertaken on it. It is a stand-alone end-product.
- One other limitation: there *might not be one most popular value*, or some values might share top spot, so that there might be two or more modes.

 Key point: The difference between means, medians and modes
When describing data, social researchers need to be aware of the difference between the three measures of central tendency and decide which is most appropriate for their specific purpose.

Describing the spread of data

If researchers wish to describe a set of frequencies it will help if they can provide not only a measure of central tendency but also some idea of the way the data are spread out from that central point – *a measure of dispersion*.

The range

This is the most simple way of describing the spread of data. It is none the less effective, and a valuable method of giving an instant image of the dispersion of the data. The range of the data is calculated by subtracting the minimum value from the maximum value. In the set of values below, the *range* is 44 (i.e. 47 minus 3).

$$3 \quad 4 \quad 7 \quad 11 \quad 12 \quad 17 \quad 17 \quad 47$$

Although a statement of the range has value as an instant picture of how wide the data are spread it does have a rather serious limitation as a statistic. It is governed by the extreme values in any set and may consequently give a biased picture of the spread of the values between the extremes. In the example above the range of 44 is obviously determined by the outlier value of 47. Visually, it is evident that seven of the eight values lie within a range of just 14 (i.e. 17 minus 3). So although reference to the range of values is quick and easy it needs to be used cautiously and with attention paid to any extreme values and the way these might give a misleading impression of the spread.

Fractiles

Fractiles are based on the idea of dividing the range of the data into fractions. Each fraction contains the same number of data cases. When *quartiles* are used the data are divided into four sections. *Deciles* operate on the same principle but, as the name suggests, they divide the range into tenths. Where *percentiles* are used the data are divided into 100 equal parts.

There are two uses of fractiles for social researchers. First, they can be used for the selection of cases to analyse. Researchers can use them as a way of eliminating extreme highs and lows from the data they wish to examine. For example, by focusing on those cases that come in the second and third quartiles researchers know that they are dealing with exactly half of all the cases and, more than that, they are dealing with the half that are 'in the middle'. This middle part of the range is known as the 'inter-quartile range'. With incomes, for instance, use of the inter-quartile range overcomes the possibility of some very high incomes distorting the overall picture, since these would occur in the top quartile. Likewise, by not using the bottom quartile the researchers would eliminate very low incomes from their analysis.

A second use of fractiles is for comparison. They allow comparisons to be made between those cases that occur at one end of the range and those that occur elsewhere in the range. The top quarter can be compared with the bottom quarter, or the highest 10 per cent with the lowest 10 per cent. The most prominent use of this is in comparisons of income and wealth. The top decile (the 10 per cent of all earners who earn more than the other 90 per cent of earners) can have their pay compared with the 10 per cent of all earners who earn the least. The comparison can be in terms of how much is earned. Here the researchers can calculate the mean earnings of the top decile and compare this with the mean earnings of the bottom decile. Used in such a way fractiles can be a valuable tool for the social scientist in describing the spread in a frequency distribution.

Standard deviation

An alternative method of dealing with the spread of data comes in the form of the *standard deviation*. This works on the idea that if we wish to understand the dispersion of the data it would be useful to know how far, *on average*, the values varied from the mean. It is not an absolute measure of the difference between the highest value and the lowest value, as is the case with the use of ranges. More subtly, the standard deviation uses all the values (not just top and bottom) to calculate how far in general the values tend to be spread out around the mean.

There are variations in the formulae used for calculating the standard deviation and there are certain complications that set in when it is used with grouped frequencies. However, these should not detain us because computer software will generally take care of the mathematics involved. The basic point is this: the greater the dispersion, the larger the standard deviation.

Use of the standard deviation as a measure of dispersion has some distinct advantages in relation to the analysis of quantitative data. Specifically:

- The standard deviation lends itself to further mathematical analysis in a way that a straightforward description of the spread does not.
- Following from this, the standard deviation assumes huge importance in social research because it is the basis of so many other statistical procedures.

However, it is important to remember that it is not a measure of dispersion that can be used with nominal data. Because it takes the arithmetic mean as the basis of its calculations only those kinds of data that lend themselves to this measure of central tendency can be used. That is, the standard deviation can be used only with cardinal numbers (interval and ratio data). It is meaningless to use it with nominal or even, strictly speaking, with ordinal data.

Good practice: Calculating the standard deviation: the logic

Technically, we want to know 'the mean variation from the mean'. In common language, we want to know 'the average amount by which our data is spread out from the middle'. To do this we could add up the amounts by which each value on our data list varies from the mean and, to get the 'average', divide this total by the number of values on the list. If we did so, however, the result would always equal zero. This is because the positive and the negative differences from the mean, when totalled, will always cancel each other out. To get around this the differences from the mean need to be squared because this ensures that they all have a positive value and cannot cancel each other out. When these 'squares of the differences from the mean' are added together and divided by the number of cases in the data list they provide a measure of the 'average' spread around the middle. Or, to put this in statistical jargon, we can calculate the mean of 'the sum of the squares' and get a measure of the *variance* of the data. To get the units back to the same as those in the actual distribution being looked at we need to get the 'square-root of the variance' – and it is this which is known as the 'standard deviation'.

Looking for patterns and relationships in the data

Having produced a description of the profile of the data the next stage of analysis is to look for patterns and relationships in the data. This involves *looking for connections*. Researchers will want to check whether there are any patterns of association between variables within a data set or whether there are any relationships between two or more sets of data. Does one category of data match another, or does one category vary along with another? Is there a difference between two sets of data where it might have been expected that there would be a similarity?

Looking for connections, at one level, can be a very straightforward process. In essence it need only involve looking at the data in the tables or the charts to see what links are evident. However, appearances can be deceptive. For research purposes the mere appearance of a connection is not enough. Good researchers want to know:

- whether the findings were a fluke;
- how strong the connection is between the two variables;
- whether one causes the other, or whether the two are mutually interdependent.

These seem reasonable things to ask of the data. And this is where *statistical tests of significance* prove to be of enormous benefit. Such statistical tests provide an estimate of the probability that any association we find between two or more variables is the product of sheer chance rather than a genuine connection between such variables – connections that will be found on other occasions. They provide a benchmark for researchers, indicating whether to proceed on the assumption that the apparent connection is real or whether to treat the data as unreliable evidence on the point.

Good practice: A cautious approach and the null hypothesis

Social researchers should start from the premise that there is no real pattern or no real relationship between sets of data and only be persuaded to reject this position if the statistics point to a probability of less than 1 in 20 ($p < 0.05$) that the results arose by chance.

Good researchers are very cautious in their approach to the search for patterns and relationships in the data. They approach things with a sceptical mindset and start from the premise that any pattern they might detect in the data could actually be the outcome of nothing more than sheer chance. As an expression of this cautious approach researchers using statistics start with a *null hypothesis*. They approach their findings with the presumption that there is no real pattern or no real relationship between sets of data, and they will only be persuaded to reject this position if there is 'overwhelming' statistical evidence to the contrary. In the social sciences there is a convention that researchers will not accept that observed patterns or relationships are worthy of being considered 'real' unless the probability of them arising by chance is less than 1 in 20. In technical terms this involves a *significance level of $p < 0.05$*. Only if the patterns or relationships are shown to have a 'probability of less than 5%' of being due to chance (shown as $p < 0.05$) will the good researcher be persuaded to reject the null hypothesis. Like members of a jury the researcher needs to be persuaded beyond reasonable doubt and this happens where the evidence/findings is likely to be true at least 19 times out of 20.

Caution: The meaning of 'significance'

Statistical significance does not necessarily imply social significance. The researcher needs to be wary of mixing the two senses of 'significance'. Statistical significance only relates to the amount of confidence we have that the findings we obtained were not the product of pure chance. It does *not* automatically imply that the findings are 'important'. That is something to be shown elsewhere by other means.

Statistical tests for association and difference

How do I find out if two variables are associated to a significant level?

Probably the most flexible and certainly the most commonly used statistical test for this is the *chi-square test*. The chi-square test works with nominal data as well as ordinal, interval and ratio data – which does much to explain its popularity. The columns and rows can use nominal data based on things like sex, ethnicity and occupation, factors which feature prominently in data collected by social researchers (see Table 15.2).

It works on the supposition that if there were no relationship between the variables then the units would be distributed in the cells of the contingency table in equal proportion. This means that if there were three times as many women as men in a sample, we would start from the assumption that women would account for 75 per cent of the amounts or frequencies we are measuring, for instance,

Table 15.2 Chi-square and contingency tables: example

Days absent from work through illness during the previous year, by sex of employee

			Sex		Total
			Male	Female	
Days lost	0–5 days	Count	8	7	15
		Expected count	*7.0*	*8.0*	*15.0*
	6 or more days	Count	6	9	15
		Expected count	*7.0*	*8.0*	*15.0*
Total		Count	14	16	30
		Expected count	*14.0*	*16.0*	*30.0*
		Value	d.f.	(2-sided)	
Pearson chi-square		0.536*	1	0.464	

Note: *0 cells (0.0%) have expected count less than 5. The minimum expected count is 7.00.

absences from work. If there is no connection between sex and absenteeism from work we might expect the larger proportion of women in the sample to account for a larger proportion of absences – in the strict ratio of 3:1. This 'expected' distribution (based on the null hypothesis) is, in other words, a theoretical distribution based on a starting premise that the two variables concerned do not affect each other. In reality it is extremely *un*likely that the research findings will match this theoretical distribution. Almost certainly there will be a difference between what might be expected and what is actually found in practice. And this difference, the difference between what was 'observed' and what was 'expected', is the key to the chi-square test. The chi-square test uses the extent of difference (in the cells of a contingency table) between what was observed and what might have been expected in order to calculate whether we can have confidence that the observed relationship was actually due to something other than pure chance – whether it was real or a fluke.

The main restriction on the use of the chi-square test is that there needs to be a sufficiently large data set and/or a sufficiently even distribution among the various categories in order to get a minimum of five in each cell. Where cells in the contingency table have fewer than five in them it threatens the accuracy of the statistic. There are ways around this should it become a problem. There is a statistical fix which can be used (e.g. the Yates correction factor) and most computer programs will put this into operation automatically. Alternatively, the categories can be combined and reduced in number to ensure that each cell has enough data in it.

There is a danger with the use of the chi-square test that the results are heavily affected by the categories which are used. Where categories are combined (for example, to ensure a minimum of five in each cell) or where categories are based on *grouped* frequencies, the researcher needs to be very aware that:

- the 'boundaries' for the categories are creations of the researcher;
- use of different combinations or boundaries will affect the chi-square statistic.

The flexibility in terms of categories in the columns and rows, then, turns out to be both a strength and a potential weakness of the test.

How do I see if two groups or categories are different to a significant level?

Project researchers often wish to compare two sets of data to see if there is a significant difference between them. For example, a teacher might wish to compare two sets of test scores obtained from students: one set obtained at the start of the school year, the other set obtained from the same students on the same test at the end of the school year. Alternatively, he/she might wish to compare the results obtained from students in one class with those from another. In small-scale research the need to compare two such groups or categories in these ways is very common.

The most appropriate statistical test for this purpose is the *t*-test. The *t*-test provides the researcher with a statistical test of significance. It uses the means of the two sets of data and their standard deviations to arrive at a figure which tells the researcher the specific likelihood that any differences between the two sets of data are due to chance.

Researchers using the t-test take the null hypothesis as their starting point. They presume that there is no real difference until they can be persuaded otherwise by a statistical test which points to a very strong likelihood that any variation found between the two sets of data was the result of something other than pure chance. As with the chi-square test, researchers normally treat differences as 'real' (not a fluke) when they find that there is a probability of less than 1 in 20, usually expressed as '$p < 0.05$', that any difference between the two sets of data was due to chance.

Example 15.1

The t-test

We have two sets of marks obtained from two classes who have both taken the same test at about the same time. Is there a significant difference between the scores obtained by students in class A (mean = 60.25) and the scores obtained by those in class B (mean = 57.00)? The 'independent groups' t-test can be used to answer this.

Class A (%)	Class B (%)
70	55
60	45
45	70
80	75
55	50
65	55
65	40
50	60
80	75
55	50
65	55
65	40
50	60
25	70
80	55
45	
75	
70	
55	
50	

$t = 0.73$ $p = 0.471$ i.e difference is not statistically significant

The *t*-test has two notable strengths which are of particular benefit for small-scale research. The *t*-test works well with small sample sizes (less than 30) – an obvious advantage with small-scale research – and the groups do not have to be exactly the same size. A data set of 20 items can be compared with a data set of 15, for example.

There are other statistical tests which compare the results from two sets of data that will work with ordinal data rather than interval or ratio data. For example, the *Mann–Whitney U test* is a well-known test that works by using the rank-ordering of cases in each group. This is why it can work with ordinal data such as examination *grades* (A, B, etc.) if actual percentage scores are not available. The Mann–Whitney U test works by producing one overall ranking which is made from both groups being investigated. The positions of members of each group on this combined ranking are then used as the basis for calculating whether there is a statistically significant difference between the two groups.

How do I see if three or more groups or categories are significantly related?

This question is likely to be moving beyond the scope of interest for project researchers. It suggests a fairly large data set with more than two variables potentially connected and worthy of statistical test. It calls for a basic *factor analysis* such as one-way *ANOVA* (analysis of variance). This test analyses the variation within and between groups or categories of data using a comparison of means.

How do I assess the strength of a relationship between two variables?

This question is not concerned with the *likelihood* of any apparent connection between two variables being real; it is concerned with how *closely* two variables are connected. The relevant statistics here are *correlations*.

Correlations between two variables can be visualized using a *scatter plot*. These need ratio, interval or ordinal data, and cannot be used with nominal data. They also require reasonably large data sets to work best (see Figure 15.1).

Figure 15.1 Correlations and scatter plot: example

The two most commonly used correlation statistics are Spearman's rank correlation coefficient (which works with ordinal data) and Pearson's product moment correlation coefficient (which works with interval and ratio data).

These statistical tests are used to arrive at a *correlation coefficient* based on the data. The correlation coefficients range from +1 to –1 as shown in Table 15.3.

Table 15.3   Correlation coefficients range

+1	0	−1
perfect positive	no relationship	perfect negative
correlation		correlation
(one goes up,		(one goes up,
other goes up)		other goes down)

In reality, correlations are unlikely to be perfect. Researchers generally regard any correlation coefficient between 0.3 and 0.7 (plus or minus) as demonstrating some reasonable correlation between two variables. 0.3 is reasonably weak, 0.7 is reasonably strong.

 Caution: Correlation does not indicate cause

It is important to appreciate that correlation is different from cause. The connection between two variables that might be demonstrated using a correlation test says nothing about which variable is the dependent and which is the independent one. It says nothing about which is the cause and which is the effect. It only establishes that there is a connection, with a specified closeness of fit between the variables. Researchers wishing to investigate connections in terms of cause and effect need to use *regression analysis*.

Presenting the data: tables and charts

Statistical packages and spreadsheets generally contain a table-making and a chart-making facility. So 'drawing' the tables and charts does not generally pose much of a problem for project researchers. The skill of producing good tables and charts tends to revolve far more around 'design' issues and the researcher's ability to do the following:

- present enough information without 'drowning' the reader with information overload;

- help the reader to interpret the table or chart through visual clues and appropriate presentation;
- use an appropriate type of table or chart for the purpose at hand.

Vital information

There are certain pieces of information which must always be included. If these are absent, then the table or chart ceases to have much value as far as the reader is concerned. The table or chart must always have:

- a *title*;
- *information about the units being represented* in the columns of the table or on the axes of the chart (sometimes this is placed by the axes, sometimes by the bars or lines, sometimes in a *legend*);
- the *source* of the data, if they were originally produced elsewhere.

Added to this, in most cases – though not all:

- the horizontal axis is the 'x axis' and is used for the independent variable;
- the vertical axis is the 'y axis' and is used for the dependent variable.

There are some exceptions to the rule about the x axis being the horizontal axis, and these are mentioned below. When constructing a chart or table, though, it is important for the researcher to have a clear view about which variable is seen to be the 'cause' and which is the 'effect'. The variable which is treated as the 'cause' is the independent variable (normally on the horizontal axis) and the variable which is being affected is the dependent variable (normally on the vertical axis). Dates (for example, 1984, 1994, 2004, 2014) are usually on the horizontal axis and are treated as an independent variable.

If the researcher pays attention to these points, the remaining dangers to the success of the table or chart generally come from trying to be too ambitious and putting in too much detail. Simplicity is a virtue that is hard to overstress in relation to the production of tables and charts. If too much data are supplied in a table, it becomes almost impossible for the reader to decipher the meaning of the data. Too many patterns, too many words, too many figures, and the impact of the table or chart is lost.

Good practice

Simplicity is a virtue when it comes to the presentation of tables and charts.

Tables

One of the main virtues of tables is their flexibility. They can be used with just about all types of numerical data. Computer software offers a variety of templates for tables, which aid the presentation of data in a visually attractive fashion.

The degree of complexity of the table depends on two things: the audience being addressed and the restrictions imposed by the format of the document in which the table appears. For the purposes of most project researchers it is likely that tables will remain fairly simple in structure. If the table *does* need to involve a considerable number of rows, the researcher should be prepared to insert horizontal and vertical 'breaks' or blank lines to ease reading and to avoid the eye slipping to the wrong line of data (see Table 15.4).

Table 15.4   Table (example)
Days absent from work through illness during the previous year, 30 employees

Days	Frequency	Days	Frequency	Days	Frequency
0	4	5	2	10	3
1	1	6	3	12	1
2	1	7	1	13	1
3	6	8	2	15	1
4	2	9	1	36	1

Source: Human Resources Dept, Healthy Life Insurance Co.

One particularly common use of tables is to present a comparison of sets of nominal data. Such tables are known as *contingency tables* (see Table 15.5). They allow a visual comparison of the data and also act as the basis for statistical tests of association, such as the *chi-square test*.

Table 15.5   Contingency table (example)
Days absent from work through illness during the previous year, 30 employees

Days lost	Male (n = 14)	Female (n = 16)
0–5 days	21	18
6 or more days	74	82

Source: Human Resources Dept, Healthy Life Insurance Co.

Bar charts

Bar charts are an effective way of presenting frequencies, and they are very common in reports of small-scale research. They can be used with nominal data and with discrete data. The principle behind them is that the bars should be of equal width, with the height of the bars representing the frequency or the amount for each separate category. Conventionally, there is a space between each bar. Their strength is that they are visually striking and simple to read – provided, that is, that not too many categories are used. The fewer the categories (bars), the more striking the impact. Beyond ten categories bar charts tend to become too crowded and confusing to read. Figure 15.2 shows a simple bar chart.

Figure 15.2 Simple bar chart (example)

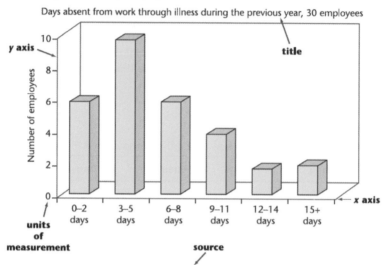

Source: Human Resources Dept, Healthy Life Insurance Co.

There are many variations on the standard bar chart. The *pictogram* embellishes the basic idea by using symbols or images instead of the standard bar. It does not tell you anything more, but it catches the eye more readily.

Bar charts are sometimes turned on their sides to make it easier to label the categories (see Figure 15.3). In such *horizontal bar charts*, the vertical axis becomes the *x* axis – as an exception to the convention.

Figure 15.3 Horizontal bar chart (example)

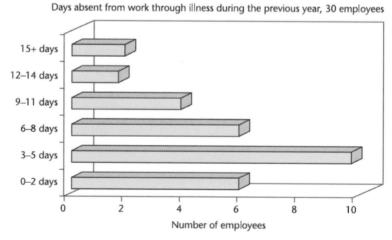

Source: Human Resources Dept, Healthy Life Insurance Co.

Sometimes each bar incorporates the component elements of the total for a category. This is known as a *stacked bar chart* (see Figure 15.4). Interestingly, stacked bar charts can be used as an alternative to pie charts (see below) because

Figure 15.4 Stacked bar chart (example)

Days absent from work through illness during the previous year, 30 employees

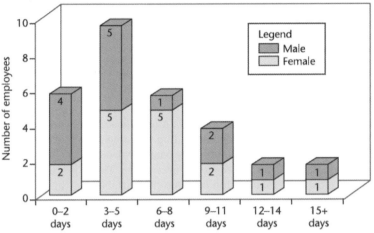

Source: Human Resources Dept, Healthy Life Insurance Co.

they clearly show the relative proportions of the factors that make up the total. They have an advantage, too. A number of stacked bars can be incorporated into the same chart, allowing a more direct visual contrast than could be achieved by placing a similar number of pie charts together.

Histograms

A histogram, like a bar chart, is a valuable aid to presenting data on frequencies or amounts (see Figure 15.5). Like a bar chart, the bars are normally of equal

Figure 15.5 Histogram (example)

Days absent from work in the previous year by age* of employees

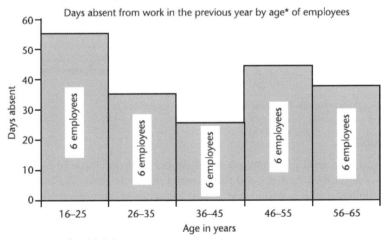

Note: *Age at last birthday
Source: Human Resources Dept, Healthy Life Insurance Co.

width and where they *are* of equal width, the height of the bar is used to depict variations in the frequencies or amounts. What distinguishes a histogram from a bar chart is that the *histogram is used for continuous data*, whereas a bar chart is used for discrete data or nominal data. In contrast to the bar chart:

- there are no gaps between the bars;
- the data 'flow' along the x axis, rather than being distinct and separate items.

Scatter plots

A scatter plot is used to display the *extent of a relationship* between two variables (see Figure 15.6). The data are represented by unconnected points on a grid, and the clustering or spread of such points is the basis for detecting a close co-variation between two variables, or a not so close co-variation. The closer the points come together, the closer the relationship between the variables on the x axis and the y axis. The more spread out the points are, the less closely the variables are connected. The extent of the relationship is made nicely visible; indeed the scatter plot is particularly good at showing patterns and deviations. There is a drawback, however. It does need a reasonable amount of data to reveal such a pattern.

Figure 15.6 Scatter plot (example)

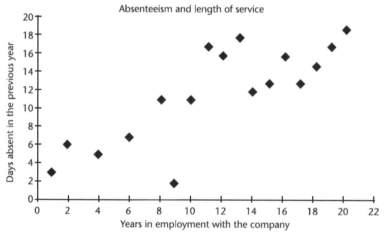

Source: Human Resources Dept, Healthy Life Insurance Co.

Line graphs

A line graph is used for depicting development or progression in a sequence of data (see Figure 15.7). It is good for showing *trends in data*. The most common use of the line graph is with dates. A time sequence is plotted left to right on the x axis. The line varies in height according to the frequency or the amount of the units. Line graphs work better with large data sets and big variations. A bar chart can be used to do the same thing, and sometimes bars and lines are combined within the same chart.

Figure 15.7 Line graph (example)

Total days absent from work through illness per year (2007–2014), all 30 employees

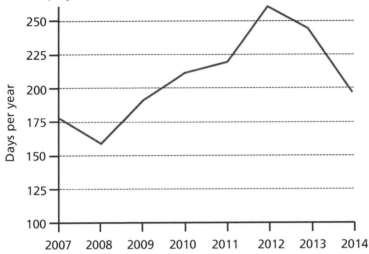

Source: Human Resources Dept, Healthy Life Insurance Co.

Pie charts

Pie charts, as their name suggests, present data as segments of the whole pie (see Figure 15.8). Pie charts are visually powerful. They convey simply and straightforwardly the *proportions* of each category which go to make up the total. In most cases, the segments are presented in terms of percentages.

Figure 15.8 Pie chart (example)

Proportion of employees absent from work through illness during the previous year, by total days absent, 30 employees

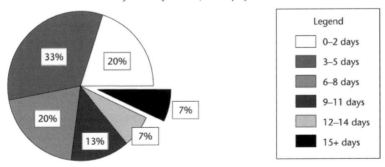

Source: Human Resources Dept, Healthy Life Insurance Co.

To enhance their impact, pie charts that wish to draw attention to one particular component have that segment extracted from the rest of the pie. On other occasions, all segments are pulled away from the core in what is known as an *exploded pie chart*.

Weighed against their visual strength, pie charts can only be used with one data set. Their impact is also dependent on not having too many segments. As a rule of thumb, a pie chart should have no more than seven segments and have no segment which accounts for less than 2 per cent of the total.

As a form of chart they tend to take up quite a lot of space on a page. The labels need be kept horizontal, and this spreads the chart out across the page. As good practice, incidentally, the proportions should be shown as a figure, where possible, *within the segments*.

 Caution: Avoid distorting the data

The presentation of quantitative data in graphs and charts can be used to mislead and give the wrong impression. Playing around with the scales on the x axis and the y axis can artificially exaggerate or underplay the appearance of differences in the data. Care needs to be taken to avoid distorting the data in this way.

Tables and charts: which one to choose?

When it comes to choosing which kind of chart or table to use researchers are faced with a range of possibilities. Their choice, however, is not simply a matter of picking 'the best'. There is no hierarchy with particular kinds of tables and charts being inherently better or worse than others. The choice, instead, needs to be based on the fact that some are better suited than others for portraying particular features of the data. As Table 15.6 indicates, when it comes to the presentation of quantitative data, certain kinds of table or chart work for certain purposes. It is important to get this right and to present the data appropriately.

Table 15.6 The use of suitable charts or tables

Purpose	Suitable chart or table
Amounts or Frequencies	tables bar charts histograms
Extent of a relationship	scatter plots contingency tables
Covering a span of time	line graphs
Proportions of a total	pie charts stacked bar charts

Reliability and validity: quantitative research

The credibility of quantitative data depends on how good the research methods are at producing data that are accurate and consistent. The data must be valid and the methods must be 'reliable', and these things are normally judged according to the following criteria.

Validity of the data

Validity refers to the accuracy and precision of the data. It also concerns appropriateness of the data in terms of the research question being investigated. The basic question is 'Are the data the right kind for investigating the topic and have they been measured correctly?'

Whether the right questions have been asked is something that the researcher needs to consider in relation to the existing theories and knowledge on the area. The data can be analysed, however, to gauge the extent to which the data are an accurate reflection of 'the truth' in the following ways:

- use 'check questions' within a questionnaire to see whether people's responses are the same to a very similar question;
- check for consistency in the profile of answers within the dataset, based on the assumption that similar respondents should provide the same kind of answers to similar questions.

The validity of the data, of course, will also depend on checking the data to make sure that they contain no errors arising from mistakes with data entry. This can be quite a laborious process but it is vital (unless the data files are constructed automatically). Where the data files have been entered via a manual process, with people typing in data from one source to another, there is the prospect of errors. It is the duty of the researcher to inspect the data files and check them against the sources.

Reliability of the methods

Reliability refers to whether a research instrument is neutral in its effect and consistent across multiple occasions of its use. This is frequently translated as the question 'Would the research instrument produce the same results on different occasions (all other things being equal)?'

There are a variety of ways researchers can analyse their data to check on reliability. They can, for example:

- use the research instrument on a later occasion and then compare the results. The *test–retest* approach should produce results that are very similar;
- split the dataset in half and compare one half with the other in terms of the findings they contain. Again, there should be a good level of consistency using this *split-half* approach;

- for data based on observations efforts can be made to find out whether different researchers would arrive at similar conclusions when looking at the same event. The level of *inter-observer reliability* should be high.

Generalizability of the findings (external validity)

Generalizability refers to the prospect of applying the findings from research to other examples of the phenomenon. It concerns the ability of research findings to explain, or occur in, similar phenomena at a general level rather than being something that is unique to the particular case(s) used for the research. Where the data are based on a large representative sample then there are good grounds for generalizing from the findings.

Objectivity of the researcher

Objectivity refers to the absence of bias in the research. It denotes research that is impartial and neutral in terms of the researcher's influence on its outcome, and it denotes processes of data collection and analysis that are fair and even-handed. Researchers are expected to address this by:

| Link up with
Reliability and
validity: qualita-
tive research,
p. 297.

- treating the data in a fair and impartial manner;
- giving due consideration to competing theories and alternative views in relation to the data;
- giving details of any sponsors of the research;
- declaring any vested interests in the outcomes of the research.

Advantages of quantitative data analysis

Scientific status

Quantitative data lend themselves to various forms of statistical techniques based on the principles of mathematics and probability. Such statistics provide the analyses with an aura of scientific respectability. The analyses *appear* to be based on objective laws rather than the values of the researcher.

Confidence in the findings

Statistical tests of significance give researchers additional credibility in terms of the interpretations they make and the confidence they have in their findings.

Precise measurement

The analysis of quantitative data provides a solid foundation for description and analysis. Interpretations and findings are based on measured quantities rather than impressions, and these are, at least in principle, quantities that can be checked by others for authenticity.

Analysis of large volumes of data

Large volumes of quantitative data can be analysed relatively quickly, provided adequate preparation and planning have occurred in advance. Once the procedures are 'up and running', researchers can interrogate their results relatively quickly.

Concise presentation of data

Tables and charts provide a succinct and effective way of organizing quantitative data and communicating the findings to others. Widely available computer software aids the design of tables and charts, and takes most of the hard labour out of statistical analysis.

Disadvantages of quantitative data analysis

Quality of data

There is a danger that appearances might be deceptive if the positive aspects of analysis and presentation associated with quantitative data flatter research that is actually based on weak data. The data need to be valid if the analysis is to have any value.

Technicist

There is a danger of researchers becoming obsessed with the techniques of analysis at the expense of the broader issues underlying the research. Particularly with the power of computers at researchers' fingertips, attention can shift from the real purpose of the research towards a blinkered concern with the technical aspects of analysis.

Data overload

Large volumes of data can be a strength of quantitative analysis but, without care, it can start to overload the researcher. Too many cases, too many variables, too many factors to consider – the analysis can be driven towards too much complexity. The researcher can get swamped.

Quantitative analysis is not as scientifically objective as it might seem on the surface

Researchers have an element of discretion and choice when conducting their data analysis, just as they do with qualitative data. And their decisions can influence the findings. Although the analysis of quantitative data might seem to be technical and scientific, in reality the researcher still has the ability to influence the findings in subtle ways.

Further reading

Balnaves, M. and Caputi, P. (2001) *Introduction to Quantitative Research Methods: An Investigative Approach.* London: Sage.

Field, A. (2013) *Discovering Statistics Using IBM SPSS Statistics,* 4th edn. London: Sage.

Gorrard, S. (2006) *Using Everyday Numbers Effectively in Research.* London: Continuum.

Rowntree, D. (1981) *Statistics Without Tears: An Introduction for Non-mathematicians.* London: Penguin.

Walker, I. (2010) *Research Methods and Statistics.* Basingstoke: Palgrave Macmillan.

Checklist for the use of quantitative data

When using quantitative data in your research you should feel confident about answering 'yes' to the following questions:　☑

1　Is it clear which type of quantitative measure is being used (nominal, ordinal, interval, ratio)?　☐

2　Have frequency distributions been described in terms of their midpoint and their range (e.g. mean, standard deviation)?　☐

3　Has the research explored patterns and relationships between variables?　☐

4　Are the results of data analysis presented in appropriate types of table or chart?　☐

5　Are the tables or charts clear and thoughtfully designed?　☐

6　Has all necessary information been supplied on the units being represented in the columns of the tables or on the axes of the charts?　☐

7　Have basic statistical tests been used to check on associations and correlations within the data?　☐

8　If so . . . Is the dataset sufficiently large to warrant statistical analysis?　☐

9　Are any statistical procedures used for data analysis suitable for:
  • the type of data collected (i.e. nominal, ordinal, interval, ratio)?　☐
  • looking for connections (e.g. correlation, chi-square, t-test)?　☐

10　Have any statistical tests of significance achieved a satisfactorily low probability ($p < 0.05$) to justify conclusions based on the data?　☐

16 Qualitative data

Types of qualitative data (words and images)

Qualitative data take the form of words (spoken or written) and visual images (observed or creatively produced). They are associated primarily with strategies of research such as case studies, grounded theory, ethnography and phenomenology, and with research methods such as interviews, documents and observation. Qualitative data, however, can be produced by other means. For example, the use of open-ended questions as part of a survey questionnaire can produce answers in the form of text. It is important to bear this point in mind and to recognize that qualitative data can be produced by a variety of research methods, as Table 16.1 indicates.

Preparing qualitative data for analysis

Qualitative data need to be prepared and organized before they can be analysed. It is important to appreciate that in a 'raw' condition qualitative data are likely to be difficult to interrogate in any systematic and meaningful fashion. Before the data can be used for research purposes, therefore, they need to be processed in a way that makes them amenable to analysis.

First, the *original data should be protected*. Back-up copies should be made of all original materials and it is generally advisable to use these back-up copies during the process of data analysis so that the originals can be preserved and protected against any unintentional corruption or damage.

Table 16.1 Types of qualitative data

Source of data	Research method	Format of data
Interviews	Interviews	Talk, transcript
Reports, diaries, minutes of meetings, scripts (e.g. for political speeches or media programmes)	Documents	Text, image
Interactions between people (including naturally occurring actions, responses, language) Events (e.g. ceremonies, rituals, performances) Artefacts, symbols, cultural objects (e.g. paintings, advertisements)	Observation	Photographs Pictures Video recordings
Answers to open-ended questions	Questionnaires	Text

Good practice: Make back-up copies

Because qualitative data tend to be irreplaceable, it is good practice to make a duplicate of any recordings, to make copies of computer files and to photocopy any visual images or documents such as field notes or transcripts.

Second, *the data should be catalogued and indexed.* Each piece of 'raw data' should be identified with a unique serial number for reference purposes. The importance of this is that when analysing the data it is vital that the researcher is able to return to points in the data which are of particular interest. Without an adequate reference system it will be virtually impossible for the researcher to navigate back and forth through the data or to record which bits of data are significant. There are various ways of doing this but, to illustrate one possibility, when indexing page 10 of a transcript of an interview that took place with Ms Hallam at Dovedale High School, Ms Hallam might be allocated T07 (the seventh teacher interviewed, perhaps), Dovedale High School might be allocated the code 13 (as school number 13), so that the actual code added to the transcript would be anonymized as [T07:13: p.10].

Transcribing audio recordings of interviews

Audio recordings normally need to be transcribed and annotated. Transcriptions help with detailed searches and comparisons of the data. They are also necessary when using qualitative data software (see below). The amount of the raw data that needs to be transcribed will depend on the use to which the data is being put. If the contents of an interview are being used for the factual information they provide,

Link up with Chapter 12 Interviews.

then the researcher can be quite selective; transcription might only be needed for the purposes of small extracts that can be used as 'quotes' to illustrate particular points when writing up the findings. If the researcher is looking for the underlying structure of the talk or the implied meanings of a discussion, the audio recordings will need to be transcribed quite extensively – possibly in their entirety.

Transcribing audio recordings is very time-consuming. For every hour of talk on an audio recording it will take several more to transcribe it. The actual time will depend on the clarity of the recording itself, the availability of transcription equipment and the typing speed of the researcher. When you are planning interview research it is important to bear this in mind. From the point of view of the project researcher the process of transcribing needs to be recognized as a substantial part of the method of interviewing and not to be treated as some trivial chore to be tagged on once the real business of interviewing has been completed.

Transcription might be laborious but it is also a very valuable part of the research because it brings the researcher 'close to the data'. The process brings the talk to life again and is a real asset when it comes to using interviews for qualitative data. Added to this the end-product of the process provides the researcher with a form of data that is far easier to analyse than the audio recording in its original state.

Good practice

Allow sufficient time for the transcription of audio recordings. The transcription of audio recordings is a time-consuming activity. For every one hour of interview recording it can easily take three hours or more of work to transcribe the talk into text.

Annotations

When transcribing an audio recording, the researcher should put informal notes and comments alongside the interviewee's words. These annotations can draw on field notes taken during the interview or notes made soon afterwards about the interview. They should include observations about the ambience of the interview and things like gestures, outside interferences, uncomfortable silences or other feelings that give a richer meaning to the words that were spoken. These annotations should be placed in a special column on the page.

Line numbering and coding

To locate different parts of the transcript and to help navigate through to particular points in it, each line in the transcript should ideally have a unique line number by which to identify it. Qualitative data analysis software always includes a facility to do this but it is also easily accomplished using basic word processing software such as MS Word. The page layout for the transcript should include a reasonable amount of clear space on which to write notes and there should be a wide margin on the side of the page that can be used later for coding and classifying the data and for writing notes. Qualitative data analysis software allows this automatically.

Problems of transcription

The transcription of audio recordings is rarely a straightforward mechanical exercise in which the researcher simply writes down the words that are spoken by research participants. In practice, it can be quite challenging, and there are three main reasons for this:

- *The recorded talk is not always easy to hear.* Especially with group interviews, but also with one-to-one versions, there can be occasions when more than one person speaks at the same time, where outside noises interfere or where poor audio quality itself makes transcribing the words very difficult. There is a fine dividing line here between the need to ditch these parts of the interview records and disregard them as worthless data and the need to exercise some reasonable interpretation about what was actually said.
- *People do not always speak in nice finite sentences.* Normally, the researcher needs to add punctuation and a sentence structure to the talk so that a reader can understand the sequence of words. The talk, in a sense, needs to be reconstructed so that it makes sense in a written form. This process takes time – and it also means that the raw data get cleaned up a little by the researcher so that they can be intelligible to a readership who were not present at the time of the recording.
- *Intonation, emphasis and accents used in speech are hard to depict in a transcript.* There are established conventions which allow these to be added to a written transcript but the project researcher is unlikely to be able to devote the necessary time to learn these conventions. The result is that transcripts in small-scale research are generally based on the words and the words alone, with little attempt to show intonation, emphasis and accents. Nor are pauses and silences always reported on a transcript. The consequence is that, in practice, the data are stripped of some of their meaning.

 Key point

Transcription is not always simple and straightforward. Transcription is not a mechanical process of putting audio-recorded talk into written sentences. The talk needs to be 'tidied up' and edited a little to put it in a format on the written page that is understandable to the reader. Inevitably, it loses some authenticity through this process.

Example 16.1: Interview transcripts

Part of the transcript of a group interview conducted with 15- and 16-year-olds about peer pressure and alcohol consumption. The names have been changed.

Notice how, typical of a group interview, more than one person is trying to talk at once. Elise cuts across James, and then gets interrupted in turn by Gordon, who manages to hold the spotlight for a moment or two. When more than one person is talking at one time, it makes transcription difficult because it is hard to capture on tape what is being said. ▶

▶

Line of the transcript		Code for the content	Notes
46	*Interviewer:* Do you feel under pressure to drink when		
47	you go out with your mates because they are drinking?		
48			
49			James looked
50	*James:* Yeh, but it's not always . . . (untranscribable)		annoyed as
51			Elise
52	*Elise:* . . . it's worse with the lads, I think, because. . .		and Gordon
53			talked over him
54	*Gordon:* . . . I was on holiday, and I don't like beer, and		
55	all my friends were drinking. I was drinking half a glass		
56	and I thought I can stick that out because I don't like it	08	
57	at all. I was drinking it and thinking this is horrible, just		
58	to look like one of the crowd, because I felt a bit left		Gordon says
59	out. My brother came up to me in front of the crowd		later that he
60	and said 'Gordon you don't like lager!' So all my		drinks beer
61	friends found out, and they said 'Look, we understand	15	regularly now.
62	if you don't like it' – and some of the people there were		
63	just like me, they didn't like it.		
64			
65			

Computer-assisted qualitative data analysis

A number of computer software packages have been developed specifically to help with the analysis of qualitative data. These are generally known as CAQDAS which stands for *computer-assisted qualitative data analysis software*. Some of these are more popular than others and some are more expensive than others. The best-known is *NVivo*, but there are many others that can be used and there are some valuable sites online which review the many alternatives and there are also a number of books that provide detailed guidance on the use of software like NVivo (e.g. Gibbs 2002; Di Gregorio and Davidson 2008; Bazeley and Jackson 2013; Lewins and Silver 2014).

It is advisable for the project researcher to use one of these computer software packages because, apart from anything else, they are designed to ensure that qualitative data are organized and stored in an appropriate fashion. In effect, using one of the packages obliges the researcher to prepare the data suitably and to take advantage of the computer's abilities to manage:

- *the storage of data.* Interview transcripts, field notes and documents can be kept in text files. Copies are quick and easy to make.
- *the coding of data.* The data can be easily coded – in the sense of both *indexing* the data (serial codes) and *categorizing* chunks of the data as a preliminary part of the analysis.
- *the retrieval of data.* The search facilities of the software make it easy to locate data once it has been coded and to pluck it out for further scrutiny.

> **Good practice**
>
> Use computer software for qualitative data analysis. Qualitative researchers should make use of CAQDAS packages because they help with the preparation, organization and storage of qualitative data.

CAQDAS packages, however, should not be regarded as a quick and easy fix for the task of analysing qualitative data. For one thing, *they do not actually do the analysis* – the researcher still needs to decide the codes and look for the connections within the data. The software helps with this – but there is no automatic processing of the data comparable with the way that statistics packages analyse quantitative data. And, of course, the use of computer software, no matter how straightforward, involves some start-up time. For the first-time user, there is the time taken in getting to know the package and understand its potential. There is also the time taken to input the data.

Analysis of talk and text

Qualitative data analysis is predominantly concerned with the analysis of talk and text, and the following sections of this chapter outline the main options available to the project researcher through a discussion of content analysis, grounded theory, discourse analysis, conversation analysis and narrative analysis. Table 16.2 summarizes the different purposes of the approaches and how these are reflected in their treatment of data. The analysis of image-based data occupies more of a niche position within social research and the specific issues concerned with the analysis of images and artefacts, therefore, are covered separately at a later stage in this chapter.

Across the range of approaches it is evident that there are different visions of the *work done by words*. The philosophy behind this is fundamental to the social sciences but from the position of the project researcher it is perhaps only necessary to appreciate that words do a lot more than simply describe something. As reflected in the different approaches, words can be analysed in terms of the background assumptions needed to interpret the words (what they imply and what they presume) or in terms of how words underlie social structure and interaction (how they produce things and construct things). So, whereas the text and talk might be treated at a surface level for the facts and information they contain, the words can also be used as a basis for 'reading between the lines' to see what lies beneath the surface. This can allow the researcher to interpret the hidden meanings contained in the talk and text or it can enable the researcher to see how things like speeches or stories or conversations are structured and sequenced in a particular fashion.

There is also a difference between the approaches in terms of the extent to which bits of the talk and text are used in separation from their context. The distinctions here are not hard and fast but the project researcher should be aware of

Table 16.2 Analysis of text and talk: a comparison of five approaches

	Content analysis	Grounded theory	Discourse analysis	Conversation analysis	Narrative analysis
Purpose of analysis	Look for hidden message	Develop concepts or theory	Show how power is exercised through language	Reveal underlying rules and structure of talk and interaction	Depict constructions of personal identity and social worlds
Data	Text and talk	Text and talk	Text and talk	Text and talk	Text and talk
Work done by words	Denote things	Imply things	Presume things	Produce things	Construct things
Significance of data	Frequency of occurrence	Derived meaning	Implied meaning	Displayed meaning	Implied meaning
Focus of attention	Surface content	Meaning of content	Content in context	Structure of content	Structure or meaning of content
Units of analysis	Words and phrases	Sentences and paragraphs	Paragraphs and whole documents	Blocks of text or talk	Whole story or text
Treatment of data	Measured (based on frequency and position)	Coded (using constant comparative method)	Related (to wider social structures and processes)	Deconstructed (to display underlying rules)	Deciphered (to find symbolic significance of story)
Data analysis	Quantification of text	Interpretation of text	Implication of text	Sequence and structure of talk	Structure or social implications of the text

© M. Denscombe, *The Good Research Guide*. Open University Press.

the *different levels of contextualization* to be found in the approaches. The unit of analysis can sometimes be individual words, sometimes sentences or paragraphs, other times the whole text, and the difference here revolves around how far the different approaches tend to isolate bits of text from (1) the words that surround them or from (2) the social context in which the words were used. For some kinds of content analysis it is not a problem to focus on instances of individual words extracted from the text. For approaches like discourse analysis and narrative analysis it is important not to separate units of the text from their wider social context. And with conversation analysis there is a particular importance given to the location of the unit of analysis within the rest of the text or talk within which it occurs.

Finally, a word on the underlying philosophies of the various approaches. In the case of content analysis there is a strong focus on measurement and it is interesting that although it is used in conjunction with qualitative data, it produces quantitative measurements. In this respect it might be seen as quite positivistic in its approach. Likewise with grounded theory the reliance on an inductive approach suggests an affiliation with positivism – although as we saw in Chapter 7, this is mainly the case with a specific branch of grounded theory. Discourse analysis, conversation analysis and narrative analysis, however, have little to do with positivism. Their assumptions about social reality and their preferences in terms of how the data should be treated are based, instead, on elements of critical realism, pragmatism and postmodernism. Broadly speaking, they are approaches to the analysis of qualitative data that are based on *interpretations*.

Content analysis

Content analysis can be used with any 'text' whether it is in the form of writing, sounds or pictures. It is used as a way of *quantifying* the contents of that text. Political scientists might use it to study the transcripts of speeches, educationists to study the content of children's books, and historians to study statesmen's correspondence. Whatever its specific application, content analysis generally follows a logical and relatively straightforward procedure:

1 *Choose an appropriate sample of texts or images*. The criterion for the choice of such a sample should be explicit. If the choice involves sampling, then there needs to be a justification for the kind of sampling technique used (see Chapter 2).

2 *Break the text down into smaller component units*. The unit for analysis can be each and every word. Alternatively, the analysis can use complete sentences as the unit, whole paragraphs or things like headlines. It can also be based on visual images or the content of pictures.

3 *Develop relevant categories for analysing the data*. The researcher needs to have a clear idea of the kinds of categories, issues and ideas that he or she is concerned with and how these might appear in the text. This might take the form of 'key words' associated with the theme. So, for example, a search for

sex bias in children's stories might look for instances of boys' names and girls' names – the names being treated as indicative of the nature of the content. The researcher might also wish to code the text in terms of the kinds of names, rather than just how many times such names occur.

4 *Code the units in line with the categories.* Meticulous attention to the text is needed to code all the relevant words, sentences, etc. These codes are either written on the text and subsequently referred to, or entered via a computer program specially designed for the purpose.

5 *Count the frequency with which these units occur.* The first part of analysis is normally a tally of the times when various units occur.

6 *Analyse the text in terms of the frequency of the units and their relationship with other units that occur in the text.* Once the units have been coded, a more sophisticated analysis is possible which links the units and attempts to explain when and why they occur in the way they do.

Link up with
Chapter 14
Documents.

Content analysis has the potential to disclose many 'hidden' aspects of what is being communicated through the written text (Table 16.3). The idea is that, quite independent of what the writer had consciously intended, the text carries some clues about a deeper-rooted and possibly unintentional message that is actually being communicated. You do not have to base the analysis on what the author *thought* he/she was saying when the text contains more tangible evidence about its message (Gerbner et al. 1969; Krippendorf 2013).

The main strength of content analysis is that it provides a means of quantifying the contents of a text, and it does so by using a method that is clear and, in principle, repeatable by other researchers. Its main limitation is that it has an in-built tendency to dislocate the units and their meaning from the context in which they were made, and even the intentions of the writer. And it is difficult for content analysis to deal with the meaning of the text in terms of its *implied* meanings, how the meaning draws on what has just been said, what follows or even what is left unsaid. In many ways it is a rather crude instrument for dealing

Table 16.3 Content analysis

Content analysis reveals . . .	By measuring . . .
What the text establishes as relevant	What is contained (e.g. particular relevant words, ideas)
The priorities portrayed through the text	How frequently it occurs; in what order it occurs
The values conveyed in the text	Positive and negative views on things
How ideas are related	Proximity of ideas within the text, logical association

with the subtle and intricate ways in which a text conveys meaning. In practice, therefore, content analysis is at its best when dealing with aspects of communication which tend to be more straightforward, obvious and simple. The more the text relies on subtle and intricate meanings conveyed by the writer or inferred by the reader, the less valuable content analysis becomes in revealing the meaning of the text.

Grounded theory

The grounded theory approach is primarily associated with the analysis of interview transcripts (although it can be used with a variety of types of qualitative data). The analysis requires a detailed scrutiny of the text and involves a gradual process of coding and categorizing the data. The ultimate goal of the analysis is to derive concepts and theories that capture the meaning contained within the data. The grounded theory approach tends to be 'inductive' in the sense that it seeks to use findings from particular instances as the basis for developing statements that apply at a general level.

Link up with Chapter 7 Grounded theory.

Explore the data

The first task for the researcher is to become thoroughly familiar with the data. This means reading and re-reading the transcripts. It entails getting a feel for the data and becoming immersed in the minute details of what was said, what was done, what was observed and what is portrayed through the data. To start with the researcher can take a fairly superficial look at the text (or images). Because some time might have elapsed since the data were collected, and because there is likely to be a considerable amount of data to work on, the aim should be to refresh the researcher's memory about the content of the data and to remind him/her about the broad scope of the material that is available. Returning to the data for further inspection, the researcher should begin to cross-reference the material with field notes to enable a better understanding of the data *in context*. Subsequent re-readings of the data should allow the researcher to identify *themes* in the data.

Memos

As the analysis progresses new things will emerge as relevant or new interpretations might spring to mind. As new insights come to the researcher, the ideas need to be noted. Brief thoughts can be appended to the data but more detailed insights are easier kept as *memos*. These memos are of practical value as a means for logging new thoughts and exploring new possibilities in relation to the analysis of the data. Such memos, in addition, are valuable in the way they provide a documented record of the analytic thinking of the researcher as they refine the codes and categories. In this sense memos are a note pad on which the researcher records how and why decisions were taken in relation to the emerging analysis of the data. In effect, they render the process of analysis explicit and accountable, and can form part of the 'audit trail' (see below).

Good practice: The use of memos

Researchers should write memos as a way of keeping track of their decisions in relation to the analysis of the data. The memos provide a permanent record and can be referred back to as a reminder about the researcher's thinking at specific points during the research.

Code the data

Codes are tags or labels that are attached to the 'raw' data. They can take the form of names, initials or numbers; it does not matter as long as the code is succinct and is used systematically to link bits of the data to an idea that relates to the analysis. The use of codes in connection with the interpretation of data is quite distinct from the process of putting a *reference* code on the various pieces of data so that the parts can be identified and stored in an organized manner. During the interpretation of the data the researcher engages in *analytic* coding.

Whatever the form of the data – interview transcripts, field notes, documents, photographs or video recordings – the first thing the researcher needs to do is decide on the *units* that will be used for coding the data. This process is sometimes known as 'unitizing' the data. With text data the units could be as small as individual words, they could be lines in the text, complete sentences or they could be paragraphs. Whichever, a decision needs to be made on what chunks of the data are to have codes attached to them.

Next, a decision needs to be made about the kind of thing that will be coded. Obviously, this will be guided to a considerable extent by the nature of the research problem but, to give an indication of the coding decision involved at this point, the researcher could base his/her coding on things like:

- a kind of event;
- a type of action;
- a shade of opinion;
- an instance of the use of a particular word or expression;
- an implied meaning or sentiment.

Finally, a decision needs to be made on the choice of initial codes that might usefully be applied to the data. The researcher can use respondent categories for this purpose; that is, base the initial codes on something that springs from the contents of the data. Or, the initial codes can be based on personal/professional hunches about what will prove useful for the analysis. The choice is not crucial at the initial phase of analysis because the codes are subject to a continual process of refinement during the research, so if the initial codes are 'incorrect', later versions will be refined and improved.

Categorize the codes

The next task is to identify ways in which the codes can be grouped into categories. The categories act as an umbrella term under which a number of individual codes can be placed. The terms 'taxonomy' and 'typology' are sometimes applied to this stage in the analysis, reflecting the general idea of classifying the various components of the data under key headings. The task for the researcher is to 'make the link'.

Reduce the number of codes and categories

At the beginning there are likely to be a large number of codes and categories – too many to be useful for any meaningful analysis. Part of the analysis, then, is to identify where there is sufficient congruence between them to allow some to be merged and others to be brought together within a broader category. Each of the codes brought together within the category will have some feature that is shared with the others and, of course, this feature will be particularly relevant for the emerging analysis. At this point some decisions also need to be made about which parts of the data are more important than others. Attention has to be focused on these parts, with other parts of the data being relegated to the sidelines. The importance of such parts of the data, it should be stressed, is determined solely by their significance for the emerging analysis.

Develop a hierarchy of codes and categories

Making sense of the data will involve differentiating among higher level and lower level codes. The higher level codes will be broader and more inclusive. Crucially, though, the task for the researcher is to develop hierarchical pyramids of codes by subsuming some (lower level) codes under other broader codes (higher level). The categories will necessarily operate at a higher level of generality which will allow them to cover a number of lower-level, more specific codes (see Figure 16.1).

Figure 16.1 The grounded theory approach to the analysis of qualitative data

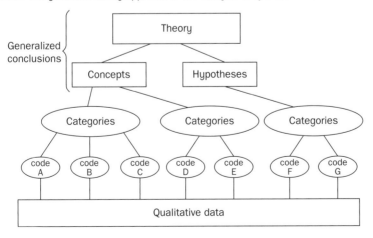

Check the emerging codes, categories and concepts with the data

The steps towards refining the categories and concepts form part of an iterative process. They are steps in the 'data analysis spiral' which means that each task is likely to be revisited on more than one occasion as the codes, categories and concepts are developed and refined.

Good practice: Check the emerging analysis against competing theories and alternative explanations

Researchers should review their analysis in the light of other explanations of similar data. Competing theories should be considered, and the analysis should be evaluated in relation to the alternatives. Particular attention should be paid to any instances within the researcher's own data that might appear to contradict the emerging analysis.

Move towards key concepts

In principle, grounded theory analysis aims to use the higher level codes and categories as the basis for identifying key concepts. The development of these concepts is the main purpose of the analysis because the concepts provide some new understanding of the data and constitute the foundations for any theory or general conclusions to emerge from the research.

Discourse analysis

Discourse analysis approaches qualitative data with the view that they should never be taken 'at face value'. Instead, they should be 'deconstructed' to reveal the hidden messages that they contain. It is an approach to the analysis of qualitative data that focuses on the *implied meaning* of the text rather than its explicit content. It is concerned with what is accomplished through the use of words – what words 'do' rather than what they literally represent – and draws on the philosophical influence of people like Wittgenstein (1968) and Austin (1962). Discourse analysis has been developed by postmodernists such as Foucault and Derrida and is familiar within the fields of social psychology, sociology and linguistics. It is used in relation to a wide range of social research areas including cultural studies, marketing (especially advertising), education and feminist studies.

In line with other approaches to qualitative data analysis, discourse analysis likes to keep *close to the data*. The task of the researcher is to interrogate the data with the aim of showing just how the discourse can be discerned through the particular data being studied. Discourse analysis, in this sense, does not differ from the kind of qualitative data analysis outlined elsewhere in this chapter to the extent that it relies on:

• a close scrutiny of the text/image;
• a firm grounding of conclusions within the data.

However, discourse analysis differs from approaches like content analysis and grounded theory in the way its analysis goes beyond the 'evidence' to be found within the text, talk or images being used as data. This is almost inevitable because discourse analysis, in its attempt to reveal the cultural assumptions that need to come into play in order to understand the data, looks at what is *absent* from the text or image as well as what is contained. It looks at what is *implied* as much as what is explicit. The question arises: 'How would you know what was missing if you did not have some idea of what should be expected to "fill the gaps" and "speak the unspoken"?' The answer to this is that researchers who undertake discourse analysis need to bring into play 'outside' factors in order to complete the picture and read between the lines. They must use existing knowledge about society, culture, politics, etc. and incorporate more general, background knowledge to decipher the significance of the message contained in the data.

Critical discourse analysis tends to add a political bite to the approach. It explores the ways the hidden, background meanings that are used to make sense of a text or image serve the interests of some groups more than others. In fact, this approach explores how power in society is achieved through discourse and how this is evident in particular instances of text or images. In doing so, it relies quite heavily on the use of political, economic and social ideologies as its frame of reference for understanding the meanings embodied in the data.

One limitation of using discourse analysis is that it does not lend itself to the kind of *audit trail* (see below) that might be needed to satisfy conventional evaluations of the research. It is not easy to verify its methods and findings. This is because the approach places particularly heavy reliance on the insights and intuition of the researcher for interpreting the data. Some discourse analysts eschew the idea that their research can, or should, be subject to any process of verification. They argue, in effect, that the findings stand as just 'the researcher's interpretation' – no better and no worse than anybody else's. No more scientific; no more credible. This is a controversial stance and it is one that could prove unwise for a project researcher to adopt. But, unless the researcher is prepared to risk taking this 'postmodernist' position, they need to be aware of the difficulties of verification inherent in the approach. With this in mind, what practical guidance can be given in relation to discourse analysis?

Be clear about which aspects of discourse are being studied

The researcher needs to specify whether the particular talk, text or image is being used in relation to:

- the shared background meanings and cultural assumptions necessary to make sense of the data themselves (micro);
- the wider ideology and cultural relations that are created and reinforced through the data (macro).

Be clear about which aspects of deconstruction are best applied

There is no hard and fast process involved in discourse analysis, but the researcher who embarks on deconstructing the data needs to have a clear vision of the things he/she is looking for and the way these link with the micro and macro aspects of discourse. A number of relevant questions to be asked include:

- Is there evidence of a wider ideology being communicated via the talk, text and images?
- Do the data reflect particular social, political or historical conditions in which they were produced?
- In what way does the talk, text or image stem from other sources ('intertexuality')?
- How is power or influence being exerted through the talk, text or image?
- Whose version of reality is being portrayed through this talk, text or image?
- How are people, processes and objects categorized and defined through the talk, text or image?
- Are there people, processes or objects that are notably absent or excluded?
- Are there contradictions within the talk, text or image? How are these coped with?
- What things are missing from the talk, text or image?
- Are there views that appear to be suppressed?
- Are there things that are not said that might have been expected to be stated?
- What rhetorical or linguistic devices are being used to argue the point?
- What version of things is being portrayed as normal/abnormal, legitimate/illegitimate, moral/immoral, natural/unnatural, etc.?
- Would alternative interpretations of the talk, text or image be possible or likely depending on the particular audience?

Conversation analysis

Conversation analysis focuses on the structure and sequencing of everyday talk. It is often considered to be a variant of discourse analysis because it focuses attention on how things get done through language use. In this instance researchers look at naturally occurring talk and the way that routine aspects of everyday life get accomplished through language (Hutchby and Wooffitt 2008; Sidnell 2010). There have been studies of things like taking turns in everyday conversation, greeting people, starting a school lesson – apparently mundane and minute parts of social life but ones that advocates of *ethnomethodology* stress are the fundamental building blocks of social interaction – without which there would be no such thing as social life.

Conversation analysts are inclined to underplay the extent to which they draw on presuppositions. However, their analysis must still rely on cultural insights. Indeed, the researcher's background knowledge can be argued to be absolutely essential to the sensible interpretation of routine conversation. For any reasonable interpretation, it is vital that the researcher has appropriate background knowledge, shared with those doing the talking. Otherwise, they would literally have no way of knowing what was going on.

Narrative analysis

A narrative relates to a story. A story can be told in many forms; in writing through books and in speech through interviews, as well as a whole host of other mediums perhaps less commonly used as sources of data by social researchers such as visual images, music and drama. Treated as a narrative, though, the story needs to have certain properties (Riessman 2003, 2008; Elliott 2005; Andrews et al. 2013). Normally, it would be expected to do the following:

- *have some specific purpose.* This could be a moral message or it could be an account of personal circumstances. Whatever the subject matter of the story, it has to be leading somewhere.
- *contain a plot line linking the past to the present.* There is normally some sense of development and change over time in which past events are recounted and linked explicitly to the present.
- *involve people.* The theme needs to have a human element to it, referring to feelings and experiences in the context of social events and human interaction.

For qualitative research such stories can be useful in two ways. First, they can be analysed in terms of how they *construct the social world.* The point here is that stories can have a special importance in culture which can go well beyond that of entertainment. They might be parables with strong moral lessons involved. They might be contemporary news stories built on underlying beliefs about rights and wrongs in politics. Or they might be 'classics' with great symbolic significance, handed down from generation to generation as part of the transmission of culture, telling of how things were and why things happened and serving to bolster the beliefs and values that bind a society together. Second, they can be analysed in terms of how they *construct a personal world.* This aspect of narrative analysis links quite closely with research on life histories and oral histories. It is concerned with the way that stories are used by people as ways of representing themselves and their lives to others. The stories are used, consciously or not, as a device through which people describe and explain themselves and the circumstances surrounding their existence.

Narrative analysis applied to any such stories is not overly concerned with whether the content of the story is built on truth or myth; the focus is more on how those stories *work*. The stories are analysed to reveal the way the story constructs and interprets the social world, and the focus of attention is on:

- the meanings and ideology the story conveys;
- the techniques and communicative devices the story-teller uses;
- how the story links with the cultural and historical context within which it is told.

Analysis of image-based data

The kind of analysis used for image-based data depends on the purposes for which the data were collected. Broadly, images are used for either, or both, of two reasons:

- for the factual information they contain;
- for the cultural significance and symbolic meaning that lie behind their content.

There are various strands to the analysis of visual images. Without becoming embroiled in the detail of the differences it is perhaps possible to identify three elements to the analysis of image-based data:

- *the image itself:* contents, genre, styles;
- *the producer:* intentions and context (by whom, when, under what circumstances, why, the intention of the creator);
- *the viewer:* interpretation and context.

The image itself can be valuable as a source of *factual information*. There is a case to be made that images provide a relatively reliable source of data – preferable, at least, argues Collier (2001: 59) to the 'deceptive world of words'. Objectively frozen in time, the image contains evidence of things with a clarity that words could never hope to match. Photographs from archives, film from distant fieldwork settings, snapshots from a family album, each contains a firm record of events that can be subsequently analysed by the researcher. 'Such images are produced to serve as records of reality, as documentary evidence of the people, places, things, actions and events they depict. Their analysis is a matter of extracting just that kind of information from them' (van Leeuwen and Jewitt 2001: 4).

Link up with Image-based research, p. 234.

To help get to grips with the information contained in large collections of images researchers can use *content analysis*, and it is quite possible to produce quantitative data as part of the analysis of images (see Bell 2000, for a detailed account of this). In practice, however, image-based research has largely favoured a qualitative approach. The key reason for this is that social researchers in recent years have become reluctant to take the content of images entirely 'at face value'. Rather than accepting images as neutral depictions of reality (along with the positivistic connotations this has), most social researchers in the twenty-first century would acknowledge, as Rose (2012) argues, that images do not contain 'one right meaning'. What they depict is open to interpretation and it would be rather naïve to presume that the contents of visual images are self-explanatory. Without entirely abandoning the use of images in terms of their ostensive content (the 'facts' they portray), researchers have become more inclined to treat the contents as something that needs to be interpreted. The meaning of the image is the thing of value for the researcher, the meaning as given within a particular culture, within a given time, within a social context within which it was produced.

Another way of interpreting an image is as a *cultural artefact*. As a cultural artefact the focus moves away from just the content of the image and what this can tell the researcher to incorporate, also, questions about the context in which the image was produced. What purpose did/does it serve? Why was it produced? As a source of evidence the value of the image is in what lies behind the surface appearance. To give an illustration, a photograph might appear to show a family on a seaside beach. At one level the researcher could use the image to get factual information about the style of beachwear worn at the time the photograph was taken. Provided the photograph was authentic, the image acts as a source of factual data. However, that same image might be interpreted as a cultural artefact by asking questions about how and why it was produced. Who took the photograph? Why was it taken? What importance is attached to it that might explain why it has been kept over a long period of time? What equipment was used to take the photograph? Such lines of enquiry could help researchers to understand the significance of family holidays, the role of photo albums and the nature of leisure activity in their cultural context. The meaning of the photograph, that is, goes beyond the superficial content depicting two adults and two children at the seaside.

Another approach to the analysis of images interprets them in terms of what they denote. It probes the image as a *symbolic representation* whose interest lies not so much in the 'facts' contained in the image as in the significance attached to the contents by those who view it. Images, used in this way, provide a source for uncovering ideologies and cultural codes. Drawing on the field of 'semiotics' the researcher first considers the various aspects of the content to see what they denote. Taken at face value, what do they 'say'? Next the researcher considers the connotations of the key elements in the image. What associations spring to mind when looking at those elements? Then, in the final stage of analysis, semiotics moves towards drawing contrasts and similarities with other signs in a way that helps us to understand the symbolism of the image. (See Penn 2000, for further information on the semiotic analysis of still images.)

It is important to note that reading the message is not entirely an individual, personal thing in which each viewer interprets things differently. While there is certainly some scope for variation, semiotics and cultural studies operate on the premise that there is a degree of consensus among viewers about the meaning of an image. People who come from a similar cultural background, who are members of the same society or who have been brought up within a particular ideological tradition (e.g. democracy, Christianity), might be expected to make sense of images in roughly the same way. As members of social groups they will have been *socialized* into ways of seeing what is meant by visual images – learning from others since their early years how to make sense of visual clues contained in things like signs, advertisements, portraits and music videos.

Caution: Context is important

When using images for research purposes there is always the danger that they might be 'taken out of context'. Events prior and subsequent to the moment captured by the image might have a crucial bearing on the meaning that can be attributed to it.

Presenting the data

An explanation of statistical techniques and data manipulation always accompanies the use of quantitative data in research yet, all too often, an account of the comparable processes is missing or very scant when it comes to reports that have used qualitative data. The process that leads from the data to the researcher's conclusions gets ignored, with the reader of the research report being given little or no indication of how the data were actually analysed. The quality of qualitative research is increasingly coming under the microscope in this respect (Seale 1999; Seale et al. 2007; Silverman 2011) and, quite rightly, those who use qualitative data are now expected to include in their accounts of research a description of the processes they used to move from the raw data to their findings.

Key point

Researchers need to be explicit about the analytic procedures they have used. It is not acceptable to say 'this is how I collected the data' (methods) and 'these are my results' (findings) without giving an account of *how* the data were analysed.

Qualitative researchers, however, face a special challenge when it comes to depicting the process involved in the analysis of their data (Woods 2006). Partly, this is because qualitative data analysis is 'a messy, ambiguous, time-consuming, creative, and fascinating process. It does not proceed in a linear fashion: it is not neat' (Marshall and Rossman 2011: 207). Partly, it is because the data are not as amenable to being presented in a concise fashion as is the case with quantitative data. Quantitative data can be represented using statistics and tables. These provide a succinct and well-established means enabling researchers to encapsulate the findings from large volumes of data and provide the reader with explicit information about the techniques used for data analysis. The challenge for qualitative researchers is to depict their kind of data analysis within the confines of a relatively few pages when dealing with:

- a fairly complicated and messy process of data analysis;
- a relatively large volume of data based on words or images.

To deal with this challenge, qualitative researchers need to come to terms very quickly with the fact that it is not feasible for them to present all of their data. They need to be selective in what they present and acknowledge that they have to act as an editor – identifying key parts of the data/analysis and prioritizing certain parts over others.

Next, and linked with the editorial role, it needs to be recognized that the data chosen for inclusion within a report does not constitute evidence that proves a point. It is more likely to be introduced as an illustration of a point that is being made. Because the reader of the report does not normally have access to all the data, they have no way of knowing whether the selection was a fair reflection of the data or not. Further discussion of this point can be found in relation to the use of extracts from interview transcripts.

Finally, the representation of qualitative data/analysis involves an element of 'rhetoric'. That is, the credibility of the research owes something to the skill of the researcher in managing to produce a persuasive account of the research that 'touches the right buttons' and conveys a sense of authority and authenticity. There are some different styles of writing that qualitative researchers can employ to achieve this (van Maanen 1995; Woods 2006). Without delving into the rhetorical devices themselves, the point to note is that the credibility of qualitative research, although it still depends on providing relevant factual details relating to the research procedures, also relies on the literary skills of the researcher to write a convincing account.

> **Link up with** Chapter 18 Research reports.

The use of interview extracts in research reports

Extracts from transcripts play an important role in qualitative research. They can be interesting in their own right, giving the reader a flavour of the data and letting the reader 'hear' the points as stated by the informants. Or they can be used as a piece of evidence supporting the argument that is being constructed in the report by the researcher. What an extract is very unlikely to do, however, is provide proof of a point. There are two reasons for this:

- *The significance of extracts from transcripts is always limited by the fact that they are, to some extent, presented out of context.* Extracts, as the very word itself suggests, are pieces of the data that are plucked from their context within the rest of the recorded interview. This opens up the possibility that the quote could be taken 'out of context'. Everyone knows the danger of being quoted out of context. The meaning of the words is changed by the fact that they are not linked to what came before and what was said after. The shrewd researcher will try to explain to the reader the context within which the extract arose but, inevitably, there is limited opportunity to do this in research reports.

• *The process of selecting extracts involves a level of judgement and discretion on the part of the researcher.* The selection of which parts of the transcript to include is entirely at the discretion of the researcher, and this inevitably limits the significance which can be attached to any one extract. It is an editorial decision which reflects the needs of the particular research report. How does the reader know that it was a fair selection, representative of the overall picture?

As a result, in the vast majority of reports produced by project researchers, extracts will serve as illustrations of a point and supporting evidence for an argument – nothing more and nothing less. It is important that the project researcher is aware of this when using extracts and avoids the temptation to present quotes from interviewees as though they stand in their own right as unequivocal proof of the point being discussed.

Having made this point, there are some things the researcher can do to get the best out of the extracts that are selected.

• Use quotes and extracts verbatim. Despite the points above about the difficulty of transcribing recordings, the researcher should be as literal as possible when quoting people. Use the exact words.
• Change the names to ensure anonymity (unless you have their explicit permission to reveal the person's identity).
• Provide some details about the person you are quoting, without endangering their anonymity. The general best advice here is to provide sufficient detail to distinguish informants from one another and to provide the reader with some idea of relevant background factors associated with the person, but to protect the identity of the person you quote by restricting how much information is given (e.g. teacher A, female, school 4, geography, mid-career).
• Try to give some indication of the context in which the quotation arose. Within the confines of a research report, try to provide some indication of the context of the extract so that the meaning *as intended* comes through. As far as it is feasible, the researcher should address the inevitable problem of taking the extract 'out of context' by giving the reader some guidance on the background within which the statement arose.

Good practice: The use of diagrams

In reports based on qualitative research it is particularly useful to include diagrams that show the link between the concepts that are developed. This provides the reader with a visual picture of what can often be complex links. It also gives some transparency to the process of data analysis.

Reliability and validity: qualitative research

The credibility of qualitative research is not easily judged using the criteria conventionally used for quantitative research. It is not feasible, for instance, to check the quality of research and its findings by replicating the research in the same way that scientists might repeat an experiment. The first reason for this is that it is virtually impossible to replicate a social setting. Time inevitably changes things and the prospects of assembling equivalent people in similar settings in a social environment that has not changed are, to say the least, slim. The second reason is that the researcher tends to be intimately involved in the collection and analysis of qualitative data, so closely involved that the prospects of some other researcher being able to produce identical data and arrive at identical conclusions are equally slim.

Link up with Reliability and validity: quantitative research, p. 271.

Recognizing such difficulties, some qualitative researchers have suggested abandoning any commitment to these conventional ways of judging the quality of research. The majority, though, have been rather more reticent to abandon the conventional criteria used by the positivistic research. They make the point that, although the nature of qualitative research means that it will never be possible to be verified in the same way as quantitative research, there is still a need to address the need for verification (e.g. Kirk and Miller 1986; Seale 1999; Gibbs 2007; Silverman 2011; Miles et al. 2014). Such qualitative researchers have adopted a more pragmatic or 'subtle' realist perspective 'that does not give up on scientific aims as conventionally conceived, but also draws on the insights of post-scientific conceptions of social research' (Seale 1999: x). The discussion and guidance that follow are rooted in this point of view.

Credibility (validity)

The issue here is the extent to which qualitative researchers can demonstrate that their data are accurate and appropriate. Lincoln and Guba (1985) make the point that it is not possible for qualitative researchers to prove in any absolute way that they have 'got it right'. (As a consequence, they prefer to use the term 'credibility' in relation to this aspect of the verification of research.) There are, though, steps to be taken that can help with the task of persuading readers of the research that the data are *reasonably likely* to be accurate and appropriate. These steps provide no guarantee, because none are available. They offer, instead, reassurances that the qualitative data have been produced and checked in accord with good practice. It is on this basis that judgements can be made about the credibility of the data. To address the matters of accuracy and appropriateness of data qualitative researchers can use:

- *Respondent validation.* The researcher can return to the participants with the data and findings as a means of checking the validity of the findings. This allows a check on factual accuracy and allows the researcher's understandings to be confirmed (or amended) by those whose opinions, views or experiences are being studied.

- *Grounded data*. One of the key benefits of qualitative research is that the findings will have been grounded extensively in fieldwork and empirical data. Qualitative research tends to involve relatively long times spent 'on location' conducting the fieldwork and it builds on a detailed scrutiny of the text or visual images involved. This provides a solid foundation for the conclusions based on the data and adds to the credibility of the research.

| Link up with |
| Triangulation, |
| p. 154. |

- *Triangulation*. Avoiding any naïve use of triangulation, the researcher can use contrasting data sources to bolster confidence that the data are 'on the right lines'.

Dependability (reliability)

With qualitative research the researcher's 'self' tends to be very closely bound up with the research instrument – sometimes an integral part of it. As a participant observer or interviewer, for example, the researcher becomes almost an integral part of the data collecting technique. As a result, the question of reliability translates from 'Would the research instrument produce the same results when used by different researchers (all other things being equal)?' to 'If someone else did the research, would he or she have got the same results and arrived at the same conclusions?' In an absolute sense there is probably no way of knowing this for certain. Yet there are ways of dealing with this issue in qualitative research – ways that accord broadly with what Lincoln and Guba (1985) call 'dependability'. Principally, these revolve around the demonstration that their research reflects procedures and decisions that other researchers can 'see' and evaluate in terms of how far they constitute *reputable procedures and reasonable decisions*. This acts as a proxy for being able to replicate research. Only if such information is supplied is it possible to reach conclusions about how far another researcher would have come up with comparable findings. As a check on reliability, this calls for an explicit account of the methods, analysis and decision-making and 'the provision of a fully reflexive account of procedures and methods, showing the readers in as much detail as possible the lines of enquiry that led to particular conclusions' (Seale 1999: 157). In effect, the research process must be open for audit.

Good practice: An audit trail

An audit trail should be constructed and mapped out for the reader – allowing them to follow the path and key decisions taken by the researcher from conception of the research through to the findings and conclusions derived from the research. But, as Lincoln and Guba (1985: 319) stress, 'An inquiry audit cannot be conducted without a residue of records stemming from the inquiry,

▶ just as a fiscal audit cannot be conducted without a residue of records from the business transactions involved.' This is why it is good practice to keep a fairly detailed record of the process of the research decisions. The principle behind the audit trail is that research procedures and decision-making could be checked by other researchers who would be in a position to confirm the existence of the data and evaluate the decisions made in relation to the data collection and analysis.

Transferability (generalizability)

Qualitative research tends to be based on the intensive study of a relatively small number of cases. Inevitably, this raises questions about how representative those cases are and how likely it is that what was found in the few cases will be found elsewhere in similar cases. The thorny issue is often raised through the question; 'How can you generalize on the basis of such a small number?' Statistically speaking, this is a reasonable question. It is one that is difficult to dodge.

Some qualitative researchers try to side-step the issue by asserting that it is not their business to make such generalizations. They argue that the findings from things like case studies are worthwhile in their own right simply as a depiction of the specific, possibly unique, situation. This, however, is a minority position. The majority of qualitative researchers accept that the issue is relevant but argue that it needs to be approached in a different way when being used in relation to qualitative research. They point out that generalizability is based on the statistical probability of some aspect of the data recurring elsewhere, and it is a probability that relies on a large sample that is representative of the wider population. Research based on small numbers and qualitative data needs an alternative way of addressing the issue. This alternative way is what Lincoln and Guba (1985) have called 'transferability'. This is an imaginative process in which the reader of the research uses information about the particular instance that has been studied to arrive at a judgement about how far it would apply to other comparable instances. The question becomes 'To what extent *could* the findings be transferred to other instances?' rather than 'To what extent *are* the findings likely to exist in other instances?'

Good practice: Transferability of findings

The researcher needs to supply information enabling others to infer the *relevance and applicability of the findings* (to other people, settings, case studies, organizations, etc.). In other words, to gauge how far the findings are transferable, the reader needs to be presented with relevant details on which to base a comparison. If, for example, the research is on the eating habits of young people and it is based on interviews with 55 students in one school, ▶

▶ the findings might not be generalizable to the population of students in all schools. However, armed with appropriate information about the age/sex/ethnicity of the students and the social context of the school, it becomes possible to think about how the findings might apply to similar students in similar schools. Armed with the appropriate information, the reader can consider the transferability of the findings.

Confirmability (objectivity)

This issue of objectivity concerns the extent to which qualitative research can produce findings that are free from the influence of the researcher(s) who conducted the enquiry. At a fundamental level it needs to be recognized straight away that no research is ever free from the influence of those who conduct it. Qualitative data, whether text or images, are always the product of a process of interpretation. The data do not exist 'out there' waiting to be discovered (as might be assumed if a positivistic approach were adopted) but are produced by the way they are interpreted and used by researchers. This has consequences for the prospects of objectivity. First, it raises questions about the involvement of the researcher's 'self' in the interpretation of the data and, second, it raises questions about the prospects of keeping an open mind and being willing to consider alternative and competing explanations of the data.

The researcher's 'self'

The researcher's identity, values and beliefs cannot be entirely eliminated from the process of analysing qualitative data. There are, though, two ways in which qualitative researchers can deal with this involvement of the self. On the one hand, they can deal with it by saying:

> The researcher's identity, values and beliefs play a role in the production and analysis of qualitative data and therefore researchers should be on their guard to distance themselves from their normal, everyday beliefs and to suspend judgements on social issues for the duration of their research.

At this end of the scale researchers know that their self is intertwined with their research activity but proceed on the basis that they can exercise sufficient control over their normal attitudes to allow them to operate in a detached manner, so that their investigation is not clouded by personal prejudices. In this case the researcher needs to suspend personal values and beliefs for the purposes of the production and analysis of the data.

On the other hand, qualitative researchers could take the position that:

> The researcher's identity, values and beliefs play a role in the production and analysis of qualitative data and therefore researchers should come clean about the way their research agenda has been shaped by personal experiences and social backgrounds.

At the extreme, this approach can take the form of celebrating the extent to which the self is intertwined with the research process. There are those who argue that their self gives them a privileged insight into social issues, so that the researcher's self should not be regarded as a limitation to the research but as a crucial resource. Some feminist researchers and some researchers in the field of 'race' make the case that their identity, values and beliefs actually *enable* the research and should be exploited to the full to get at areas that will remain barred to researchers with a different self. So some feminists argue that only a woman can truly grasp the significance of factors concerned with the subordination of women in society. Some black researchers would make a similar point in relation to 'race' inequality.

Between the two positions outlined above lie a variety of shades of opinion about the degree to which the researcher's self can and should be acknowledged as affecting the production and analysis of qualitative data. However, there is a general consensus on the key point: *the role of the self in qualitative research is important*. To ignore the role of the researcher's self in qualitative research, then, would be ill-advised.

A reflexive account of researcher's self

The analysis of qualitative data calls for a reflexive account by the researcher concerning the researcher's self and its impact on the research. There is a growing acceptance among those involved in qualitative data analysis that some *biographical details about the researcher warrant inclusion as part of the analysis*, thus allowing the writer to explore the ways in which he or she feels personal experiences and values might influence matters. The reader of the research, by the same token, is given valuable information on which to base a judgement about how reasonable the writer's claims are with regard to the detachment or involvement of self-identity, values and beliefs.

An open mind

Qualitative researchers, like all researchers, need to approach the analysis of the data with an open mind. If they do not, they can be accused of lacking objectivity. In practice, a way of demonstrating such openness is for the researcher to take seriously the possibility of having 'got it wrong'. This is actually a fundamental point in relation to the production of knowledge. It is linked to the argument that good research is concerned not with the verification of findings but with their 'falsification'. For the project researcher there are perhaps two aspects of this which can be addressed quite practically. Qualitative researchers should:

- *Avoid neglecting data that do not fit the analysis.* Qualitative researchers such as Seale (1999) and Silverman (2011) have argued that good research should not ignore those instances within the data that might appear to disconfirm the researcher's analysis. There might be only a few such 'outliers'. There might be just the occasional bit of data that does not fit nicely or that contradicts the general trend. These should not be ignored, but should be actively investigated to see if there is an explanation for them that can be accommodated within the emerging analysis, of whether there is some genuine significance in them. Looking for, and accounting for, negative instances or deviant cases that contradict the emerging analysis are important.

- *Check rival explanations.* Alternative possible explanations need to be explored. The researcher needs to demonstrate that he or she has not simply plumped for the first explanation that fits, rather than seeing if rival theories work or whether there are hidden problems with the proposed explanation.

Good practice: The need to be open about the researcher's 'self'

Qualitative researchers should provide some biographical details about themselves and their interest in the research. They should also address the issue of objectivity by demonstrating the extent to which they have approached the research with an 'open mind'.

Advantages of qualitative data analysis

There is a richness and detail to the data

The in-depth study of relatively focused areas, the tendency towards small-scale research and the generation of 'thick descriptions' mean that qualitative research scores well in terms of the way it deals with complex social situations and the subtleties of social life.

The data and the analysis are 'grounded'

With qualitative research the findings are based upon evidence drawn from real-world settings. There is little scope for 'armchair theorizing' or 'ideas plucked out of thin air'.

There can be alternative explanations

Qualitative analysis, because it draws on the interpretive skills of the researcher, opens up the possibility of more than one explanation being valid. Rather than a presumption that there must be, in theory at least, one correct explanation, it allows for the possibility that different researchers might reach different conclusions, despite using broadly the same methods.

There is tolerance of ambiguity and contradictions

To the extent that social existence involves uncertainty, accounts of that existence ought to be able to tolerate ambiguities and contradictions, and qualitative research is better able to do this than quantitative research. This is not a reflection of a weak analysis. It is a reflection of the social reality being investigated.

Disadvantages of qualitative data analysis

Generalizability of the findings

One repercussion of qualitative research's tendency to rely on the detailed, in-depth study of a small number of instances is that it becomes more difficult to establish how far the findings may be generalized to other similar instances.

The analysis takes longer

Computer programs can assist with the management of the data and they can even help with the analysis, but nowhere near to the extent that they can with quantitative data. A key factor here is that qualitative data are generally unstructured when they are first collected in their 'raw' state (e.g. interviews, field notes, photographs) and need to be coded before they can be analysed.

Questions can be raised about the objectivity of the findings

Qualitative research recognizes more openly than does quantitative research that the researcher's own identity, background and beliefs have a role in the creation of data and the analysis of data.

There is the danger of taking the data 'out of context'

The analysis of qualitative data needs to be wary about wrenching the data from its location (1) within a sequence of data (e.g. interview talk) or (2) within surrounding circumstances. Both things have a bearing on the meaning of the text or image.

Further reading

Bazeley, P. (2013) *Qualitative Data Analysis: Practical Strategies*. London: Sage.

Gibbs, G. (2002) *Qualitative Data Analysis: Explorations with NVivo*. Buckingham: Open University Press.

Grbich, C. (2013) *Qualitative Data Analysis: An Introduction*, 2nd edn. London: Sage.

Miles, M. B., Huberman, A. M. and Saldana, J. M. (2014) *Qualitative Data Analysis: A Methods Sourcebook*, 3rd edn. Thousand Oaks, CA: Sage.

Richards, L. (2009) *Handling Qualitative Data: A Practical Guide*, 2nd edn. London: Sage.

Silverman, D. (2011) *Interpreting Qualitative Data*, 4th edn. London: Sage.

Checklist for the analysis of qualitative data

When analysing qualitative data you should feel confident about
answering 'yes' to the following question: ☑

1 Does the data analysis do one or more of the following:
   - Look for hidden messages – content analysis? ☐
   - Develop concepts or theories – grounded theory?
   - Expose the workings of power through language – discourse
     analysis?
   - Reveal underlying rules and structures of talk – conversation
     analysis?
   - Give an account of the construction of self and social world –
     narrative analysis?
   - Explain the meaning and cultural significance of images –
     image-based analysis?

2 Does any report of the findings include an explicit account of the
   process of data analysis? ☐

3 Have sufficient details been incorporated to allow an 'audit' of key
   decisions in the process of the research? ☐

4 Has the data analysis taken an iterative approach? ☐

5 Has the analysis been based on a depth scrutiny of the data? ☐

6 Have relevant details been supplied to permit readers to think
   about the transferability of the findings? ☐

7 Has the topic been approached with an 'open mind'? ☐

8 Have alternative explanations been considered? ☐

9 Does the research report include some reflexive account of the
   researcher's self and its possible impact? ☐

Part 4

Context

Social research takes place within a context that shapes the possibilities of what can be done. That context is society. Society places limits on what researchers can do in the pursuit of knowledge and it has expectations about how research should be conducted.

The most obvious way in which such limits and expectations confront the researcher is through the duties and obligations associated with *research ethics*. Society sets certain standards of conduct which researchers are expected to maintain and good research must meet these standards. Its methods must be acceptable within the cultural norms of the society in which it takes place and accord with a variety of moral, legal and safety considerations. Chapter 17 outlines the expectations that operate in the western world in the twenty-first century and provides guidance on how these expectations can be met.

The context of research is also significant in terms of the accountability of researchers and the obligation this places on researchers to make their research findings available for scrutiny by a wider public. As the twenty-first century progresses, an increasing emphasis is being placed on the dissemination of findings from research and the need to make findings easily accessible to other researchers or anyone who has an interest in the outcomes from a research project. This brings into the foreground the role of the research report as the means by which researchers communicate their work. Chapter 18 outlines the general features of research reports. It also suggests ways in which project researchers can provide an account of their research to an audience with a specific interest in evaluating the quality of the research that has been undertaken.

17 Research ethics

Social researchers are expected to approach their task in an ethical manner. On moral grounds, this expectation stems from the belief that the public should be protected from researchers who might be tempted to use any means available to advance the state of knowledge on a given topic. It rests on the assumption that researchers have no privileged position in society that justifies them pursuing their interests at the expense of those they are studying – no matter how valuable they hope the findings might be.

 Key point

Research ethics is not an option – it is a fundamental feature of all good research.

Ethics Committee approval

The importance attached to research ethics is evident in the fact that social researchers will normally need to get prior approval for their investigation from an *Ethics Committee*. Even with small-scale research, it is increasingly the case that before the research can be conducted it will need to have been scrutinized by a committee of suitably qualified experts to ensure that the design of the research includes appropriate measures to protect the interests of the people and groups covered by the research. Researchers in the field of health will find that medical ethics committees are powerful in this respect, and those conducting investigations as part of any academic qualification will normally be required to have their plans vetted by an Ethics Committee within their university before they are allowed to start the investigation. Submissions to Ethics Committees will be judged according to the broad principles for ethical research outlined below, and might include further specific stipulations depending on the field of the research.

> **Good practice: Get ethics approval before commencing data collection**
> Approval from an Ethics Committee should be obtained *before* any primary data is collected from the people involved in the research. The approval process can take weeks, sometimes months, to complete and this needs to be taken into consideration when planning the data collection phase of the research.

The kinds of research that need ethical approval

Research that involves data collection from or about living individuals generally requires ethical scrutiny. This means that projects will normally need to be considered by an Ethics Committee if they plan to collect data directly from or about people using the following methods:

- questionnaires;
- interviews or focus groups;
- participant observation or systematic observation.

This scrutiny is intended to ensure that no harm is caused by the investigation. Why is this necessary? In many cases social research might seem fairly innocuous involving perhaps some market research questions about people's purchasing habits or some other kind of enquiry that would not appear to pose much of a risk to the well-being of those who take part in the research. However, the dangers of social research can be real and substantial. It is the role of an Ethics Committee to consider the potential risks entailed in carrying out a proposed piece of research and to arrive at a conclusion about whether the risks have been considered, whether effective precautions will be taken to minimize the risks, and whether the plan of work is likely to produce worthwhile results without endangering the well-being of participants involved.

Ethics Committees will pay particular attention to any kinds of research that, in the words of the Economic and Social Research Council (ESRC), 'involve more than minimal risk' to participants. This is the kind of research that involves:

- vulnerable groups (e.g. children, people with a learning disability);
- sensitive topics (e.g. sexual, religious or illegal behaviour);
- deception or carried out without the informed consent of participants;
- use of confidential information about identifiable individuals;
- processes that might cause psychological stress, anxiety, humiliation or cause more than minimal pain;
- intrusive interventions (e.g. administration of drugs or vigorous physical exercise that would not be part of participants' normal lives).

Exceptions to the rule

There are certain kinds of research that do not need to go through a process of formal scrutiny by an Ethics Committee. First, there can be exceptions when the investigation is regarded as part of routine and normal work, and therefore not really 'research' as such. In the National Health Service, for instance, data collection and analysis undertaken as part of the routine work and management of the organization would not normally need to be submitted to an Ethics Committee for approval (Department of Health 2005). The kind of investigations and data collection which would *not* need approval include:

- audits;
- service evaluation;
- clinical case studies;
- equipment testing;
- customer satisfaction surveys.

Second, there can be exceptions when the research draws exclusively on published secondary source material. Library-based research, archive research, historical research, the use of official statistics and economic data are the kind of research that fall into this category. If the research uses aggregated data where individuals cannot be identified, if it uses data that are already in the public domain, or if relates to historical or fictional characters, then it might be treated as involving little risk and therefore permissible without the need for prior approval by an Ethics Committee. The thinking here is that there are no problems that can arise in the data collection phase (because the data have already been collected on a previous occasion) and no privacy issues because the data are in the public sphere and widely available to anyone.

The risks associated with social research, however, are not limited to the harm that might potentially occur during the data collection phase. As we shall see, research ethics is also concerned with the repercussions for participants resulting from the publication of findings. These things apply whatever the kind of social research that is being conducted and, for this reason, there is an increasing tendency to require *every* social research project to go through some initial vetting, some kind of scrutiny, before it is allowed to proceed. Even if the data collection appears to be unproblematic, institutions need to feel assured that any research conducted under their auspices (for a university degree, or by an employee) equally meets the required ethical standards when it comes to the analysis of the data and the dissemination of the data.

 Caution

Be aware that research ethics applies to *all* social research, even if formal approval from an Ethics Committee is not required.

Codes of research ethics

Codes of research ethics provide guidance on the kind of actions that should be taken and the kind that must be avoided when undertaking research. Professional research associations almost always publish a code of conduct that they expect their members to abide by. Research funding bodies and government departments that commission research have similar guidelines governing acceptable practice in the context of research. There is some difference in emphasis between these codes. Market research associations approach things in a slightly different way from medical associations, reflecting the different nature of the procedures the researchers are likely to use and the potential harm that might be done to participants. Market researchers collecting data on consumer preferences are not likely to be exposing participants to the same kind of risk, psychological or physical, as health researchers investigating the effectiveness of a new drug or surgical procedure.

Good practice: Abide by a specific code of research ethics

Project researchers should identify a code of ethics that represents their academic discipline or professional association. This code should be used in relation to the research and, importantly, should be explicitly referred to in any account of the methods used in the research.

Key principles of research ethics

There are four key principles which underlie codes of research ethics. These principles have their origins in medical research and were established initially in response to atrocities committed during the Second World War which purported to have been done in the name of science and the progress of medical knowledge. Through the Nuremberg Code (1947–49), and later the Declaration of Helsinki (1964), the international community established the foundations for research ethics and enshrined the fundamental principle that *the ends do not justify the means in the pursuit of knowledge.*

The Nuremberg Code and the Declaration of Helsinki have been developed over the years and various professional bodies, academic disciplines and government departments have adapted them for use in the context of social research as distinct from medical research. These codes of ethics for social research stick to the core principle (that in their pursuit of knowledge researchers must not ruthlessly use any means at their disposal) and they develop this along four lines. Social researchers are expected to conduct their investigations in a way that:

- protects the interests of the participants;
- ensures that participation is voluntary and based on informed consent;
- avoids deception and operates with scientific integrity;
- complies with the laws of the land.

Principle 1: Participants' interests should be protected

There is general agreement that people should not suffer as a consequence of their involvement with a piece of research. Those who contribute to research as informants or as research subjects should be no worse off at the end of their participation than they were when they started. Nor should there be longer-term repercussions stemming from their involvement that in any sense harm the participants.

In accord with this principle, researchers have a duty to consider in advance the likely consequences of participation and to take measures that safeguard the interests of those who help with the investigation. First of all, they need to ensure that participants do not come to any *physical harm* as a result of the research. With some kinds of research there needs to be careful consideration of the physical safety of participants, anticipating any threats arising from the time/location of meetings, travel to such locations, or even the possibility of the participant suffering retribution from people who feel threatened by the participant's involvement in the research or the disclosure of particular information. The possibility might seem quite remote, but researchers have a responsibility to anticipate such risks and avoid any physical harm from occurring.

Second, care needs to be taken to *avoid psychological harm* resulting from research. Any investigation that is potentially going to lead to trauma, stress or other psychological harm will be considered unethical. Researchers therefore need to anticipate the likelihood that their investigation might be perceived as intrusive, touch on sensitive issues, or threaten the beliefs of the participants because these are the kinds of thing that could give rise to psychological harm.

Third, participants should suffer *no personal harm* arising from the disclosure of information collected during the research. Disclosure of personal information could be embarrassing for the participants and, depending on the type of information, it could also involve economic loss or even the prospect of legal action being taken against participants on the basis of the disclosed information if it was to come to the attention of relevant authorities (e.g. employers, Inland Revenue, social security inspectors, the police, customs officials). There is broad agreement, therefore, that researchers need to protect the interests of the participants by ensuring the confidentiality of information that is given to them. When publishing results, care needs to be taken not to disclose the personal identities of individuals who have contributed to the findings.

Fourth, the participants should stand to benefit from the outcomes from the research. This does not mean that each participant is expected to gain personally from taking part in the research but that, in principle, a person *such as them* might benefit at some point in the future as a consequence of the research. The idea is that the participants are not just 'guinea pigs' whose sole value is that of providing data. Their willingness to devote time and effort, indeed their willingness to expose themselves to risks in the case of medical research, should be done on the basis of getting something back. Not money, but some other form of benefit for people like them. This stems from the ethical principle of 'beneficence' which states that research on people should always be done 'for the good of people', never frivolously or for malicious purposes.

Fifth, and linked to this, participants should be treated *fairly and equally* in terms of the participation in the research. People should not be included in the research, nor excluded from the research, on grounds which are unfair or irrelevant. And this is not just a matter of good practice in terms of gaining a representative sample: it is an ethical point based on the idea that any benefits or risks associated with a piece of research should be shared equally amongst all those concerned. The reasoning is easy to see in the case of medical research. As Goldacre (2012) argues, it is unfair to trial Aids vaccines in Africa if the prime beneficiaries of any breakthrough will be residents of rich countries in the West and where the risks are taken by those who, in all likelihood, will not be able to afford any new breakthrough vaccine that results from the research. In social research, this translates as meaning that researchers need to ensure that their research design does not discriminate against the involvement of parties whose voices ought to be heard and whose interests need to be represented through their inclusion as participants in the research. For ethical reasons, that is, the research design should be sure to represent the interests of all relevant people, including the underprivileged, the weak, the vulnerable and minority groups.

Good practice: Protecting participants' interests

Researchers should:

- anticipate any threats to the *personal safety* of participants, and take steps to avoid these occurring;
- respect participants' privacy and sensitivities, and *avoid undue intrusion* when collecting data;
- treat all information disclosed to them during research as *confidential*, and not disclose it to other participants or people not connected with the research;
- guarantee the *anonymity* of individuals and organizations in any published documents arising from the research – unless participants give explicit (and written) consent to identify them by name;
- ensure that the benefits and risks associated with inclusion in the research are spread *fairly and equally* among relevant groups.

Principle 2: Participation should be voluntary and based on informed consent

People should never be forced or coerced into helping with research. Their participation must always be voluntary, and they must have sufficient information about the research to arrive at a reasoned judgement about whether or not they want to participate. These are the premises of 'informed consent'. Particularly where the kind of information collected is of a sensitive nature, there is a need to get informed consent. But, more than this, there is often a need to get that consent *in writing*. When the consent is in writing, it acts as a way of formally recording the agreement to participate and confirming that the participant has been informed about the nature of the research. This protects the researcher from any possible accusation that he or she acted improperly when recruiting people to take part in the research.

Good practice: Informed consent

For participants to be able to give informed consent researchers need to:

- make it very clear that participation is *voluntary*;
- provide participants with *adequate information* about the research;
- specify what kind of *commitment* is being required of participants.

A formal way to confirm that participation is on the basis of informed consent is to use a *consent form* (see the template below).

What if it is not possible to get written consent?

It may not always be possible to gain consent from all those who take part in a research project. Research on crowd behaviour at football matches or observation of the movements of visitors to art galleries are clearly instances where it would prove impossible to get everyone to complete a consent form. There are other occasions where it may not be deemed practical or, indeed, necessary to get written consent. Approaching people in the street to ask a few questions about their shopping habits, for example, might not be seen as requiring the completion of a consent form. In this case there is some tacit consent. The agreement to answer the questions clearly indicates that their participation is voluntary and, because the nature of the participants' involvement in the research is rather 'low risk', under the circumstances this 'verbal consent' might be deemed sufficient. The codes of conduct of the professional associations generally recognize this and include clauses that acknowledge that exceptions might need to be made to the general rule about written consent. Normally, the conditions under which researchers can collect data ethically without getting written consent are those where:

- the form of data collection is unlikely to involve much by way of personal risks to the informant, and
- it is not realistically possible to get such consent.

Principle 3: Researchers should operate in an open and honest manner with respect to the investigation

Researchers are expected to avoid deception or misrepresentation in their dealings with participants. They are expected to be open and explicit about what they are doing – to let people know that they are researchers and that they intend to collect data for the purposes of an investigation into a particular topic.

Furthermore, they are expected to tell the truth about the nature of their investigation and the role of the participants in that research.

Good practice: Openness in the conduct of research

Researchers should:

- produce a *brief summary* of the aims of the research and the nature of the data that are to be collected. This should be no more than one page in length and written without jargon so that the purpose of the research can be clearly understood by potential participants and others who might have an interest in the research;
- where possible, develop a *website* for the project so that information about the project can be widely available to interested parties. Links from the Home page can be used to provide further information about the researchers (their credentials and experience) and more details about the background to the project for those who might want to know more.

There is also an expectation that researchers operate with 'scientific integrity'. This means, in effect, that researchers are expected to uphold the highest standards of professionalism and honesty in terms of their treatment of the data and dealings with other researchers. On the first point, working ethically means doing the best possible job to collect and analyse data in an objective and honest way. Researchers should not be swayed to supply findings that suit the needs of those who fund or sponsor the research. Nor should they allow personal preferences and ideals to cloud their judgement and get in the way of providing a balanced and dispassionate interpretation of their findings. They should be 'fair' and unbiased. On the second point, there is an expectation that researchers should acknowledge the contribution of others and not 'steal' their work through plagiarism. Researchers certainly need to 'use' the work of others – either by way of building upon it or by criticizing it – but when doing so they should always explicitly acknowledge the source of the other work.

Scientific integrity covers two further obligations on the researcher. First, the researcher is expected to have the appropriate experience and *competence* to undertake the investigation. Without this there is a danger that the participants might be harmed. Thinking of medical research the point behind this is easy to see. With social research too, however, Ethics Committees will look to be reassured that researchers will restrict their investigations to those styles of research for which they are qualified and for which their experience makes them well prepared. And second, as we have already noted, there is a clear expectation that researchers should not engage in research which is frivolous or whimsical, or for which there is not a good 'scientific' reason to believe that something of value will be learnt as an outcome. Behind both these points there is the principle that participants should not be exposed to the risk of harm or inconvenience by being asked to participate in research that is not likely to be beneficial. This is the principle of 'beneficence'.

Good practice: Honesty and integrity in the conduct of research

Researchers should:

- avoid deception or misrepresentation in their dealings with participants;
- provide fair and unbiased interpretation of their findings;
- explicitly acknowledge any sponsorship or vested interests relating to the research;
- avoid plagiarizing other researchers' work;
- have the necessary skills and experience to carry out the research;
- show that real benefits are likely to emerge from the research.

What if some deception is necessary?

There are occasions when it is not feasible for the researcher to be completely open and honest with participants. To be so would automatically jeopardize any prospect of the investigation actually taking place or would cause participants to react to the research in a way that would contaminate the results. Many psychology experiments, for example, would be ruined if the subjects knew in advance what the researcher was investigating, and it has been estimated that about three-quarters of psychology experiments involve giving participants information that, in one respect or another, actually misleads them about the purpose of the experiment. Some types of ethnographic study, likewise, involve fieldwork where the researcher needs to disguise his/her true role because if people knew that research was being conducted they would act differently from normal, and the 'naturalness' of the setting would be destroyed.

When some form of deception is seen as necessary, researchers face an ethical dilemma: from the point of view of good research design, deception is regarded as essential, yet from the point of view of ethical research such deception is bad practice. The codes of conduct published by professional associations, however, generally acknowledge that, on certain occasions, some deception by researchers might be warranted as absolutely necessary for the purposes of the research. Such occasions, though, need to be treated as exceptions to the rule – ones that can be justified only on the basis of the very special circumstances surrounding the particular investigation. The conditions under which it might be acceptable generally require the researcher:

- to provide an explicit justification for why the deception is vital and why there is no suitable alternative approach that would permit full disclosure about the nature of the research;
- to use a 'debriefing' session in which, after the event, participants are put in the picture about the true nature of the enquiry and why they could not be informed about this at the beginning.

Principle 4: Research should comply with the laws of the land

Researchers do not stand above the law nor should they put themselves outside the law. Operating within the law, of course, does not necessarily make an action ethical. Indeed, there are many actions a researcher could take that might be perfectly legal but which would be considered to be absolutely unethical in the context of conducting research. And a case could be made that a researcher who breaks the law might, nonetheless, be doing something that is ethical. Like an investigative journalist who needs to use unscrupulous methods in order to expose a case of corruption or organized crime, it is possible that a social researcher might make a similar case for stepping outside the law. However, this would be a dangerous thing for any but the most experienced researchers and for project researchers would be most ill-advised. Most codes of research ethics are quite clear on the point: social researchers are expected to abide by the laws of the land.

Bearing this in mind, there are some laws which are of particular relevance for social researchers. First, there are those laws that set bounds to what is acceptable in terms of the topic of the research. There are areas where the nature of any research project is likely to 'cross the line' in terms of the law, and for this reason project researchers should steer well clear of such areas. Obvious examples would be the way that research involving empirical investigation into topics such as terrorism, drug trafficking, paedophilia, prostitution or pornography could all too easily, and unintentionally, end up breaking the law. Second, there are certain ways of collecting data that could fall foul of the law. There are data protection laws that need to be considered, laws against hacking into computers, laws against fraud, and copyright laws, all of which set boundaries around what can be legitimately used as a means for collecting data. The data protection laws also have a bearing on the way that researchers need to store their data and the extent to which personal data can be distributed to third parties not actually involved with the research (see below).

Link up with
Data protection, p. 317.

> **Good practice: Compliance with the law**
>
> To help them stay within the law, researchers should:
>
> - avoid researching *sensitive topics* where the methods of data collection and analysis might lead them to break the law;
> - take care on matters relating to the ownership of the data, *intellectual property rights* and copyright matters;
> - take reasonable measures to ensure that *data are kept private and secure*.

Written consent form

'Informed consent', as we have seen, is a cornerstone of research ethics. Basically, anyone participating in research should know what they are agreeing to do. Yes, there are exceptions to the rule. And there are times when consent might need to be tacit rather than explicit. But on those occasions when researchers are able to seek informed consent on a more formal basis it is standard practice to use a 'consent form'. This form does two things. First, it provides the potential participant with enough information about the research and their involvement for them to make an *informed* decision. Second, it provides the researcher with some documented evidence that the participant has agreed to take part in the research – *written consent*. The forms vary in length and detail according to the nature of the research, but generally include the following sections.

Identity of the researcher

Participants are entitled to know who is conducting the research and where they can be contacted. The consent form, therefore, should include:

- the name(s) of the researcher;
- an address and other contact details at which he or she can be contacted;
- where appropriate, the name of the organization under whose auspices the research is being conducted.

Information about the research

There needs to be a statement providing enough detail for the participant to understand, in broad terms, the aims, methods and anticipated outcomes of the research. This must be brief since participants will not normally wish to spend a lot of time reading page after page of details. Some researchers present the information on a separate sheet that can be left with the participant for future reference. At other times, the statement is limited to a few sentences on the consent form itself. Either way, participants need to be provided with a brief description of:

- what the research is investigating;
- how it is to be conducted;
- who, if anybody, is sponsoring the research;
- what benefits are likely to emerge from the investigation.

Expectations about the participant's contribution

Informed consent presumes that participants know in advance what tasks the researcher expects them to undertake and what, if any, reward they might expect for their efforts. They will need to be told whether they are expected to take part in an interview, take part in a laboratory experiment, or complete a questionnaire. And they should be given some indication of how much time this is likely to take. They might also need to know whether any expenses they incur will be paid for by the researcher, and whether they will receive some kind of payment or other incentive (such as a free copy of the final report of the research). The consent form, then, should specify:

- why they were selected for inclusion in the study;
- what tasks the participant will undertake;
- how much of their time this is likely to take;
- what general benefits or specific incentives there might be for taking part in the research.

The right to withdraw consent

Signing a consent form does not oblige participants to continue in the role if, at some subsequent stage, they no longer wish to do so. The consent form is not a contract that binds a person to the task of helping with the research – and this should be made clear on the consent form itself. Participants should be made aware that, should they wish to do so, it is their right to withdraw their consent at any time.

Confidentiality and security of data

The consent form needs to incorporate some commitment by the researcher with regard to the conduct of the research and the treatment of the data. Any agreement to take part in research ought to be made with an understanding of what code of ethics the researcher will use and what measures will be taken to safeguard the data and protect participants from any disclosure of their individual identity. Such assurances could include:

• specifying which professional association's code of ethics will be used to during the course of the research;
• what security measures will be taken to ensure the confidentiality of the data;
• how anonymity of the data will be guaranteed (if appropriate).

Ownership and use of the data

It can be prudent to get participants' formal approval for the researcher to use the information they provide and the words they use for the purposes of academic research and publications arising from the project.

Signature of the participant, with date

This signature can incorporate an acknowledgement that the participant has been advised about the requirements of the research and has understood what is involved (e.g. 'I have read and understood the written details provided for me about the research, and agree to participate in the project. Signed . . .').

Counter-signature of the researcher, with date

It is good practice for the researcher, as well as the participant, to sign the consent form effectively committing the researcher to uphold his or her side of the agreement.

Data protection

Prompted by the potential of computers to store and process vast quantities of information, and given further impetus by the growth of the Internet, most societies have *data protection laws* that are designed to protect the public from the unscrupulous collection and use of personal data. In the UK, as in many other countries, Human Rights legislation and Freedom of Information laws have imposed certain controls on the misuse of data, but the main piece of relevant legislation is the Data Protection Act (1988). This law relates to 'personal data' - data that includes personal details from which living individuals can be identified – and covers data held on any 'relevant filing system'. This includes paper records as well as computer files if they are kept systematically.

The Data Protection Act says that anyone storing such data is acting as a 'data controller' and this carries with it three responsibilities. First, data controllers must 'notify' the *Information Commissioner's Office* (http://www.ico.org.uk/) about the kind of data they hold, the purpose for which it is being used, and who the data will be disclosed to. This provides the Information Commissioner's Office with a national picture of what data is being held, who holds the data, and how that data is being used. Second, data controllers assume responsibility for keeping the data *secure* and ensuring the data are *accurate* and up-to-date. The legislation is designed to ensure that data held about individuals is handled properly and that the organizations involved take steps to ensure that the information on their database is correct. And third, data controllers become responsible for making the data *available* if, and when, any individual applies to see the data that is held about them. From a civil liberties point of view this is the key aspect of the legislation: it allows individual citizens to find out what data is held about them and, if necessary, challenge the validity of the data.

The implications for small-scale research

At first glance it might seem that, to comply with the law, social researchers will need to go through the process of notifying the Information Commissioner's Office (or equivalent regulatory body if not in the UK) about the data they hold. In reality, though, this is unlikely to be the case – particularly for small-scale social researchers conducting research as part of a university course. There are three reasons for this.

First, the Act does not apply to anonymized or aggregated data. Provided it is not possible to identify individuals from the data that are being held, and that the process of anonymization cannot be reversed, the data are not regarded as 'personal'. Bearing this in mind, researchers might ask themselves whether they really need to have personal identifying information attached to their dataset. Is it vital to directly link personal details (name, address, telephone number and email address, etc.) to each participant's data? If not, it makes sense to ensure that the data are duly anonymized.

Second, where research is conducted under the auspices of a large organization the organization itself might have a 'notification' that already covers the activity of the individual researchers who study with, or work for, that organization. Students and staff at universities are likely to be covered in this way particularly with respect to research conducted for academic dissertations and coursework.

And third, the Act includes a number of exemptions, meaning that certain kinds of data held by certain kinds of organization do not need be 'notified' to the Information Commissioner's Office. '*Personal data that is processed only for research, statistical or historical purposes*' is one of them.

In practice, then, individual small-scale social researchers in the UK do not normally need to go through the process of notifying the Information Commissioner's Office about the data they hold.

Data protection principles

Although small-scale researchers may not need to formally notify the Information Commissioner's Office about the data they hold, this does not mean that the legislation simply 'does not apply' or that the standards for data protection established through the Act can be ignored. It is important to recognize that the legislation identifies some fundamental principles about data protection and effectively sets a benchmark for good practice when it comes to the storage and dissemination of personal data. To meet these standards social researchers should:

- *Collect and process data in a fair and lawful manner.* There is an obligation on researchers to stick within the law in the way they collect their data and, equally, to avoid deception or subterfuge in order to get their information.
- *Use data only for the purposes originally specified.* It is not legitimate to collect data for one purpose and then use them for some other purpose that was not stated at the time the data were collected.
- *Collect only the data that are actually needed.* Researchers should not collect vast amounts of data anticipating that some of it might come in useful now or at some time in the future. The data collection should be targeted at the current and actual needs of the project.
- *Take care to ensure the data are accurate.* Researchers, like other data collectors, have a duty of care to make sure the data they hold are accurate and, where appropriate, kept up to date.
- *Keep data no longer than is necessary.* Although researchers do not need to erase data after any given time, the legislation establishes the principle that data should be kept for use rather than simply accumulated. Obviously, in research terms there is some real value in retaining data for future comparison and checking, and for large projects there is generally some stipulation that all data must be kept for a minimum period following the completion of a project (ranging from 2 years to 10 years and upwards depending on the nature of the data).
- *Keep the data secure.* Very importantly, data should be kept safe. Depending upon the sensitivity of the data, appropriate measures need to be taken to avoid the possibility of them falling into the wrong hands by being lost or stolen. With data held on computers, this entails a suitable use of passwords or encryption to prevent unauthorized access to the data. With paper documents, the data need to be kept under lock and key.
- *Control the distribution of the data.* It is legitimate for researchers to give copies of their data to other researchers for specifically research purposes but data should not be distributed to third parties who might use the data for other purposes.

- Where possible, *anonymize the data*. The researcher should consider whether it is really necessary to collect data that are linked to identifiable individuals since anonymized data are exempted from the legislation. Data that are anonymous cannot be traced to any particular individual.

Ethics and Internet research

Internet-based research involves the same principles of research ethics as all other research but it brings with it some issues that warrant particular attention. A considerable amount of attention has been paid to the new kinds of challenge faced by Internet research in terms of things like informed consent, privacy and deception, confidentiality and legislation (e.g. McKee and Porter 2009; Heider and Massanari 2012; Farrimond 2013; Ess 2014).

Informed consent and 'Internet surveys'

When Internet research takes the form of *surveys, questionnaires or interviews*, then the issues of consent and anonymity follow the lines of traditional research in the sense that the role of the researcher is explicit and expectations about consent can be met in an open and relatively unproblematic fashion. An outline of the research can be emailed to them. Alternatively, they can be asked to visit a website where the information is held. Or, again, with forums and chat rooms the information and consent details can be posted ahead of the time when it is proposed to begin the research.

Confirming that the would-be participant has read the information, and understands it, is rather more difficult. One possibility here is to ask for the email, the attachment, the posting or the web page containing the information to be sent back to the researcher as a way of confirming that it has been read and understood, and that there is agreement to participation. If sent back from email or a web page, the form could contain a tick box (yes/no) that allows the would-be participants to confirm their willingness to take part – a kind of proxy signature that, though it is not as good as a formal signature, at least signals agreement to take part in a project whose details have been made available. Alternatively, those who have been contacted could be asked to print off a copy of the downloaded form, sign it and return it to the researcher through the ordinary post. This provides a more robust kind of informed consent, but takes more effort on the part of the would-be participant and might well have the effect of deterring them from agreeing to participate.

Special care needs to be taken in the case of research that, intentionally or otherwise, includes children and young people. Permission from parents or someone with equivalent parental authority is needed according to most codes of conduct for research and this applies just as much to Internet research as it does to conventional data collection methods. Although it is difficult to be certain about the age of contacts on the Internet, researchers are still expected to:

- use their best endeavours to identify any respondents who might be aged under 16;

- where appropriate, seek parental permission (or its equivalent) on behalf of such young people;
- abide by relevant national laws relating to contact with children and young people.

Privacy and the use of 'online documents'

Internet research that involves the study of online documents can pose interesting questions in terms of privacy. Such research focuses on various forms of texts and images that have been put online – but were not produced with research in mind. The motive for putting the material online could be commercial, political, religious or personal and they might take the form of web-pages, blogs, discussion forums or messages on social network sites. A crucial point, though, is that wherever they appear and whatever form they take they were not intended as things that would form the basis for research data.

The decision to seek consent for the use of the material needs to be made on the basis of how *public or private* the communication was intended to be. If the material was intended for public consumption and intended to reach a wide audience then there would not normally be a requirement to gain consent before using that material as data for a research project. It is published work in the public domain. Analysis of company websites, online journals, tweets and the like fall into this category. In the case of more private material the situation becomes more murky. Contributions to a discussion forum, for example, might be intended for a particular online community and things said on social network sites might be intended for a restricted group of 'friends'. Ethically speaking, the researcher needs to think about how far the writer *intended* the words for unrestricted public consumption and how personal the material is in terms of its content. The more personal and private the communication is, the more the researcher should be inclined to seek consent before using the material as research data.

Deception and the study of online communities

Internet research that involves participation in an online community can involve issues surrounding the use of deception by the researcher. Such issues do not occur if the researcher chooses to be explicit about the reasons for joining in with the group and openly seeking the consent of the members to his/her participation. However, the nature of online communities means that it is often possible to conduct covert research and observe the workings of a community without openly declaring a presence in the group. It allows researchers to monitor and record events secretly by hiding in the background and not declaring their presence. It enables them to enter chat rooms and observe proceedings by 'lurking' rather than joining in. Researchers can read postings to bulletin boards, again observing proceedings without disturbing the natural course of events.

The question is, does this involve a form of *deception*? Should Internet researchers be morally obliged to declare their presence and state openly the purpose for observing events? There is a position on research ethics that would say 'yes'. Others, however, would argue that the information provided through these channels has been made open and public by those who supplied it, arguably removing any need on the part of the researcher to disclose the existence of the research activity or to try to get consent from those who are to become the objects of study. On the understanding that such information is 'public', some Internet researchers (e.g. Denzin 1999) have chosen to proceed without being open about who they are and what they are doing. Under specific circumstances they argue that it is not necessary to get permission to use the postings as data for research. Any researcher contemplating such Internet research needs to be aware of the alternative views and should explicitly state their considered position on this issue.

Separate from the issue of not declaring a presence, the Internet also makes it relatively easy to adopt an alias or take on a false (online) identity for the purposes of the research. This sidesteps the need for researchers to be fully honest about who they are and why they wish to participate in the group's online interactions and it can pave the way for actively engaging with a community without destroying the naturalness of the communication between the members. But is this simply a matter of deception and can it be ethical? Well, as with any research, there can be situations where researchers argue that some degree of deception is unavoidable; when it is *not expedient* to disclose research activity because to do so would be to jeopardize the research aims. A good illustration of this is provided by Glaser et al. (2002), who collected data from chat rooms associated with white racist groups. They wanted to find out what kind of events or circumstances triggered such people into advocating physical violence against ethnic groups, and covertly conducted semi-structured interviews with 38 participants through these chat rooms. The sensitivity of the issue meant that they did not seek informed consent. They argued that racists appear to 'express their views rather freely [on the Internet], at least when they are interacting with those they perceive to be like-minded' (p. 181) and that revealing the researchers' identity and purpose would have been likely to deter such openness. In this specific case, under these special circumstances, they were able to gain the approval of the relevant Ethics Committee (at Yale University) on the grounds that:

- the respondents' statements were made in a public forum under conditions that were entirely normal for the chat room and so were naturally occurring data;
- the deception was absolutely necessary in order for the research to be undertaken;
- respondents' identities were carefully protected.

Confidentiality

It is difficult, arguably impossible, for researchers using the Internet to *guarantee* that respondents' contributions will be private and will not be traced back to them. Despite the efforts of individuals and organizations to protect the anonymity of sources of Internet communications, and despite the potential of encryption, the reality is that governments and security agencies have the power and the ability to trace just about any kind of Internet communication should they wish to do so. Researchers, therefore, should be wary about making promises they are not in a position to keep, and should word statements about the confidentiality of data supplied via the Internet in a way that acknowledges the point, yet also reassures the respondent that all reasonable precautions will be taken to avoid the disclosure of identities.

Legislation

The laws that need to be observed vary from country to country and are evolving to meet the repercussions of the spread of the Internet. Mann and Stewart (2000) suggest that, in the face of this uncertainty, researchers are best advised to make a clear statement to participants about which country's legal jurisdiction is being applied as far as the research is concerned – normally the country in which the researcher is based. Complications arise when researchers wish to base their research in more than one country – for example, with collaboration between universities in the UK, Russia and the USA. Such complications, however, are fairly unlikely to arise in the context of a small-scale research project. Broadly, though, there are three aspects of legislation that are likely to affect Internet research and that need to be reflected in the researcher's use of the Internet for data collection:

- *Data protection*: the data should be collected, stored and used in accord with relevant data protection legislation.
- *Copyright*: downloading text and images is simple, but the *use* of text and images needs to be in accord with copyright conventions and legislation concerned with things like trademarks and intellectual property rights.
- *Sensitive issues*: researchers hold no special position in the eyes of the law and need to exercise particular caution when investigating topics that are politically sensitive or that involve things like pornography or terrorism.

Summary

Researchers are expected to operate in accord with ethical standards and within boundaries set by the law. These expectations manifest themselves at four stages in the research process.

At the planning stage *approval* needs to be obtained by an Ethics Committee. Before any empirical research gets under way, the plans for the research are normally scrutinized by people with relevant experience and expertise to check that appropriate measures will be in place to enable the research to meet the required ethical standards.

During the data collection stage researchers need to be vigilant to ensure that *no harm* is caused to participants. Potential risks, possible dangers and unwanted by-products from the research should have been predicted and preempted through the design of the research but, none the less, as the data collection progresses there needs to be a constant monitoring of events to prevent any unforeseen circumstances from causing harm to participants.

At the data analysis stage there is a need to act with *integrity* and high professional standards. Researchers are expected to be honest in the way they analyse the data and must avoid any temptation to manipulate the data or approach things in a biased manner. It also means that care should be taken not to plagiarize the work of other researchers.

At the dissemination stage there is a need to consider the *impact* of publication of findings. The harm that can be done to participants is not confined to the data collection stage as the researcher goes about the business of eliciting information. With social research there is possibly more chance of harm arising from what is done with that information. Particular care needs to be given to keeping the data secure and treating it as confidential. And when it comes to publishing findings from the research, consideration needs to be given to the potential impact on the lives of those who contributed to the research findings.

Further reading

Farrimond, H. (2013) *Doing Ethical Research.* Basingstoke: Palgrave Macmillan.

Israel, M. and Hay, I. (2006) *Research Ethics for Social Scientists: Between Ethical Conduct and Regulatory Compliance.* London: Sage.

Oliver, P. (2010) *The Student's Guide to Research Ethics,* 2nd edn. Maidenhead: Open University Press.

Wiles, R. (2013) *What Are Qualitative Research Ethics?* London: Bloomsbury.

Checklist for research ethics

When considering the ethics of the research you should feel confident about answering 'yes' to the following questions: ☑

1 Will prior *approval* for the research be obtained, or has it already been obtained, from a relevant Ethics Committee? ☐

2 Will the research be conducted in accord with a specific (and named) *code of research ethics*? ☐

3 Will *informed consent* be obtained from participants? If not, can this be justified in relation to the nature of the research? ☐

4 Will reasonable steps be taken to safeguard the *security of the data?* ☐

5 Will the data collection process:
   • avoid harm, stress or emotional upset to those taking part? ☐
   • respect the privacy of individuals and *avoid undue intrusion?* ☐

6 Will the interests of participants be protected through:
   • maintaining the *confidentiality* of information? ☐
   • protecting their *anonymity?* ☐

7 Does the process of selecting participants ensure that the *benefits and risks are spread fairly* and equally among relevant groups? ☐

8 Will the research *avoid the use of deception?* If not, can this be justified in relation to the nature of the research? ☐

9 Will data be collected using only *legal* and legitimate means? ☐

10 Will the research be conducted with professional integrity in an *honest,* objective and unbiased fashion? ☐

11 Will the research *respect social values and cultural norms* of the society within which it is conducted? ☐

12 Has consideration been given to the likely *impact of publishing* research findings on those who contribute to the research? ☐

© M. Denscombe, *The Good Research Guide.* Open University Press.

18 Research reports

- *The structure of research reports • Writing up qualitative research*
- *The research methods section • Referencing • Guidelines on style*
- *Guidelines on presentation • Writing for an audience • Producing accounts of research • Further reading • Checklist for writing research reports*

Research is not complete until the aims, methods and findings have been written up in some form of research report (e.g. a dissertation, a thesis or an article). Such reports are vital because the purpose of research is to contribute to knowledge and this means that the findings from a research project need to be distributed, disseminated and discussed in the wider world rather than being kept private. Some military research and research on commercially sensitive topics, admittedly, might involve special efforts to keep the results secret, but these instances need to be regarded as exceptions to the general rule which is this: *research findings should be distributed and made available for scrutiny by other researchers.*

Writing a research report, though, is not a simple, mechanical process of 'writing up' what happened. It requires a degree of *writing craft* in order to present the details of the research in a fashion that is interesting and accessible to the specific *audience* for whom the report is produced. The report also needs to conform to certain *conventions* and adopt a format that is readily recognized by those who will evaluate the work. This chapter, therefore, provides some guidelines to the relevant conventions and writing styles that are associated with good research reports.

The structure of research reports

There is a conventional structure to research reports (Figure 18.1). The order in which they present material, and even the headings used, tend to conform to a familiar pattern – a pattern which is dictated largely by the need to present information in a logical order, with each new section building on information that has been provided earlier.

Figure 18.1 The structure of a research report

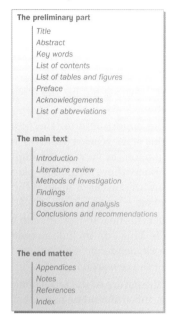

The conventional structure for reporting research divides the material into three parts: the preliminary part, the main text and the end matter. This is as true for a full-length book as it is for a PhD, for a brief journal article and for a workplace project.

The preliminary part

- *Title.* The title itself needs to indicate accurately the contents of the work. It also needs to be fairly brief. A good way of combining the two is to have a two-part title: title and subtitle. The first part acts as the main title and gives a broad indication of the area of the work. The second part adds more detail. For example, 'Ethnicity and friendship: the contrast between sociometric research and fieldwork observation in primary school classrooms'.

- *Abstract.* An abstract is a synopsis of a piece of research. Its purpose is to provide a brief summary which can be circulated widely to allow other people to see, at a glance, if the research is relevant to their needs and worth tracking down to read in full. An abstract is normally about 250–300 words in length, and is presented on a separate sheet.

- *Key words.* Researchers are often asked to identify up to five 'key words'. These words are 'identifiers' – words that capture the essence of what the report is all about. They can combine two, sometimes three, words if necessary. For example, 'employee motivation' can be used as a key word.

It identifies a concept in a way that any single, individual key words do not. Key words are needed for bibliographic searches.

- *List of contents*. Depending on the context, this can range from being just a list of chapter headings and their starting page through to being an extensive list, including details of the contents within the major section of the report, for instance, based on headings and sub-headings.
- *List of tables and figures*. This should list the titles of the various tables and figures and their locations.
- *Preface*. This provides the opportunity for the researcher to give a personal statement about the origins of the research and the significance of the research for the researcher as a person. In view of the importance of the 'self' in the research process, the Preface offers a valuable place in the research report to explore, albeit briefly, how the research reflects the personal experiences and biography of the researcher.
- *Acknowledgements*. Under this heading, credit can be given to those who have helped with the research. This can include people who acted as 'gatekeepers' in relation to fieldwork, academic supervisors, and those who have commented on early drafts of the research report.
- *List of abbreviations*. If the nature of the report demands that many abbreviations are used in the text, these should be listed, usually alphabetically, under this heading, alongside the full version of what they stand for.

The main text

The main text is generally divided into sections. The sections might be chapters as in the case of a larger piece of work or headings as in the case of shorter reports. In either case, they are normally presented in the following order.

- *Introduction*. For the purposes of writing up research there needs to be an introduction. On most occasions this will be a stand-alone section or chapter, but it might be incorporated in other ways. The important thing to recognize is that, at the beginning, the reader needs to be provided with information about:
  - the *background* to the work (in relation to significant issues, problems, ideas);
  - the *aims* of the research;
  - key *definitions* and concepts to be used;
  - optionally, in longer pieces, an *overview* of the report (mapping out its contents).
- *Literature review*. This might be presented as an integral part of the 'Introduction' or it might appear as a separate chapter or section. It is, though, essential that in the early stages of the report there is a review of the material that already exists on the topic in question. The current research should build on existing knowledge, not 'reinvent the wheel'. The literature review should

demonstrate how the research being reported relates to previous research and, if possible, how it gives rise to particular issues, problems and ideas that the current research addresses.

- *Methods of investigation.* At this point, having analysed the existing state of knowledge on a topic, it is reasonable to describe the methods of investigation. See the section on 'The research methods section' (below) for guidance on how this should be done.

- *Findings.* This is where the reader is presented with the relevant findings. The idea at this stage is to describe the findings rather than launch immediately into a discussion of what they might tell us. First things first: let's see what we have found.

- *Analysis and discussion.* In this section of the report the findings are analysed. The findings are reviewed and interrogated to see what they imply. And then this leads on to a discussion that connects the emerging ideas to the theories and ideas, issues and problems that were noted earlier in the report as providing the context in which the research was conceived. The researcher 'makes sense' of the findings by considering their implications beyond the confines of the current research.

- *Conclusions and recommendations.* Finally, in the main text, the researcher needs to draw together the threads of the research to arrive at some general conclusion and, perhaps, to suggest some way forward. Rather than let the report fizzle out as it reaches the end, this part of the report should be constructive and positive. It can contain some of the following things:
  - a retrospective evaluation of the research and its contribution;
  - recommendations for improving the situation, guidelines or codes of practice;
  - identification of new directions for further research.

The end matter

- *Appendices.* This is the place for material which is too bulky for the main body of the text, or for material which, though directly relevant to the discussion, might entail too much of a sidetrack if placed in the text. Typical items that can be lodged in an appendix are:
  - extensive tables of data;
  - questionnaires used in a survey;
  - extracts from an interview transcript;
  - memos or minutes of meetings;
  - technical specifications.

- *References.* Sources cited in the body of the text are listed in this part of the report. See the guidance on referencing below.

- *Index.* Provision of an index is usually restricted to large reports and books. It is unlikely that the kind of report produced by a project researcher would require an index.

Writing up qualitative research

For the qualitative researcher the presentation of research in sections under the headings of 'methods', 'findings', 'discussion' and 'conclusions' might seem inappropriate and not in keeping with the way the research actually evolved. Headings like these might seem to accord with a design and execution of research more in line with experiments and surveys than ethnography or grounded theory. Rather than totally rejecting the conventional headings, however, qualitative researchers can benefit from *adapting* them for their own purposes. The headings may not provide a means for faithfully depicting what actually happened in the process of research but they can provide a means for presenting the research in a way that:

Link up with
Presenting
qualitative data,
p. 294.

• addresses and highlights the key issues;
• is logically ordered;
• is comfortably recognized by those coming from different traditions within the social sciences.

The research methods section

Research reports normally include a description of the methods used to collect the data. In larger works this appears in a separate chapter. In shorter reports and articles it tends to be limited to a section under a 'research methods' heading or to a clearly identifiable paragraph or two. This account of the methods is vital in order for the reader to make some informed evaluation of the study. Basically, if the reader is *not* told how and why the data were collected, he or she cannot make any judgement about how good the research is and whether any credibility should be given to its findings or conclusions.

Within the confines of the space available the methods section should do three things.: (1) describe how the research was conduced; (2) justify these procedures; and (3) acknowledge any limitations to the methods employed.

Describe how the research was conducted

Precise details need to be given, using specific and accurate numbers and dates. These should address basic questions about the data collection process such as:

• *what* methods were used (the technical names)?
• *when* did the research take place (month and year, duration of research)?
• *where* did the research take place (location, situation)?
• *how* was access to the data or subjects obtained?
• *who* was involved in the research (the population, sample, cases, examples)?
• *how many* were involved in the research (precise numbers)?
• *how* were they selected (sampling technique)?

Justify these procedures

An argument needs to be put forward supporting the choice of methods. The methods should be justified as being:

- *reasonable* in terms of the resources and time available;
- *reliable* and *appropriate* for collecting the necessary type of data;
- *suitable* for addressing the issues, problems or questions that underpin the research and likely to produce data that are *valid*;
- conforming with *ethical* standards.

Acknowledge any limitations to the methods employed

Good research evaluates the weaknesses as well as the strengths of its methodology. The researcher should acknowledge:

- any inherent limitations of the methodology;
- the scope of what can, and cannot, be concluded on the basis of the research that was undertaken;
- any ways in which resource constraints had a direct influence on the volume or kind of findings produced;
- any reservations about the authenticity, accuracy or honesty of answers;
- the ways in which, in retrospect, alternative methods might have proved to be more useful;
- any unexpected factors which arose during research that influenced the outcome.

Referencing

It is essential to acknowledge the original sources of the ideas, arguments and supporting evidence that are directly mentioned in a research report. These sources must be 'referenced'. Broadly speaking there are two conventions that can be used for this: the *numerical system* (e.g. the Vancouver system) or the *author-date system* (e.g. the Harvard system). The numerical system involves placing a number in the text at each point where the author wishes to refer to a specific source. The full references are then given at the end of the book or individual chapters, and these can be incorporated into endnotes. It is the other system, the author-date system, however, which is more common in social research and, for that reason, further details in this chapter will concentrate on this convention.

Citing sources

In the author-date system the sources are referenced by citing the name of the author and the date of publication of the relevant work. This is done at the appropriate point in the text – immediately connected to the idea, argument or supporting evidence that has been introduced to the discussion. To avoid cluttering the text, full details of the publication are not given at this point. They are subsequently given at the end of the report where readers who might wish to do so can see all the details of the author(s) and publication. The author-date system involves referring to authors in the text in the following ways:

- Baker (2014) argues that communism has a dubious future.
- It has been argued that communism has a dubious future (Baker 2014).
- The point has been made that 'it is not easy to see what contribution communism will make in the twenty-first century' (Baker 2014: 131).

In the References section towards the end of the research report, the full details of 'Baker 2014' are given, as they are for all the authors' works cited in the report. For Baker, it might look like this:

Baker, G. (2014) The future of communism in a globalised economy, *International Journal of Politics and Economics*, 25: 249–66.

Listing references

Using the author-date system the References section contains a list of the works cited in the research report. This list appears in (1) *alphabetical order* based on (2) *the surname of the authors* and includes (3) *all the sources cited*. The list is restricted to just those sources that have been referred to within the report and does not include other works that, though they might be relevant, have not actually been cited. The information supplied about the sources covers:

- *Author's name and initial(s)*. Surname followed by forename or initial. If the book is an edited volume, then (ed.) or (eds) should follow the name.
- *Date of publication*. To identify when the work was written and to distinguish different works published by the same author(s).
- *Title*. The title of a book is put in italics and uses capital letters for the first letter of the main words. Papers and article titles are not in italics and have titles in lower case.
- *Journal name* (if applicable). This is put in italics and details are given of the number, volume and page numbers of the specified article.
- *Chapter in an edited volume*. If the source is a contribution to an edited volume, then details are given about the book in which it appears (i.e. editor's name, title of edited volume).
- *Place of publication*. This is usually the city in which the publisher is located.
- *Publisher*. This is included for books but not for journals.
- *Edition*. If the work appears in a second or subsequent edition this needs to be specified.

Look at the References section towards the end of this book to see examples of how the author-date system presents information about the sources that are cited. Further guidance on referencing techniques can be found in sources such as the *Publication Manual of the American Psychological Association* and Turabian's (2013) manual for writers.

Good practice: Use referencing software

Software packages help with the organization of references and with citing sources referred to in research reports. Packages like *EndNote, Mendeley, RefWorks, Reference Manager, and Zotero* allow the researcher to adhere to any one of the many styles that might be required.

Guidelines on style

The conventions associated with writing research reports are rather like the rules of writing which operate for the English language. Experienced writers might occasionally break the rules, but the assumption is that they realize they are breaking the rules and are doing so consciously for a particular purpose – to achieve a specific effect. Inexperienced writers, however, are better advised to play safe and stick to the rules. The same applies in relation to research reports: unless you are experienced, it is safer to abide by the conventions.

• *Use the third person.*

This means adopting the following style: 'Research involved the distribution of 164 questionnaires . . .; A response rate of 46 per cent was achieved . . .; Findings from the research indicated that . . .'. This is particularly the case for formal reports such as dissertations and theses. This style contrasts with use of the first person which takes the form:'I distributed 164 questionnaires . . .; I received 46 per cent back . . .; From the research I found that . . .'.Sometimes this style is to be found in qualitative research when researchers are keen to emphasize their personal involvement and the role of their personal identity in the collection and analysis of the data. Or, it might be used in the context of an informal report intended for restricted distribution. It is more conventional, however, to use the third person.

• *Use the past tense.*

For the most part this convention poses little trouble because researchers are reflecting upon events that happened in the past. It might be the recent past, but none the less the writing up refers to things that were done and events that happened.

Guidelines on presentation

For the production of dissertations and theses each university will have its own specific regulations and guidelines that stipulate the technical requirements in terms of
things like the layout of the text and the referencing system, and publishers always
include guidance to authors which spell out their own particular policy as far as the
presentation of work is concerned. These requirements must be followed. The general advice about presentation, however, is that research reports should:

- *Ensure good standards of spelling and grammar.*

Perhaps obvious, this requirement is still worth stressing. Spell-checkers are normally built into word-processing packages and can be used to eliminate typing errors
as well as helping with awkward spellings. Scrutiny of the text by the researcher is
still needed, however, to avoid those text errors which cannot be picked up by the
spell-checker; where 'at' has been typed instead of 'an', for example.

- *Develop logical links from one section to the next.*

A good report is one that takes the reader on a journey of discovery. The path-
ways of this journey should be clear, and the reader should never be left in doubt
about the direction of the discussion or the crucial points that are being argued.
The logic of the discussion should build point on point towards a final conclusion.

- *Use headings and sub-headings to divide the text into clear sections.*

Judicious use of headings and sub-headings can separate the text into blocks in
a way that makes the reader's task of understanding the overall report far easier.
They act as signposts. As with signposts, too few and the reader gets lost, too
many and the reader gets confused. As with signposts, their success depends on
being clear and being in the right place.

- *Be consistent in the use of the referencing style.*

Whether the *author-date* or the *numerical* style is used there should be consistency throughout the report. Use one or the other, not a mixture of the two.

- *Use care with the page layout.*

The visual element of the presentation is important and the researcher should
give some consideration to things like the page layout and the use of graphs,
tables and illustrations to enhance the appeal of the report.

| Link up with |
| Presenting quan- |
| titative data, |
| p. 263. |

- *Present tables and figures properly.*

Tables and figures should be presented in a consistent style
that provides the reader with the necessary information to
decipher the meaning of the data contained in them.

Writing for an audience

Research reports need to be tailored to meet the expectations of the audience for whom they are produced. For example, research reports produced for an academic qualification – an undergraduate project, a master's dissertation, a doctoral thesis – will be assessed by supervisors and examiners who will be focusing on detail, rigour, precision, coherence and originality as top priorities. A different audience might hold different expectations. In the case of commissioned research the audience might be more concerned with reading a report that is succinct, easy to digest and strong on practical outcomes. When writing a report, then, the researcher has to think carefully about who will read it and how best to make sure that the report is pitched at the right level. Different kinds of audience will have a bearing on:

- the style of presentation;
- the detail and length of the account;
- the amount of technical detail included;
- the terminology used.

Good practice: Meet the readers' expectations

Research reports should be tailored to meet the expectations and abilities of the audience for whom they are written.

Producing accounts of research

Finally, there is a fundamental point worth bearing in mind in relation to the nature of research reports. When writing a research report it is important to recognize that the task is not one of simply recording what happened during the project. Writing up is actually a skilful process of distilling the key events and decisions that occurred during a project and, within the confines of the space that is available, capturing and presenting these for a particular audience. A research report can never be a literal description of what took place. No matter how scrupulous the researcher might be, the end product – even if it is a dissertation or thesis – will always be an edited *account* of the research. There are four reasons for this. First, there are always limitations to the space available to provide the account of what happened, which means the researcher needs to provide an *edited version* of the totality. Decisions need to be made about what details are included and which are considered less important and can be missed out of the account.

Second, the editorial decisions taken by the researcher are likely to be shaped by the researcher's need to present the methods in their best possible light. Quite rationally, the researcher will wish to put a positive spin on events and to bring out the best in the process. Without resorting to deceit or untruths, the account of research will almost certainly entail some upbeat *positive filtering*. The point, after all, is to justify the procedures as 'good' research.

Third, although research notes will be used to anchor the description of what happened during the course of the research, the writing up is inevitably *a retrospective vision*. Situations and data are likely to have a different meaning when viewed from the end of the research process from that at the time they occurred. They will be *interpreted with the wisdom of hindsight*.

Fourth, the impact of social norms and personal values on the way we interpret events pretty well guarantees that, to a greater or lesser extent, any account of research should be regarded as a *version of the truth* rather than a literal depiction of what happened. Within the social sciences, the idea of a purely objective position is controversial, and a researcher would be naïve to presume that his or her account can stand, without careful consideration, as an 'objective' description of what really occurred.

Further reading

Denscombe, M. (2012) *Research Proposals: A Practical Guide*. Maidenhead: Open University Press.

Murray, N. and Hughes, G. (2008) *Writing Up Your University Assignments and Research Projects: A Practical Handbook*. Maidenhead: Open University Press.

Murray, R. (2013) *Writing for Academic Journals*, 3rd edn. Maidenhead: Open University Press.

Reid, M. (2012) *Report Writing*. Basingstoke: Palgrave Macmillan.

Turabian, K. (2013) *A Manual for Writers of Research Papers, Theses, and Dissertations*, 8th edn. Chicago, IL: University of Chicago Press.

Checklist for writing research reports

When writing a research report you should feel confident about answering 'yes' to the following questions: ☑

1 Is there a suitable structure and logical development to the report? ☐

2 Is the text written in a clear style, free of spelling and grammatical errors? ☐

3 Have the necessary conventions been followed in the writing up of the research? ☐

4 Does the report meet the expectations of the main audience for the research (format, style, length, detail)? ☐

5 Has an appropriately detailed and precise description of the research process been provided? ☐

6 Has the choice of method(s) been justified in relation to the type of data required and the practical circumstances surrounding the research? ☐

7 Have the limitations of the research methodology been acknowledged? ☐

8 Are the references complete and do they follow a recognized style (e.g. author-date system)? ☐

9 Are the tables, figures, illustrations and diagrams properly labelled? ☐

© M. Denscombe, *The Good Research Guide*. Open University Press.

References

Ahmed, S. (2006) *Queer Phenomenology: Orientations, Objects, Others*. Durham, NC: Duke University Press.

Alaszewski, A. (2006) *Using Diaries for Social Research*. London: Sage.

Andrews, M., Squire, C. and Tamboukou, M. (2013) *Doing Narrative Research*, 2nd edn. London: Sage.

Austin, J.L. (1962) *How to Do Things with Words*. Oxford: Clarendon.

Bakeman, R. and Gottman, J.M. (1997) *Observing Interaction: An Introduction to Sequential Analysis*, 2nd edn. Cambridge: Cambridge University Press.

Balnaves, M. and Caputi, P. (2001) *Introduction to Quantitative Research Methods: An Investigative Approach*. London: Sage.

Banks, M. (2001) *Visual Methods in Social Research*. London: Sage.

Banks, M. (2007) *Using Visual Data in Qualitative Research*. London: Sage.

Barnett, V. (2002) *Sample Survey Principles and Methods*, 3rd edn. Chichester: Wiley.

Bazeley, P. (2013) *Qualitative Data Analysis: Practical Strategies*. London: Sage.

Bazeley, P. and Jackson, K. (2013) *Qualitative Data Analysis with NVivo*, 2nd edn. London: Sage.

Becker, H. and Geer, B. (1957) Participant observation and interviewing: a comparison, *Human Organization*, 16(3): 28–35.

Bell, P. (2000) Content analysis of visual images, in T. van Leeuwen and C. Jewitt (eds) *The Handbook of Visual Analysis*. London: Sage.

Berger, P. and Luckmann, T. (1967) *The Social Construction of Reality*. London: Allen Lane.

Bergman, M. (ed.) (2008) *Advances in Mixed Methods Research: Theories and Applications*. London: Sage.

Bettis, J.D. (1969) *Phenomenology of Religion*. New York: Harper & Row.

Bhaskaran, V. and LeClaire, J. (2010) *Online Surveys for Dummies*. Hoboken, NJ: Wiley.

Birks, M. and Mills, J. (2011) *Grounded Theory: A Practical Guide*. London: Sage.

Bloor, M., Frankland, J., Thomas, M. and Robson, K. (2001) *Focus Groups in Social Research*. London: Sage.

Boellstorff, T., Nardi, B., Pearce, C. and Taylor, T. (2012) *Ethnography and Virtual Worlds: A Handbook of Method*. Princeton, NJ: Princeton University Press.

Brace, I. (2013) *Questionnaire Design*, 3rd edn. London: Kogan Page.

Bradburn, N.M., Sudman, S. and Wansink, B. (2004) *Asking Questions: The Definitive Guide to Questionnaire Design*, 2nd edn. San Francisco, CA: Jossey-Bass.

Brewer, J. (2000) *Ethnography*. Buckingham: Open University Press.

Brickman-Bhutta, C. (2012) Not by the book: Facebook as a sampling frame, *Sociological Methods and Research*, 41(1):57–88.

Brown, G., Cherrington, D.H. and Cohen, L. (1975) *Experiments in the Social Sciences*. London: Harper & Row.

Bryant, A. and Charmaz, K. (2010) *The Sage Handbook of Grounded Theory* (paperback edition). London: Sage.

Bryman, A. (1988) *Quality and Quantity in Social Research*. London: Unwin Hyman.

Bryman, A. (2006) Integrating quantitative and qualitative research: how is it done? *Qualitative Research*, 6(1): 97–113.

Bryman, A. (2007) *Qualitative Research*. London: Sage.

Bulmer, M. (1984) *The Chicago School of Sociology: Institutionalization, Diversity, and the Rise of Sociological Research*. Chicago, IL: University of Chicago Press.

Burgess, R.G. (1984) *In the Field: An Introduction to Field Research*. London: Allen & Unwin.

Campbell, D.T. and Fiske, D.W. (1959) Convergent and discriminant validation by the multitrait-multimethod matrix, *Psychological Bulletin*, 56(2): 81–105.

Charmaz, K. (2000) Grounded theory: objectivist and constructivist methods in N. Denzin and Y. Lincoln (eds) *Handbook of Qualitative Research*, 2nd edn. Thousand Oaks, CA: Sage, pp. 509–35.

Charmaz, K. (2014) *Constructing Grounded Theory*, 2nd edn. London: Sage.

Clarke, A.E. (2005) *Situational Analysis: Grounded Theory after the Postmodern Turn*. Thousand Oaks, CA: Sage.

Coghlan, D. and Brannick, T. (2010) *Doing Action Research in Your Own Organization*. London: Sage.

Collier, M. (2001) Approaches to the analysis of visual images, in T. van Leeuwen and J. Jewitt (eds) *Handbook of Visual Analysis*. London: Sage.

Cook, T.D. and Campbell, D.T. (1979) *Quasi-Experimentation: Design and Analysis Issues for Field Settings*. Chicago, IL : Rand McNally College Pub. Co.

Corbin, J.M. and Strauss, A.L. (2008) *Basics of Qualitative Research: Techniques and Procedures for Developing Grounded Theory*. Thousand Oaks, CA: Sage.

Couper, M.P. (2000) Web surveys, *Public Opinion Quarterly*, 64(4): 464–95.

Couper, M.P. (2011) The future of modes of data collection, *Public Opinion Quarterly*, 75: 889–908.

Creswell, J.W. (1998) *Qualitative Inquiry and Research Design: Choosing Among Five Traditions*. Thousand Oaks, CA: Sage.

Cresswell, J.W. (2013) *Research Design: Qualitative, Quantitative and Mixed Methods Approaches*, 4th edn. Thousand Oaks, CA: Sage.

Creswell, J.W. and Plano Clark, V. (2010) *Designing and Conducting Mixed Methods Research*, 2nd edn. Thousand Oaks, CA: Sage.

Crotty, M. (1996) *Phenomenology and Nursing Research*. Melbourne: Churchill Livingstone.

Daniel, J. (2012) *Sampling Essentials: Practical Guidelines for Making Sampling Choices*. Thousand Oaks, CA: Sage.

Delamont, S. (1992) *Fieldwork in Educational Settings*. London: Falmer.

Denscombe, M. (1983) Interviews, accounts and ethnographic research on teachers, in M. Hammersley (ed.) *The Ethnography of Schooling: Methodological Issues*. Driffield: Nafferton Books.

Denscombe, M. (2006) Web-based questionnaires: an assessment of the mode effect on the validity of data, *Social Science Computer Review*, 24(2): 246–54.

Denscombe, M. (2009) Item non-response rates: a comparison of online and paper questionnaires, *International Journal of Social Research Methodology*, 12(4): 281–91.

Denscombe, M. (2008) The length of responses to open-ended questions: a comparison of online and paper questionnaires in terms of a mode effect, *Social Science Computer Review*, 26(3): 359–68.

Denscombe, M. (2010) *Ground Rules for Social Research*, 2nd edn. Maidenhead: Open University Press.

Denscombe, M. (2012a) *Classroom Control: A Sociological Perspective*. London: Routledge.

Denscombe, M. (2012b) *Research Proposals: A Practical Guide*. Maidenhead: Open University Press.

Denyer, D. and Tranfield, D. (2009) Producing a systematic review, in D. Buchanan and A. Bryman (eds) *The Sage Handbook of Organizational Research Methods*. London: Sage, pp. 671–89.

Denzin, N.K. (1970) Strategies of multiple triangulation, in N.K. Denzin (ed.) *The Research Act in Sociology: A Theoretical Introduction to Sociological Method*. New York: McGraw-Hill, pp. 297–313.

Denzin, N.K. (1999) Cybertalk and the method of instances, in S. Jones (ed.) *Doing Internet Research: Critical Issues and Methods for Examining the Net*. Thousand Oaks, CA: Sage.

Denzin, N.K. (2012) Triangulation 2.0, *Journal of Mixed Methods Research*, 6(2): 80–8.

Department of Health (2005) *Research Governance Framework for Health and Social Care (England)*, 2nd edn. London: Dept of Health.

Devault, M. (1990) Talking and listening from women's standpoint, *Social Problems*, 37(1): 96–116.

De Vaus, D. (2001) *Research Design in Social Research*. London: Sage.

De Vaus, D. (2014) *Surveys in Social Research*, 6th edn. London: Routledge.

DeWalt, K.M. and DeWalt, B.R. (2011) *Participant Observation: A Guide for Fieldworkers*, 2nd edn. Lanham, MD: AltaMira Press.

Dey, I. (1993) *Qualitative Data Analysis: A User-friendly Guide for Social Scientists*. London: Routledge.

Diamante, T. (2013) *Effective Interviewing and Information Gathering: Proven Tactics to Increase the Power of Your Questioning Skills*. New York: McGraw-Hill/Business Expert Press.

Di Gregorio, S. and Davidson, J. (2008) *Qualitative Research Design for Software Users*. Maidenhead: Open University Press.

Dillman, D.A., Smyth, J.D. and Christian, L.M. (2009) *Internet, Mail, and Mixed-mode Surveys: The Tailored Design Method*. Hoboken, NJ: Wiley.

Dixon-Woods, M., Bonas, S., Booth, A., Jones, D., Miller, T., Shaw, R., Smith, J., Sutton, A. and Young, B. (2006) How can systematic reviews incorporate qualitative research? A critical perspective, *Qualitative Research*, 6: 27–44.

Dunning, T. (2012) *Natural Experiments in the Social Sciences: A Design-Based Approach*. Cambridge: Cambridge University Press.

Edwards, A. and Talbot, R. (1999) *The Hard-pressed Researcher: A Research Handbook for the Caring Professions*, 2nd edn. Harlow: Pearson.

Eisenhardt, K.M. (1989) Building theories from case study research, *Academy of Management Review*, 14(4): 532–50.

Eisenhardt, K.M. and Graebner, M.E. (2007) Theory building from cases: opportunities and challenges, *Academy of Management Journal*, 50(1): 25–32.

Elliott, J. (1991) *Action Research for Educational Change*. Buckingham: Open University Press.

Elliott, J. (2005) *Using Narrative in Social Research: Qualitative and Quantitative Approaches*. London: Sage.

Emmel, N. (2013) *Sampling and Choosing Cases in Qualitative Research: A Realist Approach*. London: Sage.

Emmison, M., Smith, P. and Mayall, M. (2012) *Researching the Visual*, 2nd edn. London: Sage.

Ess, C. (2014) *Digital Media Ethics*, 2nd edn. Cambridge: Polity Press.

Facebook (2011) *Anatomy of Facebook*. Available at https://www.facebook.com/notes/facebook-data-team/anatomy-of-facebook/10150388519243859 (accessed 30 October. 2013).

Farrimond, H. (2013) *Doing Ethical Research*. Basingstoke: Palgrave Macmillan.

Festinger, L., Reicken, H. and Schachter, S. (1956) *When Prophecy Fails*. Minneapolis: University of Minnesota Press (republished London: Harper & Row, 1964).

Field, A. (2013) *Discovering Statistics Using IBM SPSS Statistics*, 4th edn. London: Sage.

Fink, A. (2009) *How to Conduct Surveys: A Step by Step Guide*. Thousand Oaks, CA: Sage.

Flick, U., Garms-Homolová, V., Herrmann, W.J., Kuck, J. and Röhnsch, G. (2012) 'I can't prescribe something just because someone asks for it . . .': Using mixed methods in the framework of triangulation, *Journal of Mixed Methods Research*, 6(2): 97–110.

Fowler, F.J. (2009) *Survey Research Methods*, 4th edn. Thousand Oaks, CA: Sage.

Gallagher, S. (2012) *Phenomenology*. Basingstoke: Palgrave.

Galton, M., Simon, B. and Croll, P. (1980) *Inside the Primary Classroom*. London: Routledge & Kegan Paul.

Geertz, C. (1973) Thick description: toward an interpretive theory of culture, in C. Geertz (ed.) *The Interpretation of Cultures*. New York: Basic Books.

Gerbner, G., Holsti, O., Krippendorf, K., Paisley, W. and Stone, P. (eds) (1969) *The Analysis of Communication Content*. New York: Wiley.

Gibbs, G. (2002) *Qualitative Data Analysis: Explorations with NVivo*. Maidenhead: Open University Press.

Gibbs, G. (2007) *Analysing Qualitative Data*. London: Sage.

Gibson, B. and Hartman, J. (2014) *Rediscovering Grounded Theory*. London: Sage.

Gillham, B. (2005) *Research Interviewing: The Range of Techniques*. Maidenhead: Open University Press.

Gillham, B. (2007) *Developing a Questionnaire*, 2nd edn. London: Continuum.

Gillham, B. (2008) *Observation Techniques: Structured and Unstructured Approaches*. London: Continuum.

Glaser, B. (1978) *Theoretical Sensitivity*. Mill Valley, CA: Sociology Press.

Glaser, B. (ed.) (1995) *Grounded Theory, 1984–1994*. Mill Valley, CA: Sociology Press.

Glaser, B. (1999) The future of grounded theory, *Qualitative Health Research*, 9(6): 836–45.

Glaser, B. (2003) *The Grounded Theory Perspective II: Description's Remodelling of Grounded Theory Methodology*. Mill Valley, CA: Sociology Press.

Glaser, B. and Strauss, A. (1967) *The Discovery of Grounded Theory*. Chicago, IL: Aldine.

Glaser, J., Dixit, J. and Green, D. (2002) Studying hate crime with the Internet: what makes racists advocate racial violence, *Journal of Social Issues*, 58(1): 177–93.

Goldacre, B. (2012) *Bad Pharma*. London: Fourth Estate.

Gorard, S. (2006) *Using Everyday Numbers Effectively in Research*. London: Continuum.

Gorard, S. and Taylor, C. (2004) *Combining Methods in Educational and Social Research*. Maidenhead: Open University Press.

Gough, D., Oliver, S. and Thomas, J. (2012) *An Introduction to Systematic Reviews*. London: Sage.

Grbich, C. (2013) *Qualitative Data Analysis: An Introduction*, 2nd edn. London: Sage.

Greene, J.C. (2007) *Mixed Methods in Social Inquiry*. San Francisco, CA: Jossey-Bass.

Greene, J.C., Caracelli, V.J. and Graham, W.F. (1989) Toward a conceptual framework for mixed-method evaluation designs, *Educational Evaluation and Policy Analysis*, 11(3): 255–74.

Griffin, J. (1962) *Black Like Me*. London: Collins.

Guest, G. (2013) Describing mixed methods research: an alternative to typologies, *Journal of Mixed Methods Research*, 7(2): 141–51.

Haglund, K. (2004) Conducting life history research with adolescents, *Qualitative Health Research*, 14(9): 1309–19.

Hammersley, M. (1990) What's wrong with ethnography? The myth of theoretical description, *Sociology*, 24: 597–615.

Hammersley, M. (1992) *What's Wrong with Ethnography?* London: Routledge.

Hammersley, M. (1996) The relationship between qualitative and quantitative research: paradigm loyalty versus methodological eclecticism, in J.E.T. Richardson (ed.) *Handbook of Qualitative Research Methods for Psychology and the Social Sciences*. Leicester: British Psychological Society, pp. 159–74.

Hammersley, M. and Atkinson, P. (2007) *Ethnography: Principles in Practice*, 3rd edn. London: Tavistock.

Harrits, G.S. (2011) More than method?: a discussion of paradigm differences within mixed methods research, *Journal of Mixed Methods Research*, 5(2): 150–66.

Heidegger, M. (1962) *Being and Time*. Oxford: Basil Blackwell.

Heider, D. and Massanari, A.L. (eds) (2012) *Digital Ethics: Research and Practice*. New York: Peter Lang Publishing.

Higgins, J. and Green, S. (eds) (2011) *Cochrane Handbook for Systematic Reviews of Interventions* Version 5.1.0 [updated March 2011]. The Cochrane Collaboration, 2011. Available at: www.cochrane-handbook.org.

Hine, C. (2000) *Virtual Ethnography*. London: Sage.

Hine, C. (ed.) (2005) *Virtual Methods: Issues in Social Research on the Internet*. Oxford: Berg.

Ho, K. (2009) *Liquidated: An Ethnography of Wall Street*. Durham, NC: Duke University Press.

Hoinville, G., Jowell, R. and Associates (1985) *Survey Research Practice*. Aldershot: Gower.

Hoonakker, P. and Carayon, P. (2009) Questionnaire survey nonresponse: a comparison of postal mail and Internet surveys, *International Journal of Human–Computer Interaction*, 25(5): 348–73.

Howell, N. (1990) *Surviving Fieldwork: A Report of the Advisory Panel on Health and Safety in Fieldwork*. Washington, DC: American Anthropological Association.

Humphreys, L. (1975) *Tearoom Trade*. New Brunswick, NJ: Aldine Transaction.

Husserl, E. (1931) *Ideas: General Introduction to Pure Phenomenology*. London: George Allen & Unwin (reprinted 2012, London: Routledge).

Husserl, E. (1950) *Cartesian Meditations: An Introduction to Phenomenology*. The Hague: Martinus Nijhoff (reprinted 1999, Dordrecht: Kluwer).

Hutchby, I. and Wooffitt, R. (2008) *Conversation Analysis*. Cambridge: Polity Press.

Israel, M. and Hay, I. (2006) *Research Ethics for Social Scientists: Between Ethical Conduct and Regulatory Compliance*. London: Sage.

Johnson, R.B. and Gray, R. (2010) A history of philosophical and theoretical issues for mixed methods research, in A. Tashakkori and C. Teddlie (eds) *Sage Handbook of Mixed Methods in Social and Behavioral Research*, 2nd edn. Thousand Oaks, CA: Sage, pp. 69–94.

Johnson, R.B. and Onwuegbuzie, A.J. (2004) Mixed methods research: a research paradigm whose time has come, *Educational Researcher*, 33(7): 14–26.

Johnson, R.B., Onwuegbuzie, A.J. and Turner, L.A. (2007) Toward a definition of mixed methods research, *Journal of Mixed Methods Research*, 1(2): 112–33.

Jorgensen, D.L. (1989) *Participant Observation: A Methodology for Human Studies*. Thousand Oaks, CA: Sage.

Kamberelis, G. and Dimitriadis, G. (2013) *Focus Groups: From Structured Interviews to Collective Conversations*. London: Routledge.

Keats, D.M. (2000) *Interviewing: A Practical Guide for Students and Professionals*. Maidenhead: Open University Press.

Kemmis, S., McTaggart, R. and Nixon, R. (2014) *The Action Research Planner: Doing Critical Participatory Action Research*. Singapore: Springer.

Kirk, J. and Miller, M. (1986) *Reliability and Validity in Qualitative Research*. Beverly Hills, CA: Sage.

Koshy, V. (2010) *Action Research for Improving Educational Practice*, 2nd edn. London: Sage.

Kosinski, M., Stillwell, D.J. and Graepel, T. (2013) Private traits and attributes are predictable from digital records of human behavior, *Proceedings of the National Academy of Sciences USA*, 110(15): 5802–5.

Kozinets, R.V. (2010) *Netnography: Doing Ethnographic Research Online*. London: Sage.

Krippendorf, K. (2013) *Content Analysis: An Introduction to its Methodology*, 3rd edn. Thousand Oaks, CA: Sage.

Krosnick, J.A. (1991) Response strategies for coping with the cognitive demands of attitude measures in surveys, *Applied Cognitive Psychology*, 5: 213–36.

Kugelmann, R. (1999) Complaining about chronic pain, *Social Science and Medicine*, 49(12): 16–63.

Layder, D. (1993) *New Strategies in Social Research*. Cambridge: Polity Press.

Layder, D. (1998) *Sociological Practice: Linking Theory and Social Research*. London: Sage.

Lee, R. (1995) *Dangerous Fieldwork*. Thousand Oaks, CA: Sage.

Leech, N.L. and Onwuegbuzie, A.J. (2009) A typology of mixed method research designs, *Quality and Quantity*, 43: 265–75.

Lewin, K. (1946) Action research and minority problems, *Journal of Social Issues*, 2: 34–46.

Lewins, A. and Silver, C. (2014) *Using Software in Qualitative Research: A Step-by-Step Guide*, 2nd edn. London: Sage.

Lewis, M. and Staehler, T. (2010) *Phenomenology: An Introduction*. London: Continuum.

Lincoln, Y. and Guba, E. (1985) *Naturalistic Enquiry*. Newbury Park, CA: Sage.

Lipscomb, M. (2008) Mixed method nursing studies: a critical realist critique, *Nursing Philosophy*, 9(1): 32–45.

Loizos, P. (2000) Video, film and photographs as research documents, in M.W. Bauer and G. Gaskell (eds) *Qualitative Researching with Text, Image and Sound*. London: Sage.

Lozar Manfreda, K., Bosnjak, M., Berzelak, J., Haas, I. and Vehovar, V. (2008) Web surveys versus other survey modes: a meta-analysis comparing response rates, *International Journal of Market Research*, 50(1): 79–104.

Madden, R. (2010) *Being Ethnographic: A Guide to the Theory and Practice of Ethnography*. London: Sage.

Malinowski, B. (1922) *Argonauts of the Western Pacific*. London: Routledge & Kegan Paul.

Mann, C. and Stewart, F. (2000) *Internet Communication and Qualitative Research: A Handbook for Researching Online*. London: Sage.

Marion, J.S. and Crowder, J.W. (2013) *Visual Research: A Concise Introduction to Thinking Visually*. London: Bloomsbury Academic.

Marshall, C. and Rossman, G.B. (2011) *Designing Qualitative Research*, 5th edn. Thousand Oaks, CA: Sage.

Mayo, E. ([1933] 2003) *The Human Problems of an Industrial Civilization*. London: Routledge.

McCabe, S.E. (2004) Comparison of web and mail surveys in collecting illicit drug use data: a randomized experiment, *Journal of Drug Education*, 34(1): 61–73.

McKee, H.A. and Porter, J.E. (2009) *The Ethics of Internet Research: A Rhetorical, Case-based Process*. New York: Peter Lang.

McNiff, J. (2013) *Action Research: Principles and Practice*, 3rd edn. London: Routledge.

Mead, M. (1943) *Coming of Age in Samoa: A Study of Adolescence and Sex in Primitive Societies*. Harmondsworth: Penguin.

Mertens, D.M. (2009) *Transformative Research and Evaluation*. New York: Guilford.

Miles, M.B., Huberman, A.M. and Saldana, J.M. (2014) *Qualitative Data Analysis: A Methods Sourcebook*, 3rd edn. Thousand Oaks, CA: Sage.

Milgram, S. (1974) *Obedience to Authority*. New York: Harper & Row.

Morgan, D.L. (2006) Focus group, in V. Jupp (ed.) *The Sage Dictionary of Social Research Methods*. London: Sage, pp. 121–3.

Morgan, D.L. (2014) *Integrating Qualitative and Quantitative Methods: A Pragmatic Approach*. Thousand Oaks, CA: Sage.

Morley, J. (1998) The private theater: a phenomenological investigation of daydreaming, *Journal of Phenomenological Psychology*, 29(1): 116–35.

Moustakas, C. (1992) Firebrand: the experience of being different, *The Human Psychologist*, 20(2/3): 175–88.

Moustakas, C. (1994) *Phenomenological Research Methods*. Thousand Oaks, CA: Sage.

Murchison, J. (2010) *Ethnography Essentials: Designing, Conducting, and Presenting Your Research*. San Francisco, CA: Jossey-Bass.

Murray, N. and Hughes, G. (2008) *Writing Up Your University Assignments and Research Projects: A Practical Handbook*. Maidenhead: Open University Press.

Murray, R. (2013) *Writing for Academic Journals*, 3rd edn. Maidenhead: Open University Press.

Natasi, B.K., Hitchcock, J.H. and Brown, L.M. (2010) An inclusive framework for conceptualizing mixed methods design typologies: moving towards fully integrated synergistic research models, in A. Tashakkori and C. Teddlie (eds) *Handbook of Mixed Methods in Social and Behavioral Research*, 3rd edn. Thousand Oaks, CA: Sage, pp. 305–38.

NHMRC (1999) *How to Review the Evidence: Systematic Identification and Review of the Scientific Literature*. Canberra: National Health and Medical Research Council. Available at: http://www.nhmrc.gov.au/_files_nhmrc/publications/attachments/cp65.pdf.

Oakley, A. (1981) Interviewing women: a contradiction in terms, in H. Roberts (ed.) *Doing Feminist Research*. London: Routledge & Kegan Paul.

O'Connell Davidson, J. (1995) The anatomy of 'free choice' prostitution, *Gender, Work and Organization*, 2: 1–10.

Oktay, J. (2012) *Grounded Theory*. Oxford: Oxford University Press.

O'Leary, M. (2014) *Classroom Observation*. London: Routledge.

Oliver, P. (2010) *The Student's Guide to Research Ethics*, 2nd edn. Maidenhead: Open University Press.

Onwuegbuzie, A.J. (2012) Putting the 'mixed' back into quantitative and qualitative research in educational research and beyond: moving toward the 'radical middle', *International Journal of Multiple Research Approaches*, 6(3): 192–219.

Onwuegbuzie, A. and Combs, J.P. (2010) Emergent data analysis techniques in mixed methods research: a synthesis, in A. Tashakkori and C. Teddlie (eds) *Sage Handbook of Mixed Methods in Social and Behavioral Research*, 2nd edn. Thousand Oaks, CA: Sage, pp. 397–430.

Onwuegbuzie, A.J. and Frels, R.K. (2013) Toward a new research philosophy for addressing social justice issues: critical dialectical pluralism, *International Journal of Multiple Research Approaches*, 7(1): 9–26.

Oppenheim, A.N. (2000) *Questionnaire Design, Interviewing and Attitude Measurement*, 2nd edn. London: Continuum.

O'Reilly, K. (2012) *Ethnographic Methods*, 2nd edn. London: Routledge.

Pawson, R. (2006) *Evidence-Based Policy: A Realist Perspective*. London: Sage.

Pawson, R. (2013) *The Science of Evaluation: A Realist Manifesto*. London: Sage.

Pawson, R. and Tilley, N. (1997) *Realistic Evaluation*. London: Sage.

Penn, G. (2000) Semiotic analysis of still images, in M.W. Bauer and G. Gaskell (eds) *Qualitative Researching with Text, Image, Sound*. London: Sage.

Perry, G. (2013) *Behind the Shock Machine: The Untold Story of the Notorious Milgram Psychology Experiments*. Melbourne: Scribe.

Petticrew, M. and Roberts, H. (2006) *Systematic Reviews in the Social Sciences: A Practical Guide*. Oxford: Blackwell.

Plummer, K. (2001) *Documents of Life 2: An Invitation to a Critical Humanism*, 2nd edn. London: Sage.

Polsky, N. (2006) *Hustlers, Beats and Others*. New Brunswick, NJ: Aldine Transaction.

Pope, C., Mays, N. and Popay, J. (2007) *Synthesizing Qualitative and Quantitative Health Research: A Guide to Methods*. Maidenhead: Open University Press.

Porter, S. (1993) Critical realist ethnography: the case of racism and professionalism in a medical setting, *Sociology*, 27: 591–601.

Prior, L. (2003) *Using Documents in Social Research*. London: Sage.

Prosser, J. (1998) The status of image-based research, in J. Prosser (ed.) *Image-based Research: A Sourcebook for Qualitative Researchers*. London: Falmer.

Prosser, J. and Schwartz, D. (1998) Photographs within the sociological research process, in J. Prosser (ed.) *Image-based Research: A Sourcebook for Qualitative Researchers*. London: Falmer.

Ragin, C. and Amoroso, L. (2011) *Constructing Social Research*, 2nd edn. Thousand Oaks, CA: Pine Forge Press.

Ragin, C. and Becker, H. (1992) *What Is a Case? Exploring the Foundations of Social Enquiry*. New York: Cambridge University Press.

Ramo, D.E. and Prochaska, J.J. (2012) Broad reach and targeted recruitment using Facebook for an online survey of young adult substance use, *Journal of Medical Internet Research*. Jan.–Feb.; 14(1): e28. Available at: http://www.jmir.org/2012/1/e28/ (accessed 28 October 2013).

Rapley, T. (2007) *Doing Conversation, Discourse and Document Analysis*. London: Sage.

Reason, P. and Bradbury, H. (eds) (2013) *Handbook of Action Research*, 2nd edn. London: Sage.

Reichardt, C.S. and Rallis, S.F. (1994) Qualitative and quantitative inquiries are not incompatible: a call for a new partnership, in C.S. Reichardt and S.F. Rallis (eds) *The Qualitative–Quantitative Debate: New Perspectives*. San Francisco, CA: Jossey-Bass, pp. 85–92.

Reid, M. (2012) *Report Writing*. Basingstoke: Palgrave Macmillan.

Richards, L. (2009) *Handling Qualitative Data: A Practical Guide*, 2nd edn. London: Sage.

Riemer, J. (1979) *Hard Hats: The Work World of Construction Workers*. Beverly Hills, CA: Sage.

Riessman, C.K. (2003) *Narrative Analysis*. Newbury Park, CA: Sage.

Riessman, C.K. (2008) *Narrative Methods for the Human Sciences*. Thousand Oaks, CA: Sage.

Roethlisberger, F.J. and Dickson, W.J. ([1939] 2003) *Management and the Worker*. London: Routledge.

Rose, G. (2012) *Visual Methodologies*, 3rd edn. London: Sage.

Rowntree, D. (1981) *Statistics Without Tears: An Introduction for Non-mathematicians*. London: Penguin.

Sanger, J. (1996) *The Compleat Observer?: A Field Research Guide to Observation*. London: Falmer Press.

Sartre, J.-P. (1956) *Being and Nothingness: An Essay on Phenomenological Ontology*. New York: Methuen.

Savage, M., Devine, F., Cunningham, N., Taylor, M., Li, Y., Hjellbrekke, J., Le Roux, B., Friedman, S. and Miles, A. (2013) A new model of social class? Findings from the BBC's Great British Class Survey experiment, *Sociology*, 47(2): 219–50.

Schön, D. (1983) *The Reflective Practitioner: How Professionals Think in Action*. New York: Basic Books.

Schonlau, M., Fricker, R. and Elliot, M. (2002) *Conducting Research Surveys via E-mail and the Web*. Rand Monograph MR-1480-RC. Available online at: http://www.rand.org/pubs/monograph_reports/MR1480.html.

Schutz, A. (1962) *Collected Papers*, Volume 1. The Hague: Martinus Nijhoff.

Schutz, A. (1967) *The Phenomenology of the Social World*. Evanston, IL: Northwestern University Press.

Scott, J. (1990) *A Matter of Record*. Cambridge: Polity Press.

Seale, C. (1999) *The Quality of Qualitative Research*. London: Sage.

Seale, C., Gobo, G., Gubrium, J. and Silverman, D. (eds) (2007) *Qualitative Research Practice*. London: Sage.

Sidnell, J. (2010) *Conversation Analysis: An Introduction*. Chichester: Wiley-Blackwell.

Silverman, D. (1985) *Qualitative Methodology and Sociology.* Aldershot: Gower.

Silverman, D. (2010) *Doing Qualitative Research: A Practical Handbook*, 3rd edn. London: Sage.

Silverman, D. (2011) *Interpreting Qualitative Data: Methods for Analyzing Talk, Text and Interaction*, 4th edn. Thousand Oaks, CA: Sage.

Silverman, D. (2013) *Doing Qualitative Research: A Practical Handbook*, 4th edn. London: Sage.

Simons, H. (2009) *Case Study Research in Practice.* London: Sage.

Smith, J.A., Flowers, P. and Larkin, M. (2009) *Interpretative Phenomenological Analysis: Theory, Method and Research.* London: Sage.

Smith, T.W. (2013) Survey-research paradigms old and new, *International Journal of Public Opinion Research*, 25(2): 218–29.

Somekh, B. (1995) The contribution of action research to development in social endeavours: a position paper on action research methodology, *British Educational Research Journal*, 21(3): 339–55.

Somekh, B. (2006) *Action Research: A Methodology for Change and Development.* Maidenhead: Open University Press.

Spencer, S. (2011) *Visual Research Methods in the Social Sciences: Awakening Visions.* London: Routledge.

Stake, R. (1995) *The Art of Case Study Research.* Thousand Oaks, CA: Sage.

Stanton, J. and Rogelberg, S. (2001) Using Internet/intranet web pages to collect organizational research data, *Organizational Research Methods*, 4(3): 200–17.

Stevens, S.S. (1946) On the theory of scales of measurement, *Science*, 103(2684): 677–80.

Strauss, A. (1987) *Qualitative Analysis for Social Scientists.* Cambridge: Cambridge University Press.

Strauss, A.L. and Corbin, J. (1990) *Basics of Qualitative Research: Grounded Theory Procedures and Techniques.* London: Sage.

Strauss, A.L. and Corbin, J. (1998) *Basics of Qualitative Research: Techniques and Procedures for Developing Grounded Theory*, 2nd edn. Thousand Oaks, CA: Sage.

Sue, V.M. and Ritter, L.A. (2012) *Conducting Online Surveys.* Thousand Oaks, CA: Sage.

Swanborn, P. (2010) *Case Study Research: What, Why and How?* London: Sage.

Tashakkori, A. and Teddlie, C. (1998) *Mixed Methodology: Combining Qualitative and Quantitative Approaches.* Thousand Oaks, CA: Sage.

Tashakkori, A. and Teddlie, C. (eds) (2003) *Handbook of Mixed Methods in Social and Behavioral Research.* Thousand Oaks, CA: Sage.

Teddlie, C. and Tashakkori, A. (2009) *Foundations of Mixed Methods Research: Integrating Quantitative and Qualitative Approaches in the Social and Behavioral Sciences.* Thousand Oaks, CA: Sage.

Tesch, R. (1993) Software for qualitative researchers: analysis needs and program capabilities, in N. Fielding and R. Lee (eds) *Using Computers in Qualitative Research*, 2nd edn. London: Sage.

Thomas, G. (2011) *How to Do Your Case Study: A Guide for Students and Researchers.* London: Sage.

Thyer, B.A. (2012) *Quasi-Experimental Research Designs.* New York: Oxford University Press.

Tourangeau, R., Conrad, F. and Couper, M. (2013) *The Science of Web Surveys.* Oxford: Oxford University Press.

Tranfield, D., Denyer, D. and Smart, P. (2003) Towards a methodology for developing evidence-informed management knowledge by means of systematic review, *British Journal of Management*, 14: 207–22.

Truell, A.D., Bartlett, J.E. and Alexander, M.W. (2002) Response rate, speed and completeness: a comparison of Internet-based and mail surveys, *Behaviour Research Methods, Instruments and Computers*, 34(1): 46–9.

Turabian, K. (2013) *A Manual for Writers of Research Papers, Theses, and Dissertations*, 8th edn. Chicago, IL: University of Chicago Press.

Urquhart, C. (2013) *Grounded Theory for Qualitative Research: A Practical Guide*. London: Sage.

van Leeuwen, T. and Jewitt, J. (eds) (2001) *Handbook of Visual Analysis*. London: Sage.

van Maanen, J. (ed.) (1995) *Representation in Ethnography*. Thousand Oaks, CA: Sage.

van Manen, M. (1990) *Researching Lived Experience: Human Science for an Action Sensitive Pedagogy*. London, Ontario: Althouse.

van Manen, M. (2014) *Phenomenology of Practice: Meaning-Giving Methods in Phenomenological Research and Writing*. Walnut Creek, CA: Left Coast Press.

Walker, I. (2010) *Research Methods and Statistics*. Basingstoke: Palgrave Macmillan.

Webb, E.J., Campbell, D.T., Schwartz, R.D. and Sechrest, L. (1966) *Unobtrusive Measures: Non-reactive Research in the Social Sciences*. Chicago, IL: Rand McNally.

Webster, M. and Sell, J. (2007) *Laboratory Experiments in the Social Sciences*. London: Academic Press.

Whyte, W.F. ([1943] 1993) *Street Corner Society: The Social Structure of an Italian Slum*, 4th edn. Chicago, IL: University of Chicago Press.

Wiles, R. (2013) *What Are Qualitative Research Ethics?* London: Bloomsbury.

Wilson, R., Gosling, S.D. and Graham, L.T. (2012) A review of Facebook research in the social sciences, *Perspectives on Psychological Science*, 7(3): 203–20.

Winter, R. (1996) Some principles and procedures for the conduct of action research, in O. Zuber-Skerritt (ed.) *New Directions in Action Research*. London: Falmer Press.

Wittgenstein, L. (1968) *Philosophical Investigations*. Oxford: Basil Blackwell.

Woods, P. (2012) *The Divided School*. London: Routledge.

Woods, P. (1993) Managing marginality: teacher development through grounded life history, *British Educational Research Journal*, 19(5): 447–65.

Woods, P. (2006) *Successful Writing for Qualitative Researchers*, 2nd edn. London: Routledge.

Worthington, H. and Holloway, P. (1997) Making sense of statistics, *International Journal of Health Education*, 35(3): 76–80.

Yin, R. (2009) *Case Study Research: Design and Methods*, 4th edn. Thousand Oaks, CA: Sage.

Yin, R. (2014) *Case Study Research: Design and Methods*, 5th edn. Thousand Oaks, CA: Sage.

Yoder, P. and Symons, F. (2010) *Observational Measurement of Behavior*. New York: Springer.

Zuber-Skerritt, O. (ed.) (1996) *New Directions in Action Research*. London: Falmer Press.

Index

RESEARCH PROPOSALS
A PRACTICAL GUIDE

Martyn Denscombe

2012
9780335244065 –Paperback

eBook also available

Whether you are an undergraduate student doing
your final year project, a Mastersstudent writing your dissertation, or a
PhD student applying for acceptance onto a doctoral programme, this
practical book will
help you to produce a successful and persuasive research proposal.

Written by an experienced and best-selling author, this handbook uniquely
draws a parallel between a research proposal and a sales pitch. The book
provides guidance on what to include and what to omit from your proposal
and demonstrates how to 'sell' your research idea. Denscombe ably guides
you through each stage of the process:

- Choosing a research topic
- Reviewing the literature
- Formulating the research question
- Explaining the research methods
- Estimating the costs and planning the time involved
- Obtaining research ethics approval

With top tips throughout, this book provides an insight to the logic behind
research pr oposals and the way that good proposals address 7 basic
questions that readers will ask when they evaluate any proposal.

www.openup.co.uk